EXPLORING RELIGIOUS MEANING

SIXTH EDITION

EXPLORING RELIGIOUS MEANING

ROBERT C. MONK

WALTER C. HOFHEINZ

KENNETH T. LAWRENCE

JOSEPH D. STAMEY

BERT AFFLECK

TETSUNAO YAMAMORI

Prentice Hall

Prentice Hall, Upper Saddle River, New Jersey 07458

Library of Congress Cataloging-in-Publication Data

Exploring religions meaning / Robert C. Monk . . . [et al.].—6th ed.
       p. cm.
    Includes bibliographical references and index.
    ISBN 0-13-092386-9
    1. Religion.   2. Religious literature.   I. Monk, Robert C.

BL50 .E98 2003
200—dc21

2002022067

VP/Editorial Director: Charlyce Jones Owen
Acquisitions Editor: Ross Miller
Assistant Editor: Wendy Yurash
Editorial Assistant: Carla Worner
Editorial/production supervision and interior design: Mary Araneo
Marketing Manager: Chris Ruel
Prepress and Manufacturing Buyer: Brian Mackey
Cover Art Director: Jayne Conte
Cover Designer: Bruce Kenselaar

This book was set in 10/12 Goudy by A & A Publishing Services, Inc.,
and was printed and bound by Hamilton Printing Co. The cover was
printed by Phoenix Color Corp.

© 2003, 1998, 1994, 1987, 1980, 1973 by Pearson Education, Inc.
Upper Saddle River, New Jersey 07458

ISBN   0-13-092386-9

Pearson Education LTD., London
Pearson Education Australia PTY, Limited, Sydney
Pearson Education Singapore, Pte. Ltd
Pearson Education North Asia Ltd, Hong Kong
Pearson Education Canada, Ltd., Toronto
Pearson Educación de Mexico, S.A. de C.V.
Pearson Education — Japan, Tokyo
Pearson Education Malaysia, Pte. Ltd
Pearson Education, Upper Saddle River, New Jersey

CONTENTS

PART IV   THE SELF AND RELIGION

8   EVIL: ITS REALITY AND MEANING   160

9   UNDERSTANDING THE SELF   173

10   FREEDOM AND THE SELF   188

11   SIN AND GUILT   195

12   DEATH AND THE SELF   203

13   SALVATION AND REDEMPTION   217

PART V   RELIGION AND THE SOCIOCULTURAL CONTEXT

14   THE RELIGIOUS MATRIX OF INTERPERSONAL RELATIONS   231

PREFACE
OR SOME WAYS
OF USING THIS TEXT

Exploring Religious Meaning is intended to serve as a set of tools and resources for exploring the many dimensions of religion as a central reality of human life. It was designed with introductory courses in religion, religion and culture, religion and society, and the humanities in mind. It has also been used successfully as a main or supplementary text for courses in comparative religion, sociology of religion, and philosophy of religion. It is indexed and formatted in ways that suggest a variety of uses. It can be used readily for independent study.

The book's design suggests an approach to inquiry that may be called inductive and integrative. Many of the readings are taken from Scriptures and classic literature of the world's religions. Others, presented in a variety of ways, are drawn from classic and contemporary sources that interpret religion in its various dimensions—theological, psychological, sociological, philosophical, cultural, and practical. Some are drawn from areas of contemporary culture in which religious experience and commitment are actualized, appreciated, or criticized.

The authors of *Exploring Religious Meaning* do not always agree among themselves on questions of interpretation. Readers will no doubt find themselves questioning or disagreeing with points of view expressed in sources or interpretative commentary. We hope that individual readers will be stimulated to address their own questions and formulate their own responses in studying the issues. Questions and discussion points are connected with readings more closely than in earlier editions. We believe they will be more useful.

To understand religion, religious phenomena must be seen in their contexts as manifested in the lives of societies and individuals. Traditional practices, organizational structures, doctrinal formulations handed down from generation to generation are important aspects of religion that receive attention in this text. Important too are individual experiences of feeling and response movements of innovation, protest and reform, and the emergence of new patterns that may modify, give new life to, or eclipse the old and established.

In the first chapter, a functional definition of religion is proposed. This definition suggests that religion is important to everyone because each person's life is shaped by —and all persons are concerned about—events that confront them with occasions that threaten or promote fulfillment of the individual's most basic values and commitments. Such basic commitments express what the individual most desires, how that person defines the meaning and value of existence. Basic commitments that involve the person's deepest loyalties, feelings, and beliefs about what is worth trying to acquire or preserve are—according to our proposed definition of religion—religious.

Exploring Religious Meaning began as an attempt in the late 1960s to communicate and illuminate religious concepts, practices, and traditions in ways that would effectively speak both to students who had religious interest and commitments and to others who had little experience of or even interest in the subject. Materials in the book have been updated many times since then. Probably the two greatest changes, beginning with the second edition, were (1) the addition of a separate chapter giving connected accounts of eight of the world's major religious traditions and (2) greater attention to unity and clarity in the structure of the book. Each subsequent edition has seen the addition of more information about individual religious traditions, including the major religions, new religious movements, and religion in ancient or simpler societies. These will be found throughout the book. Also, each edition has seen the development of a strengthened context of interpretation, giving greater clarity and a more complete set of tools for interpretation.

Chapters and Units in this new edition have been thoroughly updated. Several Units, including those dealing with religion and the arts, gender issues, religion in modernizing and postmodern societies, shamanism, magic, myth, war and peace, different ways in which religions interpret evil, and science and religion have been significantly revised, updated, expanded, and made, we believe, more adequate and relevant. A new chapter, combining materials from previously existing chapters but utilizing materials dropped from the fifth edition, restored at the request of users of the text and given a thorough updating, has been installed. This chapter deals with questions of belief, faith and reason, authority and tradition.

Recent events on the world scale are examined as they are related to terrorism and its relationship to conflict arising from certain kinds of religious reactions or responses to globalization. The integrity of religious traditions and positions is respected throughout the text. At the same time the effects on religion of a modernizing technologically dominated world order and the effects of religion on contemporary societies are explored.

We have retained the basic structure of the book, which persons who use it have told us works well. Units with materials that sometimes overlap, adding new contents while enriching previously developed ones, contribute to continuity and enhance comprehension. Each chapter deals with a major topic or subtopic by means of a brief introductory discussion followed by a series of units that explore facets of the topic. Some of the units raise major questions related to the topic. Other units deal comparatively with ways in which different religious (or religious and secular) traditions treat one major aspect of religion. Some treat or illustrate one major theme or topic in depth. Several units compare ways in which two or more religious traditions respond to a human issue or experience or concept. Each exploration of a topic is intended to enrich or supplement the others.

The book's structure gives a large degree of freedom to instructors and readers. Some may choose to omit chapters or units or combine units from one chapter with units from another.

Exploring Religious Meaning uses a rather modest set of theoretical tools that we have found useful in studying religion within a single society as well as in global context. These include a functional definition of religion adapted from such theologians, philosophers, and behavioral scientists as Martin Luther, Paul Tillich, H. Richard Niebuhr, William Blackstone, and Clifford Geertz among others. A creed/code/cult/community typology adapted from Joseph Fichter and other sociologists of religion is utilized. A typology of religious groups familiar from the work of Ernst Troeltsch but frequently modified and developed, recently by Bainbridge and Stark, is invoked. A typology of five orientations to religion is explained and examined. Instructors should feel free to evaluate these theoretical tools and introduce others.

We want to thank reviewers of the fifth edition, users of the book asked by our publisher for evaluations and suggestions for improvement. They responded with extremely useful critiques. We have incorporated most of their suggestions. We continue to be grateful to Jacques Bakke for illustrations that contribute much to the book. We are indebted to our many students in academic settings where we have taught. Several of these are now engaged professionally in teaching in areas of religious studies. Their suggestions, criticism, and encouragement have been valuable.

We also wish to express our gratitude to the religion editors and their staff members who through the years have continually supported and facilitated this text's several editions. Without their confidence and encouragement recurring revisions would not be accomplished.

EXPLORING RELIGIOUS MEANING

TOWARD A DEFINITION OF RELIGION

From earliest times, religion has been a pervasive social phenomenon. In our own complex society there is evidence of religion everywhere: religious holy days of particular groups (Christmas, Hanukkah, Mardi Gras, Ash Wednesday, Passover, Good Friday, Easter, Buddhist and Hindu rites of celebration or purification, Ramadan); national holidays that have a distinctively religious component (Thanksgiving, the Fourth of July, Memorial Day); church buildings, synagogues, mosques, and temples; and even controversial social and political issues, such as abortion and the legal and civil rights of homosexuals. Officials of religious groups take part in public ceremonies, such as presidential inaugurations, while officials of organizations and private citizens advocating separation of church and state protest such participation.

Although in opinion polls people often say they believe that the influence of religion has declined, there is evidence that participation in organized religion for the overall population of the United States has been at a high level for the past six decades. But our society also has a new awareness of religious pluralism and an increasing diversity of religious groups. There seems to be, moreover, both a return to traditional religious practices—an interest in finding one's roots—and a new individualism in religion—the individual wants to be his or her own kind of Baptist or Catholic or Jew. Organized religious groups such as Reform Judaism have restored ancient rites, whereas others such as the largest group of Presbyterians in the United States have moved in the direction of ordaining homosexuals to the ministry. Later units in the text will explore other forms of this two-sided phenomenon—for example, Native Americans, many of them committed Christians, returning to older, tribal ceremonies, sometimes incorporating them into patterns of Christian worship; and Christian feminist theologians turning to elements long considered heretical among Christians, for instance, gnosticism or "witchcraft" as authentic expressions of the feminine aspects of God and the Christian message.

At the individual level, many who have turned away from traditional religious answers, or from "organized religion" entirely, give evidence of deep religious concern. This concern often finds new outlets. Interest in Asian religions, which began at least as early as the 1700s in Western cultures, has experienced a broad renewal since World War II. The attraction to New Age groups suggests that Asian religious practices and beliefs now provide significant religious nurture for many Americans. Others find help in astrology, forms of magic, belief in previous incarnations, "channeling," and related religious phenomena. Recent patterns of immigration and the protections offered by America's guaranties of religious freedom have contributed to an extraordinary rise in the practice of Buddhism and several forms of Hinduism in the United States. Immigration from largely Muslim countries and the popularity among African Americans of Islamic patterns has made Islam the most rapidly expanding religion in the United States.

Among Christians, the strong resurgence of a conservative movement in both belief and practice during the past few decades has had several results: tension among "conservative," "liberal," and "moderate" factions within mainline Protestant churches; expansion of churches oriented toward individual experience and involvement (Bible Churches, Pentecostal churches, and Charismatic groups); and the rise of a politically active "religious right" intensely concerned about prayer and religious practice in public schools, abortion, homosexuality, and the religious commitment and practice of political leaders. On the other hand, commitments to social justice; to peace; to the rights of women and minority groups, the threatened environment, animal life; and to help the starving, famine-threatened human populations of the world give evidence of a strong religious fervor among Christians of diverse groups, which sometimes bridges the gaps among Roman Catholics, mainline Protestants, and independent Protestant groups.

There has also been increased attention to the study of religion at the academic level. In many instances, as successive editions of this book reflect, this has included a demand for increasing attention to non-Western religious traditions, especially Buddhism, Islam, and Hinduism, and to ancient and contemporary religious traditions of simpler, premodern, or pre-literate tribal groups. But there is also increasing academic interest in religious developments and trends in our own society, evidenced by such sociologists as Stark and Bainbridge, in their ambitious *A Theory of Religion*; the comprehensive study of American religion and American life by Gary Wills, *Under God*; or the insightful, provocative *The American Religion* by the controversial literary critic Harold Bloom.[1] It seems to us, the authors of *Exploring Religious Meaning*, that not only has religion never before been practiced in a greater variety of ways in America but also it has never been studied so widely and with such a variety of methods and goals. Some people study religion to understand an important aspect of human behavior, some to find antidotes for what they consider human superstition and folly, some to find greater tolerance and appreciation of the varied traditions, and some to find saving truth.

---

[1]Rodney Stark and William Sims Bainbridge, *A Theory of Religion* (New York: Peter Lang, 1987); Gary Wills, *Under God* (New York: Simon & Schuster, 1990); Harold Bloom, *The American Religion* (New York: Simon & Schuster, 1992).

We continue to believe that the investigation of religion must be broad enough to incorporate the most individualistic and nontraditional expressions of religious concern. While examining the major forms of established and emerging institutional patterns, we must be able to comprehend traditional patterns of religious expression, including those of societies other than our own. Affirming the need for such a broad perspective in religious inquiry makes necessary a concrete identification of the ways in which the term *religion* will be used in this book. This is not as easy as it may seem to be. During the past three decades many behavioral scientists—anthropologists, psychologists, sociologists—who study religious behavior and beliefs have emphasized how difficult it is to comprehend the beliefs of persons from very different societies than one's own. Some postmodern theorists (see Unit 76), such as Stanley Fish, a distinguished literary critic from Duke University, have argued that it is impossible to do so. Some scholars think that this aspect of postmodernist theory is being de-emphasized or relaxed. Be that as it may, many persons do seem to be able to grasp objectively the "thought-worlds" of people from cultural contexts very different from their own both within and beyond their own society. This usually requires patience, persistent effort, and the belief that such effort is important to make.

Religion is defined in many ways. Radoslav Tsanoff, in his book *Religious Crossroads*, surveyed the major language stocks of the modern world and noted that no language group has a word meaning "religion" as a universal, inclusive phenomenon. Some languages have terms that designate "law," "devotion," "knowledge," and other components of what in the West has been termed *religion*. In fact, the Latin *religio* itself originally designated the ancestral customs and rituals of the early Romans. It was not until the emergence of a Greco-Roman culture, encompassing the area from North Africa to the British Isles and from India to the Atlantic Ocean, that the term *religio* began to denote a phenomenon of universal import. Tsanoff considered various ways of defining religion, several of which are enumerated and discussed: (1) theistic and other beliefs, (2) practices, (3) mystical feeling, (4) worship of the Holy, and (5) conviction of the conservation of values.[2]

Everyone has had some experience of religion. Most people use the term on the basis of past experience, acquired beliefs, and favorable or unfavorable impressions. To one person, the word *religion* may produce good feelings. It may connote a close relationship to God—to the benevolent Being or Beings believed to provide life, security, meaning, and purpose. To another, the term may evoke fear or self-doubt or guilt. It may connote a threatening relationship to a stern or hostile or judging Power or Powers. People often reflect their own positive or negative feelings toward religion and toward their own past experiences of it when stating what they conceive it to be. On the one hand, the behavioral scientist—psychologist, sociologist, anthropologist—may emphasize religion's *functional* aspect. Psychologists may be interested in the role of religion in providing integration or in causing conflict in the individual personality and in the individual's group relationships. Sociologists may attempt to study ways in which religion may be a source of stability or change, unity or conflict, in societies. On the other hand, philosophers may be primarily interested in the *cognitive* claims of religion, in trying to under-

[2] Radoslav A. Tsanoff, *Religious Crossroads* (New York: E. P. Dutton, 1942), pp. 13–25.

stand the belief statements of particular religious traditions and in trying to discover what the functions and significance of those statements may be and how one might discover whether they are true. Theologians may seek to explicate the *meaning* aspect of religion, or at least of their own religious tradition. They will perhaps try to show that the religious tradition is meaningful.

The anthropologist Clifford Geertz has pointed to two major functions of religion: providing a comprehensive system of symbols for understanding the nature of reality and providing a system of values that demands complete devotion.[3] He sees these as inseparable. We may express his view by saying that ultimately we value the things we do because we see them as rooted in ultimate reality, and we see them as rooted in ultimate reality because we have learned to value them as having ultimate significance.

Accordingly, in *Exploring Religious Meaning* we define *religion* as *any person's reliance on a pivotal value or a group of related values in which that person finds essential wholeness as an individual and as a person-in-community.* For that person, all other values are subordinate to this central value (or to this group of values). The pivotal value spoken of in the definition is authentic (meaningful, real to that person, of great and unique importance to the person), though it may not be meaningful to others. Here, "reliance on a pivotal value" includes trust in an unrivaled Power or Being. The pivotal value may be shared by others. In such cases, we speak of a "religious tradition," such as Christianity, Buddhism, or Hinduism.

Generally when people profess to hold some pivotal value or values and their conduct seems to contradict their profession, we believe they are either hypocrites or superficial and immature. For a person's professed religious commitment to be authentic, his or her life must be governed by the religion's pivotal value.

For many contemporary persons the idea of total commitment has lost this core meaning. Often commitment carries with it a provisional promise—if it continues to be meaningful. Such a provisional commitment is antithetic to the traditional understanding of religious commitment.

People from very different religious traditions, in which the pivotal values at least seem to differ greatly, may have great difficulty in understanding one another. An Orthodox Jew who emphasizes (whose pivotal value is) the living of all life in accordance with God's revealed law (the Torah) may find it difficult to understand or to sympathize with a Hindu mystic or a Christian Pentecostalist for whom an overwhelming sense of the presence of God *within* is the ultimate goal. Even in the same religious tradition this difficulty may appear. A Christian fundamentalist and a theologically liberal Christian may have a difficult time understanding and accepting the authenticity of the other's differing religious commitment, conduct, and belief.

However, a religiously committed person with an open and searching attitude may understand and empathize with a person of another faith by turning inward, to his or her own experience of religious commitment. At that moment a dialogue—in its truest sense—between human beings with different backgrounds and different mind-sets may allow them to open themselves to each other. We believe that such openness to others is

[3] See Clifford Geertz, *The Interpretation of Culture: Selected Essays* (New York: Basic Books, 1973), pp. 89, 126, 140.

important, even if the intellectual differences are sharpened. We believe that even when people continue to differ in major ways religiously, the value of life for each will be enhanced by a greater understanding of the other's values and that the possibility of living in a more peaceful, constructive world, where problems can be solved cooperatively in spite of, even because of, differences in religious understanding and commitment, will be enhanced.

This definition must be seen as a preliminary one. It will receive much qualification in the following units and sections of *Exploring Religious Meaning*. Chapter 1 will attempt both to illustrate the definition of religion as "reliance on a pivotal value" and to begin to qualify it.

UNIT 1   RELIANCE UPON A PIVOTAL VALUE

> We define religion as any person's **reliance upon a pivotal value** in which that person finds essential wholeness as an individual . . .

In answer to the question "What does it mean to have a god?" Martin Luther wrote, "Trust and faith of the heart alone make both God and idol. . . . Whatever . . . your heart clings to . . . and relies on, that is what really is your God."[4] It is sometimes said by religious persons that there are in reality no atheists.

◆◆◆

In what way is this statement true?

In what ways—bearing in mind our definition of religion—might it not be true?

Do you think that the way Luther talks about what a person's "real" god is makes sense?

Is this a useful way of talking about "religious" commitment?

◆◆◆

H. Richard Niebuhr was a twentieth-century Protestant thinker who accepted Martin Luther's definition of the concept of God—what one relies on, puts his or her trust in. Commenting on the definition, Niebuhr wrote, "If this be true, that the word 'god' means the object of human faith in life's worthwhileness, it is evident that men have many gods, that our natural religion is polytheistic."[5] Niebuhr pointed out that an individual's pivotal value—that which the individual seeks or adheres to as the source of ultimate meaning or fulfillment—may shift from one value to another or may be composed of a group of values (such as health, wealth, and wisdom). An individual's central value may also be any object, subject, activity that consumes a person's attention, devotion, and commitment—such as vocation, sports, music, and any number of other realities.

◆◆◆

[4] Martin Luther, as quoted by H. Richard Niebuhr, *Radical Monotheism and Western Culture* (New York: Harper & Row, 1960), p. 119.

[5] Ibid.

Are people frequently polytheistic?

Do the terms theism, polytheism, and monotheism acquire new meanings—or at least other possible meanings—when religion is defined as "pivotal value"?

◆◆◆

The religions of the world propose supreme or pivotal values to their adherents as that will bring fulfillment and security. In later units we will focus on some major religious orientations toward pivotal value. For instance, there is a *moral* orientation, which holds obedience to the will of a Divine Being (for many adherents of Judaism) or to an eternal code of right behavior (as in Confucianism) as the supreme value to be sought. There are also *mystical* religious orientations, which hold that the pivotal goal of life is a very intense sense of union with the Divine (Hinduism) or an experience of the ultimate, overwhelming, transforming presence of God by worshipers whose will and personality are united to God in love (Christian mysticism). We will speak also of esthetic, magical, and ecstatic orientations to religion, which need not be exclusive of one another. This way of classifying orientations to a pivotal value is only a conceptual tool; it is not the only way of approaching the role of religion as the center of value and meaning in the lives of groups and individuals.

The following materials illustrate how the concept of pivotal value is present in three of the world's great religious traditions. In a passage from the Hindu *Bhagavad-Gita* (c. 100 C.E.), the Lord Krishna calls for the entire devotion and loyalty of his devotee Arjuna. In effect, the Divine Krishna asks his follower to make devotion to Krishna the supreme, the pivotal, value of Arjuna's human life.

> Cling thou to me!
> Clasp Me with heart and mind! so shalt thou dwell
> Surely with Me on high. But if thy thought
> Droops from such height; if you be'st weak to set
> Body and soul upon Me constantly,
> Despair not! give Me lower service! seek
> To read Me, worshipping with steadfast will;
> And, if thou canst not worship steadfastly
> Work for Me, toil in works pleasing to Me!
> For he that laboreth right for love of Me
> Shall finally attain! But, if in this
> Thy faint heart fails, bring Me thy failure! find
> Refuge in Me! Let fruits of labor go,
> Renouncing all for Me, with lowliest heart,
> So shalt thou come; for, though to know is more
> than diligence, yet worship better is
> Than knowing, and renouncing better still.
> Give Me thy heart! adore Me! serve Me! cling
> In faith and love and reverence to Me!
> So shalt thou come to Me! I promise true.
> Make Me thy single refuge! I will free
> Thy soul from all its sins! Be of good Cheer.[6]

[6] *The Song Celestial or Bhagavad-Gita*, Sir Edwin Arnold, trans., (London: Routledge & Kegan Paul, 1955), pp. 12.8, 18.64–66. Used by permission.

In the Christian Apostle's Creed (c. 500), powerful expression is given to the Christian belief that the God of Christian worship is Lord of all life. God is confessed as being Creator, Savior and Redeemer, Deliverer, and Lord of all life, God and Lord in the present and in every future, eternally.

> I believe in God the Father Almighty, Maker of heaven and earth. And in Jesus Christ his only Son our Lord; Who was conceived by the Holy Ghost, born of the Virgin Mary, suffered under Pontius Pilate, was crucified, dead, and buried; he descended into hell; the third day he rose from the dead; he ascended into heaven; and sitteth at the right hand of God the Father Almighty; from thence he shall come to judge the quick and the dead. I believe in the Holy Ghost; the holy catholic Church; the communion of saints; the forgiveness of sins; the resurrection of the body; and the life everlasting. Amen.

Augustine, a Western Christian theologian of the fourth and fifth centuries C.E., in a brief prayer at the beginning of his famous *Confessions* (which is the story of his conversion to Christianity), gives expression to the belief that God as proclaimed in Christian teaching is and should be the pivotal value for all humans: "Lord, you have made us for yourself and our hearts are restless till they rest in you."

The following Muslim prayer gives graphic expression to the adherent's reliance on Allah as the Supreme Source of wholeness for the individual.

> Thanks be to my Lord; He the Adorable, and only to be adored. My Lord, the Eternal, The Ever-existing, the Cherisher, the True Sovereign whose mercy and might overshadow the universe; the Regulator of the world, and Light of the creation. His is our worship; to Him belongs all worship; He existed before all things, and will exist after all that is living has ceased. Thou art the adored, my Lord; Thou art the Master, the Loving and Forgiving. . . .
> O my Lord, Thou art the Helper of the afflicted, the Reliever of all distress, the Consoler of the broken-hearted; Thou art present everywhere to help Thy servants. . . .
>
> O my Lord, Thou art the Creator, I am only created;
> Thou art my Sovereign, I am only thy servant;
> Thou art the Helper, I am the beseecher;
> Thou art the Forgiver, I am the sinner;
> Thou, my Lord, art the merciful. All-knowing, All-loving.

UNIT 2   PERSON-IN-COMMUNITY

> We define religion as any person's reliance upon a pivotal value in which that person finds essential wholeness . . . **as a person-in-community.**

TAOS, N.M. (AP)—An aging spiritual leader of the Taos Pueblo Indians, the sight in his 90-year-old eyes dimming, plans to take his tribe's plea for a religious sanctuary to the white man's Capitol.

He will renew the plea of the Taos Indians for title to 48,000 acres of forest land surrounding Blue Lake, high in the Sangre de Cristo Mountains of northern New Mexico, and sacred to the tribe.

"Our Blue Lake wilderness," Romero said, "keeps our water holy and by this water we are baptized. Without this, we have no life."

"If our land is not returned to us," Romero said, "if it is turned over to the government for its use, then it is the end of Indian life."

"Our people will scatter as the people of other nations have scattered. It is our religion that holds us together."

In religion humans find wholeness not only as individuals but also as persons-in-community—persons unavoidably related to others, with whom the individual shares an identity, purpose, and experience.

Many in contemporary—modern and postmodern—secularized society (see Unit 74)—consider religion to be a purely personal, private part of an individual's life. This has not been true throughout human history and is not true in much of the world today. Religion traditionally incorporates a person into a community and its theology defines essential elements of the individual's humanity. When Pope John Paul II visited Greece on his pilgrimage retracing the travels of the Apostle Paul, his visit was deeply resented and protested by some adherents of Greek Orthodox Christianity. They saw the presence of the Pope of Roman or Latin Christianity as an attack on their religious and cultural identity as *Greek Orthodox* Christians. Much the same feeling is present in Russia today, where Russian Orthodox leaders see the presence of Protestant, Pentecostal, and other American- or European-based missionaries as an attack on Russian religious, ethnic, and cultural identities. In many Muslim countries, the attempt to convert Muslims to other religious traditions or even to import literature promoting non-Muslim religion is punishable by death. In some religious communities persons who convert to a different religion are treated as dead by other family members. Afghanistan Muslim religious beliefs recently led to the destruction of ancient Buddhist statuary considered by many non-Muslims to be great works of art.

Unit 6 discusses additional aspects of the "community" dimensions of religious commitment. This aspect of religion raises profound questions about the significance of the individual's relationships to other individuals and groups. The point is often made that most newborn animals are far better equipped biologically to begin life than humans are. Human beings, with their long period of dependency, are in many ways products of their society and its culture and must learn from their communities how to be human. Chapter 6 of the text deals with additional issues of religion: belief, knowledge, and the roles of faith, authority, and tradition.

◆◆◆

How much of what we consider knowledge, the belief systems of our society, is simply the result of shared assumptions and a shared way of life?

If Gautama Buddha had been born in thirteenth century C.E. *Italy, might he have become a religious revivalist and reformer like St. Francis of Assisi, a late medieval poet like Dante, a medieval theologian like Aquinas?*

UNIT 3   AN INDIVIDUAL AND PERSON-IN-COMMUNITY

> We define religion as any person's reliance upon a pivotal value in which that person finds essential wholeness **as an individual and as a person-in-community.**

For the Apostle Paul, living in an idol-worshipping society, commitment to Christ—as the pivotal value—eliminated the efficacy of idols. Therefore, it made no difference for Christians if the meat sold in the marketplace had been offered to idols. Nevertheless, Paul saw that although this might be true for him as an individual, as a person-in-community he had to consider other factors. "There are some who have been so accustomed to idolatry that even now they eat this food with a sense of its heathen consecration, and their conscience, being weak, is polluted by the eating." Paul as an individual was at liberty to eat such meat, but as a member of the Christian community he was ready to restrain himself. "If food be the downfall of my brother, I will never eat meat any more, for I will not be the cause of my brother's downfall." (I Corinthians 8:7, 13, NEB)[7]

Martin Luther King's last public speech was delivered in support of a sanitation workers' strike in Memphis, Tennessee. Adapting Jesus's Good Samaritan story to the current scene, King pointed out not only the social need of the time but also that individual wholeness is never separate from corporate wholeness.

> And you know, it's possible that the priest and the Levite looked over that man on the ground and wondered if the robbers were still around. Or it's possible that they felt that the man on the ground was merely faking. And he was acting like he had been robbed and hurt, in order to seize them over there, lure them there for quick and easy seizure. And so the first question that the Levite asked was, "If I stop to help this man, what will happen to me?" But then the good Samaritan came by. And he reversed the question: "If I do not stop to help this man, what will happen to him?"
>
> That's the question before you tonight. Not, "If I stop to help the sanitation workers, what will happen to all of the hours that I usually spend in my office every day and every week as a pastor?" The question is not, "If I stop to help this man in need, what will happen to me?" "If I do not stop to help the sanitation workers, what will happen to them?" That's the question.

The speech ends with King's premonition of his own death. Nevertheless, the dominant note is a firm confidence that no matter what happens to the individual, there is an abiding triumph that the individual shares when, under God, individual and group faith and action issue in corporate and individual wholeness—"the Promised Land."

> Well, I don't know what will happen now. We've got some difficult days ahead. But it doesn't matter with me now. Because I've been to the mountaintop. And I don't mind. Like anybody, I would like to live a long life. Longevity has its place. But I'm not con-

---

[7] Scripture quotations in this publication identified by the letters NEB are from *The New English Bible.* © The Delegates of the Oxford University Press and the Syndics of the Cambridge University Press 1961, 1970.

cerned about that now. I just want to do God's will. And He's allowed me to go up to the mountain. And I've looked over. And I've seen the promised land. I may not get there with you. But I want you to know tonight, that we, as a people will get to the promised land. And I'm happy, tonight. I'm not worried about anything. I'm not fearing any man. Mine eyes have seen the glory of the coming of the Lord.[8]

King's personal commitment led to direct social action. Essential wholeness, however, manifests itself in various ways. This is seen in the experience of Dietrich Bonhoeffer, who sought meaningful wholeness as he wrote from his German prison. A committed Christian preacher who would not silence his public witness for Christ despite Nazi commands to do so, Bonhoeffer was jailed and finally martyred. Until his death, however, he maintained his faith and his loving concern for others. Affirming Christ as the Man for others, Bonhoeffer interpreted faith as "Something whole, involving the whole of one's life." Faith meant "taking risks for others."[9] For such a faith in Christ, Bonhoeffer risked himself—gave himself for others—and in this way, as he believed, experienced wholeness as an individual.

UNIT 4   OTHER VALUES SUBORDINATE TO CENTRAL VALUE

> We define religion as any person's reliance upon a pivotal value . . . **for that person all other values are subordinate to this central value.**

Most contemporary Americans do not look to a political cause or movement as something that will bring salvation to them or the world. Many politicians see politics as a way to personal accomplishment, prestige, influence, or a way of improving society or helping groups and individuals have better opportunities. However, there have been times in human history in which political movements have seemed to some to be ways to salvation—for society and for individuals. One individual who saw the political movement he was committed to as of pivotal value was Leon Trotsky.

Trotsky, who with Lenin led the revolutionary movement that produced a Communist government in Russia in 1917, was one of the most brilliant Marxist thinkers of the twentieth century. He did not become a Marxist all at once, however. The son of a prosperous farmer, Trotsky was drawn to various revolutionary movements popular among students who were concerned with improving the lot of peasants and industrial workers. After a period during which he argued strongly against the Marxist position, Trotsky was "converted" to Marxism while in prison for revolutionary activities. In the following passage of his autobiography, he describes how during a period of exile he found in his new position the key to understanding all the major aspects of life.

---

[8] Martin Luther King, Jr., "A View from the Mountaintop." c/o Writer's House, Inc. as agent for the proprietor. Copyright 1963 by Martin Luther King, Jr., Copyright renewed 1991 by Coretta Scott King.

[9] Dietrich Bonhoeffer, *Letters and Papers from Prison* (New York: Macmillan, 1958), pp. 199, 209.

Since 1896, when I had tried to oppose all revolutionary ideas, and the following year, when I opposed Marxism even though I was by that time already carrying on revolutionary activity, I had come a long way. By the time I was sent into exile, Marxism had definitely become the basis of my whole philosophy. During my exile, I tried to consider, from the new point of view I had acquired, the so-called "eternal" problems of life: love, death, friendship, optimism, pessimism, and so forth. In different epochs, and in varying social surroundings, man loves and hates and hopes differently. Just as the tree feeds its leaves, flowers, and fruits with the extracts absorbed from the soil by its roots, so does the individual find food for his sentiments, and ideas, even the most "sublime" ones—as Marxism states—in the economic roots of society.[10]

In Marxism, Trotsky found the key to the understanding of all life. For him, the "truth" of Marxist teaching was so central to life that it changed his understanding of everything else. He believed that for a Marxist, the ordinary relations and activities of life—work, marriage, friendship, hobbies, recreation—would be very different than they would be for non-Marxists: They would have different meanings and would call for different behavior. For example, he saw marriage in a feudal society as a "sacred" relationship; in a capitalist society it was a contractual agreement; for Marxists, it would be a free relationship for companionship based on common political activities and friendship. Even after his expulsion from Russia and from the Russian Communist party, he believed that the Marxist theory fully explained why backward economic and social conditions in Russia had inevitably produced a deterioration of Russian communism into the Stalinist dictatorship. Trotsky remained a committed Marxist revolutionary. He was assassinated in 1940 by a Stalinist agent in Mexico.

We have stressed that religions provide a unifying value or system of values by which all other values and all parts of life may be interpreted. Did Trotsky's Marxist theory—his Marxist beliefs—express this kind of value orientation? Could Marxism for Trotsky be called a religious orientation? Note how Trotsky's beliefs about the central questions of life are interpreted by and subordinated to the central, unifying beliefs provided by Marxist theory.

The sociologist J. Milton Yinger has written

Major religious differences can persist in a functionally unified society only at the cost of sharp conflict on the one hand or by the reduction of the significance of these religions to their adherents on the other, or by some mixture of these processes. Insofar as it is reduction in the significance of traditional beliefs that occurs, men do not thereby give up the search for a unifying system of values. They develop a quasireligion to do the job. Most often in our time it is nationalism, sometimes pursued with an almost desperate sense of urgency for the conviction of unity.[11]

Sociologists often use the term quasi-religion to describe something—like nationalism or Marxism—that is ordinarily thought of as "nonreligious" in content but that functions or acts like a religion. What analogies are there between the unifying role that Marxism played in the life of Trotsky and the role that Marxism or nationalism might play in the life of a society? (See Figure 1.1)

[10] Leon Trotsky, *My Life* (New York: Grosset & Dunlap, 1960), p. 127.
[11] J. Milton Yinger, *Sociology Looks at Religion* (New York: Macmillan, 1963), p. 31.

"Why did you become a crusader? You don't even go to church."

Figure 1.1

For both traditional religions and secular quasi-religions there usually will be symbols that express the meaning and importance of the religion's pivotal value or system of values. What might happen to adherents of a religion or quasi-religion when they perceive conflicts among the values their religious tradition or political movement advocates?

Religious symbols usually express and appeal to the emotions of the adherents of the religion in a powerful way. The cross for Christians; the words of the sacred Scriptures, the Torah, for Jews; the city of Mecca for Muslims—these are powerful religious symbols.

UNIT 5   AUTHENTIC TO THE INDIVIDUAL

> This pivotal value . . . **is authentic to the individual though it may not be meaningful to others.**

Can participation in sports—for athletes and their fans—be a religion? With the tremendous emphasis on sports in contemporary society—from Little Leagues, to colleges with their bowl games and March Madness, to professionals with their World Series and the Super Bowl—the rituals and fervor of teams and crowds may *seem* religious.

Many athletes publicly or privately *do* engage in acts of religious devotion before or after games. Some express gratitude to God for wins or acquiesce in what they regard as God's will when they lose.

Possibly a case intermediate between "making a sport a religion" and expressing attitudes of a traditional religion during participation in a sport (giving thanks for victory or repeating the Lord's prayer) is to be seen in the life pattern of Phil Jackson, a remarkable figure in professional basketball. A successful player, as a coach Jackson led two teams, the Chicago Bulls and the Los Angeles Lakers, to multiple NBA championships. In his autobiography, *Sacred Hoops*, Jackson tells the story of a life devoted to success in a major sport that has been guided by practices and principles that transcend the sport but find the sport an adequate way of expressing the religious principles.[12] Jackson's parents were Christian Pentecostal preachers. He pays tribute to the positive influence of their lives and teaching on him.

As an adult, Jackson has been influenced by the teachings and practices of Eastern religious traditions. He often calls himself a Buddhist, but he has also adopted Native American attitudes and values and symbolism in major ways. As a coach, he has inculcated the values of selflessness, concern for the group, and concern for participation in basketball as an expression of a selfless holistic activity expressive of at-one-ness with reality. He has taught his players techniques of meditation to help their concentration, selflessness, and empathy with teammates and their sport while playing a very physically and mentally demanding game. This cannot have always been easy with players who often are *prima donnas*, with salaries in the millions, where emphasis often has been on each individual trying to be a *star* more concerned with his own statistics than with team welfare.

For Jackson, basketball is not a religion or a substitute for religion but an authentic way of expressing religion.

◆◆◆

Can a sport be someone's religion?

Can a sport be in conflict or in competition with someone's religion?

Can you name other life commitments that might be seen as a religion?

Unit 6   Religious Tradition

> The pivotal value may be shared by others. **In such cases we speak of a "religious tradition."**

Religion may be an intensely personal dimension of an individual's life, but even the most personal and individualistic religious experiences will have been drawn from the social setting. New religious movements, movements of reform or renewal or new direction in religious life, draw to some extent on a common body of beliefs and practices in the larger society. Thus we can speak of at least two important phases of religious tradition. First, it refers to those things handed down from the past that are shared to some extent by the members of a social group. In this phase, religious tradition becomes the basis of present and future religious life, for whatever new or deeper or repetitive elements an individual

---

[12] Phillip Jackson and Hugh Delehanty, *Sacred Hoops* (New York: Hyperion, 1995).

or group may experience. In a second phase, religious tradition may refer to that which, on the basis of the old traditions—perhaps in opposition to them, perhaps in the desire to renew them—becomes in a new way a religious possibility for people.

In the New Testament accounts of the origins of the Christian movement, there is an interesting blending of these two phases of religious tradition. On the basis of traditional and newly interpreted expectations in Judaism for deliverance from foreign oppressors, many Jews responded to a call by John the Baptist for repentance, for a renewal of life and intention in expectation of God's soon-to-be-accomplished act of judgment and deliverance. According to the earliest Christian accounts, some of those who first responded to John's interpretation and reinterpretation of the traditional messianic hope of Israel then responded to the message and activity of Jesus. In the Gospel according to John is the following account of how some of Jesus's first disciples or followers began to spread the beliefs and hopes they had acquired about Jesus:

> One of the two who followed Jesus after hearing what John said was Andrew, Simon Peter's brother. The first thing he did was to find his brother Simon. He said to him, "We have found the Messiah" (which is the Hebrew for "Christ"). He brought Simon to Jesus, who looked at him and said, "You are Simon son of John. You shall be called Cephas" (that is, Peter, the Rock).
> The next day Jesus decided to leave for Galilee. He met Philip, who, like Andrew and Peter, came from Bethsaida, and said to him, "Follow me." Philip went to find Nathanael, and told him, "We have met the man spoken of by Moses in the Law, and by the prophets: it is Jesus son of Joseph, from Nazareth." "Nazareth!" Nathanael exclaimed; "Can anything good come from Nazareth?" Philip said, "Come and see." When Jesus saw Nathanael coming, he said, "Here is an Israelite worthy of the name; there is nothing false in him." Nathanael asked him, "How do you come to know me?" Jesus replied, "I saw you under the fig-tree before Philip spoke to you." "Rabbi," said Nathanael, "you are the Son of God; you are king of Israel." Jesus answered, "Is this the ground of your faith, that I told you I saw you under the fig-tree? You shall see greater things than that." Then he added, "In truth, in very truth I tell you all, you shall see heaven wide open, and God's angels ascending and descending upon the Son of Man." (John 1:40–51, NEB)

In a similar way, later units in the text (Units 11 and 18) describe how Prince Gautama, dissatisfied with life and tortured by unanswered questions about human suffering, began the kind of religious quest that the Hinduism of his day taught those seeking religious enlightenment to pursue. He sought answers from the holy men and the teachers of philosophy. He withdrew to the forest, fasted, and meditated. A number of other seekers after enlightenment were so impressed by his devotion and his efforts to find the answers he was seeking that they attached themselves to him, hoping that when the answers came, they too would be enlightened through their contact with Gautama. When Gautama modified his approach, rejecting the prescribed fasting, mortification, and asceticism, these disciples were shocked and withdrew from him. But when the experience of enlightenment did come, they returned, became his disciples, and began to be part of a community that eventually preserved and handed on the teachings of Gautama.

A new religious tradition very often arises as a result of the activity and teachings of a powerful personality who has reinterpreted an older body of tradition. In later units of the book, such figures as Confucius, Martin Luther, Mohammed, and Teresa of Avila will be examined. In each case the pattern just described is present: Through a powerful reinterpretation of existing religious tradition, something new emerged, followers were attracted, and a new or renewed religious tradition began to be an effective influence in the societies and lives of individuals reached.

✦✦✦

What individuals from our own time have you heard or read of who are creators or renewers of religious traditions?

UNIT 7   LIFE-GOVERNING VALUE

> For a person's professed religious commitment to be authentic, the person's life must **be governed by the religion's pivotal value.**

The value systems we consciously espouse as authentic may fail to coincide with those from which we subconsciously act. This inauthenticity is often transparent. The Hebrew prophet Amos lived in a time when many of his co-religionists made a show of devotion to God. Amos believed that their acts of worship often failed to express an inner reality of commitment to the God they claimed to worship since they were not concerned about God's demands for justice and compassion in society. Speaking for God, Amos condemned outward practices of religion that did not express authentic inner commitment.

> I hate, I despise your feasts,
>   and I take no delight in your solemn assemblies.
> Even though you offer me your burnt offerings
>   and cereal offerings,
> I will not accept them,
>   and the offerings of well-being of your fatted
>   animals
> I will not look upon.
> Take away from me the noise of your songs;
>   I will not listen to the melody of your harps.
> But let justice roll down like waters, and
>   righteousness like an everflowing stream.
>   (Amos 5:21–24, NRSV)[13]

Current criticism of religion usually concentrates on the hypocrisy of inauthentic religion, or pseudoreligion. It often finds expression in popular art forms—cartoons, TV sit-coms, songs. Criticisms of religious hypocrisy are often based on claims that religion-affirming groups and individuals are often more concerned with power, possessions, and prestige than affirming the pivotal values of the religion.

What one might do on the basis of an authentic religious commitment within this Christian religious tradition possibly is expressed in a New Testament passage:

[13] NRSV indicates the *New Revised Standard Version* of the Bible (copyright © 1989, Division of Christian Education of the National Council of the Churches of Christ in the United States of America).

Tell them [who trust in this world's goods and goals] to hoard a wealth of noble actions by doing good, to be ready to give away and to share, and so acquire a treasure which will form a good foundation for the future. Thus they will grasp the life which is life indeed. (I Timothy 6:18–19, NEB)

As should be clear from earlier units, though frequently people are not genuinely or fully committed to the religious values they profess, there are many examples of persons who have been authentically and powerfully committed to the values espoused by religious traditions. Martin Luther King, Jr., and Bonhoeffer have already been cited, as well as others. In succeeding units people from a great variety of traditions—among them St. Teresa and St. Francis, Martin Luther, Gandhi, Moses, Martin Buber, and Gautama—will be presented, people whose lives were transformed in and through wholehearted commitment to the central values of one or another of the world's great religious traditions.

UNIT 8   UNDERSTANDING BASED ON DIALOGUE

> For its adherents a religion usually is held to be absolute, not relative. This means **it is often difficult for one to understand the faith commitment of someone with a different faith perspective,** either within or outside one's own religious group or tradition. In this situation a religiously committed person with an open and searching attitude may understand and empathize with a person of another faith by turning inward, to his or her own experience of religious commitment. **What is demanded is willingness of the participants in dialogue to open to each other.**

Martin Buber, a twentieth-century Jewish philosopher and religious writer who had great influence on Protestant and Catholic as well as Jewish thought, recounts two talks that involved him in religious disagreement with others. After one of Buber's public lectures, a French workingman presented an argument favoring atheism. Buber refuted the man's position.

Figure 1.2   (PEANUTS reprinted by the permission of United Features Syndicate, Inc.)

When I was through . . . the man . . . raised his lids, which had been lowered the whole time, and said slowly and impressively, "'You are right.'. . ." Buber was dismayed. "What had I done? I had led the man to the threshold beyond which there sat enthroned the majestic image which the great physicist, the great man of faith, Pascal, called the God of the Philosophers. Had I wished for that? Had I not rather wished to lead him to the other, Him whom Pascal called the God of Abraham, Isaac, and Jacob, Him to whom one can say Thou? . . ."

On another occasion, Buber and an older man whom he greatly admired argued about religion and never came to verbal agreement with each other. The older man criticized Buber for clinging to the use of the word "God."

"What you mean by the name of God is something above all human grasp and comprehension, but in speaking about it you have lowered it to human conceptualization. What word of human speech is so misused, so defiled, so desecrated as this! All the innocent blood that has been shed for it has robbed it of its radiance. All the injustice that it has been used to cover has effaced its features. When I hear the highest called 'God,' it sometimes seems almost blasphemous. . . ." "Yes," I said, "it is the most heavy laden of all human words. None has become so soiled, so mutilated. Just for this reason I may not abandon it. Generations of men have laid the burden of their anxious lives upon this word and weighed it to the ground: it lies in the dust and bears their whole burden. The races of man with their religious factions have torn the word to pieces; they have killed for it and died for it, and it bears their fingermarks and their blood. Where might I find a word like it to describe the highest? If I took the purest, most sparkling concept from the inner treasure-chamber of the philosophers, I could only capture thereby an unbinding product of thought. I could not capture the presence of Him whom the generations of men have honoured and degraded with their awesome living and dying. I do indeed mean Him whom the hell-tormented and heaven-storming generations of men mean. Certainly, they draw caricatures and write 'God' underneath; they murder one another and say 'in God's name.' But when all madness and delusion fall to dust, when they stand over against Him in the loneliest darkness and no longer say 'He, He' but rather sigh 'Thou,' shout 'Thou,' all of them the one word, and when they then add 'God,' is it not the real God whom they all implore, the One living God, the God of the children of man? Is it not He who hears them? . . ."

We cannot cleanse the word "God" and we cannot make it whole; but defiled and mutilated as it is, we can raise it from the ground and set it over an hour of great care.

It had become very light in the room. It was no longer dawning, it was light. The old man stood up, came over to me, laid his hand on my shoulder and spoke: "Let us be friends." The conversation was completed.[14]

Buber believed that the first of these two talks had been a failure. Although he had communicated with the man on the level of ideas, the two had failed to meet at the deeper level that gave force and meaning to the ideas. In the second talk there was apparently little or no agreement at the intellectual level, but Buber and the older man had come to understand each other. Each had come to understand the force of meaning and personal depth of the other's beliefs and ideas about religion and the term God.

---

[14] Specified excerpts from pp. 5–9 in *Eclipse of God* (Harper Torchbook edition) by Martin Buber. Copyright 1952 by Harper & Row, Publishers, Inc. Reprinted by permission of the publisher.

Unit 9   Communication

The cartoon in Figure 1.3 illustrates an attempt at communication that fails because of the attitude of one participant toward the other. Failure to achieve meaningful communication generally rests on the inability of the persons involved to respect and trust each other. True dialogue and honest encounter mean willingness to respect each other and to share ideas without an attempt to minimize honest disagreements.

Some may wonder whether it is valuable or necessary for persons holding to different religious traditions or beliefs to discuss religion with each other. Won't differences and disagreements be minimized if people simply agree to be different in religion and concentrate on areas in which they do agree? In some cases, if the differences are great and mutually disturbing, can't people simply keep entirely apart from each other?

◆◆◆

Can you think of other options besides these—agreeing to disagree while leaving religious differences undiscussed, or keeping entirely separate from those whose religious beliefs or practices disturb us?

◆◆◆

In the unit on Islam in Chapter 2, it is suggested that if there had been better understanding of the meaning of Islamic religious beliefs and the value placed on them by their adherents, some present conflicts between the United States and the nations and groups in the Middle East might have been avoided, or at least lessened in scope and intensity. Many believe that in a world that is increasingly interconnected, and in a society as increasingly diverse and pluralistic in ethnic and cultural makeup as the contemporary United States, we cannot afford the luxury of failing to understand diverse and contrasting religious positions.

In addition, some ethical or religious positions adhere to and advocate the need to try to understand, in both of Buber's senses—at the level of ideas and at the level of personal depth—those who differ from us religiously, as did the Christians who formulated

Figure 1.3   *The Born Loser* by Art Sansom. (Reprinted by permission of Newspaper Enterprise Association [NEA].)

the following statement concerning dialogue with those committed to other religious traditions or positions. (Participation in the process does not assume that agreement in belief will be achieved or that all differences will be found to be unimportant.)

> We believe that Christ is present whenever a Christian sincerely enters into dialogue with another man: the Christian is confident that Christ can speak to him through his neighbour, as well as to his neighbour through him. Dialogue means a positive effort to attain a deeper understanding of the truth through mutual awareness of one another's convictions and witness. It involves an expectation of something new happening—the opening of a new dimension of which one was not aware before. Dialogue implies a readiness to be changed as well as to influence others. Good dialogue develops when one partner speaks in such a way that the other feels drawn to listen, and likewise when one listens so that the other is drawn to speak.[15]

The Search for God at Harvard is the best-selling account of the author's becoming more open both to his own and to others' religious traditions. The author, Ari Goldman, grew up in New York and Connecticut in a very sheltered Orthodox Jewish environment. He attended Orthodox Jewish schools, rather than the public schools, and then a Jewish university. He knew little or nothing about religious traditions other than his own; in fact, he had been warned to avoid them (especially Christianity). When he wanted to become a newspaper reporter, he was advised by many, including rabbis, that such work would be impossible for an Orthodox Jew living in full conformity to the commandments of the Torah. Nevertheless, Goldman tried to do both. Eventually he was put in charge of religious news for *The New York Times*. As preparation for that responsibility he requested and received from the *Times* a year away from work to study the world's religions, including Buddhism, Hinduism, Islam, Christianity, and Judaism, at a Christian theological seminary. *The Search for God at Harvard* is Goldman's account of his developing awareness of the variety and diversity both among and within these religious traditions and an increasing appreciation of them as well as of his own Orthodox Jewish tradition.[16]

---

[15] The Kandy Consultation on "Christians in Dialogue with Men of Other Faiths" was held from February 27–March 3, 1967, at Kandy, Ceylon, under the sponsorship of the Division of Studies, Department of World Mission and Evangelism, World Council of Churches.

[16] Ari Goldman, *The Search for God at Harvard* (New York: Random House, 1992).

2

RELIGIOUS TRADITIONS

In the preceding chapter the term *religion* was given a functional definition. That is, *religion* was defined in terms of what it does, of how it functions in the life of an individual or a group. It was defined as that which provides unifying power, a center of meaning, a supreme, or pivotal, value in the life of the individual or group. It was also stressed, however, that religious traditions, clustered around the unifying center of a pivotal value, tend to crystallize, to develop and attain objective status, so that a religious tradition can be defined in terms of a number of characteristic features:

1. A set of beliefs (creed), which may be specifically formulated or may be rather informal and indefinite but still important in shaping the lives of the religion's adherents
2. A code of conduct (code), which, again, may be rigidly formulated in terms of taboos or may be relatively undefined, more a matter of life-style
3. Devotional or ritual practices for corporate or individual worship, meditation, or self-discipline (cult)
4. Conceptions of inclusiveness or exclusiveness of the religious group and the significance of belonging to it (community)

In this chapter we briefly examine seven of the major religious traditions of the world. We have two major purposes. The first is to provide relevant background material about seven of the world religions that are frequently referred to, discussed, or utilized in the later sections of the book. (The summary to this chapter contains a table of the major aspects of these traditions, as well as a table contrasting major emphases of Western and Eastern religious traditions.) Our second purpose is to illustrate the way in which the various features or elements of a religious tradition may cluster around its central emphasis—its pivotal value.

The seven units of this chapter are intentionally very brief and limited descriptions of multifaceted religious traditions, which will be augmented by later chapters. We do not include comments on the vast complex of prehistoric and preliterate religions, elements of which are incorporated in many modern-day African, Latin American, and South Asian cultures. Many of these religions embody an association of the divine with the natural order, a worship of nature, and a stress on humanity's cooperation with the natural order. Although some contemporary ethnic groups are presently attempting to recapture many of these traditions, they are too diverse for description here. Specific insights from such religions are discussed in later units (see Unit 82). Also, many elements of these traditions have been absorbed in the major religions addressed in this chapter.

Unit 10   Hinduism

Many would insist that oversimplification is always involved in trying to define the "essence" of a living religious tradition, that every living religion is a cluster of beliefs, practices, and attitudes held together in a certain bond of resemblance yet without definable or essential identity. The philosopher Wittgenstein used the term "family resemblance" to characterize the way in which similar things—for example, games (football, baseball, chess, capture the flag)—may be like one another without necessarily sharing a group of precisely identifiable common features. Wittgenstein's term can apply to religions, and to no religion more than to Hinduism, which in one sense is not a religion at all (see Tsanoff's discussion of the term religion in Chapter 1) and in another sense is a whole family of religions—sects, cults, and creeds—and of religious practices.

Unlike some of the historic religions—Buddhism, Christianity, Islam, Confucianism—Hinduism has no specific founders. The complex of rites, images of the gods, and beliefs that characterize it stretch very far back into human history. Of the hundreds of millions of Hindus in the world today, the vast majority live on the subcontinent of India, though there are Hindus in other parts of Asia. During the nineteenth and early twentieth centuries, Hinduism, responding to contact with Western Christian missionaries, experienced a resurgence of vitality. Some intellectuals in Europe and America, attached to Hindu philosophy and spirituality, embraced Hinduism. The broader world contact that has occurred since World War II allowed various forms of Hinduism to become more widely known and accepted. Hindu sects, such as Krishna Consciousness (also known as Hare Krishna), have been particularly successful among young Americans and Europeans and claim adherents around the world.

In contrast to some other religions, the doctrines, beliefs, and practices of Hinduism are not exclusive, nor is Hinduism dogmatic or doctrinaire in creed or code. It is not organized in any institutional way, though many of its sects, cults, and movements are so organized. Perhaps the prime characteristic of Hinduism is its tolerance. Willing to recognize truth in any religious creed or way of life, Hinduism grants that anyone who is sincerely religious—a Jew, a Christian, a Muslim, or a member of some other faith—is by the very fact of this religious sincerity also a devout Hindu. (Both Gautama the Buddha and Jesus the Christ are recognized by Hindus as among the *avatara*—incarnations—of the great God *Vishnu*.) Along with Hinduism's religious tolerance goes a certain skepticism and permissiveness in doctrinal formulation and practice. Since the ultimate Divine One—*Brahman*—is beyond all finite characterizations, almost anything asserted about the Divine is both true and false (incomplete). Hinduism has shown a remarkable ability to absorb and transform—to incorporate into itself—elements of other religions. Thus, though Buddhism began as a reform, and in some ways secessionist, movement in the India of the sixth century B.C.E., Hinduism was able to transform and incorporate elements of Buddhism, as it was to do millennia later with elements of Christianity.

GODS

Westerners may find Hinduism bewildering. In one sense it is extremely polytheistic, to the extent that literally millions of gods are worshipped in Hindu cults, but in another sense Hinduism is so purely monotheistic as to be monistic or pantheistic (see Unit 40). There is One Divine Reality and nothing else exists at all, since every reality—individual human being, cow, rock, tree—in its deepest essence (*Atman*) is not a separate entity or soul but is identical with the universal Self or Soul (*Brahman*).

The many gods, whose stories are told in bewildering detail in the Hindu scriptures, are themselves held philosophically to be aspects of the One Underlying Reality (Brahman), who is beyond all distinctions and characteristics, even beyond personality or personal existence. Though Brahman is described as the One or Supreme Self, Brahman is not to be thought of as a literal being or person, certainly not as having sexual character or personality. This non-personal understanding of the Divine is often difficult for Westerners, since the Divine is almost always understood in the West as having personal characteristics.

Although Brahman is understood to be the One Universal Supreme Self, in Hindu tradition the manifestations of Brahman are myriad. The many gods of Hinduism were originally related to the natural order, to natural functions and natural processes of the universe. There are gods and spirits from the realms of animal life, for example, elephant gods, monkey gods, and human hero gods, and there continues to be great spiritual reverence for certain animals, such as the cow. The roots of Hinduism go back to an ancient Indian culture, the Dravidian, whose gods often represented and corresponded to natural phenomena. Human hero gods, gods of battle, and other nature gods were introduced to the society by Aryan invaders in approximately 1500 B.C.E. as they overran the Dravidians. Gods of the two groups, while certainly not identical, over time merged and intermingled with each other preserving names and functions as well as exchanging and sharing them. At the popular level, modern Hinduism preserves a vast complex of gods and religious functions from these ancient periods.

Most important among the gods is the so-called Trinity of *Brahma* (Creator), *Vishnu* (Preserver), and *Shiva* (Destroyer and Renewer); each represents Brahman, the Supreme Self. Brahma, as the Creator, is rarely an object of cultic worship and is often depicted as dependent on, or derived from, Vishnu. Vishnu and Shiva, in their many forms and with their female consorts, are of all Hindu divinities the most frequent objects of devotion.

Shiva is a god closely identified with the forces of the natural world, with fertility, the river, and the monsoon rains. (A Shiva temple is shown in Figure 2.1.) Though a part of the great Hindu Trinity, Shiva has several aspects. Known as the "destroyer," his destruction is for the purpose of renewal or purification, so he not only destroys but also creates. He is often considered life itself, that is, the force or energy that sustains life. He

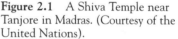
Figure 2.1 A Shiva Temple near Tanjore in Madras. (Courtesy of the United Nations).

and his many female consorts, such as Kali, a goddess particularly worshipped in her destructive and violent character, are popular objects of cultic worship.

Vishnu, the other god of the Trinity, is known for his compassion and is most often represented as the "preserver" of life. In this role, he intervenes in human history by means of *avatara*—divine representatives in animal or human form—showering humanity with benevolent love and compassion and exerting his influence on their behalf. *Krishna* and *Rama*, two principal avatara (incarnations) of Vishnu, are celebrated in legend and ritual, and their stories, along with those of their female consorts, are told in Hindu scripture and art. They themselves are objects of cultic devotion, even though they are derivative figures representing Vishnu.

The patterns found in the worship of these and the many other gods of Hinduism are varied. There are important daily rites in the home and at the numerous temples where gods are honored. Elaborate religious festivals commemorate important events in history, honor natural phenomena, and celebrate the activities of divine beings. Purification rites are important in all worship, and pilgrimages to temple shrines and other sacred places, such as the river Ganges, are central in Hindu worship.

The Hindu scriptures (the *Vedas*) are an enormous body of literature of different types—from epic poetry to cultic rites and prayers—composed over several centuries. Among the *Vedas* the *Upanishads* contain the most characteristic statement of the philosophical concepts underlying Hinduism.

KARMA

Some scholars have suggested that the basis of all later Hinduism is to be found in early rites of sacrifice, from which the concept of *karma* developed. Whether the source is in sacrifice or in other traditions, the belief in *karma*, and its complementary doctrine of *samsara*, is essential to Hinduism. In the Hindu view of life, the separate existence of particular entities is the result of a kind of ignorance (nescience) on the part of the individual. An entity, or *jiva* (*atman*, "soul"), becomes separated from the great ground of Being, Brahman, through ignorance of the nature of Brahman itself. In truth the Divine and the Self (Brahman/Atman) are one spiritual reality. However, the physical separation of individual beings (*jiva*, *atman*) leads to an illusion (*maya*)—an illusion that true life is the endless cycle of birth, death, and rebirth (as insects, animals, humans) that one experiences in physical life. This cycle is known as *samsara* and in Hindu teaching is what one must be released from to experience true spiritual life—the recognition that one is identical with Brahman, that the *atman* and Brahman are one.

How does one cast off such ignorance? The paths to release are many, but each involves *karma*. For the Hindu *karma* is a law of cause and effect. Every action, both spiritual and physical, carries consequences (*karma*); therefore, as one lives, good or bad *karma* accumulates. Good actions lead toward *moksha* (release) from the illusion of the rebirth cycle. Bad actions simply keep one trapped in that cycle (*samsara*) and may lead to lesser life forms. *Karma* then determines what one will be in a future life—whether one will rise or fall in the scale of beings when one is reborn, after death, in a particular existence. Release, *moksha*, or salvation from this cycle of rebirths and its illusion, is sought through a variety of paths or disciplines (each called a *yoga*, or "yoke"). Principal paths or yogas are the way of religious devotion to a particular deity like Vishnu or Shiva (*Bhakti-yoga*), the way of action or good works (*karma-yoga*), the way of knowledge or intellectual enlightenment (*jnana-yoga*), and the way of spiritual self-discipline through meditation (*raja-yoga*). Each of these paths eliminates bad karma and leads toward *mokska* (release) from the traps of *samsara* (rebirth).

CASTE

The theory of *karma* just sketched underlies the traditional Hindu caste system. According to the theory of *karma*, many incarnations—many births, lives, and deaths—may be required before an individual *atman* (*jiva*) achieves enlightenment and its resultant reunion with Brahman. Among humans there are four major states or levels of caste, although there developed over centuries a multitude of subcastes within the major groupings. One was born into a caste and could not leave it, except by becoming a complete outcaste, during a given lifetime. One's caste status determined what one's vocation would be, whom one could marry, and one's religious and social duties. Highest among the castes, traditionally, was that of the *Brahmins*, the priestly and intellectual leaders of India. Next came the *Kshatriyas*, the caste of political rulers and military leaders. Third were the *Vaisyas*, the caste of persons engaged in commerce and agriculture. Fourth were the *Shudras*, the servant caste. Below these and their numerous subcastes were the outcastes, those who had sunk to a level that excluded them from most opportunities to participate in society, whose very presence was religiously contaminating to members of the higher castes, and to whom only the most degrading and menial forms of livelihood were allowed.

Since India gained independence from British rule shortly after the end of World War II, the Indian government has attempted to correct some features of the caste system—outlawing, for instance, the outcaste status. Social change has also greatly modified the caste system; nevertheless, it continues to have great impact on Indian life.

Basically one's caste status specified one's religious duties. A vast number of rituals—often involving rites of washing for purification, sacrifices of various kinds, and prayers to be said or chanted—were associated with the various castes, particularly with the Brahmins. Although Hindus of every caste might choose a life of perpetual religious quest or devotion, a typical pattern for Hindus of the three highest castes—again particularly for those of the Brahmin caste—was (and to some extent still is) to close a life that passes through several stages. From the life of a student one becomes a married person and a head of family as well as a householder and participant in economic and public life (all according to one's caste status) until finally becoming a religious pilgrim or hermit, a life of complete religious devotion or meditation.

INTERCONNECTION OF ALL THINGS

Another characteristic emphasis of Hinduism, along with the importance of behaving according to one's caste status and duties, is an emphasis on the kinship and interconnection of all things. According to Hinduism, one whose eyes have been opened, one who is sufficiently enlightened, always sees only the One True Reality, the One Divine and Wondrous Brahman. From the lowest to the highest, everything is God, and life, with all its difficulties and tragedy, is therefore full of beauty and sacredness.

UNIT 11   BUDDHISM

Buddhism, emerging in the sixth century B.C.E., began as a reform movement within Hinduism that sought to renew its essential core during a period when Hindu vitality had become static and ritualized. Accepted by powerful political leaders and understood to have relevance to all people, it became a missionary religion. Over several centuries it spread through Asia, where it became an important, if not dominant, religion in China, Japan, Korea, Indochina, Nepal, Tibet, and Sri Lanka. Hinduism ultimately absorbed Indian Buddhism, so that in the modern world Buddhism is hardly represented in India. Buddhist groups in other countries were to become the conveyors and molders of modern Buddhism. Buddhism, in the last century, has experienced a resurgence of missionary zeal, spreading in some forms throughout the world.

THE BUDDHA

The founder of Buddhism, Siddhartha Gautama, lived from 563 to 480 B.C.E. His life is surrounded by legend, yet it would appear that he was a member of the Kshatriya caste. His father protected him in his youth from the realities of suffering and evil in life—from *dukkha*, life's disjointedness and dislocation. Once Gautama discovered the tragedies and difficulties present in the world, he began a quest to understand why life should include such things and what they meant. Lasting several years, the quest led him through the disciplines of philosophy and Hindu religious asceticism, but he found no lasting solace in these. Eventually, through meditation, he became "enlightened"—that is, he found answers to the riddles of life—and subsequently began a new way of life. (For a more detailed discussion of his experience, see Unit 18.) He later would be called either the *Buddha*, the enlightened or awakened one; or Gautama the Buddha.

Having found release from the anxieties of life, Buddha chose to share this knowledge with others who had joined his original quest. Five ascetics who had been with him accepted his new insights and formed with him a *sangha*, a monastic order that would become the Buddhist movement. Enlightened at approximately 35 years of age, he spent the rest of his life in a wandering existence, teaching others the insights he had gained. Although he had gathered a large following by the end of his life, even to the extent of establishing orders for women, the development of Buddhism as a distinct religion became the work of his disciples.

Some of Buddha's insights contrasted significantly with the philosophical and popular Hinduism of that time; nevertheless, he also began with certain assumptions inherent in Hinduism. Hinduism's basic understanding of the universe was accepted:

1. The concept of the material world as an illusion (*maya*) to be ultimately discarded by the true believer
2. The belief in reincarnation in a continuous round of existence (*samsara*) from which one is to be freed
3. The acceptance of the law of *karma*—the universe is governed by cause and effect, all actions have their reward, good or evil, and one's actions determine what one will be.

Accepting this framework, Buddha made major transformations in the religious thought of his own day. He was convinced that all persons, whatever their stage or station in life, could achieve the enlightenment he enjoyed. Consequently, he rejected the caste system of Hinduism, which required that one advance through a large number of reincarnations to a status where release would be possible. Hindu philosophy and religious theory was highly complex and intricate during Buddha's lifetime. Since Buddha saw no practical applications through these avenues that would offer enlightenment to ordinary people, he summarily rejected metaphysical speculation. He went so far as to reject any comment or speculation on the Divine because in his understanding human words or thoughts were not adequate to express the Divine. For Buddha all human discussion of divinity was speculation, and therefore impractical, since it could not lead to enlightenment. This hesitancy caused some later forms of Buddhism to question belief in the Divine and has sometimes raised questions about whether Buddhism should be considered a religion or simply a philosophical and ethical system.

PRINCIPAL TEACHINGS

The principal teachings of Buddha revolved around several insights into the nature of humanity and its life. He was particularly interested in helping people become "aware" of themselves and the world—the *dukkha* of life—and how they might overcome this disorientation. He is reputed to have said, "I teach only two things, O disciples, the fact of suffering and the possibility of escape from suffering." According to Buddha, one must recognize not only the reality of suffering but also that it is caused by ego-centered patterns—selfish desires (*tanha*). To alleviate suffering one must learn to redirect these desires until ultimately they are extinguished—so that one is not bound by mental, emotional, or physical desires but is released simply to "be."

To achieve release was not, however, a simple matter, for one must redirect one's whole attitude toward reality. The method formulated by Buddha to overcome suffering involved two direct steps. One must, first, recognize the truth concerning the nature of life—the *Four Noble Truths*—and, second, live by the instructions contained in the fourth truth, or by the *Eight Fold Path*.

The Four Noble Truths:

1. That life inevitably involves *dukkha* (suffering)
2. That the cause of suffering is *tanha* (desire or selfish craving)
3. That the suffering can be cured by overcoming selfish craving
4. That the way to overcome selfish craving is through following the Eightfold Way, or Path

The Eightfold Path:

1. Right View—Awareness of the need to overcome selfish desire
2. Right Thought—Determination to solve this problem
3. Right Speech—Abstention from lies and evil language
4. Right Action—Abstention from killing, stealing, and immoral conduct
5. Right Mode of Livelihood—Noninvolvement in the professions that harm living things
6. Right Endeavor—Suppression of wrong states of mind and creation of right states of mind
7. Right Mindfulness—Self-knowledge and self-mastery
8. Right Concentration—The experience of being freed from the false sense of selfhood and the isolation of selfish motivation

Such insights as taught by Buddha meant that Buddha was far more interested in the ethical patterns of life than in religious rites, rituals, and theologies. In Buddha's teachings one is challenged to work out one's own "salvation," or release; others may help by pointing the way, but each person is personally responsible for the attitudes and patterns that determine one's ultimate existence. Though high ethical action is the method for moving toward enlightenment, enlightenment is far more than a matter of ethics; rather, it is insight into the very essence of life and freedom to live on the basis of that insight.

A person who has experienced this insight or enlightenment has entered into a state of being most often described as *Nirvana* (extinction of desire). According to Buddha, when one enters Nirvana there is no need for a continuing soul or self; one simply is. Enlightenment also ends the round of reincarnations since, for Buddha, what is passed from life to life is the accumulated *karma* attached to one's consciousness. Having entered Nirvana, one no longer has need of individual consciousness (see Unit 18).

Buddha's forty years of teaching elaborated these insights and others into a wealth of sayings and instructions. In his own eyes and in those of his immediate successors, he was only "the enlightened one," giving insights into life. In his own life he treated all persons and living things with compassion and taught others to do the same. Later, others were to make much more of Buddha's teachings and patterns of living, seeing them as providing insight into human life and the nature of reality. Hence, in some patterns of Buddhism, he was elevated to divine status.

Immediately after his death, some of the leading monks among his followers joined in council and began to recite and memorize his teachings. The result was the formulation of dogma and tradition, which Buddha had criticized in Hinduism. These developments led, first, to the standardization of the teachings into scriptural writings and, second, to the formulation of two great branches, or patterns, of Buddhism.

The scriptures are written forms of the oral tradition passed down through the centuries. First written after a fourth council in the first century, they were recorded in the *Pali* tongue (an ancient Indic language). Today this text is a basic orthodox version of the scriptures. Other forms also emerged in *Sanskrit*, another ancient Indian language and the official language of the northern branch of Buddhism. Codifications of these scriptural texts have been numerous and controversial.

BUDDHIST SCHOOLS

The history of Buddhism as a religious tradition (in contrast to the teachings and life of Guatama the Buddha) revolves around changing answers to two basic questions: "What is a Buddha?" and "What is enlightenment?" Answers to these questions led to the development of several Buddhist schools, or branches, within the tradition.

Theravada, or the School of the Elders, understands Buddha to be one who points the way to enlightenment; he was a teacher who helped others by giving instruction, but ultimately it is by the individual's efforts alone that enlightenment can be reached. Enlightenment for the Theravadist essentially means wisdom—consciousness of human desire, the anxiety it causes, and the suffering it inflicts, accompanied by a personal commitment to follow the paths to the elimination of all desire. Such consciousness and commitment ultimately result in the abandonment of selfhood. The Theravadist, therefore, adheres to a strict interpretation of Buddha's teachings, insisting on an austere following of traditional rules and disciplines. The ideal followers in this form of Buddhism are the monks (known as *arhats*) who give themselves fully to the pursuit of enlightenment, usually through elaborate forms of meditation. Laypersons in Theravada understand their religious role as being primarily supportive of the monk's quest, yet any person may become a monk. In return for material support, the monks perform ritual and festival functions on such occasions as holidays, weddings, and funerals—functions often carried out by priests in other religions—although the monks still stress meditation rather than these duties. Theravada became the religion of Ceylon, Burma, Thailand, and Indochina—the southern branch. Because of its austerity, Theravada is also known (by its adversaries) as *Hinayana* ("small vehicle" or "raft") since relatively few people (the monks) would be expected to follow its path immediately to ultimate enlightenment.

Mahayana ("large vehicle") developed from a different impulse within Buddhism.

It stresses the infinite compassion of Buddha: his willingness to share his insights and his helping others to achieve Nirvana. The goal is still the same—release—but within Mahayana, Buddha assumes the role of a savior and becomes deified, for he and others assist persons toward enlightenment. Buddha shares with others his divine grace or compassion. This branch tends to be much more flexible and allows a permissive attitude toward a number of developments in ritual and theology.

A most significant development within Mahayana is the concept of the *bodhisattva*, which refers to persons or beings who are "awakening" and are far along the path to full enlightenment, such as that enjoyed by the Buddha. They have not fully achieved Nirvana but are close. What is distinctive about them is that they have chosen not to enter Nirvana but to share their insights and help those who have just begun their quest for enlightenment. The *bodhisattvas*, both male and female, are many in number and as bearers of a divine grace offer immense help to the ordinary believer and strength to achieve enlightenment. Compassion is their chief characteristic and they are destined to be future Buddhas.

The layperson carries a larger role in the religious life of Mahayana, cooperating with the monks in elaborate and exquisite ritual patterns, art, and personal worship. This form of Buddhism more readily adapted itself to native patterns and forms, often incorporating national or cultural emphases. As a result it took significantly different patterns in differing cultures. This pattern of Buddhism spread north and east into China, Japan, and Korea. It is called the large vehicle, or raft, for the obvious reason that many more might expect salvation.

Although these two branches of Buddhism have dominated the development of the religion, other forms have arisen over the centuries, and all branches have adapted many native customs and practices as the religion has moved through the various countries of the East. In the seventh century C.E., Buddhism was introduced into Tibet, where it took on a significantly different form, becoming a distinct branch. Although this form of Buddhism has been known by several names through the centuries, the most common being *Vajrayana* ("Vehicle of the Thunderbolt"), it is best described as a Buddhist representative of *tantric* religious patterns. Concerned with the interrelationship of all life, it asserts that the energies of the body as well as the mind and spirit may be used in the spiritual quest for enlightenment. Elaborate esoteric rituals perfecting body energies, *mandalas* (the use of sacred designs to focus the mind), *mudras* (hand rituals signifying feelings), and *mantras* (chanting or reciting spiritual formulas or words) all contribute to seeking enlightenment. Using these resources, the negative karmic patterns of life are transformed into the positive perfections of the Buddhas and *bodhisattvas* wherein enlightenment occurs as a perfect combination of wisdom and compassion. Their religious leader, known as the Dalai Lama, is understood to be the earthly manifestation of infinite compassion and wisdom, a *bodhisattva* now in his fourteenth successive human incarnation. In more recent times, other forms of Buddhism have arisen, such as *Zen*, which combines insights of both older branches, as well as elements of Chinese Taoist tradition and practice.

The diversity of Buddhism is evident, yet Buddha's basic insistence on enlightenment, which leads one from selfish desire to a state of selfless bliss and compassion for others, binds the various branches and interpretations together.

UNIT 12   TAOISM

For centuries, the religious principle of the *Tao* (usually pronounced "Dow") has been intertwined with dominant attitudes and themes of Chinese life and culture. The term *Tao* itself designates both a way of living that humans should follow to be in harmony with nature and the Power or Principle or Overall Governing Presence that is manifested in the universe. Thus, to follow the Tao is to live in harmony with the Governing Power or Principle that brings harmony, unity, and balance to all things. For human beings to be striving, ambitious, self-seeking, overly refined, or overly civilized (artificial) disrupts the natural harmony according to which they should, unaggressively, blend into the life that flows through all things. Understood in this manner, the Tao, or "the way," lies at the core of all Chinese culture and is claimed by the two major religious traditions that arose in China—Taoism and Confucianism.

Equally important for Chinese culture and religion is the concept of *yin and yang*, the two major components or principles that must be blended to give reality to everything. Figure 2.2 is an artistic expression of this concept. When they are blended harmoniously in accordance with Tao, peace, harmony, and fruitfulness result. Yang (in representations it is given the color red) is the positive, assertive, masculine force. It is the source of warmth, brightness, hardness, dryness, firmness, and strength. Fire and sunlight are particularly associated with yang. Yin is feminine and dark, passive, cold, moist, and mysterious. Water, shadow, shade, and night are associated with yin. Neither of these is seen as competitive or evil. Both are necessary ingredients of all that exists. Yin and yang, in fact, contain each other in a hidden or scarcely discernible way. Anything

Figure 2.2 *Yin and Yang* by Jacques Bakke.

possesses its own natural goodness and health when there is a proper balance of yin and yang in its makeup.

From very early times, a primary characteristic of Chinese society has been a reverence and a positive appreciation for nature and the powers, or spirits, inhabiting it. Good and evil spirits were worshipped with rites and sacrifices to secure good fortune and ward off evil. The spirits of departed ancestors were worshipped in the belief that this would ensure good fortune in the present life. A failure to worship the ancestors would turn them into avenging Furies. Many natural phenomena, both real and legendary, were worshipped as manifestations of powers and spirits—mountains, rivers, and various kinds of animals. For instance, building one's home above the nest of a dragon was supposed to bring good luck. Ritual—sacrifices, celebrations, colorful festivals—was very important, both in placating the spirits and as enactments of the harmony between the earthly (human) and the heavenly realms, both seen as parts of one whole.

LAO-TZU

The religious tradition that took the name of Taoism is often traced to the legendary writings and doctrines of Lao-Tzu, a teacher who was supposed to have lived during the first half of the sixth century B.C.E. Taoism also incorporates elements of much earlier Chinese tradition and has greatly influenced (and been influenced by) later religious movements, especially Buddhism.

Little, if anything, is known with certainty of the life of Lao-Tzu. This name literally means "the Old Boy" and is used affectionately to designate one who is revered as a master teacher, or sage, whose lifestyle was marked by spontaneity, lack of pretense or pretentiousness, and a mischievous, paradoxical manner. According to tradition, Lao-Tzu was a government official who resigned his post after becoming convinced of the futility of a life of ambition, striving, and conformity to artificial social conventions. For Lao-Tzu a life of harmony with nature in its unvarnished simplicity was best. Again according to tradition, he was prevailed upon, before leaving the borders of the civilized world for good, to commit his doctrine to writing. He is supposed to have done this in the thin volume called the *Tao Te Ching*, one of the classics of the world's religious and mystical literature.

The *Tao Te Ching* is characterized by a style of thought and writing that is crisp, playful, profound, and paradoxical. The central concepts of Taoism are expressed in ways that show their continuity with earlier and later Chinese attitudes, foremost of which is a feeling of harmony and kinship with nature.

A basic virtue or positive quality stressed by Lao-Tzu's Taoism is *wu wei*, a kind of creative passivity, an attitude of selfless non-action according to which one flows with the life present in all things. Just as Lao-Tzu is supposed to have withdrawn from the corrupt and artificially overcivilized world of his day to return to the simplicity of nature, there are many such stories of Taoist "conversions." In one, a harried government official, impressed by the teachings of Lao-Tzu, is supposed to have resigned his office and titles, stripped off his clothes, and walked naked into the woods to spend the rest of his days beside a stream quietly fishing without using bait (in order not to disturb the fish, the stream, or the peaceful harmony of the natural setting). Passivity; non-action; the absence of striving; and the utility of quiet receptiveness, spontaneity, and appreciation of the simple beauty of life—these are the qualities exalted in the *Tao Te Ching*. In a sense, *nothing*—non-action, non-being—is more useful than being: It is the empty space that makes a cup useful. The hardness of a rock may impress us, but a steady stream of water—what could be more yielding than water?—can wear down the hardest rock.

CHUANG-TZU

The teachings of Lao-Tzu were popularized by Chuang-Tzu, a disciple who lived in the fourth century B.C.E., whose accomplishment in the preservation and interpretation of Lao-Tzu's work was similar to that of Mencius in preserving and elaborating Confucius's teachings. Chuang-Tzu extended the teachings of the *Tao Te Ching* in his own similar small volume of sayings. For Chuang-Tzu two concepts were central: (1) All opposites and values are relative in the flow of change (the *Tao*) in the universe, so even death can be seen as only one more great change. When he was asked why he did not mourn the death of his wife, he simply suggested that just as she had changed by being born, so in death she changed again; therefore mourning is inappropriate because death is simply part of the Tao. (2) All religious insights and knowledge are real only when they are recognized and played out in the secular and daily activities of individuals. Cooking, crafts, art, and any other activity, at its core, express the activity of the Tao. The Tao is discovered or uncovered in all life (for an example of this teaching, see Unit 24).

DOCTRINE

The Taoist doctrine taught by Lao-Tzu and Chuang-Tzu is sometimes referred to as *philosophical* Taoism to distinguish it from *popular* Taoism, which has for centuries involved both the worship of ancestral and other spirits; and belief in and practice of magic and other rituals oriented to good luck and prosperity. A third form of (or really a third element within) Taoist tradition is sometimes designated by the term *esoteric* Taoism, which refers to teachings and practices of physical and spiritual self-discipline, resembling the meditation of Buddhist monks and Hindu yogis. Techniques of concentration and meditation, and claims of methods to attain remarkable physical as well as occult spiritual powers, are characteristic of this element of Taoism. Popular Taoism developed a priesthood, shrines, temples, cultic worship, and a number of divine beings to be worshipped, all to some extent modeled on Buddhist counterparts.

Taoism also interacted with, sometimes complementing and at times criticizing, Confucianism, another Chinese religious tradition that arose in the same century and emphasized the social hierarchy, law, and rational order. If Lao-Tzu emphasized yin in order to temper an overemphasis on yang, Confucius was the great champion of yang tempered with yin. For many centuries, Chinese culture was characterized by the two traditions of Taoism and Confucianism, which more or less balanced or complemented each other. In fact, for most Chinese there was no inconsistency in being Confucian (with respect to one's social duties), Taoist (with respect to elements of personal lifestyle as well as to secure good fortune in the present life), and Buddhist (since many Chinese Buddhist sects provide assurance of continuing life beyond death).

Elements of Taoist philosophy influenced Buddhist thought, too, particularly Chinese and Japanese Zen sects; and elements of popular Taoism can perhaps be recognized in the traditional Japanese popular religion called Shinto. With the rise of Mao Tse-tung's version of Marxism in China after World War II, there were strong efforts to eradicate Chinese popular religion. Taoism, Buddhism, and Confucianism, as well as religious philosophies such as Philosophical Taoism and Confucianism, were all threatening because they provided obstacles to the Marxist secular transformation, or modernization, of Chinese society. With the emergence of more permissive attitudes in post-Maoist communism, the opposition to traditional and popular religion has lessened. Citizens are now allowed, within rather stringent limits, to practice religion openly, although the official position of the regime remains atheistic.

Unit 13   CONFUCIANISM

Of the two major Chinese religious traditions, Taoism and Confucianism, Confucianism, with its emphasis on the virtues of propriety and reverence for tradition, has been the more influential in Chinese civilization. The teachings of Confucius and his disciples and later interpreters molded the social patterns and mores that were to dominate the culture for centuries.

CONFUCIUS

Confucius was born during the middle of the sixth century (c. 551) B.C.E., apparently in humble circumstances. He worked diligently to acquire an education, studying the classics of Chinese literature and music and meditating on the virtues of the great teachers and sages of an earlier period, whom he took to have been more virtuous and noble than those of his own time. The period into which Confucius was born was one that he believed to be characterized by moral and social anarchy caused by crude and selfish behavior, especially on the part of rulers motivated by vain personal ambitions—greed, desire for prestige and power, and self-indulgence. Confucius envisioned a reformation of society through a reformation of its rulers. He believed that if princes could be persuaded to live exemplary lives and to show justice and compassion to their subjects, the whole of society might be reshaped in accordance with the good, tested ways of the past. Here Confucius reflected, in a more sophisticated way, the ancient and later Chinese belief that there should be a harmony between the heavenly and the earthly kingdoms. The ability of the ruler to conform to the eternal pattern of the heavenly sphere determined whether his subjects would be blessed with peace and prosperity. Confucius himself sought positions in government to try to influence princes by precept and example. According to tradition, his moral standards, his insistence on propriety, were felt to be overly rigorous, and he spent most of his life outside government service as a teacher whose doctrines and personality attracted and influenced an increasing number of disciples.

DOCTRINE

The primary emphasis of Confucianism is on sincere adherence to a moral and social code of propriety. The Chinese term *li* designates one of the primary concepts (and virtues) exalted by Confucius. *Li* means propriety—the way things should be done. It refers to good behavior, that is, conformity to a moral and social code of appropriate behavior by doing what is customary, traditional, and required by social usage. In a more limited usage, *li* means rite or ritual. Confucius taught that the rites of Chinese traditional religion should be observed, not so much because he believed in the ancestral and other spirits to whom sacrifices were offered, but because he believed in the value of ritual, rite, and ceremony—a stylized pattern of life—for a society's stability. Confucius hoped to correct the anarchy of his own time by establishing a highly stylized, ritualized code of conduct by which each individual at each moment of life and in any conceivable relationship or situation would know exactly what to do and would do exactly what was expected. Thus, the two meanings of *li* tend to converge in Confucian teaching.

Crucial to the Confucian concept of propriety are the five great relationships: ruler to subject, father to son, husband to wife, older brother to younger brother, and older friend to younger friend. In each case, one member of the relationship is dominant and the other subordinate, yet ideally there is reciprocity of respect. The ruler, the father, the husband, the older brother, and the older friend should show concern, courtesy, and consideration for the subordinate partner. The subject, son, wife, younger brother, and younger friend should show respect, reverence, and obedience to the dominant partner. The Confucian code is not unlike codes of chivalry of medieval Europe, in which the highborn and strong were supposed to protect the lowborn and weak, to care for them and show courtesy in all things, whereas the lowborn and weak were supposed to obey uncomplainingly and with gratitude.

In addition to *li*, Confucius spoke of other virtues and characteristics that one should possess. *Jên*, which he valued so highly that he spoke of it less frequently than he did of some other virtues, designates an attitude of benevolence that produces courtesy, good will toward others, and loyalty to those to whom loyalty is due. *Jên*, for instance, produces service to one's parents and to one's ruler. It includes an attitude of respect and good will toward others and a proper respect for oneself, for one's own dignity and value as a human being.

Another important Confucian concept is *Chun-tzu*, which designates a kind of ideal humanity—the kind of fulfilled humanity that one should seek to achieve in one's own life. *Chun-tzu* is sometimes translated as "Superior Manhood," "Ideal Man," "Man-at-His-Best" or even as "the Gentleman." The person who is a *Chun-tzu* is someone who possesses the Confucian virtues, who conforms to the code of propriety, who is generous, unselfish, benevolent, loyal, and courteous—the opposite of someone who is petty, selfish, grasping, and untrustworthy.

Confucius was convinced that the major means of acquiring this virtue, of becoming a *Chun-tzu*, was through study of and meditation on the classics of Chinese literature and music and through study of the ancient rites. Thus, Confucius placed great emphasis on correct education to create good character in individuals and to restore good order to society. Confucius, reflecting positive Chinese attitudes toward nature and the natural realm, believed in the essential goodness of human nature, an innate potential that can be realized through correct education in a well-ordered society. Confucius left sayings of his own as well as edited versions of earlier Chinese writings to provide a basis for an educational curriculum that for more than 2,000 years shaped Chinese civilization. Mencius, a later interpreter of Confucius, did much to systematize the Confucian teachings, classifying the virtues—*li, Jên, Chih* (wisdom), and *I* (justice). Mencius taught that the seeds or origins of the virtues were "in the nature of things," the way the world was, and that their effects would restore harmony to the present world.

The question is frequently raised about the appropriateness of regarding Confucianism as a *religious* tradition. Is it not primarily a code of ethics and a social philosophy? Bearing in mind the definition of religion as a "pivotal value," one can see that Confucianism can be regarded as having a profoundly religious dimension. Being in harmony with and in conformity to the eternal moral code, that is, being in conformity with "heaven," was a pivotal value for Confucius. It should be remembered that for him even the rites of traditional religion were of value because observing them was demanded by propriety, the eternal moral code. Confucius, like Buddha, had nothing to say about the nature of heaven, the origin of the universe, and such matters. These questions simply were not relevant to how one lives in conformity to propriety. But for Confucius the moral code was itself a part of the very nature of the universe—a pivotal value.

INFLUENCE

The influence of the Confucian writings (some going back to Confucius himself; others, though attributed to him, probably coming from other hands) as a foundation of Chinese culture cannot be overestimated. Perhaps the best known outside China is the *Lun yü* (translated into English as *The Sayings of Confucius*), though in recent years the *I Ching* (sometimes translated as *The Book of Changes*) has received much attention in the West. In fact, the sayings of Confucius, many of them memorable proverbs and epigrams, as well as the other "canonical" Confucian writings, functioned in China much as sacred writings have functioned in other societies—as the basis of a moral and social code, as folk wisdom, as history, and as literary models, even (as the *I Ching* did and does) providing methods of divination, foretelling, and deciding about conduct to meet future situations.

Because Confucian teachings sustained the traditional and, in Mao's view, decadent government and social patterns, Mao Tse-Tung, leader of the 1950s Chinese Communist revolution, frequently attacked the influence of Confucius and Confucianism. He declared that it had to be rooted out before China could be transformed into a progressive, politically and technologically modernized society. (At times he insisted that some of the Confucian virtues, such as certain forms of courtesy, were nevertheless necessary.) More recently the Chinese government has stressed the importance of Confucius and his teachings as an integral part of China's cultural heritage.

Unit 14 Judaism

Judaism, for the purposes of this unit, refers to the faith, worship, and life of the Jewish people. Judaism arose among Semitic peoples who lived in the ancient Near East around the eastern edges of the Arabian Desert. Migrating to the West, they settled in the Palestinian area of the eastern Mediterranean now occupied by Israel, Jordan, and Syria. After occupying this land for a number of centuries, the Jews, following a period of exile in Babylon, began to scatter throughout the ancient Mediterranean world, although Judea in Palestine remained their homeland. In 70 C.E. the Romans destroyed the Jewish Temple in Jerusalem and in 135 C.E. the city itself. Without a Palestinian base, Judaism thus became a religious community spread throughout parts of Asia, Africa, and later Europe and America. Its Palestinian homeland was not restored until 1948, with the establishment of the modern state of Israel. Modern Jews, bound together by their religious and cultural heritage, live over much of the world, with Israel itself containing a relatively small portion of their total number.

Historically, Judaism traces its heritage to one patriarch, Abraham, and his family. Abraham was a Semitic wanderer who migrated into Palestine around 2000–1800 B.C.E. Central to his family tradition was the belief that he had been led into this migration by a God who promised him a land and that his family would become a "mighty nation." Some centuries later (1290 B.C.E.), again at God's instigation, Moses led the descendants of Abraham out of slavery in Egypt. It is as a result of this exodus from Egypt and subsequent developments that the distinctive patterns of Jewish faith and life began to emerge. Whereas Abraham and his sons were patriarchs of the community, Moses emerged as the architect of later Judaism. Beginning as a familial and tribal grouping, Judaism later incorporated others into the community if they were willing to accept the requirements of the "covenant" that bound them to God.

The basic beliefs of Judaism are rooted in the historical elements that created the community. In Jewish tradition, *Yahweh*, the God who led Moses and Abraham, chose Abraham and his descendants (the Israelites) to be his unique and particular people. By acting in their history to form the community and by sustaining it through the centuries, Yahweh revealed himself as a God intimately related to the world and involved in its activities. Judaism affirmed that this God was the God of the universe (creator and all-powerful), thereby establishing a monotheistic faith. In the exodus from Egyptian slavery, Yahweh further revealed himself and the nature of complete life through the Ten Commandments and the laws of Moses—the Pentateuch—the first five books of what Christians refer to as the Old Testament. He bound himself to the Israelites by promising to be "their God" and expecting that they in return would be "his people" by following the Commandments and laws given. Created in this manner, Judaism expresses its loyalty and solidarity by a corporate life in which every aspect of life, public and private, is permeated by God's presence and human response to that presence. Through this relationship, Yahweh, although transcendent in the fullest sense, is revealed as being personal and exhibiting characteristics of love and concern as well as justice (when disobedience occurs). For Judaism this choice by Yahweh has still another implication: Through Israel God reveals himself and his nature to *all* humanity so that the estrangement that exists between himself and humanity can be overcome.

In Jewish understanding, humanity is created to be responsible for its actions and as such is given freedom of will—freedom to be obedient or disobedient to the universal laws established by God. Given this freedom, humanity has a propensity to be disobedient or self-oriented, thereby becoming evil. In receiving God's commandments and responding in faithfulness, Israel overcomes this propensity, thus becoming truly a "light to the nations." According to Jewish understanding, the Israelites have not always been faithful to this ideal and have been disobedient; yet the uniqueness of their relationship to God remains. In its best sense this is to be a source not of pride but of responsibility for the Israelites. Historically the relationship has produced among Israelites two perspectives often held in tension—an extreme exclusiveness and a sense of world mission.

TORAH

The relationship depends ultimately on God's initiative, his gracious choice of the Israelites, with whom he seals the connection by giving them a *Torah*—"teachings," or more commonly, "the law." Through the Torah, all of human life is given a normative pattern by God's gracious guidance. In the broadest sense, the Torah is that guidance expressed in every aspect of life. In its written form it refers to the Pentateuch, the first five books of Jewish scripture.[1] It may also refer to an oral tradition of revelation as well as to oral and written interpretations of the tradition (*Talmud*). Rabbinic Judaism, the form of Judaism that survived the Roman destruction of Jerusalem in the years 70 and 135 C.E., understands that the Torah was transmitted in two forms through the centuries—an oral Torah and the written Torah. Both are components in the adequate interpretation of God's will for daily living. Use of oral and written Torah among the rabbis, the teachers, and ultimately among the religious, social, and political leaders of the community produced interpretative commentaries—the *Talmud*. The earliest stratum of this Talmud is the *Mishnah* redacted around 200 C.E. Early and modern forms of Rabbinic Judaism, using Torah and Talmud, interpret and adapt the law to ever-changing historical and social conditions, seeking to retain its uniqueness. In doing so they attempt to protect distinctive Jewish ethical and ritual patterns within their communities. Historically, this practice set the members of such communities apart from their non-Jewish neighbors (creating in Europe Jewish "ghettos," where the Jews lived apart from others), while at the same time guaranteeing the survival of the traditions that were severely tested through intense persecution in the medieval and modern periods. In these Jewish areas rabbis often served both as spiritual and political leaders since the legacy of the Torah did not distinguish between civil and religious law. Ancient ritual and ethical practices, as well as demanding and exacting food laws established in the Exodus period and later, have survived into the modern day through this insistence on obedience to the Torah.[2]

RITES AND FESTIVALS

The assumption that God guides all of life, added to the familial origins of Judaism, meant that the family emerged as a central element in the religion. Primary religious services and teachings, as well as the enforcement of ethical codes, take place in the home. It is here that the community of the faithful has its roots; therefore, some major religious festivals, as well as regular worship, take place in the home. Arising in the family is another central concern—insistence on education: to know and interpret the Torah and to prepare oneself as completely as possible for life.

[1] *Tanak* is the name given to the total Jewish scripture and encompasses the Law, Prophets, and Writings.

[2] For additional information on modern Rabbinic Judaism, see Jacob Neusner, *The Way of the Torah* (Belmont, CA: Wadsworth, Inc., 1979).

Related to the familial emphasis are several rites of passage: circumcision for male children as a sign of the covenant relationship; *bar mitzvah*, when the son, at age 13, recites Torah benedictions in the synagogue to mark his acceptance of the responsibilities of the covenant (also practiced among some Jews is bas mitzvah for girls); marriage, with appropriate rites and scripture readings; and burial, a simple but significant service. Each of these events, though a milestone in the individual life cycle, is also a family, and often a community, event celebrated in the synagogue. (The synagogue, formed by any ten adult male Jews, first arose as a place for teaching the Torah but also became a place of worship.)

In addition to these ceremonies, the feasts and festivals of Judaism play an important part in the religious life of the community. These include: *Pesach* (Passover), commemorating the exodus from Egypt; *Shavuot* (Pentecost), celebrating the grain harvest and commemorating the giving of the Torah; *Sukkot* (tabernacles), an autumn harvest festival; *Simchat Torah*, concluding and beginning a new annual round of Torah readings; *Rosh Hashana*, celebrating the new year; Yom Kippur, the Day of Atonement; *Hanukkah*, a feast of dedication commemorating victory in 165 B.C.E. over the Syrians, commonly celebrated by use of the seven-candle menorah shown in Figure 2.3; and *Purim*, celebrating deliverance from the Persian Empire. Other lesser festivals and fasts are also observed by many Jews. Central to all such cycles and to the regular life of the Jew is the *Sabbath*, instituted in earliest times as a day of rest and worship.

Figure 2.3 A menorah, used to celebrate the Jewish Feast of Hanukkah. (Courtesy Consulate General of Israel in New York.)

THREE BRANCHES

The impact of cultural and intellectual developments in Western civilization during the eighteenth and nineteenth centuries drastically changed the economic and political situation of European and American Jews. For the first time in their European history they were able to move freely, and they gradually abandoned the ghettos to be amalgamated into the larger society. The results have been varied. Among the traditionalists, the heritage of Rabbinic Judaism has survived to become incorporated into modern Orthodox synagogues, where ancient ritual and ethical practices are still understood to be operative, though some modifications have been allowed to meet urban and non-ghetto situations. Nevertheless, every decision and situation in life can be the topic of rabbinic interpretation.

The intellectual ferment of the Enlightenment and its aftermath led some Jews, however, to question the ancient traditions and abandon certain laws (such as food laws and exclusive dependence on the Hebrew language in religious services) and to change some elements of their theological positions. These and other changes led to the establishment of Reform synagogues—those of the more liberal Jewish religious community. Reform Judaism basically abandoned dependence on a total religious-political-ethical code but retained emphasis on the moral law along with traditional religious practices when appropriate.

Conservative Judaism forms a third major Jewish community, which, though willing to make concessions regarding certain aspects of the law, nevertheless insists on a more conservative formulation and practice than that found within the Reform community. Each of these major groups contains many smaller subgroups, which often reflect ethnic differences. With this diversification there is still a strong cohesiveness among the Jewish community. The sense of a unique culture and relation to God is present. Although the unifying core of Jewish culture has traditionally been its religion, many modern Jews, through identification with patterns of Jewish culture, affirm their continuing identity as Jews without actively participating in, or necessarily accepting, the theological implications of the religious tradition.

Unit 15   CHRISTIANITY

Arising from Palestinian Judaism but eventually separating from it, Christianity gradually spread throughout the Mediterranean cultures, becoming the religion of the Roman Empire by the fourth century. Dominating medieval Europe, Christianity became the major religious tradition of modern Europe and America, spreading from these bases throughout the world in the past three centuries. At present it claims over 2 billion believers worldwide.

JESUS

The foundation for Christianity was laid in the teachings and ministry of Jesus of Nazareth, a Palestinian Jew who lived during the reigns of the Roman Emperors Augustus and Tiberius Caesar. As a Jew, Jesus accepted without major modification many of the traditional Israelite beliefs: a monotheistic faith in one universal God, a confidence that this God acts significantly and graciously in human history, a belief in humanity's propensity to disobey the will of God, and a concept of salvation (restoration of loving relations between God and humanity) in which human disobedience can be overcome.

Jesus taught within the patterns and traditions of the Jewish rabbis (teachers), yet he reinterpreted the Jewish Torah on the basis of his own authority, claiming to teach what Yahweh originally intended in the insights and proscriptions of the Torah. He insisted on looking behind the multitudinous applications and interpretations of the Torah common among his contemporary rabbis to the *intent* of the law—the theological and ethical principles fundamental to that law and what they indicated about the relationship of God to humanity. Jesus also taught that the long-expected Jewish "kingdom of God" had begun in his own ministry. In this affirmation the popular Jewish expectation of an earthly but divine *Messiah* (anointed one of God) was substantially modified. Contemporary Jews expected a Messiah who would manifest God's graciousness within their own history by the restoration of a politically and religiously powerful Israel. For Jesus, God's kingdom was to come when God's will—the total commitment of one's life to God and the unrestricted love of one's neighbor—became manifest in the lives of the people. Therefore, the long-expected kingdom of God had already begun in those who, following Jesus' teachings, did God's loving will. It would come to full fruition in the future when all persons joined in living out God's will. Such teachings said little of the Jewish expectation of a politically restored Israel wherein one lived, according to Jesus, a restricted view of God's will. Added to these teachings was Jesus' ministry of caring—a ministry of healing and restoration to wholeness of broken human lives.

Jesus' teachings and lifestyle, which accepted all persons as God's chosen people, were controversial among Jews. He gave many of the common people great hope, but many, particularly the religious leaders, became his adversaries. After a brief ministry, he was charged with blasphemy by the Jewish leaders because of his claim to be speaking with God's authority. He was taken before Roman authorities and charged with treason for supposedly claiming to be "king of the Jews." Although the Romans crucified Jesus as a common criminal, his followers testified that he arose from the dead and appeared to them on several occasions.

For Christians, this event of resurrection, along with Jesus' life and teachings, means that Jesus was the very *incarnation of God in human form* (a unique and unrepeatable event). By the resurrection the power of death was broken, not only for Jesus but for all believers. They were offered the promise of this gracious love in their own lives and the hope that their personal lives would continue in God's love beyond death. Christians also proclaimed that through this event God offers salvation to all humanity by overcoming disobedience and its consequences. They further affirmed that the God who had revealed himself in Jesus continued his ministry by actively participating in their daily lives and communities as a unique spiritual presence—the Holy Spirit. The later church would combine these insights into a doctrine of the *Trinity*: belief in God the Father (and Creator), God the Son (God manifest in Jesus the Christ), and God the Holy Spirit (God present in history)—a triune manifestation of one God. Subject to a great variety of interpretations by believers through the centuries, these concepts form the core of Christian theology.

CHRISTIAN COMMUNITY

Immediately after the death of Jesus, his followers formed a community and in doing so provided an ongoing embodiment for his teachings and proclamations. Spreading the "Good News" (Gospel) of God's gracious love revealed in Jesus gave the new religious movement a missionary, or evangelical, pattern in a world where many religions sought adherents. Although first arising among the Jews and claiming many Jewish adherents, by the end of the first century after Jesus' death this community had gained converts throughout the Mediterranean cultures, with non-Jewish members outnumbering their Jewish colleagues.

As Jews, the first Christians retained profound respect for and dependence on the Hebrew scriptures—the *Torah*, the written forms of Jewish law, writings of the prophets, and historical writings. These became for the Christians the Old Testament (Covenant), embodying basic truths about humanity and God. Alongside these scriptures arose Christian writings recounting Jesus' life and teachings, expositions of faith, sermons, and apocalyptic materials. The most significant of these became the New Testament (Covenant) and were understood to be divinely inspired. Within the community these Scriptures constitute a principal source of information, inspiration, and interpretation of the Gospel. For some Christians, they are the sole authority in matters of faith. For others, along with faithful church tradition and the inspiration of the Holy Spirit, these Scriptures form one significant source of authority.

The diversity of the Christian community and its accommodation to hundreds of social settings resulted in a great diversification of practices and patterns of worship. Most Christians accept two sacraments: *Baptism*, a rite recognizing God's gift of his love and forgiveness, the acceptance by the believer of that grace, and the incorporation of the believer into the community of the faithful; and *Eucharist* (the Lord's Supper, Holy Communion), which is a rite commemorating the life, death, and resurrection of Jesus, giving the believer an opportunity to participate symbolically in that event. Interpretations of the meaning and form of the sacraments have been numerous and often divisive, yet these sacraments remain characteristic of Christianity. Certain branches of the church (particularly the Roman Catholic and Orthodox) recognize other sacraments in addition to these two (usually seven in all). Though there is great diversity among Christian celebrations, the veneration of Jesus' life, death, and resurrection is embodied in Easter rites by most Christian churches, as is his birth at Christmas and the coming of the Holy Spirit to the first disciples at Pentecost.

THE CHURCH

Patterns of church organization, governance, and theology have also been diverse. From the earliest period, the church found itself ministering to variant groups with differing intellectual, cultural, and ethical impulses. The result has been the formation of many subgroupings, but most of them can be incorporated into three major branches: Orthodox, Roman Catholic, and Protestant.

During its first several hundred years, the church was a loosely organized community with local leaders (bishops) having responsibility and authority in local questions of doctrine and practice. When a universal or churchwide issue arose, representatives from the various local churches formed a council to make authoritative decisions. However, because the eastern and western sections of the Mediterranean contained significantly different cultural traditions, distinct theological and ritual practices emerged in each section. The differences between the eastern and western sections ultimately became acute, and two branches of Christianity emerged: Orthodoxy in the east and Roman Catholicism in the west. The process was slow, and an official final split did not occur until 1091 C.E.

Orthodoxy emphasized the spiritual aspects of worship by stressing the poetic and the mystical, accepted a loose regional autonomy of "equal" metropolitans (archbishops), and saw the Eucharist as the celebration of Christ's resurrection from the dead. Roman Catholicism insisted on a more precise rationalistic theology and on the authority of one bishop over the church (the bishop of Rome, known commonly as the Pope) and understood the Eucharist as a remembrance and reenactment of Christ's redemptive death on the cross. Once separated, these branches had little contact with each other until modern times.

Called on to provide stabilization in the West as the Roman Empire disintegrated, the Roman Catholic church with its strong papacy and expansive monasticism became a primary component in the political as well as spiritual fabric of medieval Western Europe. By the late medieval period (1400–1500), however, the hierarchy of the church had become rich, corrupt, and indifferent—out of touch with new intellectual, scientific, and spiritual trends in the society and removed from the needs of the common people.

In the sixteenth century, several Christian groups rose in protest against abuses of faith and governance in the church. Collectively known in history as the Protestant Reformation, the criticisms of the Church raised related questions as to the nature of religious faith and the power of the Pope. Protestants insisted that God's grace was available through faithful trust in him as well as through the sacraments and that the primary religious authority resides in the Scriptures rather than in the church. Accompanying the protest was the resolute affirmation that a person is saved by God's gracious love recognized and accepted in personal faith, an affirmation that questioned the traditional capacity of Roman Catholic priests to define spiritual and moral works, which were understood to renew one's relation to God. Insistence on personal, direct access to God led to the development of numerous independent voluntary congregations and churches. Proliferation of separate denominations, each establishing its own interpretations, beliefs, and practices, became a hallmark of the Protestant branch of Christianity.

In modern times many of the differences among the three major Christian branches have been recognized by all involved as being historical, ecclesiastical, and cultural rather than substantial matters of faith. Recent changes in theology and practice within each group, the threat of secular culture, and competition with other religions have contributed in recent years to the rise of numerous ecumenical movements providing conversations, study, and joint projects among the variant Christian branches. Protestantism has during this period experienced a number of mergers and reunions of variant subgroups. It is to be expected, nevertheless, that a religion covering the many cultures of the world will continue to have major differences among its adherents.

Unit 16 Islam

In the sixth century the ancient civilizations of the Mesopotamian valley and adjacent areas had become decadent and were loosely governed by tribes living on the Arabian peninsula. The religion of these tribes was a polytheist amalgam of nature religions drawn from surrounding cultures. Prominent was the *Ka'ba*, a shrine containing many holy objects and images located in an important trade center, Mecca. One of the most conspicuous of these relics was a large black stone or meteorite.

MUHAMMAD

Muhammad, the prophet through whose teachings the Islamic religion began, was born in 570 C.E., part of an aristocratic clan responsible for the care of the *Ka'ba*. Although closely identified with religious practices of the community through his family, as a young man Muhammad was repelled by the patterns of a religion in which caprice and change were prominent and sacrifices influenced or directed the divine spirits. Orphaned early and raised in the households of his grandfather and uncle, he traveled extensively throughout the region, working in merchant caravans. In these travels Muhammad was exposed to Judaism and Christianity and attracted to their monotheistic emphasis on the revealed will of *one* all-powerful God communicating through spokespersons (prophets). Concerned by issues of human existence and given to personal meditation, he was encouraged in his religious interests by Khadija, his wife. Once, while meditating in a desert cave, Muhammad had a vision in which the angel Gabriel appeared and commanded him to "recite." This was the first of a number of such occasions, which Muhammad understood to be direct expressions of God's will—the will of *Allah*, the Arabic high God. Khadija, with whom he shared these revelations, became his first convert to a new religion. Others soon joined her, forming a small community of believers in Mecca.

Central to Muhammad's teachings was the belief in one all-powerful, supreme God—Allah, on whom all creation depended. Humanity's proper relation to Allah was submission to Allah's will. The literal meaning of the word *Islam* is "submission." One who so submits becomes a *Muslim*. Allah's revelations to Muhammad were written down over a period of years and became the 114 *suras* (chapters) of the *Qur'an*, the Islamic scriptures. Muslims look upon these revelations, and therefore the Qur'an that records them, as direct communication from Allah given through his greatest prophet, not as the original thoughts of Muhammad. The content of the Qur'an is wide-ranging, from teachings about the nature of Allah and humanity to instructions for daily living.

Muhammad's new message to the citizens of Mecca contrasted greatly with their traditional religious beliefs because it demanded that they abandon the worship of many gods to give devotion to Allah alone. Many responded with hostility, in part because they felt Muhammad's message was a threat to the economic benefits of the religious rites and shrines that attracted pilgrims to Mecca. For their own safety, Muhammad and his followers abandoned Mecca, taking up residence in a nearby city, Yathrib. Here the citizenry was much more receptive to the Islamic message, and Muhammad was soon made governor. In Muslim tradition this escape to Yathrib in the year 622 became known as the Hegira, the "flight." From this Hegira Muslim calendars are dated. Yathrib's name was later changed to Medina, or "City of the Prophet."

Gaining support in Medina, Muhammad sought to reenter Mecca with his message. Conquering the city without a major battle, Muhammad's followers suppressed its polytheistic worship, cleansing the Ka'ba of all of its religious images and relics, with the exception of the black stone. In Muslim teaching, the stone had been placed there by Abraham, forefather of Arabs as well as Jews, as a symbol of Allah; thus, the Ka'ba became the holiest shrine of the new religion, and Mecca and Medina became holy cities. The Dome of the Rock Muslim shrine in Jerusalem shown in Figure 2.4 is the third most important Muslim shrine.

During the remainder of Muhammad's life and in the years after his death, the Islamic religion spread rapidly across the eastern Mediterranean and North Africa and into parts of Europe. Islam forbade wars of aggression, but recognized the right of defensive war and did not hesitate to suppress polytheism, while tolerating other monotheistic religions among conquered populations. During the seventh and eighth centuries Muslims

Figure 2.4 *The Dome of the Rock.* Located in Jerusalem, this seventh-century building continues to be a principal sacred place of revelation. (Courtesy Israel Ministry of Tourism.)

occupied Portugal and Spain and a part of present-day France. Islam also spread across all of the Arabian peninsula, across large parts of Asia—covering present-day Turkey, Syria, Iraq, Iran, Afghanistan, Pakistan, and parts of India, Malaya, and Indonesia—and into China. Though Muslims were later driven from France, Spain, and Portugal, Muslim influence remained in the architecture, medicine, and philosophy of medieval Europe. At present, there are large numbers of Muslims in parts of southern and eastern Europe—Bosnia, Albania, and Bulgaria—as well as Africa and Asia. Immigration from these areas and the attraction of Americans of African descent to Islam has contributed to a recent large expansion of the Muslim community.

Muslims regard Muhammad as the last and greatest of the prophets in a line extending from Abraham and other figures whose lives and teachings are recorded in the Jewish scriptures down through Jesus. In no sense a divine being, Muhammad is regarded as the *Seal of the Prophets*. Muslims recognize kinship with Christians as well as with Jews since each religion is a monotheistic faith worshipping the same God as the one and only Divine being. Nevertheless, Muslims are critical of elements that they consider polytheistic in Christianity—including the doctrine of the Trinity and the recognition of Jesus as Divine, the unique Son of God. They see the Jews as unfaithful to the revelation that they received through their own prophets.

DUTIES

Combining the belief in one supreme, all-powerful, eternal God, creator of all things with the concept of Allah revealing his will through Muhammad, the Muslim demand that one submit to Allah's will became the hallmark of Islamic doctrine. Based on this affirmation, Muslims are enjoined in the Qur'an to observe five supreme duties, called the *Five Pillars of Islam*. The first of these incorporates the central belief—one is to confess (profess) and sincerely hold a belief in one God and in the revelation of his will through Muhammad. Anyone who can confess sincerely, "There is no God but Allah, and Muhammad is his Prophet" is regarded as a Muslim and has fulfilled the first duty of the Islamic religion.

A second duty is to offer prayer to Allah, at prescribed times, five times daily. Although ideally prayer is best offered in a mosque (a building dedicated to the worship of Allah), Muslims can pray anywhere. In Muslim countries followers are summoned to prayer by the chant of a *muezzin* (one who calls the populace to prayer, usually from the tower of a mosque). In prayer, Muslims, facing toward Mecca, prostrate themselves to symbolize their total submission to Allah, usually on a specially designed prayer rug (to symbolize or confer sacredness on the site where the prayer is made). Though women may attend services at mosques, it is especially important for men to do so; and if at all possible, men and boys are present in the mosque for prayer at midday on Fridays, when an *imam*—a mosque official—leads the worship.

A third duty prescribed for Muslims is to give alms for the benefit of the poor and for the upkeep of the mosque.

A fourth duty is to observe a strict fast during daylight hours of the Muslim month of *Ramadan*, the month that marks the anniversary of the beginning of Allah's revelations to Muhammad. The month also calls for a special conscientiousness in fulfilling one's moral and religious duties. In addition, as much daylight time as possible is to be devoted to prayer and meditation and food may be eaten only at night.

A fifth duty—the fifth Pillar of Islam—is the duty of making, at least once during one's lifetime, a pilgrimage (called a *hadj*) to the holy city of Mecca. The hadj is supposed to be made with great reverence and with strict obedience to all moral and ritual requirements of the Islamic religion. Only Muslims are allowed inside the sacred city. A number of ritual duties must be performed during the trip to Mecca if the hadj is to fulfill its purpose. For instance, on arrival, the pilgrim must run around the Ka'ba seven times, each time kissing or touching the black stone. A pilgrim also reenacts the "flight" of Muhammad's first followers to Medina. Because of the encounter of believers from around the world Muslim pilgrims often testify to the sense of brotherhood experienced during the hadj.

These Five Pillars constitute primary duties, but daily life of the Muslim is defined much more fully by elaborated duties and rules derived from the Qur'an and *hadith*—reports of what Muhammad said and how, as one inspired by Allah's will, he acted in his personal daily life. Trained Muslim jurists (*fuguha*), using the Qur'an and hadith, formulated the *sunna* or moral law that, for the vast majority of Muslims, defines their daily life.[3] These laws and moral codes determine justice and truthfulness, require abstinence from alcoholic beverages, reject the eating of pork, and above all condemn any worship that seems remotely connected with idolatry. No representations of divine, human, or animal beings may be made.

To those who are faithful to its moral and cultic demands, Islam promises endless rewards in a blissful Paradise after the present earthly life. The rewards are often presented as involving both material and spiritual benefits. Those who are unfaithful are threatened with endless punishment in Hell, represented in graphic physical detail in the Qur'an (see Unit 58).

BRANCHES OF ISLAM

After Muhammad's death Islam rapidly spread throughout the Middle Eastern and Mediterranean worlds and yet was accompanied by significant schisms. The largest group, known today as *Sunnis*, arose from the followers of Muhammad who accepted Abu Bakr, one of Muhammad's principal lieutenants, as his legitimate successor and identified their community characteristics by embracing the sunna based on the Qur'an and hadith. Abu Bakr was elected to succeed Muhammad after Muhammad's death and was given the title *caliph* ("leader"). Abu Bakr and his successor caliphs were largely responsible for the effective and energetic spread of Islam. Minority groups, however, have existed from the beginning of the religion. Members of Muhammad's family and their colleagues resisted the rule of the early caliphs, contending that leadership should have been retained among Muhammad's descendants. From this group arose the present-day *Shi'ite* branch of Islam, which places great emphasis on the charismatic qualities of their leaders, understood to be the proper spiritual heirs of Muhammad. This group is traditionally the more conservative of the two major branches in its refusal to accommodate Islam to the non-Muslim influences of the modern world.

---

[3] For further elaboration of the development of Islamic law, commonly known as the *sharia* (way or path) built upon the *sunna*, see John L. Esposito, *Islam: The Straight Path* (New York: Oxford University Press, 1988).

In most Muslim countries there are rival Muslim groups and rival interpretations of the meanings of important aspects of the Islamic religion. There have recently been militant revivals of traditional, or "fundamentalist," Islamic practices and beliefs in some Islamic countries—particularly Iran and Afghanistan—in opposition to adoption of Western, non-Islamic influences. The necessity of developing technological societies to meet the challenges of the modern world has created great tension, with a strongly felt need to resist Western encroachment and to retain distinctive Muslim patterns and traditions while still embracing these technological advances. Muslims who have felt traditional patterns of belief and practice threatened by non-Muslim influence have often surprised outsiders by their willingness to attack even their fellow Muslims for what they consider to be secular modernization and false belief. *Shi'ite* Iran, for instance, has supported efforts, sometimes including violence, by Shi'ite minorities to secure greater influence in Muslim countries where the Sunni tradition is predominant.

Islam in recent decades has experienced significant revival both in areas where it has long been dominant and in many other areas of the world. Notable expansion of the tradition has taken place in Europe and America. The conservative renewal of Islamic cultural and social law has caused significant change, as well as conflict, in the present social and government patterns of many traditionally Muslim countries.

One major strand of Islamic faith that has been influential in many forms of Islam is that of the *Sufis*, a pattern of religious mysticism that first arose in the ninth century and continues to the present. The influence and strength of the Sufi tradition has been varied throughout history and was strongly criticized and persecuted by more traditionally oriented Muslims in the nineteenth century (see Unit 19).

Muslim contact with the Christian West has often involved great tension, yet Muslim theologians and philosophers helped to preserve the teachings of the great Greek philosophers of antiquity, transmitting them, with monotheistic elaboration and interpretation, to the Christian philosophers and theologians of the Middle Ages. To the outside observer, the Islamic tradition may appear stern and demanding, yet it is rich and varied. It has supported and encouraged subtle and powerful expressions of religious devotion and creativity in the arts, in science, in poetry, and in speculative philosophical and religious thought.

SUMMARY

Since this book does not seek to exhaust the content of all of the living religions, the charts that follow are intended to serve as aids in comparing and differentiating basic concepts and thrusts in today's major religions.

The material in these categories cannot be considered complete or fully representative of any of the religions in content and practice. One must constantly remember that there are problems in oversimplification. If one keeps in mind the complexity that is characteristic of any religious perspective, the chart may be helpful in reminding the reader of important emphases in the various religions. In addition to the seven religious traditions found in this chapter, information is included here on the native Japanese religion Shinto, which is discussed in several units of *Exploring Religious Meaning*.

Basic Tenets of the Major World Religions

	HINDUISM	BUDDHISM	
		Hinayana	Mahayana
Creed			
What is the divine?	Brahman-Atman External Spirit in world and individual	——	Cosmic compassion
What is humanity?	Eternal soul in bondage to a physical body through ignorance		
	Reincarnation	Reincarnation	
	Karma: reap what you sow	*Karma:* reap what you sow	
What is nature?	Illusion arising from ignorance	Illusion rising from ignorance	Illusion yet reality, through which many may know
	Unreal	Unreal	compassion
What is salvation?	Being freed from bondage to illusion through: Knowledge Works Devotion Asceticism	Achieving enlightenment through: Four Noble Truths Eightfold Path	
Code			
How should one live?	Meditation	Eightfold Path	Eightfold Path
	Doing one's duties	Discipline	Gentleness
	Devotion to deity or deities	Gentleness and kindness	Kindness and Discipline
Cult			
How should one worship?	Prayers	Prayers	Prayers
	Offerings	Offerings	Offerings
	Sacrifices	Sacrifices	Sacrifices
	Hymns	Hymns	Hymns
	Scriptures	Scriptures	Scriptures
	Meditation	Meditation	Meditation
	Ritual directed to deity or deities	Ritual for the sake of discipline	Ritual directed toward divine beings
What should one worship?	Powers of nature Brahman-Atman symbolized by images	——	Divine beings embodying cosmic compassion symbolized by images
Community			
How is the religious group understood?	Everyone	Those seeking enlightenment through self-discipline (monks) and, to a lesser extent, laypersons abiding by the rules	Those who express compassion
How is it related to others?	Recognizes other approaches to faith. Holiest withdraw to live the life of religious hermits	Recognizes other approaches to faith. Expresses wisdom to all	Recognizes other approaches to faith. Expresses compassion to all

(continued)

Basic Tenets of the Major World Religions (cont.)

	TAOISM	*CONFUCIANISM*	*SHINTO*
Creed			
What is the divine?	Tao: the Way	Cosmic order	*Kami:* Spiritual force in all things
What is humanity?	One among many natural beings Corrupted by aggressiveness and self-assertiveness	One among many natural beings Rational Able to do good or evil Moral Educable	One among many natural beings in whom kami is present
What is nature?	Ever-changing process in which the harmony and unity of the Tao is ever present	Real and dependable order in which harmony may be realized	Expression of the kami
What is salvation?	Becoming one with the Tao through mystical union and passivity	Restoring harmony within society and the universe by restoring the old ways	Recognition and veneration of the kami: the gods of the way
Code			
How should one live?	Social passivity; intuitive, mystical oneness with Tao	Harmonious relations with living, dead, and nature	Doing one's duty and honoring the kami
Cult			
How should one worship?	——	Prayers Offerings Sacrifices Hymns Scriptures Ritual Learning directed toward Heaven, ancestral spirits	Prayers Offerings Sacrifices Hymns Scriptures Ritual directed toward the kami
What should one worship?	——	Heaven Ancestors Spirits	Kami, which may or may not be symbolized by images
Community			
How is the religious group understood?	Any who seek union with Tao	Every thinking, sensitive person in society	Everyone
How is it related to others?	Withdraws from society	Is part of society seeking to establish harmony for all	Includes all society

(continued)

Basic Tenets of the Major World Religions (cont.)

	JUDAISM	*CHRISTIANITY*	*ISLAM*
Creed			
What is the divine?	Yahweh (One God with personal attributes)	One God with personal attributes characterized by love and justice (often conceived of as triune unity—Father, Son, Holy Spirit)	Allah (one God with personal attributes)
What is humanity?	Beings created in the image of God and directly dependent on the Divine	Beings created in the image of God, renewed in relationship to God and humanity through Christ	Beings created by Allah and dependent on him
What is nature?	Created physical order with a specific beginning, end, and purpose	Created physical order with specific beginning, end, and purpose	Created physical order with a specific beginning, end, and purpose
What is salvation?	Proper recognition of Yahweh and following his will	Freedom from alienation to participation in the Divine Love through relationship to Christ presently and eternally	Proper recognition of Allah and following his will Heavenly eternal reward for following his will
Code			
How should one live?	Following the commandments of the Law derived from the Torah, the Mishnah, and the Talmud commentaries based on them	In loving fellowship with God and humanity as Jesus taught and exemplified	Following the commandments of the Law derived from Qur'an, *hadith* and the *sharia* based on them
Cult			
How should one worship?	Prayer Ritual Scriptures Offerings Festivals	Prayer Ritual Scriptures Offerings Festivals Preaching	Prayer Alms Scriptures Pilgrimage
What should one worship?	Yahweh	God	Allah
Community			
How is the religious group understood?	Those who recognize Yahweh and follow his laws	Those who affirm the Lordship of Christ and live by his precepts of love in community	Those who recognize Allah and Muhammad as his prophet
How is it related to others?	Family Recognizes other approaches to faith. Non-evangelistic	Recognizes other approaches but seeks to convert others through basic message of faith	Recognizes other approaches but seeks to convert others through basic message of faith

A Comparison Between Eastern and Western Religions

EASTERN RELIGIONS	WESTERN RELIGIONS
Hinduism	**Judaism**
Buddhism	**Christianity**
Taoism	**Islam**
Confucianism	
Shinto	

Oriented toward nature	Oriented toward history
Conceives of Divine Power(s) as impersonal	Conceives of Divine Power as personal
Places little emphasis on time	Places great emphasis on time
Believes world and humanity eternal and uncreated	Believes world and humanity created and not eternal
Believes truth is not bound to particular persons	Believes truth comes through particular persons
Tends to be inclusive	Tends to be exclusive
Has little interest in clearly defined doctrine	Has strong interest in clearly defined doctrine
Tends toward unity of reality	Tends toward duality of reality
Downgrades individual will	Exalts individual will

✦✦✦ 3 ✦✦✦

RELIGIOUS EXPERIENCE

Everyday human life is a series of experiences related to each other by occurring to a particular person. Often these experiences arise out of a community or group setting but they may also be individual or private. Some are routine while others may be extraordinary and therefore particularly important to a person. When we want to share our experiences with a friend or acquaintance we sometimes do so in story form so our experiences become something other than simply an event in our day. For example, if, on the way to work or school, a person has been involved in an automobile accident, or simply observed one, the experience may dominate his or her thoughts during the day and will likely be related to a coworker or friend. The event can be remembered for weeks or years. Depending on its continuing significance, such an experience may also become a defining event in one's life. In a related way many common experiences, being similar in form and pattern, often accumulate into what we characterize as "business experiences," "educational experiences," etc. These too may shape other elements of our lives.

In this context, relying on our basic definition of religion, we define a religious experience as any experience that initiates or strengthens, maintains or weakens, or terminates a person's reliance on or commitment to a pivotal value. Since at any one time each of us will act in accordance with our pivotal value, the variety of human religious experiences is as great as the personal uniqueness found among us. Yet, as we have seen, similar elements found within individual experiences lead to the formation of religious traditions. Communities formed within such religious traditions often create unique patterns of religious experience for their participants.

We may attach labels, or classifications, to these many types of religious experience. For example, we call the experience of the Zen Buddhist engaged in strenuous silent meditation a mystical religious experience. The crying out in joyous ecstasy of the Pentecostal Christian may be classified as an ecstatic experience. Similarly, an aesthetic experience with religious content may occur when a religious intellectual perceives an orderly and awesome universe that points beyond itself. While assigning such classifications to religious experience, however, we caution the reader that such labels should not be taken as absolutes and are at best indications of some of the various elements or dimensions of religious experience.

This chapter presents representative examples of individual religious experiences. They have been selected from a number of traditions and periods not only to show the richness of diversity but also to allow the reader to observe the intensity and significance that the experiences held for the persons involved. Corporate expressions of religious experience are included in the study of structural elements in Chapter 4. Our purpose here is to begin with specific individuals who were historically influential within their religious communities and whose experience typifies an aspect of the variety found in religious experience.

The following questions may be used as a framework to help clarify the nature of a particular religious experience. They will also be relevant to the instances of both personal and corporate religious experience described throughout the book.

1. How did the experience initiate, maintain, strengthen (intensify), or weaken the relationship of the individual or group to (a) pivotal value(s)?
2. What specific features did the experience have?
   Was it an experience nurturing religious belief or practice?
   Did it intensify or transform the individual or a religious community?
   Was it sudden or gradual?
   Was it expected or unexpected?
   Was it sought (a quest) or unsought (a call)?
3. In what context did the experience occur?
   Did it occur in familiar or in unfamiliar surroundings?
   Did it occur in relation to familiar or unfamiliar persons?
   What, if any, patterns of a religious tradition did it reflect?
4. Did the religious experience affect particular areas or aspects of the individual's life? The group's life? Were there areas or aspects that were not affected?
5. How did it affect the individual's or the group's relationships? How did it affect the role(s) of the individual in the group or the roles the group had in the larger society?

It should be remembered that while such questions may help us identify a particular experience, many other factors influence and are affected by individual or group religious experiences. Most religions involve a belief, or creedal component. Similarly, every religion contains some directives, moral or legal, relating to the way of life, or code of conduct, advocated for its adherents or the world at large. Most religions contain practices and prescriptions for public and private devotion—its worship or cultic aspect. Finally, every religious tradition contains some concept of the limits of the community—who is included and how one becomes included; who is excluded—united in (or divided by) their adherence to the particular tradition. Note how each of these factors, and others, may or may not be present in the examples that follow.

UNIT 17   GOD'S CALL, MOSES' RESPONSE[1]

Born to a Hebrew woman but reared in the pharaoh's court, Moses, the revered leader of the Hebrew exodus from Egypt, enjoyed Egyptian favor and privilege. As a young man, however, he impulsively killed an Egyptian taskmaster whom he saw mistreating one of his Hebrew kinsmen. Fearing Egyptian punishment for murder, he fled to "the land of Midian," where he married the daughter of Jethro, "the priest of Midian," and became a shepherd of Jethro's flocks (Exodus 2:15–22, NRSV).

While keeping his father-in-law's flock, Moses found himself on Mount Horeb, the traditional holy mountain of God. There he encounters a burning bush, which is not consumed by the fire, and pausing to investigate this phenomenon, discovers God speaking to him (or calling him).

> When the Lord saw that he turned to see, God called to him out of the bush, "Moses, Moses!" And he said, "Here am I." Then he said, "Come no closer! Remove the sandals from your feet, for the place on which you are standing is holy ground." He said further, "I am the God of your father, the God of Abraham, the God of Isaac, and the God of Jacob." And Moses hid his face, for he was afraid to look at God. (Exodus 3:4–6, NRSV)

Note that this is a personal, direct encounter with God. Moses does not observe God himself but is clearly aware of his holy presence, represented by the burning bush. In this historical time period, the fourteenth to thirteenth centuries, B.C.E., the Divine was often depicted as using normal human means of communication. In Hebrew tradition such encounters, while not commonplace, were accepted means of divine/human interaction. They usually conveyed a particular purpose—a call to a mission or an instruction to the people. The Lord makes the purpose of Moses' call clear.

> Then the Lord said, "I have observed the misery of my people who are in Egypt, and have heard their cry because of their taskmasters. Indeed, I know their sufferings, and I have come down to deliver them from the Egyptians, and to bring them up out of that land to a good and broad land, a land flowing with milk and honey. . . . So come, I will send you to Pharaoh to bring my people, the Israelites, out of Egypt." (Exodus 3:7–10, NRSV)

Moses responded in typical human fashion with a series of reasons why he should not be God's messenger. "Who am I that I should go to Pharaoh?" The question is never answered directly. He is simply God's choice. Next Moses objected that he does not even know the name of the God who is giving the call. God is identified as Yahweh (although the name cannot be directly translated, its closest English approximation is "I AM WHO I AM"). In revealing to Moses a "new" name, God is asserting that no ordinary name is ade-

---

[1] Unlike other experiences recounted in this chapter, which have been drawn from relatively modern historical periods, this scriptural account of Moses' call was first retained among the Hebrews through oral transmission and in that sense predates their written history. Some modern scholars have seriously questioned its historical accuracy. For purposes of this chapter it is included with other more historically verifiable materials because it expresses quite well the Hebrew understanding of religious experience as a direct engagement of humans with the Divine.

quate or necessary—this God simply "is" the transcendent Lord of the universe. But another name was also given—the "God of your fathers, Abraham, Isaac, and Jacob," or the God whom the Hebrews had followed in Israel but whose presence had been difficult for them to discern in Egypt. Having God identified, Moses is still unable to believe the Hebrews would accept him as God's messenger.

God promises a sign to the people—Moses' shepherd's rod or staff will miraculously become a serpent, convincing the Israelites (and the Egyptians) that he has God's favor and message. Moses, in desperation, asserts that he is "not eloquent . . . (but) slow of speech and tongue." God chides him, pointing out that he had made Moses' tongue, and he promises to be with Moses in his speech. Finally, Moses, driven to no more excuses, cries out, "Oh, My Lord, send, I pray, some other person." God, relentless in his call, only promises to use Moses' brother, Aaron, as his spokesperson. Moses reluctantly submits to the call.

Notice that God establishes the relationship, and yet Moses is free to struggle with his own response to that call and ultimately to accept or refuse it. Based on a personal encounter, the call is to a much broader community responsibility—the saving of all of Israel. The experience changes the direction of Moses' life and the immediate relationship of God to the people of Israel. In submitting to God's will, Moses becomes one of the central figures through whom the relationship of Israel and God is revealed and clarified.

◆◆◆

> In what ways does Moses' encounter with God both question and yet intensify his commitment to a primary pivotal value?
>
> How does Moses' membership in a religious group relate to his personal encounter with God?
>
> What does the story reveal about the Hebrew understanding of the relationships between humans and the Divine? About the divine presence in the universe?

Unit 18   GAUTAMA'S QUEST FOR NIRVANA[2]

Reputed to have been reared in a noble family in India, Siddhartha Gautama, (born c. 563 B.C.E.), in his early life, was protected from many of life's harsh realities such as disease, poverty, and death. As a young man, he ventured forth into the broader world, only to discover and be staggered by the knowledge that extreme human suffering (disease, poverty, death, widowhood) is a common occurrence. Resolved to find answers to why such conditions should exist, he entered into a philosophical/religious quest.

Like many before him in India, Gautama began a life of spiritual searching by first studying the philosophical and religious teachings of the highly educated Brahmins

---

[2] Like the Moses account quoted in Unit 17, Gautama's religious experience was orally transmitted among Buddhists long before taking written form. Its historical accuracy has also been questioned, but it is used here because it captures the essence of Buddhist understanding of religious experience.

(see Unit 10) and practicing the rigorous physical and spiritual exercises of the highly disciplined, self-denying ascetics. Even after six years of striving, his quest was not satisfied. Having exhausted the means suggested by the holy men of India, Gautama, according to traditional Buddhist teachings, sat under the Bodhi Tree (the Tree of Wisdom) in meditation, determined not to leave until he had found a solution to the problem of suffering and the riddle of existence. In this "life and death" meditation, Gautama received illumination so that he comprehended the source of suffering and its relationship to universal/timeless life. As he taught these insights and methods of achieving them to others, he became for his followers the Buddha, the Enlightened One (see Figure 3.1).

Gautama's description of the experience through which he received his enlightenment follows:

> Now having taken solid food and gained strength, without sensual desires, without evil ideas I attained and abode in the first trance of joy and pleasure, arising from seclusion and combined with reasoning and investigation. Nevertheless such pleasant feeling as arose did not overpower my mind. With the ceasing of reasoning and investigation I attained and abode in the second trance of joy and pleasure arising from concentration, with internal serenity and fixing of the mind on one point without reasoning and investigation. With equanimity towards joy and aversion I abode mindful and conscious, and experienced bodily pleasure, what the noble ones describe as "dwelling with equanimity, mindful, and happily," and attained and abode in the third trance. Abandoning pleasure and abandoning pain, even before the disappearance of elation and depression, I attained

Figure 3.1   Amida Nyorai (Amitabha), known as Great Buddha of Kamakura, thirteenth century. Kotokuin Temple, Kamukura, Japan. (Photo by M. Sakamoto; reproduced by permission of Sakamoto Photo Research Lab., Tokyo, Japan.)

and abode in the fourth trance, which is without pain and pleasure, and with purity of mindfulness and equanimity.[3]

Having progressed to a state of pure consciousness, an awareness that took him beyond reason, feeling, pain, or pleasure, Gautama began to comprehend various aspects of existence or reality. First, by reviewing his former lives he came to the realization that rebirth is the normal order of human life. Second, he understood that these rebirths were dependent on the law of *karma*, the concept that those who lead evil lives "in deed, word, and thought . . . are reborn in a state of misery and suffering" while those who live good lives are "reborn in a happy state." Embracing this teaching, shared by Hinduism, Gautama reformulated it into a primary Buddhist insight and teaching: Life contains suffering because humans selfishly desire physical, spiritual, and intellectual attainments and satisfactions. This suffering can be overcome through elimination of desire—an insight that came to be known among Buddhists as the Four Noble Truths (see Unit 11). This awareness of the nature of the universe, or "enlightenment," brought Gautama an immense sense of freedom and emancipation.

> As I thus knew and thus perceived, my mind was emancipated from the āsava of sensual desire, from the āsava of desire for existence, and from the āsava of ignorance. And in me emancipated arose the knowledge of my emancipation. I realized that destroyed is rebirth, the religious life has been led, done is what was to be done, there is nought (for me) beyond this world. This was the third knowledge that I gained in the last watch of the night. Ignorance was dispelled, knowledge arose. Darkness was dispelled, light arose. So is it with him who abides vigilant, strenuous, and resolute.[4]

Gautama then chose to share with others the freedom and knowledge obtained in this enlightenment. His religious experience and the teachings that arose from it became the foundation of Buddhism.

Freedom from the round of rebirths achieved through the Four Noble Truths brought one to Nirvana—a state of being beyond all selfish desire, intellectual comprehension, or usual human emotions. Following are descriptions from Buddhist literature of this state and suggestions about how it might be achieved.

> A wanderer who ate rose-apples spoke thus to the venerable Sariputta:
> "Reverend Sariputta, it is said: 'Nirvana, Nirvana.' Now, what, your reverence, is Nirvana?"
> "Whatever, your reverence, is the extinction of passion, of aversion, of confusion, this is called Nirvana."
>
> (*Samyutta-nikāya* IV, 251–52)

> The stopping of becoming is Nirvana.
>
> (*Samyutta-nikāya* II, 117)[5]

---

[3] Edward J. Thomas, *The Life of Buddha as Legend and History* (London: Routledge & Kegan Paul, 1927), pp. 66–68.

[4] Ibid., p. 68.

[5] Edward Conze, ed., *Buddhist Texts Through the Ages* (New York: Harper & Row, 1964), pp. 92, 94.

We are told that Nirvana is permanent, stable, imperishable, immovable, ageless, death-less, unborn, and unbecome, that it is power, bliss, and happiness, the secure refuge, the shelter, and the place of unassailable safety; that it is the real Truth and the supreme Reality; that it is the Good, the supreme goal, and the one and only consummation of our life, the eternal, hidden and incomprehensible Peace.[6]

Guatama's religious experience became not only a defining element of his own life but through his teachings the essence of a new religious tradition. Although many modern day patterns of Buddhism have emerged through the centuries, Guatama's experience is central to each of their teachings.

✦✦✦

How is Gautama's religious experience similar to and/or different from those of Saint Teresa (Unit 20) and Rumi (Unit 19)?

Is it possible to see in Gautama's experience elements of a pivotal value or group of values? What might these be?

What characterizations of religious experience, as defined in the questions offered at the beginning of this chapter, apply to Gautama's experience?

Unit 19   SUFI ENCOUNTERS

From its beginnings, Islam emphasized the transcendence and omnipotence of Allah—a teaching that made submission to the authority, power, and rule of Allah an essential element of the tradition. Such submission can be, and often has been, understood to establish a "master/servant" relationship between Allah and the ordinary believer, a predominately impersonal relationship. However, a significant segment of Muslim followers also affirm that a personal religious encounter with the Divine is not only possible but necessary and central to their faith. Such encounters are often characterized as an intuitive experience of Allah, which cannot be captured by the rational, historical, or moral patterns of religion. Taking Muhammad's own personal encounters with Allah as an example, these Muslims stress direct confrontation with God, an experience that often transports them beyond ordinary reality. Known as *Sufis* ("wearers of wool"; in their early asceticism they wore rough wool robes), through the centuries they have represented a distinct Islamic mysticism: a mysticism that stresses the union of an individual with God. Concentrating on Allah's love as his primary category of being, their poetry and other writings reflect their own personal character of devotion.

Their insights and teachings often find voice in folklore, stories, and poetry that reflects their experiences rather than the recording of their own personal encounters. In the thirteenth century, Jalal al-Din Rumi, a Persian Sufi teacher and poet, spoke to the importance of feeling God in one's heart in the following tale from his *Mathnavi*:

---

[6] Edward Conze, *Buddhism: Its Essence and Development* (New York: Harper & Row, 1959), p. 40.

Moses saw a shepherd on the way, who was saying "O God who choosest whom Thou wilt, where art Thou, that I may become Thy servant and sew Thy shoes and comb Thy head? That I may wash Thy clothes and kill Thy lice and bring milk to Thee, O worshipful One; that I may kiss Thy Hand, and rub Thy foot. . . . O Thou to whom all my goats be a sacrifice, O Thou in remembrance of whom are my cries of ay and ah!"

The shepherd was speaking foolish words in this wise. Moses said, "Man, to whom is this addressed."

He answered, "To that One who created us; by whom the earth and sky were brought to sight."

"Hark!" said Moses, "you have become very back-sliding; indeed you have not become a Muslim, you have become an infidel. What babble is this? What blasphemy and raving? Stuff some cotton into your mouth! The stench of your blasphemy has turned the silk robe of religion into rags. Shoes and socks are fitting for you, but how are such things right for One who is a Sun?"

The shepherd said, "O, Moses, thou hast closed my mouth and thou hast burned my soul with repentance." He rent his garment and heaved a sigh, and hastily turned his head towards the desert and went his way.

A revelation came to Moses from God—"Thou hast parted my servant from Me. Didst thou come as a prophet to unite, or didst thou come to sever? So far as thou canst, do not set foot in separation: . . . I do not look at the tongue and the speech; I look at the inward spirit and the state of feeling. I gaze into the heart to see whether it be lowly, though the words uttered be not lowly, because the heart is the substance. . . . In substance is the real object. How much more of these phrases and conceptions and metaphors? I want burning, burning; become friendly with that burning! Light up a fire of love in thy soul, burn thought and expression entirely away! O Moses, they that know the conventions are of one sort, they whose souls and spirits burn are of another sort.[7]

Rumi carries the image further, expressing insight into the union possible between humanity and Allah.

When God appears to His ardent lover the lover is absorbed
in Him, and not so much as a hair of the lover remains.
True lovers are as shadows, and when the sun shines in
glory the shadows vanish away. He is a true lover of God to
whom God says, "I am thine, and thou art mine."
Let me then become nonexistent, for nonexistence
Sings to me in organ tones, "To his shall we return."
Behold water in a pitcher; pour it out;
Will that water run away from the stream?
When the water joins the water of the stream
It is lost therein, and becomes itself the stream.
Its individuality is lost, but its essence remains,
And thereby it becomes not less nor inferior.[8]

Emphases on direct, dynamic, personal dedication and encounters with God are matched among Islamic Sufis by their awareness of the immanence of God in all of life's

[7] John D. Yohannan, ed., *A Treasury of Asian Literature* (New York: Mentor Books, 1957), pp. 31–32.
[8] N. H. Dole and Belle M. Walker, Flowers from Persian Poets (New York: Thomas Y. Crowell, 1901), pp. 216, 219.

experiences. The traditional Muslim stress on outward prayer, pilgrimage, and alms is subordinated to the inward encounter with and dedication to God. In a story attributed to a tenth-century Sufi, Yahye-e Mo'adh, the teaching is clear:

> Yahye-e Mo'adh had a brother who went to Mecca and took up residence near the Kaaba. From there he wrote a letter to Yahya.
>
> "Three things I desired. Two have been realized. Now one remains. Pray to God that He may graciously grant that one desire as well. I desired that I might pass my last years in the noblest place on earth. Now I have come to the Sacred Territory, which is the noblest of all places. My second desire was to have a servant to wait on me and make ready my ablution water. God has given me a seemly servant-girl. My third desire is to see you before I die. Pray to God that he may vouchsafe this desire."
>
> Yahya replied to his brother as follows.
>
> "As for your saying that you desired the best place on earth, be yourself the best of men, then live in whatever place you wish. A place is noble by reason of its inhabitants, not vice versa.
>
> "Then as for your saying that you desired a servant and have now got one, if you were really a true and chivalrous man, you would never have made God's servant your own servant, detaining her from serving God and diverting her to serve yourself. You should yourself be a servant. You desire to be a master, but mastership is an attribute of God. Servanthood is an attribute of man. . . . When God's servant desires a station proper to God, he makes himself a Pharaoh.
>
> "Finally, as to your saying that you desire to see me, if you were truly aware of God, you would never remember me. So associate with God, that no memory of your brother ever comes into your mind. There one must be ready to sacrifice one's son; how much more a brother! If you have found Him, what am I to you? And if you have not found Him, what profit will you gain from me?[9]

Extravagant Sufi expressions of love for and identification with God along with significant asceticism through the early centuries of Islamic history often set Sufis apart from many of their fellow Muslims. Persecution of Sufi teachers and practitioners occasionally became intense. Abu Hamid al-Ghazali, in the eleventh century, sought to heal the rift between the legalistic religion of the Sunnis (see Unit 16) of his time and the insights of the Sufis. His work made it possible for Muslims to embrace the self-discipline, meditation, and intuition of the Sufis, practiced within the bounds of common sense, and at the same time participate in the demands of the Five Pillars, which were to flow from a heart identified with God's will. Modern Sufism most often embraces al-Ghazali's insight and follows his example.

◆◆◆

What description of religious orientation (see p. 68) best characterizes Sufi emphases?

What particular insights concerning humanity may be gained through Sufi experiences of God? How might these compare with those of Gautama (Unit 18)?

[9]Farid Al-Din Attar, *Muslim Saints and Mystics,* translated by A. J. Arberry (London: Routledge & Kegan Paul, 1966), pp, 181-82.

Unit 20   SAINT TERESA'S ECSTASY

Christian mysticism has never been more highly developed or widely appreciated than it was in sixteenth-century Spain, when reforms were brought to the church by this mystical tradition. Central figures in this reform were Saint Teresa of Avila and her younger colleague, Saint John of the Cross. Their writings provide enduring standards for mystical discipline and have greatly influenced Christian mystical patterns. For her preeminence in this field, Saint Teresa was declared a *Doctor of the Church* in 1970—a distinction granted to only two women by the Roman Catholic Church.

Born in 1515, Teresa was a member of a prominent Spanish family. After her mother's death when she was fourteen, Teresa turned to a more serious religious life, although its full fruition came to maturity much later. At the age of 20, over her father's objections, she entered the Carmelite Monastery of the Incarnation at Avila. At the time of her entry, members of this convent practiced a rather lax religious life, including a good deal of interaction with the secular community. From her early years Teresa had experienced visions, trances, and other spiritual encounters, which intensified through the years, making her uncomfortable with the convent's lack of a rigorous spiritual life. As a result of an experience of intense compassion and sorrow at the sight of a statue of Christ being scourged, in 1555 she began a life dedicated to spiritual perfection.

Over considerable opposition, she was granted permission in 1562 to establish the Convent of Saint Joseph to follow more strictly the original disciplines of poverty and spiritual life of the Carmelite order. The community became known as the Discalced (Barefooted) Carmelites, and over the next twenty years some thirty-two houses were established for both nuns and monks. Reforms instituted by Teresa and St. John of the Cross influenced renewal of spiritual life throughout the whole Carmelite order. Teresa's mysticism exemplified a dedicated spiritual life, which prompted religious reform both in her monastic order and the Roman Catholic church as a whole, as it responded to the Protestant reformation. Mysticism, always focused in personal encounter with the Divine, did not lead Teresa to inactivity or passivity.

At the urging of her superiors, she shared her experiences by writing several books. Her *Life of Saint Teresa* is both a recounting of her own early experiences and a manual for her sisters in the disciplined spiritual life. In this work she describes several states of prayer, from the first beginnings in meditation to union with God. The metaphor of water is used to illustrate her experience. The first state of prayer is like drawing water from a well. It is difficult, requiring discipline when the result is small and slow. The second state is like the introduction of an irrigation pump. Divine aid is given and the reward is much greater. The third state is compared to a running stream. The stream runs at God's instigation, not that of the individual; one's faculties are reduced, in that one may participate in directing the flow but may have little other function. The final stage is likened to a gentle shower of rain, wherein, without human effort, the soul is freely watered by God. One's usual faculties are transcended so that the experience becomes indescribable. Ecstasy is initiated by God, is not granted to many, and results in influencing the person's subsequent life (this was the way Teresa distinguished between true and hallucinatory experience). Teresa insisted that although such experiences were of the greatest importance, they were not ends in themselves—the goal of life remained to do God's will.

The following passage from her *Life* recounts one of Teresa's best-known descriptions of an ecstatic mystical experience:

> It pleased the Lord that I should sometimes see the following vision. I would see beside me, on my left hand, an angel in bodily form—a type of vision which I am not in the habit of seeing, except very rarely. . . . It pleased the Lord that I should see this angel in the following way. He was not tall, but short, and very beautiful, his face so aflame that he appeared to be one of the highest types of angel who seem to be all afire. . . . In his hands I saw a long golden spear and at the end of the iron tip I seemed to see a point of fire. With this he seemed to pierce my heart several times so that it penetrated to my entrails. When he drew it out, I thought he was drawing them out with it and he left me completely afire with a great love for God. The pain was so sharp that it made me utter several moans; and so excessive was the sweetness caused me by this intense pain that one can never wish to lose it, nor will one's soul be content with anything less than God. It is not bodily pain, but spiritual, though the body has a share in it—indeed, a great share. So sweet are the colloquies of love which pass between the soul and God that if anyone thinks I am lying I beseech God, in His goodness, to give him the same experience.[10]

[10]*The Life of Teresa of Jesus: The Autobiography of St. Teresa of Avila*, trans. and ed. E. Allison Peers (New York: Doubleday, 1960), pp. 274–275.

Figure 3.2   The Ecstasy of St. Theresa by Gianlorenzo Bernini, in Sta. Maria della Vittoria, Rome. (Reproduced by permission of Alinari/Art Reference , N.Y.)

In the seventeenth century Gianlorenzo Bernini visualized Saint Teresa's experience of the pierced heart in a celebrated sculpture (Figure 3.2). This piece was to become one of the best-known religious artworks of the day and a celebrated representation of Saint Teresa.

◆◆◆

What distinctions do you see between Teresa's experience, described here, and those of Gautama (Unit 18)?

What similarities/differences do you find between Teresa's experience and the Sufi experience described in Rumi's poem (see Unit 19)?

Unit 21   JUAN DIEGO AND OUR LADY OF GUADALUPE

In April 1519, Hernando Cortéz and his Spanish army entered Mexico. The natives of Mexico were subjugated by these conquerors, forcing the indigenous people to accept a new culture in the name of the Cross of Catholicism and the Crown of Spain. The priests who accompanied Cortéz represented the Roman Catholic mandate to missionize, evangelize, and win pagans to Christianity. During the decade following the conquest by Cortéz, the Indians of Mexico resisted the Catholic faith. Then, in 1531, a mysterious event occurred—one that caused the Indians of Mexico to embrace Catholicism by the thousands. Virgilio Elizondo writes about this religious experience as follows:

> There is no scientific proof or disproof, or explanation, of the "apparition" of Our Lady of Guadalupe, but there can be no denying its impact on the Mexican people from that time to the present. Its inner meaning has been recorded in the collective memory of the people.
>
> According to the legend, as Juan Diego, a Christian Indian of common status, was going from his home in the barriada ("district") near Tepeyac, a hill northwest of Mexico City, he suddenly heard beautiful music. As he approached the source of the music, a lady appeared to him. Speaking in Nahuatl, the language of the conquered, she ordered Juan Diego to go to the palace of the archbishop of Mexico, at Tlatelolco, and tell him that the Virgin Mary, "Mother of the true God through whom one lives," wanted a temple to be built on that site so that in it she could "communicate all her love, compassion, help, and defense to all the inhabitants of this land . . . to hear their lamentations and remedy their miseries, pain, and suffering."
>
> After two unsuccessful attempts by Juan Diego to convince the bishop of the Lady's authenticity, the Virgin wrought a miracle. She sent Juan Diego to pick roses in a place where only desert plants grew. She then arranged the roses in his cloak and sent him to the bishop with the sign he had demanded. As Juan Diego unfolded his cloak in the presence of the bishop the roses fell to the floor and the painted image of the Lady appeared on his cloak.[11]

This sign convinced the Bishop that Diego had indeed experienced a vision of Mary and that her instructions were authentic. Because the Virgin Mary had appeared to

[11]Virgilio Elizondo, *Galilean Journey: The Mexican-American Promise* (Maryknoll, NY: Orbis Books, 1983), pp. 11, 12.

one of their own people, the Mexican natives began to broadly accept the Christian faith, not as the religion of their conquerors but as arising from Diego's, and their own, unique experience of Mary. The Basilica de Guadalupe was subsequently built where Juan Diego's apparition is believed to have occurred. Every year, thousands of people make a pilgrimage to the Basilica to commemorate this event. There they recall the story and worship Our Lady of Guadalupe. The centrality of this story for the people of Mexico and other Latin American countries cannot be overemphasized. One cannot understand Mexicans and the religious roots of Mexico without reference to Juan Diego and his vision of the Virgin.

✦✦✦

> How was the communal life of the conquered Mexicans affected (empowered) by the personal religious experience of Juan Diego?
>
> What similarities/differences are present in the experiences of Moses, Saint Teresa, and Juan Diego?

UNIT 22   MAHATMA GANDHI'S RELIGIOUS JOURNEY

Mahatma Gandhi led India to independence from England, not by the power and might of military strength, but by *Satyagraha* (nonviolent direct action). A world-renowned figure in his own lifetime, Gandhi, shown in Figure 3.3, was revered and admired by millions in both the East and the West for his courage to renounce violence and his tremendous

Figure 3.3   Mahatma Gandhi. (Courtesy United Press International.)

spiritual strength. Born in India in 1869 and reared a Hindu, he trained in England to be a lawyer and practiced law in South Africa for twenty years before returning to India. There, with creative power, he led his people to spiritual renewal and to political independence. In 1948, while on his way to prayer, Gandhi was assassinated. His last words, murmured as he was shot, were, "Hey *Rama* (oh God)."[12]

Gandhi's early glimpses of religion came from the *Vaishnava* faith, but that interpretation of Hinduism repelled him because of too much "pomp and glitter."[13] While a law student in England he studied the *Bhagavad Gita* and then the Bible, reading the Old Testament in boredom but the New Testament with deep interest, especially the "Sermon on the Mount," which he compared to the *Gita*. He was particularly impressed by Jesus's teachings:

> "But I say unto you, that ye resist not evil: but whosoever shall smite thee on thy cheek turn to him the other also. And if any man take away thy coat let him have thy cloak too," delighted me beyond measure and put me in mind of Shamal Bhatt's "for a bowl of water give a goodly meal," etc. . . . My young mind tried to unify the teaching of the Gita, the Light of Asia and the Sermon on the Mount. That renunciation was the highest form of religion appealed to me greatly.[14]

From that time forward, Gandhi's interest in religion increased and he intensified his study of various religious writers.

While he was practicing law in South Africa, friends and colleagues sought to convert Gandhi to Christianity. He willingly submitted to hearing the Gospel, discussing doctrine, and being the subject of Christian prayers. He told a colleague, a Protestant lay preacher, that "nothing could prevent me from embracing Christianity should I feel the call. . . . I had long since taught myself to follow the inner voice."[15] He even attended a convention for Protestants, during which friends prayed fervently for him, but Gandhi saw no reason to convert, for he could not believe that Christianity was the only way to salvation. Although he did not feel that Christianity was the supreme religion, neither did he believe that Hinduism was perfect. He saw great value in both religions as well as in Islam, which he also studied.

The spirituality of Hinduism and Christianity intersected in Gandhi's religious quest. The teachings of Jesus were used by him in urging his fellow citizens to practice the ancient Hindu doctrine of Satyagraha, the postulate that nonviolence to all living beings is ultimately more powerful than violent action toward another living being. Convinced that all actions have consequences and either build up or tear down life—the Hindu doctrine of karma—he led a successful nonviolent revolution, ultimately gaining India's freedom from British rule. For Satyagraha, Gandhi suffered imprisonment, attacks on his life, long fasts that threatened his survival, and, finally, a martyr's death.

Gandhi's sense of obligation to the "inner voice" required him to live under

---

[12]Homer A. Jack, ed. *The Gandhi Reader* (Bloomington: Indiana University Press, 1956), p. 475.

[13] Ibid., p. 14.

[14] Ibid., p. 23.

[15] Ibid., p. 35.

intense obligations of faithfulness. He urged the use of nonviolent resistance to South African ordinances discriminating against Indians:

> We all believe in one and the same God, the differences of nomenclature in Hinduism and Islam notwithstanding. To pledge ourselves or to take an oath in the name of that God or with Him as witness is not something to be trifled with. If having taken such an oath we violate our pledge we are guilty before God and man. Personally I hold that a man, who deliberately and intelligently takes a pledge and then breaks it, forfeits his manhood.[16]

The tenor of his whole life expressed his faithfulness to the highest and deepest truth, the truth that he held to be not only divine but also essential for being human.

✦✦✦

How do you interpret Gandhi's religious pilgrimage?

How do you understand that he could be influenced by both Hinduism and Christianity to come to his religious convictions concerning nonviolent power as the force of love?

How would you describe the pivotal value that empowered Gandhi's political and social innovations?

---

[16] Ibid., p. 62.

✦✦✦ 4 ✦✦✦

ELEMENTS OF RELIGIOUS EXPERIENCE

If we reflect on any day of our individual lives we recognize that we participate in a wide variety of experiences. We often characterize or classify those events. We attend class, work, relax with our friends, study, play with our children, volunteer in a social service program, and participate in any number of other activities. Yet within these activities there are distinctions. The content of different academic classes is often unique, so studying for one class usually develops patterns that separate it from other classes and require different intellectual tools. So we recognize differing activities in our daily lives and find diverse structures and needs within any one activity. Similarly, as noted in Chapter 3, personal religious experiences are unique but fall into recognizable structures. The questions in the introductory comments of that chapter help one detect some patterns present in particular experiences.

Discussion of religion often concentrates on theologies, creeds, organizations, institutions, traditions—all important aspects of religion. However, it is probably at the level of personal experience—what happens to the individual or to the group, what is done or felt or believed—that the vitality of religion is most evident. To more adequately understand the nature of these personal and group experiences, the materials included in this chapter focus on elements that define the religious character of particular events.

First, we examine three significant and representative elements of religious experience found in every religious tradition—symbol, ritual, and myth. Each of these provides insight into how any experience is often permeated by both conscious and subconscious elements.

Second, we examine several orientations—the moral (or legal), the mystical, the aesthetic, the ecstatic, and the magical—that often characterize particular religious experiences. These orientations may be present in various degrees in any given experience of religion. Some may be greatly prized and sought in some religious traditions and shunned in others. They may mingle and mix or appear in relatively pure forms in the lives of groups and individuals. The five orientations defined here will be illustrated throughout this chapter and in later sections of the book.

The *moral (or legal) orientation* to religion seeks to subordinate behavior and attitudes to a pattern of conduct and intention held to have ultimate significance. This pattern may have been given through the commandments of a Divine Being or Beings. It may be held to be intrinsic to basic reality, the universe, or human nature. Or it may be the moral code of society developed from such orientations. While every religious tradition may contain elements of such an orientation, Islam, Judaism, and Confucianism are examples of religious traditions where moral and legal perspectives dominate (see Chapter 14 for other examples).

The *mystical orientation* to religion attempts to negate or subordinate every reality, world, society, self, and all their relationships to Divine Reality—God or universe, absolute spirit or nature, truth, goodness, beauty—so that at its deepest level or core the self can realize oneness—union or unity—with the Divine Reality. St. Teresa and Rumi, the Sufi poet, express this orientation.

The *aesthetic orientation* to religion attempts to interpret all experiences in such a way that they are seen to manifest a divine or transcendental pattern as their underlying and guiding reality—God's mind or will, wisdom, truth, order, beauty. The nature of this orientation is evident in Taoist, Christian, and Jewish teachings that one must see manifestations of the Divine in every aspect of life.

The *ecstatic orientation* to religion seeks supernormal experiences that bring individuals or groups under control of or in close contact with transcendental power(s). Pentecostal Christians speaking in "other tongues" and some forms of Buddhism fall into this pattern.

The *magical orientation* to religion seeks to discover and exercise methods that allow the control of transcendent power(s) for human purposes. This pattern may be found in Caribbean Voodooism and some traditional African religions.

No doubt additional approaches to understanding religion may be identified. But it will be useful to keep these five in mind while reading this text. As noted, some experiences involve a moral or legal outlook, in which the individual or group seeks to subordinate self and world to a code of life and conduct expressive of the Divine Will. Conformity to this code becomes the pivotal value, or at least is closely connected with it. Similarly mystical, aesthetic, and ecstatic orientations may also take on the nature of a pivotal value. Combining an understanding of such orientations and their interaction with recognition of the significance and role of symbol, ritual, and myth is essential to understanding the many aspects of personal and group religious experience.

Unit 23   The ROLE OF SYMBOLS IN RELIGION

Oh say, can you see,
By the dawn's early light,
What so proudly we hailed,
   at the twilight's last gleaming,
Whose broad stripes and bright stars. . . .[1]

---

[1] Francis Scott Key, *The Star-Spangled Banner*, excerpt from the national anthem of the United States.

Citizens of the United States of America generally will become quiet and stand when hearing the instruments of a band play the introduction to "The Star Spangled Banner," their national anthem. Removing hats as an act of respect, often placing hands over their hearts and joining in singing, they look for a flag with patterns of red and white stripes and a field of blue with white stars representing the states of the federal union. There is legislation that regulates the employment of these flags. Proper patterns of folding the flags for storage are an established convention. Traditions of public behavior are established regarding the occasions when a flag is unfurled. To drag a flag on the ground, to stand on it, or to desecrate it in any way can lead to arrest by police and possible prosecution in court. When traveling abroad American citizens may experience a strong emotional response when seeing the flag at an embassy or other public place. A famous work of public sculpture depicts American soldiers struggling to plant the standard for the flag in the ground of the Pacific island of Iwo Jima during World War II. This piece of fabric with distinctive patterns clearly evokes powerful feelings and resulting behavior. What does the flag connote? What representative functions does it serve: It may be argued that for most Americans this flag has been accorded more than that of a mere identifier or sign, rather it has gained the status of a symbol. This symbolic function, particularly its role as a symbol of national unity, has become intensified since the September 11, 2001, terrorists' attacks on America.

Symbols long have been relied on to express truths and insights that may not be simply rational.[2] When we look for the origin of the English word symbol, we must turn to Greek. The Greek word *symballo* can be translated as "to place together" or "to bring together." Thus, we see that a central function of symbols in religion has been to unite or join truths with powerful, graphic representations.[3] Yet one problem in dealing with symbols is semantic. Some people may use the words *symbol, allegory, metaphor, sign* or other terms as if they are interchangeable. However, these words are different, and they carry differing connotations. A careful consideration of the functions of symbols requires that they be differentiated from other ways that we represent or signify.

It is a truism to say that most of our modes of expression serve some communicative functions. But in these ordinary communications, we usually can separate the meaning from its vehicle, i.e., the carrier of that communication. To illustrate this point, let us begin by considering a well-known metaphor, *the ship of state*. The intention of the phrase is readily apparent. Few people would confuse a nation with a ship, that is, the *vehicle (carrier)* with its *meaning*. Therefore, what distinguishes a symbol from a metaphor like ship of state is the peculiar representative function that is served by a symbol. Now we come to the central point of this unit: *that which is pointed to becomes one with the vehicle that serves*

---

[2] Although many people have contributed to the growing literature on the analysis of symbols, this unit depends especially on the important contributions to contemporary understanding by Rollo May, a psychologist; Paul Ricoeur, a philosopher; and Paul Tillich, a theologian. Each has had some influence on the conceptions presented here: See Rollo May, ed., "The Significance of Symbols," *Symbolism in Religion and Literature* (New York: George Braziller, 1960), pp. 11–49; Paul Ricoeur, *Interpretation Theory: Discourse and the Surplus of Meaning* (Ft. Worth: Texas Christian University Press, 1976), pp. 45–69; Paul Tillich, *Dynamics of Faith* (New York: Harper & Brothers, 1957), pp. 41–54.

[3] See also Erich Kahler, "The Nature of the Symbol," in May, *Symbolism in Religion and Literature*, p. 70.

as the pointer. Thus, some reality can become *condensed* in its symbol, enabling people to grasp part of some vast or transcendent reality so that at least they can participate in its symbolic form. Often metaphors are developed to indicate what something is like.[4] But a symbol is multidimensional; it takes us beyond words to roots deep in experience.

If we understand symbols to point to something beyond themselves, they do another thing as well: they *fuse (join)* with that which they represent.[5] For its believers, the emotion aroused by the symbolized object is attached to, or shared with, its symbol. Because of this fusion, the symbol becomes a kind of autonomous reality because it *points to and becomes a part of* the larger reality that it represents. Thus, one may perceive or encounter some essential quality of what is being represented in the representor (symbol). A symbol elicits a deep and strong response from the person who actually perceives it. The symbol demands more than cognitive recognition; it functions at the emotional level as well. Therefore, people may experience symbols at the conscious as well as the subconscious level of their experience. Indeed, symbols may not be constructed by conscious intention but may arise from individual and group unconscious experience. Furthermore, it can be observed that symbols change as both individual and group needs change.[6] So after they are established, symbols continue to grow or sometimes are replaced by new and more functional ones. Certainly, this becomes clear when one studies the history of religions.

Specifically, religious symbols may represent the ultimate—God. They can serve to make the vast, awesome, transcendent deity perceptible to adherents of the religious tradition. They are part of the language of faith. Religious symbols can have a power that distinguishes them from other symbols; they deal with issues that are the deepest of all concerns a human may have, with *ultimate meaning.*[7]

Religious symbols are supported by communities and therefore are socially rooted. Most societies support special institutions such as churches, synagogues, mosques, or temples, one of whose functions is to maintain and develop their tradition of religious symbols.

A religious image or concept that has achieved the level of symbol may be perceived and treated as the deity itself: This is called idolatry. An image or concept can function *as a symbol* only when some difference is discerned between the *representation* and the *represented*, between the object and the actual Ultimate. When this is known, a person becomes capable of employing a symbol to point to the Ultimate, to serve as an "arrow" to the Divine. It is in and through the symbol that the Divine is encountered and known. The symbol serves to "telescope" the transcendent Divine, to make it accessible, to serve as vessel or vehicle and yet not *be* the totality of the Divine. The symbol serves as a revealer, though it cannot reveal all of the Divine. In many living religions, the symbol is of God in terms of its intermediary, representational function, but the image and the words remain less than that to which they point.

---

[4] See also the more extensive discussion of metaphor in Ricoeur, *Interpretation Theory*, pp. 46–53.

[5] Cf. also Tillich, *Dynamics of Faith*, p. 42.

[6] See the characteristics of symbols, ibid., p. 43.

[7] Ibid., pp. 44–47.

A symbol arises from the depths of human experience and stands for something vast, something not fully under rational control, something at the edge of one's ability to comprehend. Yet the symbol *embodies some essential characteristic* or quality of that which it represents (see Figure 4.1). As has been suggested, the symbol "telescopes" the represented (like God) into a manageable form; hence, the represented is encountered within the symbol; it is *there*. At the same time, the symbol always points beyond itself to the represented. Both models and symbols facilitate connections. They are not absolute substitutes for what they represent, but the essential of the represented may be contained in them.

Indeed, a large part of human religious experience is mediated through symbols. The Bible, the Wailing Wall in Jerusalem, the Cross, the Ka'ba in Mecca, a footprint of the Buddha, the sacred Ganges River in India—all are powerful religious symbols, expressive of the Divine that is apprehended through them, in them, or behind them by adherents of the religious traditions involved—Jewish, Christian, Muslim, Mahayana Buddhist, and Hindu. The same may be true of works of religious art and architecture. They often function powerfully in human religious experience.

A potent *visual statement* of ancient Greco-Roman theology is the statue representing the god Apollo—god of light, music, healing, and prophecy (see Figure 4.1).

Figure 4.1   *Apollo Belvedere,* marble sculpture, Vatican Museums, Rome, second century C.E. (Alinari/Art Resource, N.Y. Used by permission.)

Intended for placement in a niche of the sanctuary of a temple to Apollo, the statue is sta-bilized by the sculpted mass of a tree stump (at the viewer's left). Crawling up the stump is a snake, the ancient Python of Delphi, symbol of earth's creation. The anthropomor-phic (human) representation of Apollo is beautifully balanced both in position and pro-portion. Rational balance and aesthetic beauty are quintessential characteristics of Apollo. The figure is nude in celebration of the Greek ideal of the human form. The for-ward movement of the figure is suggested through the placement of the right foot on the ground and the raised left one. The lips are parted as if speech issues from the mouth. The gaze of the eyes follows the arm, outstretched in gesture. The drapery of the mantle accen-tuates the gesture and movement of the body. Apollo approaches the viewer, *seeks and addresses* humanity, with his message of reason, balance, and aesthetic beauty.

Surrounded by the pre-Columbian glyphs of hieroglyphic text celebrating the scene, an idealized figure of an ancient Mayan ruler receives offerings (see Figure 4.2). The central figure is quite abstract in terms of the idealization of Mayan beauty, notably the long nose that issues from a ridge in the forehead. His head rises toward a point, with the hair arranged in a strict style with bands indicating the man's position in that soci-ety. His seated pose is one of aristocratic grace atop a platform of stylized alien subject figures. The exaltation of Mayan civilization above all others is visually enhanced by this arrangement.

Figure 4.2   Mayan ruler receiving offerings, from "Tablet of the Slaves," relief sculpture, site of ancient Palenque, Chiapas, Mexico, 730 C.E. (Photo by K. Lawrence)

Large arrangements of jewelry of symbolic significance adorn the ruler's body. Of special significance is the necklace with pendant (partially hidden by the wrist and hand) that is a symbol for a god. The power of the deity, as associated with the ruler, is of singular importance in that context.

The official at left offers the ruler a headdress with feathers, which functions like a crown. On its front, a symbol for one of the gods protrudes from the elaborate surface. At right, another functionary offers a symbol of religious significance. The abundant art of the Maya clearly indicates elaborate ritual and ceremony, accompanied on some occasions by music provided by bands of instrumentalists (cf. frescoes from nearby Bonampak). Ruler-priests wore elaborate ritual regalia of symbolic significance on such occasions and, in a certain sense, seem not only to serve as priests, but to impersonate the gods.

Most modes of religion depend heavily on symbols as expressions of the Divine, even though it may be argued that no finite symbol (a concept, a thing, or a work of art) can adequately express the Divine that transcends all symbols. Certainly the magical modes of some religions are heavily dependent on symbols (see Unit 26). Perhaps only the mystical mode of religion attempts finally to dispense with all symbols and to know God directly. But even in the mystical mode, symbols have an important role in the communication of the mystic's experience to others.

◆◆◆

In your own religious background, how are symbols understood?

Can you name instances where, as the unit suggests, symbols "fuse (join) with that which they represent"?

Illustrate how a pivotal value can be symbolically identified.

Unit 24   THE ROLE OF RITUAL IN RELIGION

Our lives are filled with patterns of personal behavior that take on the function and feeling of a ritual. Most of us perform the everyday functions of life in set patterns, patterns that from repeated use become habits. When these have become formalized to the point that we are disturbed if they are interrupted or changed, they have taken on a "ritual" function; rituals help keep us focused or oriented and provide us with a sense of meaning and purpose. Participation in group activities follows similar patterns of ritual. Many apparently "secular" activities in society, for example, football and soccer matches and graduation ceremonies, are highly ritualized events. In our present American culture the rituals of sports events perform similar functions to the roles that traditionally "sacred" rituals have had in the life of a culture.

It is not surprising then that ritual acts of piety and worship have from time immemorial been part of all recognized religions. Their variety is unlimited and their functions numerous. Because of their public nature and constant repetition, much of the content of a religion is handed down from generation to generation through ritualized religious rites; the acts and stories of ritual convey as much or more than formal religious teaching. Consequently participants may find the rituals meaningful without understanding or recognizing the teachings on which they are based. Religious ritual normally falls into three discernible categories, which although distinct are not necessarily exclusive.

RITUAL DIRECTED TOWARD THE DIVINE

Humanity, recognizing its own limitations and finitude, has through religious ritual sought to communicate with the Divine Power(s) understood to be responsible for its creation and continuing existence. Since religion permeated all aspects of life in early cultures and was not separated from any event, the rites and rituals that emerged naturally had religious overtones and functions. Thus the cultivation of crops, creation of tools, tribal celebrations, warfare, and all other events in the life of a people carried ritual forms recognizing the gifts and guidance of the deities. As with symbols (see Unit 23), their importance and power were not limited to their particular form. People often understood the rites to be humanity's participation in the divine drama of life itself so they often became elaborate, beautiful, and central to culture. In sacrificial offerings human beings gave what was theirs, a part of themselves, in recognition of what had been given to them and to express community with the divine.

Although it arose in early cultures, such an understanding continued in sophisticated civilizations, as reflected in the words of Hzün Tzu, a Chinese philosopher of the third century C.E.:

> In general, rites begin with primitive practices, attain cultured forms, and finally achieve beauty and felicity. When rites are at their best, men's emotions and sense of beauty are both fully expressed. When they are at the next level, either the emotion or the sense of beauty oversteps the others. When they are at still the next level, emotion reverts to the state of primitivity.
>
>   It is through rites that Heaven and earth are harmonious and sun and moon are bright, that the four seasons are ordered and the stars are on their courses, that rivers flow and that things prosper, that love and hatred are tempered and joy and anger are in keeping. They cause the lowly to be obedient and those on high to be illustrious. He who holds to the rites is never confused in the midst of multifarious change; he who deviates therefrom is lost. Rites—are they not the culmination of culture?[8]

In many cultures the religious aspects of every event and act in life are often celebrated in ritual forms; every religion has also developed specific forms of worship and celebration to show devotion and commitment publicly. Often these rituals are obligatory for pious believers. The *Qur'an*, the Muslim scripture, clearly illuminates this aspect of ritual. In the following passage Allah is speaking of the pilgrimage all Muslims should make at least once to the *Ka'ba*, or Holy Mosque, in Mecca (Figure 4.3).

> And when We settled for Abraham the place of the House [Ka'ba] We said "Thou shall not associate with Me anything [idols or other Gods]. And do thou purify My House for those that shall go about it and those that stand, for those that bow and prostrate them-

---

[8] Hzün Tzu, "Rationalism and Realism in Hzün Tzu," trans. Y. P. Mei, as quoted in William Theodore de Bary, ed., *Sources of Chinese Tradition* (New York: Columbia University Press, 1960), pp. 123–124.

Figure 4.3   Pilgrims at the Ka'ba in Mecca. (Courtesy of ARAMCD)

selves; and proclaim among men the Pilgrimage, and they shall come unto thee on foot
and upon every lean beast, they shall come from every deep ravine that they may witness
things profitable to them and mention God's Name on days well-known. . . . Let them
then finish with their self-neglect and let them fulfill their vows, and go about the
Ancient House." All that; and whosoever venerates the sacred things of God, it shall be
better for him with his Lord.

We have appointed for every nation a holy rite, that they may mention God's Name
over such beasts of the flocks as He has provided them. Your God is One God, so to Him
surrender. . . .

O men, bow you down and prostrate yourselves, and serve your Lord, and do good;
haply so you shall prosper; and struggle for God as is His due, for He has chosen you, and
has laid on you no impediment in your religion, being the creed of your father Abraham;
He named you Muslims aforetime and in this, that the Messenger might be a witness
against you, and that you might be witnesses against mankind. So perform the prayer, and
pay the alms, and hold you fast to God; He is your Protector—an excellent Protector, an
excellent Helper.[9]

---

[9] Reprinted with permission of Scribner, a Division of Simon & Schuster, Inc., from *The Koran Interpreted*, Arthur J. Arberry, translator, Sura XXII, verses 26–38, 75–77. © 1955 George Allen & Unwin, Ltd.

PERSONAL INWARD-DIRECTED RITUAL AS TRANSFORMATION OF THE SELF

Spiritual life expressed in public ritual is often complemented by personal ritual patterns, the purpose of which is not only communication with the Divine but also discovery and transformation of the self. In religions such as Buddhism, personal discipline is designed to "free" one from the delusions of *samsara*, the eternal round of individual existences (see Unit 11). Highly cultivated ritual patterns contribute to introspection, leading the devotee to release from *samsara* and thereby serving as a channel or means to personal transformation.

The fourteenth-century Zen Buddhist master Bassui Tokusho in the following passage recognizes the practical importance of personal ritual but also notes its transitory nature:

> To realize your own Mind you must first of all look into the source from which thoughts flow. Sleeping and working, standing and sitting, profoundly ask yourself, "What is my own Mind?" with an intense yearning to resolve this question. This is called "training" or "practice" or "desire for truth" or "thirst for realization." What is termed zazen [the actualization of the true Buddha nature] is no more than looking into one's own Mind. It is better to search your own Mind devotedly than to read and recite innumerable sutras and dharani every day for countless years. Such endeavors, which are but formalities, produce some merit, but this merit expires, and again you must experience the suffering of the Three Evil Paths. Because searching one's own mind leads ultimately to enlightenment, this practice is a prerequisite to becoming a Buddha. No matter whether you have committed either the ten evil deeds or the five deadly sins, if you turn back your mind and enlighten yourself, you are a Buddha instantly. But do not commit sins and expect to be saved by enlightenment [from the effects of your own actions], for neither enlightenment nor a Buddha or a patriarch can save a person who, deluding himself, goes down evil ways.[10]

Most religions include such pragmatic or practical personal rituals although they are not understood, as in certain forms of Buddhism, to be indispensable ritual forms.

RITUAL SPIRITUALIZING OF ORDINARY ACTIVITIES

For many religions the ideal devotee is one who recognizes and identifies the presence of the Divine in the ordinary activities of daily existence. For these people the ritual patterns of daily life become an avenue for praise of and identification with the Divine. Chuang Tzu, a third-century B.C.E. Taoist teacher, expresses the point quite well in his tale "Prince Wen Hui and His Cook":

> Prince Wen Hui's cook
> was cutting up an ox.
> Down went a shoulder,
> He planted a foot,
> He pressed with a knee,

---

[10] Philip Kapleau, *The Three Pillars of Zen* (New York: Anchor Press/Doubleday, 1980), p. 169.

The ox fell apart
With a whisper,
The bright cleaver murmured
Like a gentle wind.
Rhythm! Timing!
Like a sacred dance. . . .

"Good work!" the Prince exclaimed,
"Your method is faultless!"
"Method?" said the cook
Laying aside his cleaver,
"What I follow is Tao
Beyond all methods!

"When I first began
To cut up oxen
I would see before me
The whole Ox
All in one mass.
After three years
I no longer saw this mass.
I saw the distinctions.

"But now, I see nothing
With the eye. My whole being
Apprehends.
My senses are idle. The spirit
Free to work without plan
Follows its own instinct
Guided by natural line,
By the secret opening, the hidden space,
My cleaver finds its own way.
I cut through no joint, chop no bone. . . .

"There are spaces in the joints;
The blade is thin and keen:
When its thinness
Finds that space
There is all the room you need!
It goes like a breeze!
Hence I have this cleaver nineteen years
As if newly sharpened!

"True, there are sometimes
Tough joints. I feel them coming,
I slow down, I watch closely,
Hold back, barely move the blade,
And whump! the part falls away
Landing like a clod of earth.

"Then I withdraw the blade,
I stand still
And let the joy of the work
Sink in.
I clean the blade
And put it away."

Prince Wan Hui said,
"This is it! My cook has shown me
How I ought to live
My own life!"[11]

In Christianity this type of spiritualization of daily existence was practiced by Brother Lawrence, a monk who understood his dishwashing as an expression of praise and thanksgiving to God.

In modern cultures the role and significance of religion for the life of society has been increasingly personalized so that public religious rituals have often lost their traditional functions. Consequently, public religious rituals have been modified and substantially limited, occasionally causing consternation and conflict among those most active in religious traditions. For example, the use of manger scenes in secular settings during Christmas holidays have largely vanished because the rising plural nature of religious practice questions the relationship to and role of Christianity in the larger American society. Yet, such scenes continually appear in religious contexts and in private homes and lawns. Examples of such changing societal appropriation of religious rituals could be multiplied but all demonstrate continually changing patterns of ritual function. Rituals may take new or differing forms but they continue as crucial elements of practice and communication in both private and public religious life.

◆◆◆

Think about the rituals or rites widely practiced in our own society. Are these most often secular or religious? Can they be both?

Are ritual forms and practices necessary for religious expression?

Why do most religions urge believers to participate in public rites of worship?

From your own religious tradition name the rituals that are most significant.

Unit 25   Myth and Religious Insight

The term *myth* is often used in ordinary conversation to mean "something that is widely accepted or believed but that is in fact false." A second common use of *myth* is to designate stories that arose in primitive or naive societies that involve personified forces of nature, gods and goddesses, and legendary heroes, for example, the familiar Greek myths. In a third sense, *myth* is sometimes used to mean "primitive" beliefs about nature and the universe, "prescientific science"; for instance, the Babylonian cosmology (still the basis for systems of astrology) is sometimes called a mythological scientific system. Finally, *myth* is used by some political or social thinkers, such as R.M. MacIver and Bronislaw Malinowski, to refer to any basic belief or system of beliefs involving value claims and commitments. Thus, MacIver defines *myth* as the "the value-impregnated beliefs and notions"

---

[11] Thomas Merton, *The Way of Chuang Tzu* (New York: New Directions, 1965). Copyright © 1965 by the Abbey of Gethsemani. Reprinted by permission of New Directions Publishing Corporation.

that sustain and give unity to society. Malinowski called such myths the "charters of belief" that validate the customs and practices and code of society.[12] Originally the term *myth* referred to the spoken part of a religious ritual.

In this unit, we will suggest that a simpler and better way to understand *myth* is to begin by remembering that the word often refers to a kind of story. The story is not always about gods and goddesses or the forces of nature personified or even great legendary heroes and heroines. For example, an American myth is associated with the life of Abraham Lincoln. It tells a story of a man who grew up in poverty; who experienced hardship and failure; but who through determination, hard work, and personal integrity, attained the highest office in the nation. This story embodies one of the great myths of American society, the belief that by hard work and personal integrity a person may rise from poverty to economic and social success. The myth is rooted in historical experiences such as those of Lincoln, in which such a rise in status did indeed occur.

It is misleading to think that myths necessarily involve falsity. Myth has a very important role in the life of the individual and in society. Often, it is by means of myths that societies and individuals define or acquire their sense of identity, which is why myths have a significant role in most of the world's religions.

Perhaps one of the more helpful students of myth is the anthropologist Claude Lévi-Strauss, who studied functions of myth in both preliterate and literate societies. According to Lévi-Strauss, the essential characteristic of myth is that its structure is historical or narrative in character. A myth is the narration of a sequence of events. These events may be historical or legendary, but they are presented as being, and are felt to be, ahistorical and "eternally valid." A myth is a pattern of relationships combined in a temporal sequence and related to one another by means of transformations.

As noted earlier, the term *myth* originally meant the spoken part of a religious ritual. A myth always begins with persons, forces, or elements in conflict, an imbalance. The beginning words of a religious rite may, for instance, tell of a powerful, good, and loving god whose faithful human worshippers are weak, oppressed, and apparently forsaken. A second, or mid-stage, of ritual may show the Divine Being making himself or herself weak like his or her followers. The conclusion of the rite may show the Divine Being and worshipper-followers raised from weakness to triumph, strength, and well-being. There will always be at least three, possibly more, stages involving transformations in the ritual, story, or myth. The first stage will express a negative imbalance, with the hero or good force in a position of weakness or apparent strength that is threatened. The second stage will expose or intensify the weakness of the good force or hero. The third stage will transform the weakness into strength or show that it is or has somehow been strength all along. Or, to say this differently, the first stage will present a negative imbalance, the second either a negative imbalance or balance, and the third stage a positive balance with the elements, forces of good and evil, in right relation to each other. As noted, there may be many more stages of transformation as the story seeks to bring an appropriate balance to the originally unbalanced situation.

The result of the transformation of the elements of myth is that unlike or contradictory elements of human experience (including life and death, agriculture and war-

---

[12] See David Bidney, *Theoretical Anthropology* (New York: Columbia University Press, 1953), p. 297.

fare, and maleness and femaleness) are enacted and felt as being essentially identical. The myth allows the integration of differences that are potentially disruptive to society or to the individual because of their contradiction with other elements (such as beliefs, values, interests, expectations, and desires). The mythical resolution of the contradictions of life is not reached or apprehended reflectively or discursively; it is enacted and lived in feeling, imaginatively and affectively.

Most of the great dramatic works of ancient Greek theater have the structure of myth. At the beginning of *Oedipus Rex* by Sophocles, Oedipus, who has saved the city of Thebes, has been triumphantly crowned king; the city, however, is now being devastated by plague (negative imbalance). At midpoint, though warned not to, Oedipus seeks to discover the cause of the plague and discovers that unknowingly he has killed his father and married his mother (negative balance). By the end of the play, Oedipus blinds himself and becomes an outcast. By his action, Oedipus both purifies himself and brings health to the city, producing a positive balance.

Mythical structure appears often in what may seem to be unlikely places. A popular radio and television program of a generation ago featured a fictional hero of the American West. This was a masked man, the Lone Ranger. Because of his mask, he was often thought to be an outlaw as he rode into town, since someone was robbing the citizens. In fact, the thieves were respectable pillars of the community (negative imbalance). At the midpoint of the story, the tension became great, with the apparently powerless Lone Ranger headed for a showdown with the powerful outlaws (intensified negative imbalance). At the end of the episode, the Lone Ranger unmasked the outlaws, bringing peace and safety to the town, and revealing his identity only as he galloped away on his great horse Silver, shouting, "Hi-yo Silver, away," leaving someone in the town who asked, "Who was that masked man?" to be answered in words that truly thrilled members of the young audience, "Why *that* was the *Lone Ranger*." The person who said this was obviously a citizen capable of being the myth's internal interpreter, with a gift of seeing and putting a seal on the final positive balance.

A well-known Vietnamese myth, which tells of the origin of the Vietnamese people from the marriage of a beautiful and gracious fairy to an aggressive, ugly dragon, expresses through a series of transformational events the unity within diversity and the diversity within unity of the Vietnamese people. At the same time it offers an explanation for the distinctions between northern and southern Vietnam.[13]

Some Christians have objected to the use of the term *mythological* to characterize any parts of the message of the Bible. Other Christians, like Rudolf Bultmann, have asserted that mythological elements must be interpreted in such a way that the message of the New Testament can come alive in a meaningful form today. Thus, he argues that the Bible must be "demythologized." Still others, including Paul Tillich, insisted that all religious expression must involve certain mythological elements, since myth is a necessary symbolic medium in expressing reality that is transcendent. The understanding of myth presented here attempts to go beyond this debate by arguing that what makes a myth a myth is the structure of a story that allows those hearing or participating in the story to

---

[13] See Tran Van Dihn, "The Foundation of Man" in *Story in Politics*, Michael Novak, ed. (New York: Council on Religion and International Affairs, 1970), pp. 55ff.

live and relive it. The story need not be fictitious, prescientific, or unhistorical. C.S. Lewis, a twentieth-century British Christian popular apologist, once said that the unhistorical myths of ancient Greece prepared him intellectually and spiritually to accept the Christian story of the life, death, and resurrection of Jesus, events he believed to be historical.[14]

Societies usually communicate and hand on their most important "truths"—beliefs, aspirations, values, self-image—through myths, stories that do not merely describe these "truths" but allow the society's members to identify with and internalize them by living and reliving them. The courageous child of the 1950s entering a schoolyard where bullies threatened other children *became* the Lone Ranger when he resisted the bullies. The Buddhist monk imitating the path of Gautama toward enlightenment *becomes* the Buddha. The Christian sacrificing her or his comfort, pride, personal desires because she or he believes it is God's will to do so dies and is raised to new life with Jesus.

◆◆◆

> Examine the Babylonian and Japanese creation stories presented in Unit 80 and some of the familiar Greek and Native American myths in light of Lévi-Strauss's discussion of the way myths function. Note especially the transformations from imbalanced to more balanced states of affairs.
>
> What myths are important and meaningful to you?

Unit 26   MAGIC: THEORY AND PRACTICE

As myth has a critical role in a society and is often related to religion, so too has magic frequently been associated with religion. Earlier we stated that a magical orientation to religion involves attempts, either by an individual or a group, to use transhuman, often spiritual or divine beings or powers, to bring about human goals. Most societies in which magic is practiced and magical powers are believed to be available have made a distinction between good and evil (or white and black) magic. According to this distinction, good magic is used to help the group and its members.

Evil magic, often described as witchcraft, is believed to be able to do unjustified harm to group members. A witch may be male or female. In some societies, for instance among the Native American Navajo, witchcraft has been held to be a pervasive phenomenon, causing most illnesses and harmful events. When an individual becomes ill or experiences misfortune, elaborate measures are often used to discover the witch's identity to bring about or force the undoing of evil spells.

In societies where "good" magic has been institutionalized, practitioners of magic, often referred to as shamans, are held to have gained power by intense personal—mental and spiritual—discipline. Again, among the Navajo, persons recognized as shamans are held in great esteem, recognized by their impressive, dynamic personalities and by their success as healers.

---

[14] See C.S. Lewis, *Surprised by Joy* (New York: Harcourt, Brace & World, 1955).

In many societies, practitioners of magic will have undergone ordeals, such as fasting and a period of solitude in isolation from the group. Often they will have experienced visions. Usually, they will be taught by an experienced older practitioner. Knowledge and character are both important. In the ancient Roman Empire, especially in the first two centuries C.E., belief in magic was widespread. A second-century novel entitled *Metamorphoses or The Golden Ass,* by Lucius Apuleius, a priest of the goddess Isis, in this supposedly autobiographical tale tells the story of an ambitious young man who becomes a roomer in the house of the most famous woman magician of a Greek city. The novel has a serious theme but is wildly comical as well. Wanting to get power to become wise and wealthy, Lucius persuades the woman's servant to show him the books of magic. Lacking both character and knowledge, he casts a spell that turns him into a donkey and throughout the rest of the novel he wanders helplessly over the empire until the goddess takes pity and turns him back to being human.

The twentieth-century anthropologist Bronislaw Malinowski believed that a clear line of distinction can be drawn between science and magic and between magic and religion. Although many disagree that these lines can be drawn with exactness, it will be useful to give a brief account of Malinowski's theory. According to Malinowski, in societies that rely on magic, science—by which he means technology or nonmagical techniques established by experience—is used for tasks where natural causality is understood to accomplish desired social or personal goals. "Science," for example, will be used for fishing in a safe lagoon or gathering fruit. Magic, on the other hand, consists of rites used when activities involve uncertainty or danger, fishing in the ocean or going to war.[15]

Again, according to Malinowski, magic (like science) involves specific goals. The goals of religion are nonspecific. Its rites are done because they "are the right thing to do" or have been commanded by tradition, a priest, a shaman, or a divinity. Malinowski mentions funeral rites as activities that have no specific goal but that bring healing to the grief threatened community. However, in contrast to what Malinowski argued, it can be noted that, like what he calls science, magic involves technical practices thought to be validated by past experience. Also, "religious" rites may seem to have very specific goals. The funeral rites may be done to appease spirits of the dead in order that the dead will not be jealous of and harmful to the living. Also, it may be difficult to draw a line between a religious service in contemporary urban America where there are prayers for rain and a magical rain dance performed by Native Americans. Some may insist that the rain dance is supposed to produce rain automatically and that the requests of the prayer service are acknowledged to be contingent on God's will.

We may define the magical orientation toward religion as one in which control of transcendent or divine power is sought so that it may be used for manipulation of the religious adherent's environment for personal or group purposes. We can also see why some religious traditions have highly valued the magical orientation as a vital element in their religious traditions. If we examine the role of the shaman (or "medicine man"—not always a man—or "witch doctor" or "oracle") in many societies, we can see that the "expert" in magic is often highly valued. Often the term shaman is associated with prelit-

---

[15] See Bronislaw Malinowski, "Magic, Science and Religion," *Science, Religion and Reality,* ed. Joseph Needham (London: Society for Promoting Christian Knowledge, 1925).

erate or at least rather simply organized societies, such as those whose economic life is built on hunting or fishing or undiversified agriculture. But the expert in magic is not confined to simpler societies and may be highly valued for two reasons. The shaman will be seen as someone who through demanding disciplines—often physical as well as intellectual or spiritual—has acquired transcendental powers and may be seen as a kind of saint. The shaman will also be valued for the ability to provide cures for the sick and success in war or love or agriculture. However, we have seen that there can be harmful magic, and some magical experts may be seen as extreme dangers to the individual or group. Even so, the belief in malicious witches provides some relief to suffering individuals or the group: It "explains" illness, bad luck, and misfortune, thus making them more "rationally" acceptable and understandable. The belief in malicious witches also gives suffering individuals something positive to do, namely, to find a "good" shaman who can counteract the malicious witch's spells.

Still among the best sources for learning about beliefs and the practice and acquisition of the shaman's art are the fine essays in Lévi-Strauss's *Structural Anthropology*.[16] But two fictional accounts, one of them recent, do much to bring to life the shaman's powers. The first is the Nigerian novelist Chinua Achebe's *Arrow of God*, a vivid depiction of the conflict between traditional ways and modernity, in which an Igbo leader of great authority uses his reputation as a man of magical power to try to stem the erosion of tribal customs.[17] The second, *Coyote Waits* by Tony Hillerman, tells the story of a Navajo tribal police officer, Jim Chee, whose deepest desire is to become a singer, one who can exercise the healing power of one of the Navajo "ways."[18]

At one point in the story Chee remembers the ceremonial curing—an Enemy Way (a Navajo ritual conducted to cure people from contamination by contact with things "foreign" to Navajo life, such as strangers or enemies)—he attended as a child.

> The cure had been conducted by a hataalii who had been very tall and had seemed to him then to be incredibly ancient. The patient had been Chee's paternal grandmother, a woman he had loved with the intensity of a lonely child, and the event had formed one of his earliest really vivid memories. The cold wind, the starlight, the perfume of the pinon and juniper burning in the great fire that illuminated the dance ground. Even now, he could see it all and the remembered aroma overpowered the mustiness of this office. Most of all, he remembered the hataalii standing gray and thin and tall over his grandmother, holding a tortoiseshell rattle and a prayer plume of eagle feathers, chanting the poetry from the emergence story, making Old Lady Many Mules one with White Shell Girl, restoring her to beauty and harmony.
>
> And restore her it had. Chee remembered staying at the old woman's place, playing with his cousins and their sheepdogs, seeing his grandmother happy again, hearing her laughter. She had died, of course. The disease was lung cancer, or perhaps tuberculosis, and people with such diseases died—as all people do. But it had been that cure that had caused him to think that he would learn the great curing ways, the songs and the sand paintings, and become a hataalii for his people.[19]

---

[16] Claude Lévi-Strauss, *Structural Anthropology*, Vol. 1 (New York: Basic Books, 1963).

[17] Chinua Achebe, *Arrow of God* (Garden City, NY: Doubleday/Anchor Books, 1969).

[18] Tony Hillerman, *Coyote Waits* (New York: Harper Paperbacks, 1992), pp. 191–192. Copyright © 1990 by Tony Hillerman. Reprinted by permission of HarperCollins, Publishers, Inc.

[19] Ibid., pp. 191–192.

Chee wanted so much to become a singer who could bring benefits to his people that he took lessons from a highly regarded shaman and learned the curing ceremonial called The Blessing Way. As he tells a non-Navajo character in *Coyote Waits*,

> I'm a would-be shaman. A singer. A medicine man. Hataalii is the Navajo word for it. I was going to be one of the people who conducts the curing ceremonies to restore people to harmony. Or I was trying to be. Nobody seemed to want my services.[20]

Chee's comment shows both the power of the belief in shamanistic magic and the effects of modernism in corroding that power. But if we look at even the most highly modernized societies, such as the United States today, we can find remnants and pockets of belief and reliance on magic, in southern Louisiana, for instance, where voodoo is practiced, or in southern California, where magic by many names and in many forms flourishes.

◆◆◆

Many religious communities believe that their religion offers mental and physical healing to its believers. Could this also be seen by many as magical?

How would Malinowski's distinctions between magic and religion apply in such situations?

Why would a priest of Isis in the ancient Roman empire write a novel warning people of the dangers of practicing magic, as Lucius Apuleius did in his fictional autobiography Metamorphoses?

What characteristics of western mentality make it unable to accept magic as a reality?

How are magic and religion interwoven in the shamanistic cure recounted from Hillerman's novel?

Unit 27   ECSTATIC RELIGIOUS PHENOMENA

Common human phenomena include ecstatic experiences in which a person is so caught up in the excitement and emotion of the moment that he or she moves beyond the ordinary self into a state where time and place have little meaning or consequence. The event takes over all sensation and meaning. In the bliss of the moment one may act in ways that are uncharacteristically bold and different or become able to perform extraordinary physical tasks. Such moments vary widely. They may occur at sports events that then become highpoints of memory, in crisis moments of daily living, at cultural events where appreciation of music or art carry one beyond the norm, and in interpersonal relationships that change the nature of one's contact with another person. In these events a person is often in contact with her pivotal value(s) that shape and give content to the experience. So such events, even where they occur in a secular context, may have religious substance.

[20] Ibid., p. 178.

Such ecstatic events, in religious terms often referred to as "spirit-filled" experiences, are part of a universal religious phenomenon found in every major religious tradition. Mystical experiences, such as those of St. Teresa (Unit 20) and of Islamic Sufis (Unit 19), exemplify one form of the phenomenon wherein the believer, while in contemplation or meditation, understands his or her spirit to be united with the Divine Spirit. Another form is manifested in popular religion when believers, often in highly charged emotional situations, display unusual physical or emotional capacities. These are most often understood to be expressions of a Divine presence: Examples include the "Whirling Dervishes" of Islam, where the participants express the spirit through phenomenal physical feats of dance; Hindu holy men or Voodoo practitioners walking on spikes or hot coals; Native Americans evoking through song the spirits of nature; and Christian groups experiencing bodily "spirit possession" and glossalalia (speaking in tongues).

The religious campmeetings of the American frontier often included ecstatic experiences where participants believed they became possessed, emotionally and physically, by the Holy Spirit. They might lie prostrate for long periods, find their bodies responding to the event by "the jerks," discover themselves powerfully singing and praying when otherwise normally silent or reticent to speak, and occasionally speaking in tongues. Such phenomena were often understood to be the sign of a "successful" campmeeting. By the middle of the nineteenth century the settlement of the frontier meant the establishment of local churches with formalized doctrine and standardized ritual worship that discouraged such spontaneous "spirit-filled" events. Late in the nineteenth century new patterns of ecstatic worship began to emerge in urban "tabernacle" meetings (in some sense a campmeeting adapted to an urban setting). A Sacramento California meeting in 1883 illustrates the development.

> The prevailing spirit was that of expectancy, or waiting. The powers of the heavenly world seemed to settle down upon the people, and the ministers never seemed so inspired and filled with love and the Spirit of Jesus, who seemed almost to be visibly present. . . . Many were stricken down under the mighty shock. Many felt themselves beginning to go down as when metal begins to melt, and seemed forced to lie prostrate upon the ground. There was an indescribable power that went surging through the soul, until life seemed suspended on a single thread. . . . Then, also, a strange thing occurred to some. It was not a light, nothing of a cloud-form; but as it were, a haze of golden glory encircled the heads of the bowed worshippers—a symbol of the Holy Spirit; for then that company knew that they were baptized with the Holy Ghost and fire. . . . All were melted into tears and sobs, and murmurs of praise and glory. Truly the day of Pentecost had finally come—and the scene of the upper chamber was repeated, and all were filled with the Spirit."[21]

In many denominations similar experiences were expected in annual revivals in the late nineteenth and early twentieth centuries—events where lively preaching and "loosened" ritual practices led to "spirited" meetings.

Pentecostalism, another spiritually oriented movement arising at the turn of the twentieth century, expected that every believer would experience "the spirit" in ecstatic moments or events. Such events were then understood to be the basis of one's everyday

[21] Taves, Ann, *Fits, Trances, and Visions: Experiencing Religion and Explaining Experience from Wesley to James.* Princeton: Princeton University Press, 1999, p. 239.

living of the Christian life. Pentecostalism gave rise to new denominations, the Assemblies of God and the Churches of God in Christ, as well as numerous smaller churches and groups. These churches appealed initially to those of the lower economic stratum of the society, emphasized a literal interpretation of the Bible, and called for the "baptism of the spirit" as recorded in Acts: "And they were filled with Holy Spirit and began to speak in other tongues" (Acts 2:4). In recent decades these traditional Pentecostal churches have through strong evangelism become among the most rapidly expanding Christian groups throughout Latin America, some parts of Africa, and Eastern Europe.

Two examples illustrate the appeal of the ecstatic experience:

> I knew that something ought to be there which was not there, and could not be found. . . . I read in the Bible about the early church and its supernatural power and I so longed for such as that. . . . This was about two years ago. Between seventy and eighty of our people have received this glorious experience. Men and women who wearily trudged to prayer meeting and drove themselves to be faithful have become flaming evangels for Jesus![22]

> I continued to tarry for the Baptism (of the Spirit). . . . On Sunday . . . I received the Baptism. The Holy Spirit came like a torrent, as though He would tear my body to pieces. One of my besetting sins has been my unwillingness to speak out boldly for Christ, but when the Holy Spirit came in He made me shout the praises of Jesus until He verily split my throat. However, as one brother said to me, the Lord is able to repair any damage He does to the old temple. After being tossed about violently for quite awhile until I was panting for breath and wet with perspiration, I then lay for quite awhile in blessed quietness and poured forth praise to God in tongues for over half an hour.[23]

These accounts indicate crucial elements of a modern neo-Pentecostalism: dissatisfaction with perfunctory and powerless religious practice, the desire for an experience of supernatural power, baptism by the Holy Spirit, exuberant and emotional worship, contentment, and praising God in tongues.

During the 1960s–1980s the phenomenon of "tongues speaking" became more broadly accepted and was identified as a "charismatic" experience. Generally, persons participating in the movement claimed that the baptism of the Holy Spirit fulfills Christ's promise to the apostles: "But you shall receive power when the Holy Spirit has come upon you" (Acts 1:8, NRSV). Convinced that the church will receive new power only by this baptism, charismatics began to penetrate mainline Protestant denominations, including Lutheran, Presbyterian, Episcopalian, and Methodist, as well as the Roman Catholic church. They also differed from classical Pentecostalism at several points. Stressing tongues-speaking, they nevertheless recognized the diversity of spiritual gifts (Greek: *charismata*) assuming that all believers may share in any of the gifts—speaking in tongues and the ability to interpret tongues, prophesy, healing, and expelling evil spirits (I Corinthians 12–14). They included many people from the middle- and upper-class eco-

[22] Frederick D. Bruner, *A Theology of the Holy Spirit* (Grand Rapids, MI: William B. Eerdmans, 1970), p.127.

[23] *Ibid.*, p. 126.

nomic strata. Some saw the movement as cutting across denominational lines so it tended to be ecumenical or nondenominational in orientation.

This "charismatic movement" has waned in recent decades yet some aspects of its "spirit-filled" worship have become vital elements in many churches and parachurch groups. A highly participatory experience, worship often includes singing praise songs and choruses; music of guitars, drums, and keyboards in addition to pianos and organs; joyous praise; hearty handclapping; ecstatic prayer; communal witness; and testifying. Many "mainline" Protestant and Catholic churches have incorporated some of these elements in their worship services. Such "ecstatic" experiences and others similar to them have been present throughout Christian history.

As noted, comparable ecstatic experiences are found throughout the various religious traditions. They are essential in many religions. African religious traditions imported into the Caribbean islands developed into Voodooism where spirit possession is a central element of the religion. The following description of a participant in a Voodoo fire ceremony illustrates the phenomenon:

> You can't tell how or why it comes. You can't predict when it will come. It is the moment of spiritual crisis. The possessed becomes a changed personality. Even though I knew that this was to happen, it struck me with an impact beyond my expectation. I saw Apela (a young girl) step into the fire. I watched her take seven slow, shuffling steps. I studied her face for signs of pain. There were none. The glow of the fire surrounded her with an aura. The others who were possessed had also stepped in. They too registered no pain, no fright, no reaction. They came out of the flames to make a circle around the fire and then went back for seven more steps. I could see the live coals topple over their feet. Their feet sank into the fiery embers. They walked back and forth until the coals were stamped out black. . . .She and the others were offered food. She refused. Finally she consented to eat. But it was not Apela who ate. . . .The food was offered to the *loa* (the spirit) through Apela. . . . There was no evidence of blistering or burning (of her feet when the ceremony ended). Her feet were normal in every respect. I asked her whether she remembered anything about walking through the fire. 'I didn't walk through the fire,' she said. She was right. It was not Apela. It was the *loa*[24].

Such moments and practices may be found in many groups and have many similarities but they may also have very differing purposes as in Tantric Buddhism, popular Taoism, and in some forms of Hinduism.

◆◆◆

> *Think about ecstatic experiences you have experienced or observed in ordinary life. What was their character? Were they related to religious practice?*
>
> *What differences do you note between Pentecostal or Charismatic Christianity and mystical Christianity?*
>
> *Why might ecstatic occurrences such as those described occasionally take on the power of a pivotal value for those who experience them?*

[24] Marcus Bach, *Strange Altars* (New York: Bobbs-Merrill Company, Inc., 1952), p. 25.

Unit 28   MYSTICISM IN RELIGIOUS EXPERIENCE

An account of the religious experience of Teresa of Avila is given in a previous chapter (Unit 20). Teresa's experience is a classic instance of religious mysticism.

> One day, being in orison . . . it was granted me to perceive in one instant how all things are seen and contained in God. I did not perceive them in their proper form, and nevertheless the view I had of them was of a sovereign clearness, and has remained vividly impressed upon my soul. It is one of the most signal of all the graces which the Lord has granted me. . . . The view was so subtle and delicate that the understanding cannot grasp it.[25]

Mysticism as a type of religious experience has been frequent in Christianity. It is also characteristic of many Eastern religions—Buddhism, Hinduism, and Taoism—and has been represented by the Sufis in Islamic religion. The Greek philosopher Plato believed that the highest knowledge of reality must be gained in a flash of mystical insight.

> Even so, this organ of knowledge must be turned around from the world of becoming together with the entire soul, like the scene-shifting periact in the theater, until the soul is able to endure the contemplation of essence and the brightest region of being.[26]

As we suggested earlier in this chapter, mysticism is one of the major forms of or orientations to religious experience. It involves an attempt to negate self, others, and the world in order to give God, or the Divine Reality, complete power in and over the self. The result is that the self is completely surrendered to, or in union with, the Divine.

> As a deer longs for flowing streams,
>   so longs my soul for you,
>   O God.
> When shall I come and behold
>   the face of God?
> My tears have been my food
>   day and night,
> while people say to me continually,
>   "Where is your God?"
>
> Why are you cast down, O my soul,
>   and why are you disquieted within me?
> Hope in God; for I shall again praise him,
>   my help and my God.
>   (Psalm 42:1-5, NRSV)

[25] Saint Teresa of Avila, as quoted in William James, *The Varieties of Religious Experience* (New York: Longmans, Green and Co., 1912), p. 411.

[26] Plato, quoted in Walter Houston Clark, *The Psychology of Religion* (New York: Macmillan, 1958), p. 261.

Evelyn Underhill, an important twentieth-century British writer who was herself a Christian mystic, defined mysticism as follows:

> Mysticism, according to its historical and psychological definitions, is the direct intuition or experience of God; and a mystic is a person who has, to greater or less degree, such a direct experience—one whose religion and life are centered, not merely on an accepted belief or practice, but on that which he regards as first-hand personal knowledge.[27]

In describing the phenomenon of mysticism in religious experience, the psychologist and philosopher William James found these four characteristics:

1. *Ineffability*—The handiest of the marks by which I classify a state of mind as mystical is negative. The subject of it immediately says that it defies expression, that no adequate report of its contents can be given in words. It follows from this that its quality must be directly experienced; it cannot be imparted or transferred to others. In this peculiarity mystical states are more like states of feeling than like states of intellect. No one can make clear to another who has never had a certain feeling, in what the quality or worth of it consists. One must have musical ears to know the value of a symphony; one must have been in love one's self to understand a lover's state of mind. Lacking the heart or ear, we cannot interpret the musician or the lover justly, and are even likely to consider him weak-minded or absurd. The mystic finds that most of us accord to his experiences an equally incompetent treatment.
2. *Noetic quality*—Although so similar to states of feeling, mystical states seem to those who experience them to be also states of knowledge. They are states of insight into depths of truth unplumbed by the discursive intellect. They are illuminations, revelations, full of significance and importance, all inarticulate though they remain: and as a rule they carry with them a curious sense of authority for after-time. . . .
3. *Transiency*—Mystical states cannot be sustained for long. Except in rare instances, half an hour, or at most an hour or two, seems to be the limit beyond which they fade into the light of common day. Often, when faded, their quality can but imperfectly be reproduced in memory; but when they recur it is recognized; and from one recurrence to another it is susceptible of continuous development in what is felt as inner richness and importance.
4. *Passivity*—Although the oncoming of mystical states may be facilitated by preliminary voluntary operations, as by fixing the attention, or going through certain bodily performances, or in other ways which manuals of mysticism prescribe; yet when the characteristic sort of consciousness once has set in, the mystic feels as if his own will were in abeyance, and indeed sometimes as if he were grasped and held by a superior power. . . .[28]

R. C. Zaehner, in a classification of three types of mysticism, feels that in all of them, the quality or kind of experience is perhaps similar—like that described by William James—but that the object or content is different. The first type of mystical experience described by Zaehner is nature mysticism, sometimes called pantheism—the feeling of union or identity of the self with objects in the natural world or "nature" as a whole.

A second type of mysticism is that typical of certain Eastern religious traditions,

[27] Evelyn Underhill, *The Mystics of the Church* (New York: Schocken Books, 1964), pp. 9–10.
[28] James, *Varieties of Religious Experience*, pp. 380–381.

particularly Vedantic Hinduism, in which the self feels itself as identical with the Absolute Self, Brahman, the One Reality beyond the natural world of mere appearance and in which the individual self is totally merged with, absorbed in, the Absolute.

The third type is described as follows:

> Thirdly there is the normal type Christian mystical experience in which the soul feels itself to be united with God by love. The theological premise from which this experience starts is that the individual soul is created by God in His own image and likeness from nothing and that it has the capacity of being united to God, of being "oned" to Him as the medieval English mystics put it. Here again we have a third type, distinct, it would appear, from the other two.... No orthodox Christian mystic, unless he is speaking figuratively or in poetry as Angelus Silesius does, can well go farther than to say that his individual ego is melted away in God by love: something of the soul must clearly remain if only to experience the mystical experience. The individual is not annihilated, though transformed and "deified" as St. John of the Cross says: it remains a distinct entity though permeated through and through with the divine substance.[29]

❖❖❖

What difference does Zaehner see between Christian and Vedantic mystical experience? Between both and nature mysticism?

❖❖❖

Although Zaehner's threefold division of the types of religious mysticism is useful, it probably represents a simplification that, taken too far, is misleading. This can easily be seen by considering Zen Buddhism, which is based on a form of mystical experience, prepared for by instruction in rigorous techniques of meditation by a Zen teacher (or master), and leads to an experience of enlightenment called *satori*. In many ways Zen enlightenment results in attitudes similar to those of nature mysticism, a sense of overcoming the division between the self and the whole, as well as between the self and the individual concrete presence of things. Zen is rooted in Buddhist traditions that derive from Hindu pantheism (though Buddhism generally and Zen particularly do not have theological or metaphysical theories of pantheism or, for that matter, of the nature of things). Christian writers have found profound analogies between the Zen approach and that of the Hebrew-Christian Scriptures and parts of Christian mystical tradition and practice.[30]

Following is a Zen play presenting the experience leading to the Zen enlightenment of Bodhidharma, an Indian Buddhist monk who became the founder of Zen, a movement that spread to China and is now most frequently associated with Japan. The play, entitled *Bodhidharma*, is by Saneatsu Mushakoji. It is a good illustration of Zen mysticism, which is in some sense uncategorizable as one of Zaehner's types. Nevertheless, it resembles all of them, particularly if one realizes that even with the emphasis in Christian mysticism on devotion to an absolute object, most Christian mystics have stressed that God as experienced in mystical union cannot be "known" (as a subject-knower might know—perceive or understand—an object of finite experience). Note that entrance into

---

[29] R. C. Zaehner, *Mysticism: Sacred and Profane* (London: Oxford University Press, 1961), p. 29.

[30] See Thomas Merton, *Mystics and Zen Masters* (New York: Farrar, Straus & Giroux, 1967), and J. K. Kadowaki, S. J., *Zen and the Bible: A Priest's Experience* (London: Routledge & Kegan Paul, 1980).

enlightenment is the culmination of extreme personal discipline but does not depend on that discipline or reason; it comes in the intuitive moment, in this case symbolized by a blow on the head.

> The characters are A, B, and Dharma. In front of a small temple where Dharma sits in meditation, A and B enter.

A: Do you know the fellow that lives here?

B: I don't.

A: Don't you? There's a peculiar fellow living in this temple.

B: What is he like?

A: A fellow who has sat staring at nothing but the wall for eight or nine years.

B: Staring at the wall for eight or nine years? What for?

A: If we knew what he was doing that for, he would no longer be considered peculiar. But there isn't anyone who knows what he is staring at the wall for. People say he must be an idiot.

B: If you talk in such a loud voice, the fellow inside will hear you.

A: No fear. He's an idiot, and besides, he's deaf.

B: Is he deaf?

A: He is deaf.

B: Is that why he only stares at the wall?

A: Yes, that's why he only stares at the wall.

B: How does he eat?

A: His neighbors make a point of bringing meals to him, it seems.

B: How thoughtful of them!

A: I suppose they sometimes forget to bring the meals. They told me that once they purposely didn't bring his meals for three or four days, but he stared at the wall as usual as if nothing had happened. . . .

B: But is he really an idiot? I can't believe that he is.

A: But an intelligent person could not go on doing such a thing for eight or nine years at a time like this, could he? For what is the good of staring at a wall? It can't do any good, can it?

B: I think you're right. However, are you sure he didn't change color when he was beaten? Don't you think he was just pretending?

A: No, I assure you he didn't change color. I watched him intently.

B: But you saw him at some distance didn't you? Then you couldn't possibly see him roll his eyes.

A: Then I'll strike him on the head now, so watch closely.

B: Is it all right to strike him? If the fellow should suddenly roar you look as though you'd be paralyzed with terror. For we seldom see such a fearful face, you know.

A: Don't worry. Now watch me, I'll strike him.

B: Are you sure it's all right?

A: Of course it is. Watch me closely.

B: The more I look at him the stranger his face looks. He looks as if he'd choke you to death and eat you if he once got angry.

A: No, he is a mild fellow really. He looks terrible only in the face. Now I'll strike him.

B: All right.
      [A strikes Dharma on the head.]

A: How was it?

B: Strange. It surely is strange. Please strike him again. [He draws nearer.]

A: All right. [He strikes him again.] . . .
      [He approaches Dharma . . . and raises his arm. Dharma turns his head]

A:	[falling on his knees.] Please forgive me. Please forgive me.
Dharma:	What day is it today?
	[A and B are struck dumb. They try to say something but cannot.]
Dharma:	Are you two deaf?
A:	No, no.
Dharma:	What day is it today?
A:	Yes, sir. Today is the twelfth day of December.
Dharma:	Is it? Then I have been here exactly nine years!
A:	Yes sir.
Dharma:	[Standing up.] Dullard as I am, I have at last attained enlightenment after nine years! What the Buddha said was true. Thanks! Thanks!
	[The two watched in amazement.]
A:	Then you are not deaf?
Dharma:	No, I am not deaf.
A:	Please forgive us our rudeness a while ago.
Dharma:	You haven't done anything rude to me.
A:	But we struck you on the head . . .
Dharma:	Oh, then it was you? I must thank you for it. I was able to attain enlightenment because you struck me on the head. The Buddha kindly entered into you and beat me.[31]

Zen as a religion is purely a religion of human realization, or self-awakening. It teaches us, human beings, to attain satori and live a new life in this world as new men of satori. It insists that this inner conversion should be carried out by oneself, that one can attain his Zen personality by oneself by searching inwardly, not relying on anything outside. It declares that man has the potentiality for attaining satori. This should be happy tidings for human beings.[32]

The following excerpt from a longer poem expresses in poetic form the classic Zen insight into the universe and life.

All beings are primarily Buddhas
Like water and ice,
There is no ice apart from water;
There are no Buddhas apart from beings.[33]

❖❖❖

Would a Zen devotee be disturbed by a Western person suggesting that much of Bodhidharma's story seems extreme in its demands?

What similarities are there between the examples of mysticism discussed in the first part of this unit and the Zen illustrations?

What may be some of the reasons that mysticism, a universal experience in all religious traditions, seems "strange" or "challenging" in modern western culture?

---

[31] Umeyo Hirano, trans. *Buddhist Plays from Japanese Literature* (Tokyo: Cultural Interchange Institute for Buddhists, 1962), pp. 1–2, 4–5, 7–8. Used by permission.

[32] Zenkei Shibayana, *A Flower Does Not Talk* (Rutland, VT: Charles E. Tuttle, 1970), pp. 30–31.

[33] Ibid., p. 65.

✦✦✦ 5 ✦✦✦

RELIGION IN ARTISTIC EXPRESSION

Chapters 3 and 4 have concentrated on the nature and character of religious experience, using examples that mostly are verbal descriptions of religious expression. In our time, many people have difficulty grasping the full import of the meaning of value statements or religious expressions because they do not understand the differences between verbal and visual texts. Yet anyone who considers carefully the nature of communication in modern societies realizes that an enormous number of the messages transmitted today are primarily in a visual format; that is, they are visual texts. Part of our difficulty rests in our lack of formal education in analyzing and consciously "reading" these visual statements with which we are bombarded—from television, film, Internet, advertising, architecture, magazines, and various forms of mass art. Yet, in reality, human religious experience probably has been as readily expressed, perhaps sometimes more adequately expressed, in the various arts than in verbal and literary forms. People of all ages and cultures have sought to express in painting, sculpture, architecture, and music—and in our time, film and television—their deepest values, including, in symbolic form, their sense of encounter with the Divine.

Some people have suggested that artistic expression is the most reliable of all the forms of communication. In the nineteenth century, John Ruskin said that cultures present their own "autobiography: in three books. The first book is the 'book of their deeds,' that is, their histories; the second is their literature, or 'the book of their words'; and the third is 'the book of their art.'"[1] He argued that "not one of these books can be understood unless we read the two others" as well. Furthermore, "the only trustworthy one is the last: the arts." In the late twentieth century, British art historian Kenneth Clark agreed: "Writers and politicians may come out with all sorts of edifying sentiments, but they are what is known as declarations of intent. If I had to say which was telling the truth

---

[1] Quoted in Kenneth Clark, *Civilization* (New York: Harper and Row), p. 1.

about society, a speech by a Minister of Housing or the actual buildings put up in his time, I should believe the buildings."[2]

The primary purpose of this chapter is to look at some examples in which religious experience and meaning have been communicated in visual arts, including painting, mosaic, stained glass, sculpture, cinema, television, and architecture. In Unit 29 we explore some of the ways art serves as an avenue, a vehicle for the expression of religious meaning. Included in this unit is discussion of how a visual object can become a very important symbol, an *icon*, and how it may function in the lives of individuals.[3] To become more explicit, Unit 30 discusses how visual images were used to interpret Jesus as Saviour (Christ) in the very early centuries of the Christian church.

Next, a process central to the expression of virtually all religions, the *translation of ideas into visual form*, is considered in Unit 31. To help clarify that process, the unit focuses on the emergence of medieval Gothic architecture in the history of Christianity, especially in France. Thus, this chapter considers the many and varied art forms one encounters daily that may communicate values or religious meanings.

UNIT 29   ART AS SYMBOLIC VEHICLE

The arts are among the most reliable means of knowing the true characteristics of a culture or a time. The twentieth-century Spanish painter Pablo Picasso, who evidently did not wish to theorize about his work, is reported to have said, "Art is a lie that makes us realize the truth."[4] Indeed, if Picasso did utter this interpretive statement, his phrase urges us to consider how the *form* of art has everything to do with its *content*, that is, its meaning. An artist or composer designs, composes, constructs, or fabricates a form that in a *literal* sense is an illusion, albeit a carefully constructed one. Yet it is in this art form that one may encounter imaginatively something that is vastly more than the form itself. The art form may serve the function of symbol; the art object may gather into itself qualities that transcend (go beyond) the object. That is, the art object may contain some essential quality of what it represents, and thus we "see" or "know" the characteristic through the art object. Then one may argue that art is a form of "disclosure."[5] The art object discloses some essential quality of what it represents. Thus, something essential of what is being represented is "present" in the art.

When we look at paintings created by prehistoric, "primitive" peoples, often in caves, we cannot be certain of their original purpose, but we know we are not viewing art objects that are intended to be mere reproductions of something. Instead, ancient artists have *interpreted* that which is represented by their selection of subject matter and the

---

[2] Ibid., p. 1.

[3] See the unit on "The Role of Symbols" in Religion in Chapter 4.

[4] Roger Hazelton, *A Theological Approach to Art* (Nashville, TN: Abingdon Press, 1968), p. 16.

[5] Ibid., p. 17.

manner in which they present it. This can be argued to be true of virtually all art objects. Even photographs, including those not intended to serve an artistic function, such as "record shots" or "snaps," still include some element, no matter how little-considered or fleeting, of the photographer's interpretation and composition. The plethora of movies and television programs today that have as their subject the functioning of the court system repeatedly illustrate through courtoom scenes how a majority of the statements one makes contain an element of one's interpretation of reality. Consequently, when we attempt to address art as a symbolic vehicle, we speak of the way humans create symbols (some form or concept) that point beyond themselves, representing that which they themselves are not. Thus, the symbol is an image we have created, albeit often unconsciously, of some larger, complex reality.[6]

Over a period of years at the end of the twentieth and beginning of the twenty-first centuries C.E., American filmmaker George Lucas created a film series entitled *Star Wars* through which he concentrated a complex plot of mythic proportions centered on the "redemption of Anakin Skywalker" and "how he fell from Grace" as well as the web of relationships of a rather large group of principal characters.[7]

In these films Lucas employs symbols in the form of theological language, visual imagery, color symbology, and certain elements of the salvation stories from both Western and Eastern religions.

Anakin Skywalker is introduced as an extraordinary child in Episode I with possibilities for both great creativity and evil. His eventual fall from the good makes him a virtual Mephistopheles (satanic) character. He becomes allied with the "forces of darkness." His will to personal power is overwhelming and results in immense potential for destructiveness and the near death of the "Republic" of freedom, good, or "the forces of light." He becomes allied with the Emperor who has risen to power and sweeps away the republican Senate and begins a reign based on fear, military domination, centralized power, and regimentation. In what becomes a struggle between the forces of light and the forces of darkness, the scriptwriter explores elements of the nature of humanity (anthropology), the nature of the universe (cosmology), questions of what makes the "good society" (ecclesiology), personal and collective salvation (soteriology), and theology (nature of the Ultimate or God).

After establishing an identiy with the "Dark Side," Anakin takes a new name, Darth Vader. His biological offspring, twins named Luke and Leia (interestingly, these are biblical names), are reared by others, taking them out of Darth's care and influence. Among those training Luke and Leia are Obiwan (Ben) Kenobi, who is a sage or prophet figure among the "forces of light," and another powerful wiseman, Yoda. As the complicated story line develops, both Luke and Leia become involved in a rebellion against the Empire's "forces of darkness" and, consequently, against Darth Vader.

Eventually, through a learning process influenced by Kenobi and Yoda, Luke becomes almost a saviour figure and is presented as a hero, exhibiting numerous sym-

---

[6] See also Chapter 4, Unit 23.

[7] George Lucas, in videotaped interview preceding *Episode VI: The Return of the Jedi* (Beverly Hills, CA: 20th Century Fox Home Entertainment, Inc., 1995).

bols of the hero common to Western culture. His "pilgrimage" is presented as an extended and difficult struggle in which he must prevail through numerous trials, all of which serve as instruction in his unfolding enlightenment. As the story progresses, the powerful struggle between good and evil becomes concentrated in the internal enlightenment of Luke. For example, Luke visits Yoda on a planet where the environment exudes a primeval quality. Yoda instructs Luke both in the nature of the "Force" and the necessity of placing faith in it and in developing self-discipline to resist the "Dark Side," in order to differentiate the good from the bad. All of this leads Luke to insight into the good, even a kind of enlightenment (which will make him powerful in a constructive way). The writer includes an episode where Luke must "descend" to a subterranean realm as a part of his "training." Luke inquires of Yoda, "What's in there?" Yoda replies, "Only what you take with you."[8] Luke descends into the cave and eventually, in a dreamlike atmosphere, he encounters the image of Darth dressed all in black. Darth approaches Luke menacingly and begins to attack while Luke defends himself with his "light saber" and decapitates the figure. As the helmet rolls to Luke's feet, he sees his own face in it. Thus, Luke has descended into his own subterranean subconscious and recognized that in him lies the same potential that has claimed Darth. By recognizing it, he learns he can resist the temptation to egocentric power and domination. Gradually, Luke internalizes what he learns from his mentors and emerges as a powerful figure himself for the "Light" and comes to trust in the good that can reside in individuals—individuals who, because they trust the "Force of Light," can form a community for the restoration of the Republic.

By this time, the two characters, around whom so much of the story revolves (the struggle of good and evil, light and darkness), have become almost like icons themselves. Luke, often filmed from angles below him, frequently is presented visually as a hero figure, in the Greek sense. He is relatively tall, most often clothed in white (often associated with purity). The "standing tall," head held high, still but ready-for-action pose Luke adopts in the beginning of some scenes, particularly in Episode IV, is traditionally that of the Greek or Roman hero figure so ingrained in much of the Western art tradition. (It was used in the United States for heroes in Western wilderness settler or cowboy films.) By contrast, Darth Vader is the epitome of the self-centered, threatening, frighteningly mysterious and violent "prince of darkness." He is so removed from the personal that one never sees his face because of the helmet-mask he wears and his towering figure is enveloped in black. His demeanor reeks menace. Nevertheless, he becomes fascinating as he sometimes argues his justification for actions with insinuating grace.

In the final *Episode VI: Return of the Jedi*, Luke resists both the Emperor and Darth. In a protracted and dramatic sequence he convinces Darth of the good that resides in himself, and Darth turns on the Emperor and, in a climactic battle, saves his son's (Luke's) life. Mortally wounded, Darth falls while the space station they are traveling in is being attacked in a rebellion against the Empire. Luke attempts to lift Darth to carry him to safety. Darth (Anakin) tells him it is too late and Luke frantically replies, "But I've

---

[8] Ibid., George Lucas, scriptwriter, *Episode V: The Empire Strikes Back*.

got to save you." And Anakin replies, "You already have. Tell your sister; you were right."[9] Later, in the concluding scene of victory celebration, Luke and his sister Leia see a vision of Anakin Skywalker (their father, returned to his true identity), Ben Kenobi, the beloved teacher and mentor, and Yoda, the great sage, all reunited and looking down at them. Their goal has been reached.

Thus, this epic film series has been employed to express varied theological conceptions of the Ultimate (the Force), good and evil and their sources, personal and social salvation, the good society, and the nature of the universe. The extended story form bears some resemblance to the *symbolic narratives* that express the underlying theological perspective of major religions of the world (see Chapter 2).

This series of films by George Lucas clearly uses the cinematic art form to visually express numerous ideas about life and its continual encounter with basic questions concerning nature, humanity, the presence and struggle of good and evil in every aspect of life, and the eventual triumph of good over evil. Each of these issues, along with many similar ones, has traditionally been the topic of ancient and modern religious art. The following illustrations suggest, as do Lucas's films, the ability of representational art, such as paintings, mosaic representations, and sculptures, to point one visually to religious affirmation and encounter.

Representation in art perhaps reaches its greatest depth in objects that can become spiritual icons. When a picture or other artistic representation of a religious tradition, person, or story becomes so identified with the spiritual truth it depicts that it comes to be venerated as sacred itself, it becomes an icon. In such cases, the art is not just an external display; rather, it involves both internalization and participation on the part of the viewer.

The power of art as icon is illustrated by the experience of some university students who were studying religious art and architecture in Greece a few years ago. One day the group of North American students found themselves in a major square in downtown Thessaloniki, where there is a large Greek Orthodox church. The students entered the narthex (entrance area) and discovered that the many people coming and going were stopping in the church for quiet meditation or prayer rather than for a worship service. Of particular significance to the students was how virtually all the people would pause before a large painting of Jesus Christ and Mary, his mother. The people gazed up into the faces in the image and frequently would begin to mutter or whisper quietly. This action would be followed by gestures made with their right hands, touching their heads and chests, forming the shape of a cross; they would "cross" themselves. Often, the individuals would kneel before the painting, kiss their own hand, and place it at the bottom of the image. Then they would rise and advance toward the sanctuary inside.

Some of the students wanted to know how these religious people felt about the image and what their thoughts about it might be. They asked some individuals whose behavior they had observed. In most cases, the people responded in a friendly manner and explained in several ways that the painting was an icon for them and that it served as a

---

[9] Ibid., *Episode VI: The Return of the Jedi.*

Figure 5.1 *Christ Pantocrator*, mosaic in tympanum above portal in the exo-narthex of the Church of the Saviour in Chora (Kariye Camii), Constantinople (Istanbul), ca. 1320 C.E. (Photo by K. Lawrence.)

focal point for their devotional acts. The object had a sacred quality because it represented something central to their religious perspective and faith. They did not worship the object itself; rather, the object "captured" an image of historical people from their faith tradition through whom God was made known. The picture was revered because of the power of its representative function. They *encountered the represented in the representor*, and thus it had become an icon.

A large mosaic[10] image of Jesus Christ as Pantocrator (universal saviour) is placed in an arch (tympanum) above the central portal leading from the exo-narthex (an outer foyer) toward the sanctuary of a Byzantine-style church in ancient Constantinople (now Istanbul). Upon entry into the church, this image is the first thing one sees (see Figure 5.1).

This mosaic image of Christ is set off from all surrounding art in the church

---

[10] Mosaic images are composed of tiny *tesserae*, i.e., tiles that may be made of ceramic, stone, glass, or metal. The image or pattern formed by the tiles is set in an adhesive on a wall, ceiling, or floor. They may be an interior or exterior installation. Generally, mosaics remain stable for very long periods of time.

because of (1) the well-defined decorative motif that serves as a curving frame for the tympanum and (2) the gold background, which is "devoid of all spatial depth."[11] "The plane before which the painted figures appear has no equivalent in the world of reality; it is so to speak the 'nothingness' of ethereal space."[12] In sharp contradistinction, the figure of Christ is given great volume through the subtle shading in the mosaic colors, the use of lines at angles, light and shadow, and the enlargement of segments of the body, such as the hands, so that they may appear nearer to the viewer. The effect is to place the figure of Christ in a void of empty space, a realm of eternity.

Christ is dressed in a flowing blue garment (a *himation*), which is drawn from the ancient Greek traditional garb of the philosopher. It seems to flow counterclockwise around his body and encloses his right arm, from which his hand emerges. It then sweeps across his chest and waist, continues behind the left hand and over the arm to cascade down seemingly into the viewer's (your) space. This garb serves to suggest knowledge and authority.

In his left hand, Christ holds a bejeweled book of the Gospels (a principal means of knowing about him), which communicates the importance and authority of Biblical literature to the viewer. Emerging from the folds of his garment, his right hand (to the viewer's left) is raised in a gesture associated with teaching.

The open neck of the garment reveals the suggestion of a physically powerful figure. The thick, light-colored hair frames a broad face with a long nose, high cheekbones, and arching eyebrows, all of which emphasize the gaze of Christ's eyes. The artist has placed the eyes far apart in the composition of the face, which causes the viewer to feel "looked at" from almost any viewing position in the room. The irises of the eyes are rather light in color while the pupils are an absolute black (made of onyx).

If one looks for a prolonged period at the figure in the mosaic, one can develop a sensation of being gazed upon in an intense manner. One can experience an uncanny sense of this transcendent figure in a vast space openly encountering the viewer, who may also experience returning the gaze. Hilde Zaloscer, a scholar who has spent much time analyzing icons, speaks of a "face-to-face and eye-to-eye attitude, which turns into a relationship between the 'I' and the 'thou,' the person represented and the beholder."[13]

Thus, as a symbolic vehicle, an icon points to something beyond itself. An essential quality of that which is represented is *contained within* the symbol itself (the icon). Therefore, persons may experience an *encounter* with the Divine, the Beyond, through this mosaic object. And the object may become precious to those for whom this experience is possible. It can represent a sense of *presence* in the present time and place—where you are.

Frederick Jensen, a university student, articulated his responses to seeing the great icon for the first time.

---

[11] Hilde Zaloscer, quoted in Richard Temple, *Icons and the Mystical Origins of Christianity* (Longmead, Shaftesbury, Dorset, England: Element Books Limited, 1990), p. 90.

[12] Ibid.

[13] Ibid. See Unit 38 and Martin Buber's, *I and Thou* (New York: Harper and Row, 1967) from which Zaloscer gets the concept of profound relationship.

The object grabs you, stops you, everything just stops. When you walk in the door and see it there, you're stunned. You catch your breath. It overwhelms you. Certainly, it's not a rational response. For just that moment, it's the entire universe. Then you realize that you're looking at a work of art. But, in the moment, your reaction is holistic, total.

The gold surrounding his head is very bright—a photo does not capture its brilliance. The eyes are a very pale shade of brown; and this makes them somewhat mysterious. The eyes 'come at you'; they capture you. You look from one eye to another. It's as if he is looking at me, yet looking all around me. After one has been awed by this thing, you have to collect yourself.

I find myself talking about him as if this were really a man, rather than an image. The facial expression is hard to read. It's not so much a happy expression, yet it's not a frown, nor is it judgmental. The face says something; it's hard to express. This image of Christ Pantocrator acts on you. He does not invite you to speak so much as he tells you to feel. He has moved toward you; I feel known. To me, the spiritual power of this place becomes infused in you. When you leave, you take something with you because of this encounter.[14]

Seeing, as we refer to it in terms of *seeing into* or *being seen* with regard to one's grasp of an icon, is a unique experience. Jacob Needleman has said, "neither ideas nor images alone can cause us to see, but they can orient our intention and guide us towards the act of opening to the universal mystery that has neither name nor form."[15]

UNIT 30   IMAGES OF JESUS AS CHRIST IN THE EARLY CHURCH

Conceptions of the incarnation of deity have played an important role in several of the major religions of the world. Yet one could argue that Christianity has placed greater emphasis on the incarnation of God than any other religion. From this central affirmation that the essential quality of the Divine is fully present in the man Jesus comes the rest of the doctrine of Christianity.

Central to the Christian perspective is Jesus of Nazareth's affirmation that unqualified love has the power within itself to elicit a response of the same kind. His capacity to express this "no strings attached" love (Greek: *agape*) is exemplified in his forgiveness of those who were crucifying him even while they were doing it. The early Christians saw in this loving act the presence of God fully manifest in the man. Hence, the cross representing crucifixion became the central symbol of the religion, though several hundred years would pass before it did so.

To the earliest Christians, Jesus had taught that the one God in whom they placed their trust was the deity who was sovereign over all the universe, perfectly just, and personal in quality, and this God could be characterized most completely as unconditional love (*agape*). They further observed that Jesus *was* what he had taught, that in his person he exemplified perfectly what he had said about the nature of deity. Thus, the claim emerged that God is incarnate in Jesus, to whom the faithful gave the title Christ (Saviour).

[14] Frederick Jensen, Interview at Texas Christian University, February 25, 1997. Used by permission.

[15] Jacob Needleman, in the Foreword to Richard Temple, *Icons and the Mystical Origins of Christianity*, vii.

Throughout the history of Christianity, followers have developed conceptions of Jesus the Christ as Saviour and as mediator of God's love and will. Soon after Jesus' time, Christians began to express their understanding and experience of Christ in verbal (written) and visual statements (art).

Controversies arose early and have often recurred in the church regarding Christology (ideas about the nature, person, and work of Christ). Historic creeds were written that affirmed both the full humanity and divinity of Jesus Christ. Just how these characteristics were mingled, without confusion, has remained a point of continued discussion and disagreement, although orthodox Christianity continues to affirm that Jesus was fully a man in whom God was fully present.

Quite early in the history of Christianity, artists expressed varied understandings of Jesus and his ministry through painting, mosaic, and sculpture. Particular characteristics are emphasized in these works of art, which sometimes communicate with greater depth than words. The combination of the figure of Jesus Christ (especially the manner in which he is portrayed) along with various symbols and actions can be one of the most effective means of communicating conceptions of his significance.

As in Figure 5.2, one of the most frequent modes of depiction of Jesus Christ in the earliest Christian art is as the "good shepherd." Quite consistently he is presented as youthful, a common mode at that time to suggest vigor and power. Also, he is clean shaven, with a Caesarean haircut, and in the contrapposto pose (with weight supported by one leg only) frequently employed in ancient Greek and Roman art to present an active hero or deity figure. Generally, the clothing is that of a Roman shepherd with the loose-fitting tunic and short skirt (to allow rapid movement) that was so familiar in the Greco-Roman world. This shepherd's clothing (in fresco paintings on walls) frequently is white with vertical purple stripes down the front, a connotation of authority in ancient Roman society. Thus, though he is presented as a shepherd caring for his flock (the church), he is exalted with authority. Such depictions of Jesus as Christ began to appear as early as the second century C.E.

In the image that follows, Jesus Christ is the shepherd, the deliverer from death, of his flock (the Christian community). He is carrying a sheep over his shoulders, an idea that may have as its source the parable of the lost sheep, which appears in the New Testament Gospel books of Matthew and Luke. The syle of this visual image was familiar at that time, having been employed in pre-Christian art. Further, Jesus is shown carrying a container of water (possibly representing the water of new life or baptism), and his arm is extended in a very natural manner because of the weight of the object. He is surrounded by other sheep, which represent the community of the faithful (the church). Frequently, such scenes are placed in a pastoral setting; in this fresco painting, the lines suggest the earth on which the figures are standing and the trees on either side (almost lost to view by damage from moisture over the centuries).

The whole scene is enclosed in a circle, which helps to complete part of the total design. Circles frequently were used symbolically to represent the eternal. Thus, the suggestion is made that Jesus, the good shepherd, is eternally Christ the Saviour.

In the fresco painting in a lunette above a crypt in the Catacomb of Saint Domitilla at Rome, we notice the beginnings of significant shifts of emphasis in the depiction

Figure 5.2 *The Good Shepherd,* fresco, ca. 225 C.E. Detail from the ceiling of the Vault of Lucina, Catacomb of San Callisto, Rome. (Photo by K. Lawrence.)

of Jesus Christ (see Figure 5.3). The painting may be dated perhaps a century later than the visual text in Figure 5.2.

The artist has arranged the disciples of Jesus so that attention is focused on the Christ figure. Their gestures and their gazes suggest his importance to them and have the effect of exalting him. Jesus Christ is presented with an air of authority; his right hand is extended in a gesture of communication or address, and he has an intense gaze. He wears a white, togalike garment with the dark stripes that suggest authority, as in the costume in Figure 5.2. His disciples, through association with him and through his authority, gain a similar importance, as is suggested by their clothing. However, note the youthful appearance they are given in comparison with the image of Jesus Christ. Here, Jesus is no longer presented as in the earlier, familiar shepherd format but as a teacher and lawgiver, as *pantocrator,* Greek for "universal lord or saviour."

Two figures stand behind Jesus Christ, holding up and extending what appears to be a mantle (cape), with a background field of blue scattered with stars. This design subsequently was used in Christian art to refer symbolically to the cosmos; by being placed

Figure 5.3 *Jesus Christ as Pantocrator with Disciples*, ca. 350 C.E., Catacomb of St. Domitilla, Rome. (Photo by Max Hirmer. Used by permission.)

behind the figure of Jesus, possibly it began to refer to his universal significance. The position of these figures and the way they seem to lift the object suggest that they will place it on the shoulders of Jesus Christ, a gesture associated with a kind of investiture. In the church, it eventually became one of the acts used to invest Christ's authority in his vicars (representatives), the bishops of the church, who were being set apart even in New Testament times for special functions. Thus, a more exalted interpretation of Christology is suggested by the entire composition.

In 313 C.E., the Roman Emperor Constantine issued the Edict of Toleration at the city of Milan. Through this act, the Christian religion was officially recognized by the state. This act allowed complete freedom of worship, the erection of churches, and the end to persecution of Christians. Though the emperor seems to have adopted the new religion, and members of his family, especially his mother, Helena, were active in it, for a long time many were opposed to it, including some important senatorial families. Nevertheless, with an imperial sanction made official, the church could grow openly and organize itself throught the Roman empire. It would supplant officially the old Roman religions through the proclamation of Emperor Theodosius in 392.

At Ravenna, on the northern Adriatic coast of Italy, some of the finest examples of Christian art of the fifth and sixth centuries are preserved. Among these is the little Mausoleum of Galla Placidia, erected probably in 424 or 425 C.E. Originally dedicated in honor of the early Christian martyr San Lorenzo (Saint Lawrence), the building, according to a longstanding tradition, was used as a mausoleum by Galla Placidia, sister of the Emperor Honorius (who temporarily moved the western capital to Ravenna), for Hono-

Figure 5.4 *Christ as Good Shepherd*, mosaic, Mausoleum of Galla Placidia, Ravenna, Italy, ca. 425 C.E. (Scala/Art Resource, N.Y.)

rius after he died in 423. Tradition suggests that Galla Placidia may have been entombed there as well.[16]

In an interior tympanum of the mausoleum (in this case, an arch above the doorway), there is a mosaic of Christ as good shepherd (see Figure 5.4). This mosaic contains some of the finer workmanship of the period, and although strong Byzantine influences are present in this transitional work of the latter part of the early Christian era, the good shepherd figure recalls Roman catacomb art.

This mosaic was created in a time of enormous controversy throughout the Roman Empire over the interpretation of Jesus as Christ (Christology). Because of this discord, several church council meetings were deemed necessary. Finally the great Council of Chalcedon was convened in 451 in an attempt to clarify and settle the matter. An essential ingredient in the creed produced at Chalcedon included the insistence on Jesus Christ as

---

[16] For more detailed discussion of this structure and its mosaics, see Kenneth Lawrence, "An Iconological Analysis of Mosaics in the Mausoleum of Galla Placidia, Ravenna," *ARTS, The Arts in Religious and Theological Studies,* III, 3 (Summer 1991), 19-24.

. . . the same perfect in Godhead and also perfect in manhood; truly God and truly man
. . . the property of each nature being preserved, and concurring in one person (prosopon),
and one subsistence (hypostasis), not parted or divided into two persons, but one and the
same Son. . . .[17]

Although the mosaic was produced before the Council of Chalcedon, it can be
argued that the elements under discussion, regarding the manner in which Christ was
understood to be simultaneously fully human and fully divine, are incorporated in this
image by the artist.

Placed in a pastoral setting, tending and caring for the flock (the church community), as he frequently was seen in early Christian images, Jesus Christ is reaching
across his body, warmly responding to one of the sheep by chucking its chin, an intimate
gesture. All the sheep that flank him look toward the shepherd. His face is rather Roman,
instead of Eastern, in character—a facet of classical Roman art.

At the same time, the setting is elevated, not only because the tympanum mosaic
is above the entrance door, but also because the location depicted is like a dais, a raised
platform. (Note the clifflike escarpment suggested at the bottom of the image, in the fore-
ground of the picture plane.) Rather than the typical Roman shepherd costume, Jesus
wears a more priestly garb. His clothing is long, flowing, and golden, with royal purple
stripes on either side of the front—suggesting an exalted figure of authority. One might
expect the staff he holds to be a shepherd's crook; instead it has a cruciform appearance,
like the cross carried in Christian liturgical processions. In its time frame of the fifth century C.E., it probably should be interpreted as a symbol of authority, as a sceptor.[18]

Jesus is seated on three rocks, graduated in size—a thronelike arrangement and
perhaps a reference to the concept of the Trinity. The three sheep on each side are geo-
metrically arranged. An *aureole*, or halo,[19] is around his head. The complex symmetry of
the composition, the concern for order, may reflect the need for clarity in the thoughts of
the church, which was so urgent at the time.

In the vault above the tympanum, we see a strictly ordered decoration with a
deep blue background and starlike designs. Is this a symbol of the cosmos (universe), and
by association, does it suggest the *universal saviour* significance being assigned to Jesus the
Christ by Christians? The colors, geometric balance, and emphasis on ordered arrangement complement those of the tympanum image. "Thus, in this image, in *simultaneous
mutual interaction*, we observe a presentation of both the human and divine."[20]

During the reign of Emperor Justinian II (from Byzantine Constantinople), a
remarkable, if small, church was constructed in Ravenna and consecrated in 547 C.E. The
scene shown in Figure 5.5 is found in its mosaic-encrusted sanctuary apse.

---

[17] Williston Walker, *A History of the Christian Church*, rev. ed. (New York: Scribner, 1959), p. 139.

[18] Lawrence, "An Iconological Analysis," p. 23.

[19] In classical mythology, an aureole was a shining cloud sometimes surrounding a deity when on
earth. In Christian art, sometimes it refers to the "light of God," the "holiness" that is communicated by Jesus
the saviour.

[20] Lawrence, "An Iconological Analysis," p. 23.

Figure 5.5   *Christ as Pantocrator with Saint Vitalis, Bishop Ecclesius, and Archangels*, mosaic, apse of Church of San Vitale, Ravenna, Italy, 547 C.E. (Scala/Art Resource, N.Y.)

Heavily influenced by imperial court ceremony, the mosaic puts Christ at the center, enthroned as *pantocrator* ("universal ruler/saviour" or "sovereign"). He is presenting a martyr's crown to Saint Vitalis (at far left), to whom the church is dedicated.[21] An angel (second from left) is presenting the saint to Christ. At right, another angel is presenting Bishop Ecclesius, the founder of the church,[22] who in turn ceremonially is presenting a model of the church to Christ. A broad study of the art of the early church demonstrates that by the time of this building, the saints and martyrs were being represented in the very formal, ceremonial clothing of the era.

Christ himself, now more exalted in the thought of the church, is seated on a sphere, whereas the other figures are standing with their feet on the ground. Below Christ, the four rivers of Heaven flow forth. He holds the Book of Life in his left hand and is

[21] Everett Ferguson, "S. Vitale," in *Encyclopedia of Early Christianity*, Everett Ferguson, ed. (New York: Garland Publishing, Inc., 1990), p. 828.

[22] Ibid.

endowed with a bejeweled halo that incorporates the shape of the cross. The light depicted by brilliant colors on the clouds behind Christ possibly suggests sunrise. The brilliant gold background (which becomes a convention in art of this type) and the strong colors have a dazzling effect on the viewer below and connote the vastness of the eternal and the preciousness of Christ's church and its authority.

✦✦✦

Considering the stages of development in the images of Jesus discussed in this unit, does one's pivotal value or simply one's image of such a value change over time?

UNIT 31   LUMINOUS WHOLENESS IN WESTERN EUROPEAN MEDIEVAL ARCHITECTURE

How are perspectives of religious meaning expressed in physical structures? How are concepts translated into physical form? The writing of an extraordinary leader of both church and state in medieval France, as well as other available sources, make it possible to trace the development of form in one particular circumstance. What today is called Western European Gothic architecture arose in the twelfth century. Central to its development was the decision to reconstruct the Royal Abbey Church of St. Denis in the Ile-de-France, near Paris.[23] Numerous and complex factors, summarized in the text that follows, contributed to this development. Our discussion is based partly upon the work of H.W. Janson and Erwin Panofsky, art historians, and Max Miller, lecturer at the Chartres Cathedral, France, as well as on our own direct study of numerous medieval buildings.

There must have been many people who contributed to the creation of a "new" architectural statement in the first half of the twelfth century, but we are able to distinguish the experience, thoughts, and religious and political circumstances of one man: Abbot Suger of the Royal Abbey Church of St. Denis, a place where some monarchs were crowned. Suger attended the school at this abbey, where he became a close friend to the prince who would be the future king of France. One may assume that their friendship from student days provided a basis for the later great trust accorded Suger when his friend became king. Suger's efforts and his later role in both the church and the state would make him counselor to yet another king.

After his ordination into the priesthood, Suger found his way back to St. Denis, a place of learning, contemplation, and worship. Before considering further the role of the royal abbey church and the new architectural form, let us turn our attention to the Abbey Church of St. Denis. According to ancient tradition, a man named Denis was the apostle to France; that is, he brought Christianity to Gaul (France), as well as bringing several

---

[23] For a useful analysis as well as a translation of original documents by a person who more than any other brought about the creation of Gothic architecture, see Erwin Panofsky, ed. and trans., *Abbot Suger on the Abbey Church of St.-Denis and Its Art Treasures* (Princeton, NJ: Princeton University Press, 1946). Though many analyses and commentaries of substantial merit on medieval Gothic architecture are available, an especially clear, brief introduction to the form, its origins, and the surrounding religious, social, and political circumstances is provided by Janson and Janson, *History of Art, 5th edition* (New York: Harry Abrams, Inc., 1997), pp. 321–327.

important theological ideas. These ideas would later be incorporated into the physical structure of the church—creating a visual "text," a medium for expressing theology and faith. Tradition erroneously assigned the origin of these ideas to Dionysius the Areopagite, a follower of St. Paul, the missionary, teacher, and theologian of the earliest church. (That the ideas should have been assigned to a later fifth-century theologian, now referred to as the "Pseudo Dionysius," probably did not matter in terms of the tradition.)[24] The remains of Denis, the Christian apostle to France, were enshrined in the abbey church dedicated in his honor.

When Suger accepted the role of abbot at the Abbey of St. Denis, it had long been a place where pilgrims came to venerate the saint who had brought the Christian faith to their land. Suger also inherited a monastery in need of spiritual and administrative reform and physical restoraton of the buildings. Suger poured all of his considerable energy and talents into sustaining the important role of this abbey, favored by monarchs. Erwin Panofsky speaks of the manner in which Suger submerged himself into the abbey and its honored saint:

> Thus Suger, conceiving of himself as the adopted child of St.-Denis, came to divert . . . the whole amount of energy, acumen and ambition nature had bestowed upon him. Completely fusing his personal aspirations with the interests of the "mother church," he may be said to have gratified his ego by renouncing his identity: he expanded himself until he had become identical with the Abbey.[25]

Suger not only identified himself with the abbey and St. Denis but also with the nation of France. It is argued that he developed an almost "mystical nationalism," and "the French word *chavinisme*" has been applied to him.[26] Suger saw the king as having divine responsibility for concord in the land, for defending it, and especially for preserving the church and seeing to the needs of the poor. Suger's dear friend, King Louis *le gros*, vowed "at his coronation in 1108" to fulfill these roles.[27] Thus, for Suger, the abbey, St. Denis, and the central authority of the realm, invested in the king, were effectively merged.[28]

The dukes of the regions forming the French nation often were rather independent in their behavior, and the central authority of a monarch with a cooperative court was not easy to maintain. By imbuing the investiture of the monarch's office with a holy task, Suger succeeded in forming an alliance, even a union, between the mother church and the royal office.[29] The Abbey Church of St. Denis, with its holy relics of the apostle to France, was steadily forged into a symbol of that union. "Suger wanted to make the Abbey the spiritual center of France, a pilgrimage church to outshine the splendor of all the others, the focal point of religious as well as patriotic emotion."[30]

[24] See further discussion on this subject in Janson and Janson, *History of Art*, pp. 322–323.
[25] Panofsky, *Abbot Suger*, p. 31.
[26] Ibid.
[27] Ibid., p. 2.
[28] Ibid.
[29] Janson and Janson, *History of Art*, p. 321.
[30] Ibid.

Suger set out to achieve this goal partly by restructuring the church building, and from this project emerged a striking architectural accomplishment: the new style that we have come to call *Gothic*. Suger assembled the great designers and builders of the land, and gradually there emerged a physical form that reflects the theological ideas Suger drew from St. Denis. Whoever served as chief architect must have been singularly responsive to Suger's stated desires to express theology in stone. Architect and theologian must have collaborated continuously to realize this form.

Two salient features of Gothic architecture that especially reveal theological meaning are (1) *mathematical harmony*, the clear demonstration of perfect ratios and (2) *luminosity*, the use of natural light to flood the structure, especially through stained glass, with a brilliance that invades the interior space like a revelation.[31] The perfect harmony and the rationality, clearly perceptible in the building's balance and ratios, symbolizes the very mind of God. It suggests the order and balance in the God-created universe, as perceived by medieval humanity. The new form allowed the creation of huge spaces for windows, making possible the admission of great shafts of light. The deep coloration of the stained glass of the period served to transform the light, to diffuse and filter it—to change the very quality of daylight and endow it with special character. The luminosity could then symbolize the "light of God," especially seen in Christ, so that humanity might be enlightened.

How was this accomplished through the structure of a building? Before the emergence of Gothic architecture, Western buildings used for public gathering and/or worship were characterized by great mass. They appeared often as powerful and sometimes majestic edifices, which seemed to rise out of the ground. Roman building principles, long used by the church in some form or other, produced a fortresslike quality. It was necessary to use the Roman arch or a post and lintel system, with heavy walls and small windows to support the weight of the roof. If one wanted to make a building taller, it had to be widened as well, to retain stability. Otherwise, the roof weight might cause collapse, since it tended to exert pressure downward and outward. Thus, one was conscious of an enclosed, fortresslike space.

Innovation was required for Suger's goals to become possible if they were to be translated into structural form. It appears that architects under his supervision were experienced in the development of the groined arch system used in some Romanesque (Roman-like) churches of fairly recent construction. In planning the new building, they employed this system in the direct support of the roof (see Figure 5.6).[32]

The weight of the roof would fall onto a *boss* (a round, latchlike ornament) positioned at intervals along the center of the peak of the pointed arch. Radiating out from the boss were curved *ribs* to support the vault and disperse the weight in at least four directions to four or more *capitals*. Then, a fourth of the weight on the boss was received at the capital and projected down a *column* to the *column base*, which rested on a *plinth* (a square or rectangular base for the column). Thus, part of the weight was transferred to the

---

[31] Cf. discussion on this subject in Janson and Janson, *History of Art*, p. 322.

[32] Because the Abbey Church of St. Denis has been altered considerably since it was constructed, we are using pictures of Notre Dame in Paris, which clearly exemplifies the Gothic form developed by Suger and his associates.

Figure 5.6   Interior nave of the Cathedral of Notre Dame, Paris, facing east. (Alinari/Art Resource, N.Y.)

Figure 5.7 Cathedral of Notre Dame, Paris, exterior detail: flying buttresses at apse. (Photo by K. Lawrence).

foundation. However, because the architects wanted to open huge sections of the walls to windows so that the symbol of light could be used, the resulting tall, pointed arch system (a kind of skeletal structure) required further support to avoid collapse. It appears that the architects calculated that the weight and pressure received at each capital, pressing down and out, needed to be met in precise ratio by an object pressing in and up. Thus, we have the invention of the *flying buttress* (see Figure 5.7).

A structure is then possible in which the walls play a comparatively small role in its overall stability. Examination and contemplation of the exterior and interior of the structure reveal the interdependence of all the parts. The balance of ratios and the visually exhibited geometric planning—the rationality of it all—eventually may overwhelm the viewer with its seeming harmony. The building no longer suggests a fortress, a great pile of stone; instead it seems to reach up, to suggest a vast order, a unified wholeness rather like the universe in microcosm (see Figure 5.8).

Now the walls of this great, skeletal structure could be opened for windows. Frequently the glass was stained or painted to present pictures of persons, events, and symbols important to the history of Christianity. Stone tracery formed an intricate support system for sections of the glass, which were further divided into smaller segments held together by lead (metal). Much of this glass was so refined that it gathered light rather like

Figure 5.8   Cathedral of Notre Dame, Paris, exterior from west. Note especially the system of buttresses and windows. (Photo by K. Lawrence.)

a lens and transformed it into dazzling rays of widely varied colors that were projected into the interior. Luminosity, the symbol of the Divine Light, invades this universe.

Though certainly not unique to Christianity, from the very beginnings of the faith the symbol of light has been one of its central and most active symbols (see Figure 5.9). This very ancient symbolic reference is also so deeply rooted in culture that language is thoroughly permeated with it. W. Mark Gunderson, an American architect, articulates the deeper levels that give that architectural form spirituality.

> Light is a building's breath.
> Day and night are inhaling and exhaling.
> Light invests form . . .
>
> It becomes difficult . . . to speak of quality of light in a room which reflects no regard for daylight (to say nothing of moonlight).
>   *Lucid* thought, *clarity* of idea, *shedding light* on a subject, *illuminating*, etc.; all of these metaphors reiterate the importance of Light as requisite for understanding—for the need to "see clearly," literally and figuratively. Without a discipline it is impossible to *enlighten*.
>   Order allows light into situations which light would avoid through no prejudice of its own.[33]

---

[33] W. Mark Gunderson, "On Light," unpublished working notes. October 9, 1991. (Used by permission.)

Figure 5.9   Cathedral of Notre Dame, Paris, detail, north transept, rose window. At the center the Virgin Mary holds the Christ child on her knee and is surrounded by disciples of Christ, prophets, kings, ancestors of Jesus Christ, patriarchs, and high priests of Israel. (Giraudon/Art Resource, N.Y.)

Figure 5.10 Cathedral Church of St. Andrew, Wells, England; interior nave with choir and sanctuary beyond double arch. (Photo by K. Lawrence.)

The sense of the splendid balance of ratios and of harmony and the invasion of space by dazzling light are exhibited especially well by the Cathedral Church of St. Andrew at Wells, England. Smaller than many Gothic cathedrals, Wells may be judged a superlative statement of the Gothic perspective. Upon entering the nave of the church, one immediately perceives the two major ideas of the Gothic conception (see Figure 5.10).

While Christian thinkers created the theological systems of the high medieval period, the schools and cathedrals influenced the religious experience of the populace. One can imagine the communicative effect of these structures on the worshippers as they participated in the Mass and, awed by light filtering into the gloom below, perceived the massive intricacy of these houses of God. The massiveness, beauty, and luminosity all express through the structure itself religious meaning—the majesty and power, as well as the self-revealing, self-giving qualities of the one God of the universe.

✦✦✦ 6 ✦✦✦

KNOWLEDGE, BELIEF, AUTHORITY, AND TRADITION

Earlier in *Exploring Religious Meaning*, we examined religious experiences of individuals and groups; presented an analysis of some of the characteristic features and elements of religious experience; and articulated the broad aspects of religious experience, especially through art and architecture.

Now we shift from the more subjective dimension of personal—individual or group—experience to the more objective side of that which is experienced. That is, here we characterize what people who have had such experiences have believed to be their object, source, or goal. In Western religious traditions the object, source, or goal of religious experience is often characterized in personal terms as God. Since some religions do not conceive of the Ultimate Reality in strictly personal terms, we ordinarily use the term the Divine to indicate that which is sought in religious experience. In Chapter 7, we begin examining ways in which different religious traditions characterize the Divine.

Many have argued that the concepts religious persons use to indicate or to characterize the Divine and the relations that humans have with the Divine arise from the experiences of mundane human life—from the interaction of human beings with their natural environment and from the realm of interpersonal relations. Thus, the Divine may be characterized with images derived from the forces or phenomena of nature, like lightning or a storm, or from human relationships or phenomena, such as with a king or an all-powerful father. Because human images of the Divine are based on or derived from human experience of nature and of social—personal and interpersonal—life, to speak of the Divine is in some sense to speak of the human. Yet religious persons are convinced that they encounter a transhuman reality that is real regardless of the way it is imagined, conceived, or expressed.

Unit 32 examines the question of diversity in sources claimed by people of different societies and people within contemporary society of knowledge, especially religious knowledge.

Unit 33 discusses questions related to the nature, meaningfulness, and verification of religious statements and religious belief. These questions are much discussed in contemporary philosophy of religion and theology.

Three interrelated topics of particular importance to Western religious traditions—Judaism, Christianity, and Islam—are also discussed in this chapter. Naturally, the concepts of history, revelation, and faith are present in other religious traditions also. In this chapter these topics are of special importance, for if we are seeking to examine and understand human concepts and experiences of the Divine, then the question of how the Divine is present in human history, how the Divine is revealed, how the Divine is known (by faith or in other ways) becomes crucial.

Every religious tradition contains some understanding of revelation. The meaning of revelation ranges from some form of religious insight—as experienced by a Taoist in contemplation of nature or by a Hindu in transcendental meditation—to the idea of a special communication from a personal God—as when, in Jewish, Christian, and Islamic belief, God communicates the Divine will to particular individuals in unique events. Judaism, Christianity, and Islam have, in fact, frequently been called "historical" religions because of their belief that God does communicate to people in specific historical contexts through specific historical events. Unit 34 deals with these important issues under the headings of General and Special Revelation, Reason, and Faith.

Every religious community includes some concept of authority, be it by virtue of people, institutions, documents, or experience of some kind. Authority, in this sense, refers to that which is accepted as orthodox, stable, fixed. As such it becomes the touchstone of belief and action. It is used to settle questions of religious truth, questions about right conduct and right belief. Unit 35 discusses the role of authority in religion, and Unit 37 focuses again on the community as a context for religious faith and attempts to define faith as including but being more than belief.

In this book we often use the words *religious tradition* to refer to the many facets of a distinct religion. In Unit 36, tradition includes beliefs, leaders, distinctive events, structural patterns, and the host of other aspects that make up a particular religion such as Christianity, Hinduism, or Islam. (See Unit 6 for a discussion of religious tradition used in this sense.) Tradition has other meanings, however, one of which is the means by which a particular religion conveys to each new generation the knowledge and experience gained within a religious community. It is this understanding of tradition that will be the focus of our attention in Unit 36.

UNIT 32   HOW DO WE KNOW? WHAT CAN WE KNOW?

In two remarkable novels, *The Morning River* and *Coyote Summer*, W. Michael Gear imaginatively recreates conditions of life in early nineteenth century America along the Missouri River where white frontiersmen are establishing trade with many different Native American tribes.[1] The main character is Richard Hamilton, a young man who has studied

---

[1] W. Michael Gear, *The Morning River* and *Coyote Summer* (New York: Tom Doherty Associates, Inc., 1996; 1997).

the most sophisticated European Philosophy at Harvard University. Richard was sent by his wealthy father to St. Louis with a large amount of money on a business mission meant to toughen the young man and wean him from philosophy. Richard, showing contempt for the uneducated frontiersmen, is robbed and almost murdered, and to survive sells himself into temporary slavery as an indentured servant in a crew hauling a boat loaded with merchandise upriver. In the course of the journey he comes to question everything he believes: Boston society's and Harvard's ideas of right and wrong, of how to know what is true and what is false, and of religion and morality. He learns to kill without restraint when survival is at stake. He nearly starves and comes close to freezing on a long winter journey on foot.

When Richard returns to Boston, he feels he can no longer communicate with his friends and his philosophy professor because the beliefs and assumptions that form the basis of their lives are now so different from his. Many in contemporary society share Richard's question when accepted traditions no longer seem to answer present day questions.

How do we know what we know? Imagine an opinion survey in a contemporary American shopping mall asking the following individuals this question (remember, this is an imaginary exercise):

Jeremy, a seventeen-year-old student, says that he learns what he knows from the Internet: "Anything you want to know you can find there. It's a world of information. Keep going and you'll find it."

Jennifer, a twenty-six-year-old graduate student in microbiology, believes that genuine knowledge is gained through the sciences. What isn't verified by scientific theory and experiment is not really knowledge but feeling or conditioning by society. "How I live my life," she says, "questions of morals and religion, whether I can trust my friends or my fiancé are important. But we don't know these things, we have hopes or feelings that guide us or we just decide to do one thing instead of another."

Brad, a thirty-five-year-old accountant, says he learns from observing and listening to his associates at work. What they say gives him the basis for the activities he engages in, his lifestyle, his political preferences. He and his wife were members of a different denomination in the city where they lived, but now they attend St. Mega's, the church most of the members of his firm attend.

Brandi, a nineteen-year-old member of a Bible church, says she knows what is true from the Bible, which contains all truth. Her pastor has told her that even if some things in the Bible are hard to understand, if she will pray, God will reveal the truth to her. She knows that this is true because, when she went to the altar and gave her heart to Jesus, God gave her the assurance that she was born again and saved as her pastor said is promised in the Bible.

Shannon, a thirty-eight-year-old travel agent, calls herself a religious mystic. She considers the Bible and the Scriptures of most major religions to be sources of religious truth. She has especially found truth in Buddhist scriptures. "These truths," she says, "resonate in your mind and spirit." Shannon is a member of one of the traditional Protestant denominations and considers her church's two clergy, a woman and a man, to be good-hearted, helpful congregational leaders and effective counselors but not especially profound spiritual interpreters. She often suggests that they study scriptures of Eastern religions. Shannon also relies on astrology for some of the decisions of daily life. "Some people say astrology is unscientific," she says, "but it is based on some of the oldest science of all. I am a Libra, and I have all of the Libra characteristics. My husband is a Capricorn, and was there ever a Capricorn, dependable and fair-minded but slow at deciding and not very imaginative and rather conservative."

Dillon, a recently retired head librarian of a major university, says that the only thing he knows with certainty is that he knows very little. When he needs to know something he is unsure of, he tries to consult someone in a position to know. "I am a traditionalist about religion and morality," he says. "Years ago, I could make repairs on my car's engine. Now cars are so complicated I have to find a reliable mechanic. When they were giving me morphine in the hospital, I had a lot of delusions. One morning I woke up from a dream and thought I was a prisoner of war. I saw the phone by my bed and dialed my son who is a lawyer and asked him. He told me I wasn't a prisoner of war but a patient in a hospital but not to call so early in the morning next time! He also helps me with legal advice and finds a good accountant to do my taxes. As for politics, my father was a judge for many years. He told me always to vote the straight Democratic ticket. So far he has been right."

Marcia, a forty-year-old woman who is married with two teen-age children, is a physician's receptionist. She says that things she does in her daily life and in her work life are things she was taught earlier at home or at school or has learned through observation or experience at work or as a mother. About important issues of morals or religion, she depends on the teachings of her church. "Oh, I know my priest doesn't know everything," she says, "but I feel safe because I know there is someone in the Church who does. I also know the Church has the best-trained Bible scholars in the world. They know the ancient languages. They've studied the ancient manuscripts. They can tell us what in the Bible is meant to be taken historically and literally and what is symbolic or a story."

Stan, a twenty-one-year-old college student, says he relies for information on what his friends tell him, on what he sees and hears on TV, and on the information in college texts and lectures. Still, the most important source of what he believes or knows about how people act or should act and should not comes from a few powerful films he saw in earlier years: *Titanic*, *Shakespeare in Love*, *The English Patient*, and *Silence of the Lambs*. These and other films showed him deep truths about life.

During his ordeal on the American frontier, Richard encountered a very strong Native American woman named Heals Like A Willow. She knew nothing of European or Anglo-American science or medicine but was able to heal many people of wounds or diseases. Twice she saved Richard's life. She was such a capable healer that she was banished from her tribe, since they did not believe a woman could have such power without being a witch. Richard often argued with Heals Like A Willow about religious, moral, and social ideas and values since he considered her tribe's belief to be based on ignorance and superstition. He was not able to convince her that his Boston and European knowledge was superior to her tribe's beliefs. She always had stories about things that were done by Wolf or Coyote or Trout or Eagle not long after the world came into existence to explain her beliefs. She considered Richard's biblical story of Adam and Eve to be a similar but inferior story to hers about Wolf and Coyote.

Richard concluded that he and Heals Like A Willow lived in different worlds but he also concluded when he returned to Boston that he no longer lived in the thought world he had once shared with Boston people. Still, he found common knowledge between them and himself and enough common knowledge between himself and Willow to allow communication about some things that both took to be true and valuable. In this process, some of the beliefs of each changed. Richard also found some of his Boston friends willing to accept or at least examine his new beliefs.

A view of knowledge similar to Jennifer's was widely held during the mid-twentieth century by many university-educated persons. This position was called *Logical Positivism* (a broader version was called Logical Empiricism.) Strong in Austria, Germany, and England in the 1930s and in the United States in the 1940s and 1950s, Logical Positivism held that only knowledge established by sciences or ordinary sense perception is knowledge. All else—values, moral principles, preferences in the arts, politics, and religion—is the result of people's emotions or social conditioning.

This position is still held by some philosophers who argue that only the natural sciences give truth (knowledge). Even the behavioral sciences, such as psychology, anthropology, and sociology, are characterized by these philosophers as "folk wisdom." However, the Logical Positivist position was undermined by the Harvard philosopher W.V. Quine (Richard Hamilton might have liked him) as long ago as 1950 in a paper called "Two Dogmas of Empiricism" that has since become famous. Quine rejected the fundamental premise of Logical Positivism, that there are two (and only two) kinds of meaningful statements: conventional definitions and those based on sense experience. Since at the time Quine seemed to *be* a logical empiricist, his demolition of some of the tenets of that position seemed devastating to many.

The foundation of Logical Positivism was that there are only two types of sentence that can have knowledge content. There are definitions, which are merely conventions ("All bachelors are unmarried" does not give us knowledge about the world, it merely reflects how our society has chosen to categorize certain types of individuals, whether there are any bachelors or not). Definitional knowledge is meaningful but empty.

The second and only type of meaningful sentences that refer to anything beyond how we use language are sentences verifiable or falsifiable by sense experience (physical observation). With only these two types of sentences, expressions about art, morality, and religion are only empty (conventional but without content), since they are certainly not testable by sense experience. In a subtle and far reaching argument, Quine contested the view that there are only these two contrasting types of statement.

Beyond the universities, in the general population, it is generally held that not just the natural sciences but medicine, behavioral sciences, history, the arts and religion make claims to be or at least contain knowledge. Most people familiar with music in the European tradition would say that it is true that Beethoven's Third Symphony is a greater artistic achievement than his First Symphony. Within a particular society such statements may be understood to convey knowledge, still, persons from a very different society, such as Heals Like A Willow's, might find both symphonies to be meaningless explosions of noise, at least at first hearing.

◆◆◆

How similar and different from each other are the accounts of knowledge and its sources given by the respondents to the imaginary survey given in this Unit? Do some resemble and differ from each other more than others do?

Do you consider some of the respondents to be making valid points? If so, which ones?

◆◆◆

The issue of relativity of knowledge both within and between societies is one of the issues raised by postmodernism (see Unit 76). For more on Logical Positivism and other theories of the nature and sources of religious belief, see Unit 33.

A recent report in the press throws light on the position of Jeremy in the imaginary interviews. According to it, increasing numbers of persons questioned in a real opinion survey say that their primary source of religious knowledge and religious beliefs is the Internet.

◆◆◆

What implications might this last statement have for traditional patterns of religion?

Unit 33   Interpretation and Verification of Religious Knowledge

Plato, in his dialogue *Theaetetus*, may have suggested that when persons claim to know something—"I know that it rained last night"—they mean to assert at least three things: (1) that what they claim to know is true—"It really did rain last night"; (2) that they believe it is true; and (3) something else, something that the participants in Plato's dialogue were not able to define to their satisfaction—something that expresses a difference between mere *belief* and belief based on adequate evidence.

Every society has well-established methods of determining whether different kinds of statement—proposed beliefs, proposed knowledge—are true or not. Even within a single society there are widely different ways of verifying or testing the truth of different kinds of statements. Some depend on the kind of statement involved. (We use different methods for deciding whether it is true that "It rained last night" and "Beauty is truth, truth beauty—that is all/Ye know on earth, and all ye need to know.") Some depend on the context of the statements. (For some of our beliefs the statement "Well, I've always been told that" might count as good evidence, but it would not count as good evidence in a court of law.)

Most religions include a code of conduct and involve participation in some form of worship, though this may range from communal observances to solitary meditation. But religions also involve beliefs, and every religious tradition accepts some methods as legitimate ways of interpreting and verifying religious knowledge. The religion must be able to guide its adherents toward religious truth; otherwise, a crisis of belief, a crisis of truth would result.

A particular religion may appeal to wisdom or revelation handed down orally through the generations as containing ultimate truth. It may appeal to written documents—Judaism, Christianity, and Islam are often referred to as "religions of the Book." A religion may appeal to those who have had especially intense experiences of religious ecstasy or who have followed special religious disciplines as its interpreters of truth, or to persons who have been specially trained and selected by the official agencies of the group or to those with whom the spirit of the Divine seems to reside in a striking way. It may appeal to criteria of rational acceptability or to scientific methods of observation. But each of these sources requires a continual effort of interpretation, for traditions must be continually interpreted and reconciled to one another. (Navajo Native Americans often explain divergences in oral tradition by saying, "Well, that's *one* story, that's *his* story.") Scriptures like the Jewish Torah and the Christian New Testament must be interpreted: Jews and Christians and Muslims must ask themselves first what the Scriptures actually *say*, what they *mean*; then they must ask how their teachings are to be applied in present situations. Even the criteria of rational acceptability and scientific testability require a continuous effort at further clarification, reflection, and experimental observation.

Most religious traditions insist that not all religious truth can be adequately tested, established, or refuted by ordinary commonsense methods of observation or by scientific methods of experimentation. Some religions insist that much religious truth transcends and surpasses human reasoning and thus cannot be fully understood or tested by methods of reason or sense observation alone. Nevertheless, every religious tradition will make provision for methods of finding and testing proposed religious truth. It is worth noting that in a time when many contemporary societies are experiencing a profound crisis of belief, the suggestions religious traditions give about sources of truth and methods of testing it may be of the greatest value and relevance.

Most religions contain a variety of different kinds of beliefs—all of which are accepted by adherents of that tradition as containing genuine knowledge. For instance, some Christian beliefs are *historical* statements ("Jesus suffered under Pontius Pilate, was crucified, dead and buried"). Some are *metaphysical* statements ("God is the sole Creator of all that exists, and God created it out of nothing"). Some, though they sound like *predictions* or *forecasts* are more likely intended to be understood as *promises*, *assurances* to sustain faith and commitment.

Perhaps no topic has been more thoroughly investigated by contemporary theologians and philosophers of religion than the "logic" of religious language. That is, how language expressing aspects—feelings, attitudes, value judgments, beliefs—of the religious dimension of life (the dimension of ultimate or pivotal concern and commitment) is used.

Very roughly—since the issue is extremely complex—there have been four major positions taken about the logic of religious language.

1. The logical positivists, of whom A.J. Ayer is a notable example, insist that religious language (as well as moral, ethical, and aesthetic language) expresses only people's feelings and attitudes, and therefore there is no need to be concerned about how religious statements might be tested for truth value. Religious language does not even make claims or assertions about reality. This view has been called emotivism. (See the previous Unit.)

The other three views are willing to grant that some religious language may be claiming to assert truth. To oversimplify, the views can be characterized as follows:

2. There is no problem about the logic of testing the truth of at least some religious statements. We would use exactly the same kinds of procedures to discover whether they are true as we do to test statements in the sciences or history or ordinary sense experience.

3. At least some religious language makes statements that claim to be true, but the method of testing them for truth is totally unique (perhaps depending on a special kind of authority or on some inner revelation or illumination).

4. Others have argued that, though at least some expressions claim to give true accounts of reality, their logical status is neither wholly like nor wholly unlike that of statements in other areas of discourse. Although there may be some analogies between the claims made by a religious affirmation—once we have come to understand its intent and significance, say, an article of the Apostle's Creed—and the expression of a scientific hypothesis, there may also be dissimilarities. People who hold this fourth view may argue that, though it is useful to compare the way religious statements function and are verified with the way statements in science, history, ethics, aesthetic appreciation, and the law function and are verified, there should be no attempt to impose the logic of one field on statements belonging to other fields.

The issue of the nature of religious language not only has been of interest to contemporary students but also excited the intellects of the great thinkers of the Jewish-Christian-Islamic Middle Ages as well as great Hindu thinkers like Sankara and Ramanuja.

The question of whether and how religious expressions can be judged to be *true*—whether they make truth claims, and if they do, how it can be determined whether the claims they make are in fact true—is one of the most frequently discussed issues in contemporary theology and the philosophy of religion.

Some students of religious uses of language have warned us that it may be a fundamental mistake to *ask* whether uses of religious language are true or verifiable. Many twentieth-century philosophers and theologians have stressed *noncognitive* uses of religious language—that is, uses in which the speaker does not and may not intend to convey information.

> Rather, noncognitive use of language expresses feeling, makes a commitment, helps to cement the bonds of solidarity of a group, or does any other of innumerable possible things about which it would be ridiculous to suppose that questions of truth or falsity arise, as they would if the languages were assumed to have cognitive content (i.e., to claim to convey information) . . . when a minister says the words in a marriage ceremony, "I now pronounce you united in holy matrimony". . . no one would think that the purpose of the minister's expression is to give information. Rather, the minister is using language performatively, to accomplish something. Still, the position asserted by some that *all* religious language is noncognitive seems extreme and would not be accepted by most religious persons.[2]

If some religious language is cognitive—that is, makes claims to be true—by what methods or sources do we verify its truth claims? When is a belief merely a belief, and when is it knowledge? When is a belief a "fact," and when is it merely opinion?

[2] Robert C. Monk and Joseph D. Stamey, *Exploring Christianity*: An Introduction (Englewood Cliffs, NJ: Prentice-Hall, 1990), p. 153.

Ordinarily we say that we *know* a belief is true, or we say that a belief is a fact, when we possess good reasons—sufficient amounts of the right kind of evidence (that is, a sufficient amount of relevant *other* beliefs that we have good reason to accept as true).

Philosophers have sometimes attempted to establish that there are *some* facts that we know with absolute certainty, facts (beliefs) that we do not need to justify by appealing to other beliefs (facts) to support them. One candidate for a type of absolutely certain belief—a pure "fact"—has been the kind of factual statement based on immediate sense experience. How can I be mistaken that I am now seeing a patch of white or feeling a sharp pain? These philosophers argued that on the basis of such immediate sensations, we *construct* a theoretical world of objects: We infer that because we see patches of white, there is an object present *causing* us to have the experience of seeing white. The theoretical world we construct may be a world of commonsense objects—tables and chairs—or it may be the abstractly conceived, rigorously precise world of theoretical physics.

Other philosophers have argued that there is no clear-cut line between what we observe or experience and the theoretical interpretations we create to explain what we observe and experience. Ordinarily, we do not *see* patches of white; we see white objects. Thus Marx Wartofsky, a contemporary philosopher of science, points out that what we *observe* will be dependent on the language, the set of predicates we choose to interpret the observed (and the observable).

> Thus, determining what are observables may be reduced to the question of choosing the so-called basic predicates of [our] reconstructed language. For example, if one chooses as basic predicates such "phenomenal" terms as *red, heavy, hot, loud,* and such "phenomenal" relations as *longer than* or *brighter than,* then this fixes such terms as denoting the observables for that system. The only question is whether the theoretical terms of a science may somehow be reduced to these, and thus tied to observation as stipulated. On the other hand, one may choose terms of physical measurement as the basic predicates, so that everything would in principle be reducible to such predicates as measured distances, time intervals, or measurements of mass or of electrical charge.
>
> It is on pragmatic or instrumental grounds, according to this view, that one chooses among alternative languages—on grounds relating to the methodology of science, involving what scientists do when they observe, measure, etc. Nor does one simply choose among prevailing languages, which may have developed haphazardly in the history of science; rather one constructs artificial languages, ideally reconstructed languages, choosing the terms and even the logical structures best suited to scientific frameworks.
>
> What appears as an utter relativism concerning "observation" thus has certain constraints.[3]

Wartofsky emphasized the condition of being publicly verifiable that holds for what will be considered "observable." But similar, though perhaps less rigorously measurable, criteria of verification are often appealed to in the realm of religious experience. Thus, though the experience of satori (enlightenment) in Zen Buddhism is ineffable and incommunicable, the Zen master is able to validate or verify the occurrence of this experience in his disciples, presumably by seeing whether the change in manner and attitude of the disciple

---

[3] Marx W. Wartofsky, *Conceptual Foundations of Scientific Thought* (New York: Macmillan, 1968), pp. 112–113.

is coherent with the master's sense of the meaning of the experience. Apparently, the meaning of a belief can be discovered by asking what that person would consider good evidence—enough evidence of the relevant kind—to establish the truth of the belief. American philosopher Charles S. Peirce wrote,

> Consider what effects, that might conceivably have practical bearings, we conceive the object of our conception to have. Then our conception of these effects is the whole of our conception of the object.[4]

◆◆◆

Do you agree with the statement of C. S. Peirce just quoted?

◆◆◆

In most societies of the past, some forms of religious belief have been required of members of the society. This is true in parts of the world today. Since the time of the beginnings of Protestantism and independent nation-states in Europe and America, the acceptance of individual religious freedom to believe or not believe in any religious tradition has become widely accepted. This sometimes has led people to think of religious belief and commitment as something left entirely to the individual. However, even in societies where there is complete legal freedom of religion, the religious beliefs and practices of most individuals are initially shaped and frequently continually sustained by their group affiliations—family, ethnic identity, or regional background.

It is no accident that in the United States most persons of Hispanic or Italian descent are Catholic or that most people who live in certain Southern states are Methodist or Baptist. In the imaginary interviews of the previous unit, Marcia not only expresses this fact but approves of it. She is very happy to have her religious and moral beliefs guided by the recognized leaders of her church.

Many Protestants have held that all or much genuine religious knowledge comes from the Bible. This has sometimes led to highly individualistic interpretations. Southern Baptists, for instance, have traditionally stressed the spiritual or "soul competence" of individual believers to interpret the Bible. Still, Baptist preaching and teaching gives a great amount of guidance to individual believers, and it is clear that Brandi, in the imaginary interviews, relies on the teaching of her pastor.

Recently, even among some Protestants who have traditionally stressed individualism in religious interpretation, there has been a move toward the need for community leadership and guidance. The influential contemporary theologian, Stanley Hauerwas, is a United Methodist. He calls himself a Mennonite Methodist and a Catholic Mennonite and stresses the need for community authority and guidance for Christian individuals, families, and groups. Deliberately provocative and probably exaggerating, Hauerwas has said that no individual in North America should be allowed to own a Bible since no individual can responsibly interpret the Bible without the guidance of an authoritative religious community. Hauerwas does not believe that religious interpretation should be

---

[4] James Mark Baldwin, *Dictionary of Philosophy and Psychology* (New York: Macmillan, 1902).

legally enforced (as in seventeenth-century England or contemporary Iran or Afghanistan). He does believe that committed individual Christians should and will be willing to be guided by disciplines of their Christian communities.[5]

Unit 34   GENERAL AND SPECIAL REVELATION, REASON AND FAITH

❖❖❖

Is God self-revealing? If so, how can we understand revelation?

❖❖❖

> Revelation translates the Greek word apokalypsis and literally means 'an uncovering, a laying bare, making naked.'. . . So understood, R[evelation], presupposes (1) that someone or something is hidden and that (2) this someone or something has not been discovered but, rather, disclosed.[6]

We cannot find a developed concept of revelation in the Bible. Although the Bible contains numerous "images and symbols for the disclosure of God's will and purposes,"[7] revelation has developed as a doctrinal concept during the history of Christianity since the writing of the Scriptures. Alan Richardson, author of *Christian Apologetics*, interprets two kinds of revelation: general revelation, the awareness that everyone has of God, and special revelation, a designation of the unique knowledge of God that comes from a particular historical experience:

> The only kind of theory of the knowledge of God which will adequately embrace all the facts of man's experience will be one which recognizes that there are two kinds of revelation or divine disclosure of truth. There is first general revelation, which pertains to the universal religious consciousness of mankind; and there is also special revelation, which is mediated through particular episodes of definite times and places in history. The broad distinction between general and special revelation is that the former is nonhistorical, in that its content is not communicated to mankind through particular historical situations but is quite independent of the accidents of time and place, whereas the latter is historical, that is, bound up with certain series of historical persons and happenings through which it is communicated to mankind. This is broadly the distinction between biblical (Jewish-Christian) religion and the non-Christian religions.[8]

So according to Richardson, general revelation allows all people in some way to know about God, but special revelation means that God is disclosed in a very special way to spe-

[5] Stanley Hauerwas, *Unleashing the Scripture: Freeing the Bible from Captivity to America* (Nashville, TN: Abington, 1993).

[6] Van A. Harvey, *A Handbook of Theological Terms* (New York: Macmillan, 1964), p. 207

[7] Ibid.

[8] Alan Richardson, *Christian Apologetics* (New York: SCM Press and Harper & Row, 1947), p. 117.

cific people so that they personally experience God. Special revelation is the divine confrontation of God and humankind through such actual historical events as the Israelite exodus from Egypt and the life, death, and resurrection of Jesus Christ.

There are at least three dimensions of general revelation that represent different ways of knowing God: the first is reason, our capacity to think about God; for example, when our logic tells us that there must have been an ultimate first cause of all that is. The second, artistic experience that may include the use of our minds but often relates to our emotional responses, for example, when we are moved by the beauty of visual art forms, scenes in nature, or music. The third is our sense of morality, for example, a gnawing conscience in the face of hard ethical choices or a case of gross injustice. Reflect on these three forms of general revelation as you read further.

The key to a general revelation or knowledge of God, according to Richardson, relates to the moral experience.

> It is, however, in the moral sphere that the chief evidence of general revelation is found. Even though some might hold that there are certain people who are totally devoid of religious experience, it is indubitable that all people have had moral experience—the experience of knowing that one ought to do this and ought not to do that. Every human being who is not clearly an imbecile has knowledge of right and wrong.[9]

Alan Richardson claims that general revelation has redeeming power for those who experience God through philosophy, art forms, or nature. Other eminent theologians, however, such as Karl Barth and Emil Brunner (highly influential German theologians during post-World War I decades), held that special revelation alone serves as the vehicle for saving grace. Barth believed that every person is a sinner, totally devoid of any natural capacity to receive God's revelation. For him, a person may know God only because God makes that knowledge possible. Brunner agrees with Barth on this point but would argue that in every person there remains a capacity for general knowledge about God, even though such knowledge does not redeem a person from sin. Richardson feels that both Barth and Brunner neglect the saving power that comes from the knowledge of God revealed outside of Christianity.

Richardson affirms that non-Christian humanists who do good works or have some vision of God are to be considered vehicles of God's general revelation. He is quick to say, however, that Christians who recognize God-given humanist values in non-Christians should claim special revelation as essential for clarifying and correcting general revelation.

> Concerning the necessity of special revelation, Richardson writes, There is indeed a sense in which the noblest insights of the humanist are fulfilled in Christ, but there is also a sense in which they are judged and transcended by Him. . . . Although all that we have said about the necessity and value of general revelation is true, it is also true that apart from faith in Christ there is no undistorted knowledge of God or of truth at all."[10]

[9] Ibid., p. 124.
[10] Ibid., p. 129–130.

◆◆◆

Do you think everyone has a religious consciousness?

Could the concepts of general and special revelation as defined by Richardson be meaningful to those of religious traditions other than Christianity?

Reflecting on the definition of religion used in this text, may a pivotal value be appropriated through both general and special revelation?

◆◆◆

The terms faith and reason are closely related to the concepts of general and special revelation. Ordinarily, when faith means an attitude of affirming or accepting religious beliefs whose evidence transcends the ability of reason to comprehend, faith is held to be a response to events of special revelation. However, general revelation may still be thought to call for a response of faith. Also, reason may be believed to be useful in responding to and understanding special revelation. The following paragraphs explore these relationships.

The concepts of faith and reason have been particularly important in Western religious traditions. Those who stress special revelation probably tend to emphasize faith as a way to know God, and those who affirm the reality and importance of general revelation place a heavy emphasis on reason. In the West, there have traditionally been four basic ways of relating faith and reason.

REASON REJECTING FAITH

When reason rejects faith, it tends to result in skepticism about God. Reason alone has sought God but in many cases has reached an atheistic (no God) or an agnostic (no knowledge of God) position. Some interpreters who have a thoroughgoing use of reason without the help of faith have concluded that religious affirmations of God or life after death equal faith in goblins, Santa Claus, fairies, and monsters in the night. According to some thinkers, reason seeks evidence for God's existence, but in the absence of evidence for God's existence, atheism becomes obligatory.[11] A similar, though not identical, position has been proposed by A. J. Ayer:

> We conclude, therefore, that the argument from religious experience is altogether fallacious. The fact that people have religious experiences is interesting from a psychological point of view, but it does not in any way imply that there is such a thing as religious knowledge. . . . The theist, like the moralist, may believe that his experiences are cognitive experiences, but, unless he can formulate his "knowledge" in propositions that are empirically verifiable, we may be sure he is deceiving himself.[12]

Ayer refuses to accept any statements about reality as meaningful unless they are grounded in verifiable sense experiences. Others, such as Aristotle, Leibniz, and Hartshorne, have claimed to have knowledge of God through reason alone.

[11] Michael Scriven, *Primary Philosophy* (New York: McGraw-Hill, 1966), p. 103.
[12] A. J. Ayer, *Language, Truth and Logic*, 2nd ed. (New York: Dover, 1946), p. 120.

REASON EMBRACING FAITH

A number of interpreters have held the view that reason includes the way of faith. Adherents of this position have seen a common denominator of Divine Truth in both philosophy and the Judeo-Christian tradition. Justin Martyr, a second-century philosopher and Christian martyr, held "That a saving natural knowledge of God was possible through philosophy. . . ."[13] He saw a close identity between Christian teachings and much in the thought of the best philosophers. He felt Christianity inherited all the truth discerned by Greek philosophers.

Justin fathered a tradition that was articulated strongly by Clement of Alexandria (c. 150–215) and Origen. Clement tended to equate the saving power of philosophy with Jewish law and prophecy. He saw Plato as a Moses talking Attic Greek.[14] Origen, Christianity's earliest systematic theologian, developed a system of theology in which he saw a close proximity between the word of the Greek philosophers and the Word become flesh, Christ, the incarnation of God. In his classic work, *First Principles*, he relates in creative ways the message of scriptural faith to the teachings of philosophy and reason.

Peter Abelard, Christian philosopher of the twelfth century, refocused the emphasis on a reasoned faith. "He held that what had been revealed to the Jews by prophecy had been given to the Greeks by philosophy and that the doctrine of the Trinity, and other Christian truths, had been taught by Heraclitus and Plato. . . ."[15] Abelard's method emphasized doubt as a way to understand faith. He did not intend to make reason primary to faith, but his approach did open the way for more rationalism in theology, culminating in Immanuel Kant's attempt to confine "religion within the limits of reason alone."

FAITH REJECTING REASON

In reaction to the tendency of reason to suppress faith, some people of faith have tended to negate reason altogether. At times, Tertullian, an early Christian theologian, rejected reason, "denouncing Greek philosophy as the bridal gift of the fallen angels to the daughters of men and the Greek philosophers as the patriarchs of the heretics."[16] Bernard of Clairvaux, a Christian mystic, felt that Abelard threatened the true faith with his rationalism. Doubting reason as a reliable guide to God, Bernard said, "By faith I think of God. . . ."[17] Martin Luther, father of the Protestant Reformation, held that no one can enter into a right relationship with God through good works or the power of thought. Although reason may help us in practical living, such as making clothes or doing a job, human reasoning falls short in spiritual matters; other power is required here—something given only by God and made known in divine word. That which God

---

[13] Richardson, *Christian Apologetics*, p. 228.

[14] Ibid., p. 229.

[15] Ibid.

[16] Ibid., p. 228.

[17] Bernard of Clairvaux, "Selections from His Sermons," in *The Christian Reader: Inspirational and Devotional Classics*, ed. Stanley Irving Stuber (New York: Association Press, 1952), p. 106.

grants, in Luther's understanding, is faith alone, the gift of trust in God's saving strength.[18]

In the twentieth century, the theologian Karl Barth expressed serious apprehensions about reason's ability to point adequately to God: "Knowledge of God is a knowledge completely effected and determined from the side of its object, from the side of God. . . . Our concepts are not adequate to grasp this treasure."[19] We should note, however, that Barth, as well as others who rejected reason in the realm of faith, had to depend on the expressions of reason to reject reason. Although some voices may justifiably cry out against the excesses of rationalism, no one can be free completely from its use and the philosophy of the times.

FAITH EMBRACING REASON

The classical Christian answer to the conflict between faith and reason finds apt expression in the fifth-century words of Saint Augustine, bishop of Hippo in Africa:

> Understanding is the reward of faith. Therefore seek not to understand that thou mayest believe, but believe that thou mayest understand. . . . We believed that we might know; for if we wished first to know and then to believe, we should not be able to know or to believe. . . . They did not believe because they knew, but they believed in order that they might know.[20]

Here Augustine exhibits an orthodox Christian view of the relationship between faith and reason. Reason comes to creative fruition only as it is guided by faith. Faith orders understanding.

This does not mean that faith supplies factual data of sense experience. Reason must still assess and make judgments about facts of knowledge, but the power of reason to function adequately comes from faith. In knowing, "faith supplies the 'clues' or categories of interpretation by which alone the empirical data of science and religion can be rightly understood."[21] According to Augustine's approach, every philosophy must follow the lead of a faith principle to give valid meaning to existence. Faith serves as the condition of sound reasoning. In fact, according to Augustine, the person of faith is freed to exercise his reason more responsibly. Faith enables the believer to understand.

◆◆◆

Can reason operate apart from faith?

Does faith undermine reason or enhance the intellectual process?

Does faith enable understanding?

[18] Hugh Thomson Kerr, Jr., ed., *A Compend of Luther's Theology* (Philadelphia: Westminster Press, 1958), p. 3.

[19] Karl Barth, *Dogmatics in Outline*, trans. G. T. Thomson (New York: Philosophical Library, 1949), p. 24.

[20] Saint Augustine, "In Joannis Evangelium Tractatus," *An Augustine Synthesis*, ed. Erich Pryzywara (New York: Harper & Brothers, 1958), pp. 58–59.

[21] Richardson, *Christian Apologetics*, p. 230.

Unit 35   AUTHORITY IN RELIGION

Søren Kierkegaard, a nineteenth-century Danish thinker, was raised by his father in a strict Lutheran orthodox tradition. For a time he rebelled against the rigidity of his religious upbringing, but later he embraced it fully, rejecting humanistic and liberal elements that had become popular in academic Protestant circles in his day. The humanistic liberals stressed the human capacity to understand God. They emphasized human reason, conscience, and human creativity as sources of religious truth. Kierkegaard rejected such ideas. In the following passage he argues that genuine religious truth must come from God, by revelation. Thus a prophet or an apostle, like Paul—persons who are instruments of God's revelation—is in a very different category from wise or learned or brilliant or well-educated persons whose teachings, however brilliant they may be, are simply products of finite human capacities. The prophet and the apostle have authority from God; the others do not.

Kierkegaard thought that a true understanding of Christianity depended on seeing that it is paradoxical, that it negates *human expectations* and *accomplishments* (human intellect, knowledge, insight, and virtue are *not* the key to religious understanding) at the same time that it fulfills the deepest hopes by speaking of a God who reaches out to people to bring them into the presence of God's love. The paradox is that truth and fulfillment come by unexpected means and in ways that shock and surprise and humble. In the following passage, Kierkegaard's critique of the liberals (referred to as "clergymen") leads him to a forceful statement of his own interpretation of religious authority.

> When the sphere of paradoxical religion is abolished or explained back into the ethical, then an apostle becomes nothing more nor less than a genius—and then good-night Christianity. *Esprit* and spirit, revelation and originality, a calling from God and ingeniousness, an apostle and a genius, all coalesce . . . one not infrequently hears clergymen . . . in all learned simplicity, prostitute Christianity. . . .
>
> They talk in lofty tones of the cleverness and profundity of St. Paul, of his beautiful similes, etc.—sheer aesthetics. If Paul is to be regarded as a genius, it looks very bad for him. Only to clerical ignorance could it occur to praise Paul aesthetically, because clerical ignorance has no standard but thinks in this wise: If only one says something good about Paul, it's all to the good. Such good-humored and well-intentioned thoughtlessness is to be referred to the fact that the person in question has not been disciplined by qualitative dialectics, which would have taught him that an apostle is not served by saying something good about him when it is crazy, so that he is recognized and admired for being what in an apostle is a matter of indifference and what essentially he is not, while with that what he is is forgotten. It might just as well occur to such thoughtless eloquence to laud Paul as a stylist and for his artistic use of language, or still better, since it is well known that Paul practiced a manual trade, to maintain that his work as an upholsterer must have been so perfect that no upholsterer either before or since has been able to equal it—for, if only one says something good about Paul, then all is well. As a genius Paul can sustain no comparison with Plato or with Shakespeare, as an author of beautiful similes he ranks rather low, as stylist his is an obscure name, and as an upholsterer—well, I may admit that in this respect I don't know where to place him. One always does well to transform stupid seriousness into jest—and then comes the real serious thing, the serious fact that Paul was an apostle, and as an apostle has no affinity either with Plato or Shakespeare

or a stylist or an upholsterer, who are all of them (Plato as well as the upholsterer Hansen) beneath any comparison with him.

A genius and an apostle are qualitatively distinct, they are categories, which belong each of them to their own qualitative spheres: that of immanence and that of transcendence. . . . The genius may well have something new to contribute, but this newness vanishes again in its gradual assimilation by the race, just as the distinction "genius" vanishes when one thinks of eternity. The apostle has paradoxically something new to contribute, the newness of which, precisely because it is paradoxical and not an anticipation of what may eventually be developed in the race, remains constant, just as an apostle remains an apostle to all eternity, and no immanence of eternity puts him essentially on the same plane with other men, since essentially he is paradoxically different. . . . The genius is what he is by reason of himself, i.e., by what he is in himself: an apostle is what he is by reason of his divine authority. . . . A genius may perhaps be a century ahead of his age and hence stands there as a paradox, but in the end the race will assimilate what was once a paradox, so that it is no longer paradoxical. Quite otherwise with the apostle. The word itself indicates the difference. An apostle is not born, an apostle is a man called and sent by God, sent by him upon a mission. . . .

An apostle can never in such wise come to himself that he becomes conscious of his apostolic calling as a stage in his life's development. The apostolic call is a paradoxical fact which in the first as well as the last moment of his life stands paradoxically outside his personal identity with himself as the definite person he is. A genius is appraised on purely aesthetic grounds, according to the content and specific gravity his productions are found to have; an apostle is what he is by reason of the divine authority he has. The divine authority is the qualitatively decisive factor.[22]

Because the authority of the prophet or apostle rests for Kierkegaard in the Divine, and these persons are unique representatives of the Divine, their words become distinctive and binding. Only a few individuals are so called and serve as instruments of God's revelation.

In seventeenth-century England, the Quakers held a view of religious authority that, like Kierkegaard's, stressed the presence of the Divine but was also quite different. The Quakers declared that all people were blessed with divine authority: Each believer experiences the indwelling Spirit of Christ, the Inner Light, as a source of all religious truth. Embracing the Light present in all, all believers had within themselves the full religious authority of Christ. An authority on the religious history of the time has written the following:

> Many of the [seventeenth-century] Quakers took [the] doctrine of the indwelling Spirit to what by most of the [other] Puritans was felt to be a dangerous extreme. The Spirit was to be the guide by which everything, Scriptures included, was to be judged. William Penn corrected misunderstandings when he wrote: It is not our Way of Speaking to say that the Light within is the Rule of the Christian Religion; but the Light of Christ within us is the Rule of true Christians, so that it is not our Light but Christ's Light that is our rule.[23]

---

[22] Selections from Søren Kierkegaard, *On Authority and Revelation: The Book on Adler, or A Cycle of Ethico-Religious Essays*, trans. Walter Lowrie (Princeton, NJ: Princeton University Press, 1955), pp. 103–107. Copyright © 1955 by Princeton University Press. Reprinted by permission of Princeton University Press.

[23] Hugh Martin, *Puritanism and Richard Baxter* (London: SCM Press, 1954), p. 79.

In the understanding of Kierkegaard and the Quakers, religious authority resides in the Divine even when exemplified in a human personality. Yet the words, works, and writings of those who possess Divine Authority often become sources of religious authority. Paul's writings, and those of other apostles and prophets, came to be accepted as sacred Scripture because of the Divine Authority that they possessed. Nevertheless, as Scripture, these words assumed an authority of their own. They represent the presence and the will of the Divine. Similarly, religious authority often resides in several aspects of community experience: Particular historical events take on religious authority—Gautama's enlightenment; Jesus' life, death, and resurrection. Great teachers and leaders become authorities—Confucius, Buddha, the pope in Roman Catholicism, Martin Luther in Protestantism. Orthodox beliefs are formulated into creeds and confessions—the Three Refuges of Buddhism, the Apostles' Creed of Christianity, the confessions of the Qur'an. Authoritative moral codes define proper life—the Ten Commandments in Judaism and Christianity, the Eightfold Path in Buddhism, the Five Great Relations in Confucianism. Each of these sources of authority points beyond itself to the Divine, but for the ordinary believer each constitutes meaningful and real authority, defining belief and action. In so doing, these sources exemplify the multifaceted nature of religious authority as experienced in daily life.

◆◆◆

How does Kierkegaard's understanding of authority relate to the discussion (in Unit 34) of general and special revelation? Would it be accurate to say that Kierkegaard rejects the validity of the idea of general revelation?

What are the most significant sources of authority in the religious groups and traditions with which you are familiar?

Who can speak with authority in matters of religious truth? Those who are specially trained or appointed (ordained)? Those who live the best lives, morally or religiously? Those with a unique or distinctive religious experience? What do the main religious groups with which you are familiar say about this?

Does ultimate religious authority reside in the written words of a document (such as the Bible or the Qur'an)? Does it come from a special experience, such as an illumination of the heart by revelation? Does it come from some other source?

Unit 36   TRADITION: ITS MEANING AND FUNCTION

Because of the brief span of our national history, our mobility, and the fact that we are a land of immigrants, Americans have sometimes been "antitraditional"—making a virtue out of newness and often discarding the old. Only recently have we begun to understand and use our traditions in the manner that most cultures have throughout history. It may be difficult for Americans to appreciate the significant role tradition has played in human history, yet its importance can hardly be overstated.

The term tradition is derived from the Latin word *traditio*, which literally means "a handing over." In Latin culture and in later cultures, this term was used to indicate (1) content—information, teachings, doctrine, behavior patterns, or other thoughts and/or practices received from previous generations—and at times (2) the process by which such material was handed down. The term thus embraces customs, doctrines, and concepts, as well as action.

Tradition understood in this way has been an ever-present reality in the great religious movements of the world. It has been the central means by which religions ensured the transmittal of religious experience, information, beliefs, and moral codes to each new generation of believers.

Tradition is so important in Judaism that in the musical *Fiddler on the Roof,* set in a late nineteenth-century Russian Jewish community, it was idealized as perhaps the means of defining life and its relationship to God.

> A fiddler on the roof,
> Sounds crazy, no? But in our little village of Anatevka you might say everyone of us is a fiddler on a roof, trying to scratch out a pleasant simple tune without breaking his neck. It isn't easy.
> You may ask, "Why do we stay up there if it's so dangerous?" We stay because Anatevka's our home. And "How do we keep our balance?" That I can tell you in one word: tradition.
> Tradition! Tradition! Tradition!
> Tradition! Tradition! Tradition!
> Because of our traditions we've kept our balance for many years. Here in Anatevka we have our traditions for everything—how to eat, how to sleep, how to work, even how to wear clothes. For instance, we always keep our heads covered; we wear these little prayer shawls. This shows our constant devotion to God. You may ask "How did this tradition get started?" I'll tell you, I don't know. But it's tradition. Because of our traditions everyone here knows who he is and what God expects him to do.[24]

Tradition plays an important part in Judaism in yet another way. Its festivals and holy days are to a large degree the means by which Jewish faith, life, and history are perpetuated. This is evident in the Passover celebration, in which, among the components of the ceremonial practices, there is a section that recites the ancient "four questions," usually asked by the youngest male present.

> Why is this night of passover different from all other nights of the year?
> On all other nights, we eat either Chomaytz or Matzoh,
>   but on this night we eat only Matzoh.
> On all other nights, we eat all kinds of herbs,
>   but on this night we eat only Moror.
> On all other nights, we do not dip even once,
>   but on this night we dip twice.

---

[24] "Tradition," from *Fiddler on the Roof*, a musical play based on Joseph Itkin, *Fiddler on the Roof.* Copyright © 1964 Joseph Stein. Used by permission.

> On all other nights, we eat either sitting or reclining,
>   but on this night we eat reclining.

The eldest male, usually the father, answers:

> Once we were slaves to Pharaoh in Egypt, and the Lord in His goodness and mercy brought us forth from that land, with a mighty hand and an out-stretched arm. Had he not rescued us from the hand of the despot, surely we and our children would still be enslaved, deprived of liberty and human dignity.
>
> We, therefore, gather year after year, to retell this ancient story. For, in reality, it is not ancient, but eternal in its message, and its spirit. It proclaims man's burning desire to preserve liberty and justice for all.
>
> The first question asked concerns the use of Matzoh. We eat these unleavened cakes to remember that our ancestors, in their haste to leave Egypt, could not wait for breads to rise, and so removed them from the ovens while still flat.
>
> We partake of the Moror on this night that we might taste of some bitterness, to remind ourselves how bitter is the lot of one caught in the grip of slavery.
>
> We dip twice in the course of this Service, greens in salt water and Moror in Charoses, once to replace tears with gratefulness, and once to sweeten bitterness and suffering.
>
> The fourth question asks why, on this night, we eat in a reclining position. To recline at mealtimes in ancient days was the sign of a free man. On this night of Passover, we demonstrate our sense of complete freedom by reclining during our repast.[25]

Note that in both of these examples, tradition does not necessarily depend on cognitive or conscious transmission of information or patterns of behavior, but rather is incorporated in the dynamic interplay of daily life; therefore, it is often unconsciously appropriated. Tradition plays a similar role in all religions. In Chinese and Japanese religions, it has been as important as duty (see Unit 60) in defining life. Even to an outsider, the importance of traditions of Hinduism in Indian society is obvious.

Christianity, as other religions, depends greatly on tradition to define and interpret beliefs and lifestyles. Roman Catholicism and Eastern Orthodoxy heavily depend on tradition, insisting on its continuing role in defining belief and action. The following statement by the Catholic theologian Karl Adam expresses this function:

> The Church affirms, completely and entirely, the whole of holy Scripture, both the Old Testament and the New. . . .
>
> And by the side of the holy Scripture stands extra-scriptural Tradition. The Gospel itself is based upon oral teaching, upon the preaching of Christ, of his disciples and of that apostolic succession of teachers which began with the first pupils of the apostles. Therefore the formation in the Christian communities of a living stream of tradition was natural and inevitable. The New Testament is certainly an important expression, but it is by no means an exhaustive expression, of this apostolic tradition which filled and permeated the whole consciousness of the Church. Oral tradition, the apostolic teaching alive and active in the Christian communities, is prior to and more fundamental than the Bible. It attests the Bible, both in its inspiration and in its canon. It is more comprehensive than the Bible, for it attests a mass of ritual and religious usage, of customs and rules, which is

---

[25] *Haggadah for the American Family*, English Service with directions by Martin Berkowitz. Copyright © 1958, 1963, and 1966 by Martin Berkowitz. Used by permission of the copyright owner.

only slightly indicated in the Bible. And it possesses a quality which the Bible as a written document has not and cannot have, and which constitutes its pre-eminent merit, namely, that living spirit of revelation, that vitality of revealed thought, that "instinct of faith" which stands behind every written and unwritten word, and which we call the "mind of the church."[26]

◆◆◆

What principal traditions can you identify within the religious communities with which you are familiar? Do they sustain the religion from generation to generation?

Given the definition of religion used in this book, is it possible for a person to be religious with little or no dependence on tradition?

What might be the relationships, if any, between tradition and personal religious experience?

Unit 37   THE ANATOMY OF FAITH

In the preceding units, it was emphasized that many contemporary theologians, influenced by twentieth-century concepts of personality as an integrated whole, have attempted to understand the concept of faith as involving more than the cognitive dimension of belief.

Faith—for many people one of the most familiar of religious concepts—is also one of the most easily and consistently misunderstood. Paul Tillich comments, "There are few words in the language of religion which cry for as much semantic purging as the word 'faith.' It is continually being confused with belief in something for which there is no evidence, or in something intrinsically unbelievable, or in absurdities or nonsense. It is extremely difficult to remove these distorting connotations from the genuine meaning of faith."[27]

The understanding of faith as a belief "in something for which there is no evidence," though common, is a most dangerous form of misunderstanding. It unwittingly pits faith against reason and knowledge. To say that you believe "by faith" in something that is unknown or cannot be rationally proved is to affirm its existence and relevance even though you lack evidence to support your faith. In a day when rational evidence is the hallmark for accepting anything as true, it is obvious that knowledge that can be rationally validated will appear more trustworthy than faith that cannot. Therefore, in an era of expanding "knowledge," an individual with this understanding of faith assumes that he or she is less and less dependent on faith. As knowledge expands in the life of the individual, its importance tends to overpower and outweigh that of faith—faith is reduced to a wholly subjective and relatively unimportant part of life.

[26] Karl Adam, *The Spirit of Catholicism*, trans. Dom Justin McCann, O.S.B. (New York: Macmillan, 1954).

[27] Paul Tillich, *Systematic Theology*, Vol. III (Chicago: University of Chicago Press, 1963), p. 130.

So it would seem that the most common understanding of faith leads to a struggle between knowledge and faith wherein faith is the inevitable loser. Perhaps this understanding has contributed to the tendency in modern Western societies to relegate religion to a secondary (or even nonexistent) role in life. In any case, it is evident that the misunderstanding of the nature and meaning of faith has important consequences.

To understand faith as the opposite of knowledge is not only misleading but also unnecessary. Much of the difficulty arises over the tendency to use the words belief and faith as synonyms. For many people, to say "I believe in God" is to say "I have faith in God"; the two expressions are used without recognizable distinction. Yet the words do not mean the same thing. *Faith* connotes "reliance on," "trust in," "commitment to." On the one hand, having faith means being personally willing to trust or depend on something. On the other hand, *believing* in something means holding or thinking that it exists, but it does not necessarily mean trust. H. Richard Niebuhr helpfully points up this distinction:

> The belief that something exists is an experience of a wholly different order from the experience of reliance on it. The faith we speak of . . . is not intellectual assent to the truth of certain propositions, but a personal, practical trusting in, reliance on, counting upon something. So we have faith in democracy not insofar as we believe that democracy exists, but insofar as we rely upon the democratic idea or spirit to maintain itself and to influence the lives of people continuously. We have faith in the people not insofar as we believe in the existence of such a reality as "the people," but insofar as we count upon the character of what we call the people to manifest itself steadfastly in the maintenance of certain values. Faith, in other words, always refers primarily to character and power rather than to existence. Existence is implied and necessarily implied; but there is no direct road from assent to the intellectual proposition that something exists to the act of confidence and reliance upon it. Faith is an active thing, a committing of self to something, an anticipation. It is directed toward something that is also active, that has power or is power. . . . Belief as assent to the truth of propositions does not necessarily involve reliance in action on that which is believed, and it refers to propositions rather than, as faith does, to agencies and powers.[28]

Belief should be distinguished from faith in our common usage of the terms. Faith may entail belief—that is, the acceptance of something—but it goes beyond acceptance to actual dependence. Conversely, belief may be present without faith; that is, one may believe but not really trust. Such, in fact, is the case with the religious understanding of many people. They may believe many things—that God exists, that Jesus Christ is Savior, that certain religious propositions are true—yet they do not act in their daily existence on what these beliefs imply, and in failing to do so they reveal the inconsistency between their beliefs and their faith. Such inconsistency is easily recognized by others as hypocrisy, although it is seldom recognized by the individual, for the individual thinks that his or her beliefs and faith are the same.

If the proper distinction between faith and belief is kept in mind, we may return to the relation between faith and knowledge. Although it is true that knowledge is based on specific evidence, it is also true that knowledge relies on (trusts) certain

---

[28] H. Richard Niebuhr, *Radical Monotheism and Western Culture* (New York: Harper & Brothers, 1960), pp. 116–117.

presuppositions. Scientists build their store of knowledge on the assumption that the universe is ultimately orderly and that this order is discoverable. They place faith in that orderliness and work from this presupposition. Faith then lies behind their endeavors. Evidence from the universe and the knowledge built on it substantiates their initial trust. Religious faith follows a similar pattern. It also operates on an assumption—that the universe has meaning and purpose and that purpose is evident in human experience of life. Theologians then trust this assumption and think, like the scientists, that life provides evidence for the validity of the assumption. The religious experience, abundant throughout humanity's existence, may not be of the same form as that found in the physical world with which the scientist works, but it is no less valid because of this. *Meaning* in the universe may call for evidence of a different order or genre than that of *function* in the universe, but both are legitimate and necessary. In either case, faith is an active element in human experience. Science and religion depend on both faith and knowledge, and they need not oppose each other.

A more acute problem may be, instead of opposition between faith and knowledge, a conflict between opposing "faiths." We attach our trust (faith) to many objects in the course of our lives (or even in the course of one day): self, occupation, money, scientific method, distinctive religious formulations, particular political systems, and moral standards, to mention only a few. Each of these demands of us a trust and commitment resulting in the exclusion of other alternatives. We find ourselves creatures with many faiths; in Niebuhr's words, "our natural religion is polytheistic."[29] At one moment we pursue and trust one faith, and in the next another. On some occasions we find that we must choose between these faiths—one must be more important than another.

For those willing to accept a religious solution to this problem of opposing faiths, Niebuhr offers some useful insights. He points out that all of these faiths are ultimately finite—insufficient to carry the weight of full and total commitment.

> None of these can guarantee meaning to our life in the world save for a time. They are finite in time as in space and make finite claims upon us. . . . None of these beings on which we rely to give content and meaning to our lives is able to supply continuous meaning and value.[30]

When the finitude of these faiths is recognized and accepted, when each one is destroyed or loses effectiveness, we are faced with a failure of meaning or purpose. At that moment we are enabled to place our faith in "the one reality beyond all the many, which is the last power, the infinite source of all particular beings as well as their end. And insofar as our faith, our reliance for meaning and worth, has been attached to this source and enemy of all our gods, we have been able to call this reality God."[31] When all of our lesser faiths have been destroyed, we are able to trust in that which stands behind all others—the source of all meaning and purpose—God.

Such an answer is, of course, unacceptable if we affirm other faith commitments as definitive and sufficient or if we define faith as something other than trust. Neverthe-

[29] Ibid., p. 119.
[30] Ibid., pp. 120–122.
[31] Ibid., pp. 122–123.

less, any solution to the problem of conflicting faiths demands that the object of our faith be clearly identified and that faith be distinguished from belief and from knowledge. If that which can be distinguished from belief and knowledge—faith—can be seen as reliable, it may again be recognized for the role it actually plays in the human experience. This is Niebuhr's claim.

When in this study of religion we define religion as "reliance on a pivotal value," we are speaking of faith—a faith that supersedes and dominates all other claims for attention and action.

◆◆◆

Has the unit contributed to or modified your understanding of faith and belief? How?

If all humans, according to Niebuhr's definition, are normally polytheistic, why would a "pivotal value" be attractive or necessary?

Explain how or why faith might be seen as "active" and belief as "passive".

✦✦✦ 7 ✦✦✦

WAYS OF CONCEIVING
THE DIVINE

Human reason and its ability to structure knowledge so dominates Western cultures that it is often difficult to recognize that our daily experience may contain many aspects that do not conveniently fit into rational or scientific explanations (see Chapter 6). Even when we seek to consider many of these aspects, such as emotion, nonrational behaviors, and experiences of transcending the present moment, we turn to psychology and sociology to explain human behavior in rational terms. While such studies may give us insight into human action, they may not capture the fullness of particular experiences. In the same way, we often encase religion in descriptions of rites and rituals, creedal formulations and teaching formulas, or theological concepts expressing beliefs and doctrines. Religious experience is, however, too rich and varied to be captured by such manifestations of its presence. Behind these reasonable ways of talking about religion lie experiences that encompass "something greater"—something that is not grasped by human description. Yet, being social beings we want to share such experience so we attempt to describe it. To do so we have to use rational categories to point to the inexpressible; even when many believe that any description is finally inadequate.

The purpose of the units in this chapter is to probe some of the ways people talk about such experiences and encounters while examining the concepts by which they have sought to characterize them. Differing cultural views are examined to help contact the many ways an encounter with what is usually termed, in Western societies, "the Divine" may be expressed. As the units note, many non-Western religious traditions rely on intuitive experience that may not need rational explanation but must, nevertheless, be expressed in understandable terms if it is to be shared with others.

In Chapter 1 we discussed an understanding of religion that embraces not only "sacred" or "theistic" views of the Divine but also "secular" or "nontheistic" commitments. Although the following units lean toward examples of theistic conceptions (belief in one Divine Being), the reader should keep in mind our definition of religion involving a commitment to a supreme or pivotal value that becomes the focus for the whole of life.

Thus, even nontheistic religions and secular movements may involve the concept of an ultimate object or source of an individual's or a group's commitment that expresses what is, in the west, usually called the Divine.

UNIT 38   THE HOLY

Theistic religious experience in any of its many forms is grounded in an encounter with transcendent reality, which gives it a sacredness, or holiness, that distinguishes it from other human experiences. Rudolf Otto, in *The Idea of the Holy*, says this encounter includes a "moment of consciousness or a state of mind" in which one is overwhelmed by an awareness of the Divine. Such an experience gives one a feeling of "awe"—a sense of "astonishment" or "blank wonder." For Otto this encounter with the "wholly-other" lies behind and permeates all other religious consciousness.[1] In essence it is an encounter with the mystery that lies at the core of life. Otto's name for this mysterious reality is the *mysterium tremendum*, which suggests its power and centrality.

> Let us consider the deepest and most fundamental element in all strong and sincerely felt religious emotion. Faith unto salvation, trust, love—all these are there. But over and above these is an element which may also on occasion, quite apart from them, profoundly affect us and occupy the mind with a well-nigh bewildering strength. Let us follow it up with every effort of sympathy and imaginative intuition whenever it is to be found, in the lives of those around us, in sudden, strong ebullitions [outbursts or manifestations] of personal piety and the frames of mind such ebullitions evince, in the fixed and ordered solemnities of rites and liturgies, and again in the atmosphere that clings to old religious monuments and buildings, to temples and to churches. If we do so we shall find we are dealing with something for which there is only one appropriate expression, "*mysterium tremendum*." The feeling of it may at times come sweeping like a gentle tide, pervading the mind with a tranquil mood of deepest worship. It may pass over into a more set and lasting attitude of the soul, continuing, as it were, thrillingly vibrant and resonant, until at last it dies away and the soul resumes its "profane," nonreligious mood of everyday experience. It may burst in sudden eruption up from the depth of the soul with spasms and convulsions, or lead to the strangest excitements, to intoxicated frenzy, to transport, and to ecstasy. It has its wild and demonic forms and can sink to almost grisly horror and shuddering. It has its crude barbaric antecedents and early manifestations, and again it may be developed into something beautiful and pure and glorious. It may become the hushed, trembling, and speechless humility of the creature in the presence of—whom or what? In the presence of that which is a mystery inexpressible and above all creatures.

Although one confronts that which is finally a mystery, Otto suggests that what is encountered here is a distinctively positive reality, even if mystery is normally understood to carry negative connotations.

> It is again evident at once that here too our attempted formulation by means of a concept is once more a merely negative one. Conceptually *mysterium* denotes merely that which

---

[1] Rudolf Otto, *The Idea of the Holy* (Oxford: Oxford University Press, 1923), *passim*. Reprinted by permission. Otto's work is a thorough investigation of the phenomenon of "numinous" encounters with the Divine.

is hidden and esoteric, that which is beyond conception or understanding, extraordinary and unfamiliar. The term does not define the object more positively in its qualitative character. But though what is enunciated in the word is negative, what is meant is something absolutely and intensely positive.[2]

As Otto indicates, such an encounter may have many different aspects—it may take place in a dynamic moment or tranquil mood or in any number of other forms. Yet the experience itself, whatever its occasion or form, leaves one with a conviction of the reality and presence of the *mysterium tremendum*—the transcendent, the Divine, God.

Otto's suggestive analysis and description of the mystery that lies at the core of all religion helps to conceptualize this central element in religion. But conceptual descriptions, as important as they may be, are only part of such an experience. Whatever its occasion or form, such an experience demands not only recognition but also response—whether positive or negative, expressible or inexpressible. The following illustrations show how people from differing religious traditions have responded to and described this experience.

A JEWISH ENCOUNTER

The first illustration comes from Jewish literature. The Hebrew prophet Isaiah describes the encounter with the *mysterium tremendum* (God), which began and empowered his prophetic career.

> In the year that King Uzziah died I saw the Lord sitting upon a throne, high and lofty; and the hem of his robe filled the temple. Seraphim were in attention above him; each had six wings: with two they covered their faces, and with two they covered their feet, and with two they flew. And one called to another and said:
>
> Holy, holy, holy is the Lord of hosts;
> the whole earth is full of his glory.
>
> And the foundations of the thresholds shook at the voice of those who called, and the house filled with smoke. And I said: Woe is me! I am lost, for I am a man of unclean lips, and I live among a people of unclean lips; for my eyes have seen the King, the Lord of hosts!
>   Then one of the seraphim flew to me, holding a live coal that had been taken from the altar with a pair of tongs. The seraph touched my mouth with it and said: Now that this has touched your lips; your guilt has departed and your sin is blotted out. And I heard the voice of the Lord saying, "Whom shall I send, and who will go for us?" And I said, "Here I am! Send me." (Isaiah 6:1–8, NRSV)

CHINESE MYSTERIES

The second example is taken from Chinese literature and art. Lao-Tzu filled the *Tao Te Ching* with pithy images suggesting how life should properly be lived (see Unit 12). Behind these images is an acute consciousness of the *Holy*, the mystery that underlies life.

[2] Ibid., pp. 12–13.

In Chinese culture the mystery present in all of the universe is symbolized by the word *Tao*. Lao-Tzu often used the symbol in unusual ways to point beyond to the hidden mystery of the Divine found in ordinary life.

> When the highest type of men hear the Tao (truth),
>   They practice it diligently.
> When the mediocre type hear the Tao,
>   They seem to be aware and yet unaware of it.
> When the lowest type hear the Tao,
>   They break into loud laughter,—
> If it were not laughed at, it would not be Tao.
>
> Therefore there is the established saying:
>   "Who understands Tao seems dull of comprehension;
>   Who is advanced in Tao seems to slip backwards;
>   Who moves on the even Tao (Path) seems to go up and down."
>
> Superior virtue appears like a hollow (valley);
> Sheer white appears like tarnished;
> Great character appears like insufficient;
> Solid character appears like infirm;
> Pure worth appears like contaminated.
>   Great space has no corners;
>   Great talent takes long to mature;
>   Great music is faintly heard;
>   Great Form has no contour;
>   And Tao is hidden without a name.
> It is this Tao that is adept at lending [its power] and bringing fulfillment.[3]

Expressions of the Divine Mystery are certainly not limited to poetry or prose. Traditional Chinese art radiates an awareness of the Divine—the *Tao*. In the following passage, Otto Fischer describes this element as it is expressed in Chinese paintings (see Figure 7.1):

> The spectator who, as it were, immerses himself in them feels behind these waters and clouds and mountains the mysterious breath of the primeval Tao, the pulse of innermost being. Many a mystery lies half-concealed and half-revealed in these pictures. They contain the knowledge of the "nothingness" and the "void," of the "Tao" of heaven and earth, which is also the Tao of the human heart. And so, despite their perpetual agitation, they seem as remotely distant and as profoundly calm as though they drew secret breath at the bottom of the sea.[4]

A HINDU EXPRESSION

The third and final example is drawn from the Hindu classic *The Bhagavad-Gita*. In the philosophic tradition of Hindu holy men, the Divine is beyond description and grasp since any human attempt to express it is necessarily a part of the illusory world (see Unit 10).

---

[3] Lin Yutang, ed., *The Wisdom of China and India*, (New York: Random House, 1942), p. 606. Copyright 1942 and renewed 1970 by Random House, Inc. Reprinted by permission of the publisher.

[4] As quoted in Otto, *The Idea of the Holy*, p. 67.

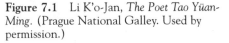

Figure 7.1   Li K'o-Jan, *The Poet Tao Yüan-Ming.* (Prague National Galley. Used by permission.)

For the majority of Hindus, however, the Divine is often expressed through an array of gods and goddesses. Each Divine Being may have many representatives or embodiments, all expressing the majesty and wonder of the *mysterium tremendum*. In the passage that follows, Krishna, a popular embodiment of one of the three great gods of Hinduism, has been asked by his disciple Arjuna to reveal himself in all his glory. Krishna grants the request, suggesting that this is indeed a very unusual gift, withheld even from the other gods.

> Then, O king, when he had spoken these words, Sri Krishna, Master of all yogis, revealed to Arjuna his transcendent, divine Form, speaking from innumerable mouths, seeing with a myriad eyes, of many marvellous aspects, adorned with countless divine ornaments, brandishing all kinds of heavenly weapons, wearing celestial garlands and the raiment of paradise, anointed with perfumes of heavenly fragrance, full of revelations, resplendent, boundless, of ubiquitous everywhere present regard.
>
> Suppose a thousand suns should rise together into the sky: such is the glory of the Shape of Infinite God.
>
> Then the son of Pandu beheld the entire universe, in all its multitudinous diversity, lodged as one being within the body of the God of gods.

Then was Arjuna, that lord of mighty riches, overcome with wonder. His hair stood erect. He bowed low before God in adoration, and clasped his hands, and spoke:

"Ah, my God, I see all gods within your body;
Each in his degree, the multitude of creatures;
See Lord Brahma throned upon the lotus;
See all the sages, and the holy serpents.
Universal Form, I see you without limit,
Infinite of arms, eyes, mouths and bellies—
See, and find no end, midst, or beginning.

Crowned with diadems, you wield the mace and discus,
Shining every way—the eyes shrink from your splendour
Brilliant like the sun: like fire, blazing, boundless.

You are all we know, supreme, beyond man's measure,
This world's sure-set plinth and refuge never shaken,
Guardian of eternal law, life's Soul undying.
Birthless, deathless; yours the strength titanic,
Million-armed, the sun and moon your eyeballs,
Fiery-faced, you blast the world to ashes,

Fill the sky's four corners, span the chasm
Sundering heaven from earth. Superb and awful
Is your Form that makes the three worlds tremble.

Into you, the companies of devas [gods]
Enter with clasped hands, in dread and wonder.
Crying 'Peace,' the Rishis and the Siddhas [disciples]
Sing your praise with hymns of adoration. . . ."[5]

Arjuna, attempting here to express the immensity of this confrontation with the Divine, clearly can only point to the fact that no description will be adequate. The power, majesty, and wonder of the God is simply overwhelming and beyond expression.

In each of these examples, drawn as they are from different religious traditions with their distinct cultural forms, the presence and experience of the *mysterium tremendum* is expressed. However, as Otto points out, the best and most poignant descriptions never really do justice to the inexpressible awe that humans, aware of their finitude, feel before God.

❖❖❖

Reflecting on your own life, have you had experiences or encounters with "the Holy?" If so, what description could you give of the experience?

Can common life experiences, as well as the "extraordinary" ones such as described in this unit, be the locus of an encounter with the Divine?

Is consciousness of the numinous a necessary experience for valid religious encounter, as Otto appears to assume?

---

[5] Swami Prabhavananda and Christopher Isherwood, trans., *The Song of God: Bhagavad-Gita* (Hollywood, CA: Vedanta Press, 1951), pp. 91–97. Used by the permission of the Vedanta Society of Southern California.

Unit 39   THE DIVINE EXPRESSED IN RELIGIOUS TEXTS

In the preceding unit, Rudolf Otto's characterization of the human encounter with the Divine as being a feeling of awe and mystery also suggests such experiences may be recurring, but often momentary, events in human life. Once statements about the Divine are given textual or written expression, however, they take on an existence that may be descriptive of momentary human experiences but is independent of those experiences. As Paul Ricoeur and other contemporary philosophers have noted, the text takes on a life of its own. As such it projects a reality (which Ricoeur calls "the world of the text") *ahead* of its readers or users that they are invited to enter (for example, many texts concerning the Divine are primarily used for liturgical or cultic purposes). Thus textual statements that originally expressed thoughts and feelings about the Divine drawn from particular experiences become the basis for an unending human dialogue with those experiences. As textual materials they become both guides and criteria for later thoughts, feelings, and experiences that humans have relating to the Divine—to their ultimate concern.

In this unit, a number of textually expressed ways of conceiving of God are drawn from different cultures, different religious traditions, and different historical periods. There is some overlap: The passages from the Jewish Scriptures can also illustrate important dimensions of Christian and Islamic understanding, since Christians and Muslims understand the God of the Jewish Scriptures to be their God, too.

From most of the traditions represented in this unit, other and differently expressed statements about the nature and reality of God could be found. There are other traditions, too, from which significant statements might have been taken. The statements included resemble one another in some ways; they also differ rather dramatically. Some are primarily conceptual philosophical expressions; others are more direct, poetic statements growing out of practical life and the experience of worship. But it would be difficult and perhaps false to say that even the most abstractly expressed textual statement about God—for instance, Aristotle's—did not grow out of personal experience and deep or intense concern.

The unit is long and contains a number of texts that lend themselves to analysis and discussion. You may be better prepared to consider these examples if you will write out your own understanding of the Divine before you begin examining these expressions. As you read, the following questions may also help you analyze and interpret the examples:

◆◆◆

How do you respond to the different views of God presented here?

Which of the views, if any, are most like ways you have heard God spoken of?

How do they differ from, and agree with, each other?

◆◆◆

GOD IN THE JEWISH SCRIPTURES

In the Hebrew Scriptures (sometimes referred to by Christians as the Old Testament), repeated emphasis is placed on the perception or conception that the Divine, that is, God, is personal in character. Further, this God is continually active and involved in the physical historical world both as creator and sustainer and as such exhibits continuing personal concern for the world and its creatures. Though writers of scripture suggest that this God is immanently present in the universe, God is also transcendent, not limited by but indeed "beyond" the universe. Following are three examples of Jewish conceptions of the Divine. The first is from the *Torah* (religious law or teachings), the revered portion of the Jewish Scripture. The second two are from prophets, whose teachings have shaped the theology of Judaism up to the present day.

> You are the people whom the Lord brought out of Egypt . . . and took for his own possession, as you are to this day. . . . Be careful not to forget the covenant which the Lord your God made with you, and do not make yourself a carved figure of anything which the Lord your God has forbidden. For the Lord your God is a devouring fire, a jealous God. . . . When you have children and grandchildren and grow old in the land, if you then fall into the degrading practice of making any kind of carved figure, doing what is wrong in the eyes of the Lord your God and provoking him to anger . . . the Lord will disperse you among the peoples, and you will be left few in number among the nations to which the Lord will lead you. But if from there you seek the Lord your God, you will find him. . . . When you are in distress and all these things come upon you, you will in days to come turn back to the Lord your God and obey Him. The Lord your God is a merciful god; he will never fail you, nor destroy you, nor will he forget the covenant guaranteed by oath with your forefathers. (Deuteronomy 4:20–32, NEB)

> Do you not know, have you not heard, were you not told long ago, have you not
> perceived ever since the world began, that God sits throned on the vaulted roof of earth,
>   whose inhabitants are like grasshoppers?
>
>   He stretches out the skies like a curtain
>   He spreads them out like a tent to live in, . . .
> Lift up your eyes to the heavens; consider who created it all, led out their host one by
> one and called them all by their names;
>   through his great might, his might and power,
>   not one is missing. . . .
> Do you not know, have you not heard?
> The Lord, the everlasting God, creator of the wide world,
>   grows neither weary nor faint;
>   no man can fathom his understanding.
> He gives vigour to the weary,
>   new strength to the exhausted.
>
> (Isaiah 40:21–29 NEB)

> What shall I bring when I approach the Lord?
> How shall I stoop before God on high?
> Am I to approach him with whole-offerings or yearling calves?
>   Will the Lord accept thousands of rams
>   or ten thousand rivers of oil?
>   Shall I offer my eldest son for my own wrongdoing,

> my children for my own sin?
> God has told you what is good;
>> and what is it that the Lord asks of you?
>> Only to act justly, to love loyalty,
>> to walk wisely before your God.
>
>   (Micah 6:6–8 NEB)

ARISTOTLE: GOD AS PURE BEING, THE UNMOVED MOVER

The view of God held by Aristotle, a Greek philosopher of the fourth century B.C.E., greatly influenced later Western thought. Joined or fused with the Jewish view of God as the active Creator, it influenced Jewish, Muslim, and Christian thought.

Aristotle's beginning point is with the world of nature that we observe. He sees natural entities—organisms—as having an innate tendency to develop. An acorn has within itself an innate tendency to grow into a fully developed oak tree, provided its environment is favorable. A newborn human baby will naturally develop into a full-grown human being, capable of self-sustaining life and rational activities. Even the stars and planets seem to move in accordance with a law of their being.

Aristotle was convinced that the motion and development characteristic of things we observe must have an ultimate source, or cause. This first cause of motion must be perfect and complete in every way. It must not be subject to change or development, for otherwise its own development would need an explanation that goes beyond it. He calls this perfect source of motion and development for the whole universe God, or the *Unmoved Mover*. For Aristotle, God does not create the world; the world is uncreated and exists eternally. God is the source of motion and development in the world, the perfect reality that exists as an object of love and desire, the standard of absolute perfection for all other things.

> The first mover, then, exists of necessity; and insofar as it exists by necessity, its mode of being is good, and it is in this sense a first principle. For the necessary has all these senses—that which is necessary perforce because it is contrary to the natural impulse, that without which the good is impossible, and that which cannot be otherwise but can exist only in a single way.
>
> On such a principle, then, depends the heavens and the world of nature. And it is a life such as the best which we enjoy, and enjoy for but a short time (for it is ever in this state, which we cannot be), since its actuality is also pleasure. (And for this reason are waking, perception, and thinking most pleasant, and hopes and memories are so on account of these.)

◆◆◆

What is God's life, his activity, like, according to Aristotle?

◆◆◆

And thinking in itself deals with that which is best in itself, and that which is thinking in the fullest sense with that which is best in the fullest sense. And thought thinks on itself because it shares the nature of the object of thought; for it becomes an object of thought in coming into contact with and thinking its objects, so that thought and object of thought are the same. For that which is capable of receiving the object of thought, i.e., the essence, is thought. But it is active when it possesses this object. Therefore, the possession rather than the receptivity is the divine element which thought seems to contain, and the act of contemplation is what is most pleasant and best. If then, God is always in that good state in which we sometimes are, this compels our wonder; and if in a better this compels it yet more. And God is in a better state. And life also belongs to God; for the actuality of thought is life, and God is that actuality; and God's self-dependent actuality is life most good and eternal.

We say therefore that God is a living being, eternal, and most good, so that life and duration continuous and eternal belongs to God; for this is God.[6]

Since, according to Aristotle, to know the world would mean to know change, and thus to change in his knowledge, God does not know the world: He knows only his own unchanging mind, yet all the changing reality humans experience depends on God.

SAINT THOMAS AQUINAS: GOD AS HE WHO IS

Thomas Aquinas, a principal leader among theologians and philosophers of medieval Christianity, drew on Christian Scriptures, tradition, and the philosophical reflections of Christian thinkers like Saint Augustine. To these he joined Aristotelian philosophy in formulating his statements about the nature and reality of God.

This name HE WHO IS, is most properly applied to God, for three reasons:

First, because of its signification. For it does not signify form, but simply existence itself. Hence since the existence of God is His essence itself, which can be said of no other (Q. III, A, 4), it is clear that among other names this one specially denominates God, for everything is denominated by its form.

Secondly, on account of its universality. For all other names are either less universal, or if convertible with it, add something above it at least in idea; hence in a certain way they inform and determine it. Now our intellect cannot know the essence of God itself in this life, as it is in itself, but whatever mode it applies in determining what it understands about God, it falls short of the mode of what God is in Himself. Therefore the less determinate the names are, and the more universal and absolute they are, the more properly are they applied to God. Hence Damascene says (de. Fid. Orth. i.) that, HE WHO IS, is the principal of all names applied to God; for comprehending all in itself, it contains existence itself as an infinite and indeterminate sea of substance. Now by any other name some mode of substance is determined, whereas this name, HE WHO IS, determines no mode of being but is determinate to all; and therefore it denominates the infinite ocean of substance.

Thirdly, from its consignification, for it signifies present existence; and this above all properly applies to God, whose existence knows not past or future, as Augustine says (De Trin.v.)[7]

THE DIVINE IN NAVAJO LIFE

The Navajo are one of the larger groups of early inhabitants of the North American continent still living in part of their original region, the southwestern United States. They retain many elements of their ancient culture, including religious traditions. Those who

---

[6] Aristotle, *Metaphysics*, Book 12, ch. 7, 1072b; from The Oxford Translations of Aristotle, Vol. 3, 2nd ed., trans. W. D. Ross, (Oxford: Oxford University Press, 1928).

[7] Thomas Aquinas, *Summa Theologica*, trans., Fathers of the English Dominican Provinces (London: Burns, Oates & Washbourne, 1920), Part 1, QQI-XXXVI (abridged).

have not been converted to Christianity, brought by the Europeans, remain polytheistic in their religious beliefs.

Navajo conceptions of the Divine may seem strange to those not familiar with polytheistic religions. If you are acquainted with the gods and goddesses of the ancient Greeks or with the stories of creation that appear in the early Babylonian or Japanese religions, you may notice similarities to Navajo beliefs. (The stories of the Navajo Holy People have primarily been preserved as an oral tradition passed on through the generations. Recently, students of Navajo life have incorporated many features of this oral tradition in textual descriptions of their beliefs.)

> The universe of The People contains two classes of personal forces. There are the Earth Surface People, living and dead; these are ordinary human beings. Then there are the Holy People. They are not "holy" in the sense of possessing moral sanctity, for often their deeds have a very different odor. They are "holy" in the meaning of "powerful and mysterious," of belonging to the sacred as opposed to the profane world. They travel about on sunbeams, on the rainbow, on the lightnings. They have great powers to aid or to harm Earth Surface People. But it is better not to call them gods because the word "god" has so many connotations which are inappropriate. The Holy People are not portrayed as all-knowing or even as all-powerful. They certainly are not depicted as wholly good. While they are supplicated and propitiated, they may also be coerced. Probably coercion is indeed the dominant note. In general, the relationship between them and the Earth Surface People is very different from what Christians think of as the connection between God and man.
>
> As described in the Navaho origin myth, the Holy People lived first below the surface of the earth. They moved from one lower world to another because of witchcraft practiced by one of them. In the last of the twelve lower worlds the sexes were separated because of a quarrel, and monsters were born from the female Holy People. Finally a great flood drove the Holy People to ascend to the present world through a reed. Natural objects were created. Then came the first death among the Holy People. About this time too, Changing Woman, the principal figure among them, was created. After she reached puberty, she was magically impregnated by the rays of the Sun and by water from a waterfall, and bore twin sons. These Hero Twins journeyed to the house of their father, the Sun, encountering many adventures and slaying most of the monsters. . . .
>
> The Hero Twins—Monster Slayer and Child of the Water (sometimes called Reared-within-the-Earth and Changing Grandchild)—are invoked in almost every Navaho ceremonial. Their adventures establish many of the Navaho ideals for young manhood. They serve especially as models of conduct in war and can almost be called the Navaho war gods. The Hero Twins slew most of the monsters, but they did not kill all of these potential enemies of mankind. Hunger, Poverty, Old Age, and Dirt survived, for they proved to have a place in human life. The exploits of the Twins, as well as those of other Holy People, define many features of the Navaho landscape as holy places. The lava fields, which are so conspicuous in the Navaho country, are the dried blood of the slain monsters.
>
> Changing Woman, the Sun, and the Hero Twins are four supernatural beings who seem to bulk largest in the religious thought and lore of The People. In the background are First Man and First Woman, who were transformed from two ears of white and yellow corn, and others prominent in the stories of life in the lower worlds. Most of The People believe that First Man created the universe, but another version of the incident, possibly due to Christian influence, pictures a being called *be'gochidi* as the creator of the world. . . .
>
> But of these beings and powers, of whom we have mentioned only a few, Changing Woman alone is consistently well-wishing to the Earth Surface People. The other beings are undependable, even though they may have given mankind many of their prized pos-

sessions. The Sun and the Moon demand a human life each day: the Hero Twins are often pitiless; First Man is a witch; Coyote is a trickster.[8]

ŚANKARA: BRAHMAN, THE ONE ETERNAL SELF

Śankara, a Hindu philosopher who lived from approximately 788 to 820, describes God—Brahman—as the *One Reality*—"One without a second." For Śankara Brahman (See Unit 10) is that source of the changing world of illusion, whose reality, in contrast to the One Reality, is only apparent or illusory, a product of nescience, a sort of false or mistaken knowledge that is really ignorance.

> Brahman as the eternal subject (*pratyagâtman*, the inward Self) is never an object, and . . . the distinction of objects known, knowers, acts of knowledge, etc. . . . is fictitiously created by Nescience.
>
> Of Brahman . . . the two following passages [from the *Upanishads*] declare that it is incapable of receiving any accretion and is eternally pure, "He is the one God, hidden in all beings, all-pervading, the Self within all beings, watching over all works, dwelling in all beings, the witness, the perceiver, the only one; free from qualities" and "He pervaded all, bright, incorporeal, scatheless, without muscles, pure, untouched by evil.". . .
>
> The Self is not to be known as manifold, qualified by the universe of effects; you are rather to dissolve by true knowledge the universe of effects, which is mere product of Nescience, and to know that one Self, which is the general abode, as uniform.[9]

JESUS: GOD AS LOVING PARENT

Jesus of Nazareth, out of whose teaching, example, and lifestyle arose Christianity, most often presented God as a loving parent. The following quotations from the New Testament exhibit this perspective.

> You have learned that they were told, "Love your neighbor, hate your enemy." But what I tell you is this: Love your enemies and pray for your persecutors: only so can you be children of your heavenly Father, who makes his sun rise on good and bad alike, and sends the rain on the honest and the dishonest. If you love only those who love you, what reward can you expect? Surely the tax-gatherers do as much as that. And if you greet only your brothers, what is there extraordinary about that? Even the heathen do as much. There must be no limit to your goodness, as your heavenly Father's goodness knows no bounds. . . . (Matthew 5:43–48, NEB)
>
> For if you forgive others the wrongs they have done, your heavenly Father will also forgive you; but if you do not forgive others, then the wrongs you have done will not be forgiven by your Father. . . . (Matthew 6:14–15, NEB)
>
> Surely life is more than food, the body more than clothes. Look at the birds of the air; they do not sow and reap and store in barns, yet your heavenly Father feeds them. You are

---

[8] Reprinted by permission of the publisher from THE NAVAHO by Clyde Kluckholm, Cambridge, MA: Harvard University Press, Copyright © 1974 by Florence Kluckholm Taylor and Dorothea Leighton.

[9] F. Max Müller, ed., *The Sacred Books of the East*, trans. George Shebaut (Oxford: Clarendon Press, 1890), p. 32.

worth more than the birds! Is there a man of you who by anxious thought can add a foot to his height? And why be anxious about clothes? Consider how the lilies grow in the fields; they do not work, they do not spin; and yet, I tell you, even Solomon in all his splendor was not attired like one of these. But if that is how God clothes the grass in the fields, which is there today and tomorrow is thrown on the stove, will he not all the more clothe you? How little faith you have! No, do not ask anxiously, "What are we to eat? What are we to drink? What shall we wear?" (Matthew 6:26–32, NEB)

EMPTINESS (*SHUNYATA*): THE VOID IN BUDDHISM

Some forms of Buddhism are often described as being atheistic since beliefs about a God or gods are not given prominent attention or are looked on as idle speculation. But students of Buddhism have noted that even in so-called atheistic forms of Buddhism, there are teachings that resemble ideas about the Divine in other religious traditions. One such Buddhist concept is that of "the Void."

> The Buddhist Void is far from being a nihilistic doctrine. The Void is not nothingness or annihilation but the very source of all life. In speaking of this theory as taught in the Buddhism of China and Japan (where it has influenced the creation of a very subtle aesthetics...), Hajime Nakamura, the Japanese Buddhist scholar, says:
> "Voidness . . . is . . . that which stands right in the middle between affirmation and negation, existence and nonexistence. . . . The void is all-inclusive; having no opposite, there is nothing which it excludes or opposes. It is living void, because all forms come out of it, and whoever realizes the void is filled with life and power and the . . . love of all beings."
> This subtle doctrine is, by its very nature—expressed in the term "Void" itself—not a matter that readily lends itself to brief or simple exposition. Perhaps, however, modern science can again be brought to our aid if we remind ourselves that in this century the nonmaterial nature of the universe has been widely accepted since Eddington in *The Nature of the Physical World* presented his two famous tables: one a seemingly solid "symbol," the other a mysteriously balanced group of invisible energies and forces. Still, though accepted as scientific fact, such knowledge as the nonsubstantiality of substance plays little part in the living of our everyday lives or the thinking of our everyday thoughts. The early Buddhists, being Indians, perhaps found less difficulty than Westerners in acceptance of the world as maya, or a kind of magical show in which what is seen is both true and not true. Buddhism would say this is not to argue that what is seen is nonexistent, but only that we take it for what it essentially is not.[10]

❖❖❖

What elements of your own description of God were captured in these descriptions? Were there different insights offered that needed to be included in your description? If so, what were they?

Among the descriptions of the Divine listed above which do you find most familiar? least familiar? most appealing? least appealing?

Contrast Aquinas' description with that of "the Void." Can you identify elements in each that may be necessary for a full understanding of the Divine?

[10] Nancy Ross Wilson, *Three Ways of Asian Wisdom* (New York: Simon & Schuster, 1968), pp. 121–122.

Unit 40   Conceptual Expressions of the Divine

The preceding two units examine many ways the Divine has been conceived and expressed throughout history. When these examples and the many others that could be discussed are compared, they fall into distinctive patterns that may help in understanding the relationship of differing conceptions of God. The following chart incorporates the most commonly used terms to reference concepts of the Divine and may be useful for considering them.

A Framework for Conceptualizing Images and Concepts of the Divine

A *DEISTIC VIEWS*	C *TRANSCENDENT-IMMANENT VIEWS*	B *PANTHEISTIC VIEWS*
1. *Polytheistic deism:* There are many divine beings. They *belong* to the natural order.		3. *Dualistic pantheism:* The natural order is a manifestation or superficial appearance of the One Divine Reality.
	5. There is One Divine Being, who both transcends the natural order as its Creator, or source, and is present and active in it.	
2. *Dualistic deism:* There is One Divine Being transcending the natural order as its Creator, or source, with a relative separation between the Divine and the natural.		4. *Materialism:* The basic physical components (matter, energy, etc.) of the natural order are what is ultimately real.

DEISTIC POSITIONS

In deistic positions, God or the gods are viewed as individual beings. In *polytheistic deism*, the gods are beings, usually possessing extraordinary powers, within the universe. They may create and maintain parts of it. They may come into being, that is, may themselves be created or born. Some of them may die; others may be immortal. Polytheistic deism is found in many religious traditions, including the following: popular Hinduism, popular Taoism, the Babylonian and Japanese creation stories (see Unit 80), and the Navajo religion (see Unit 39). Ordinarily in polytheistic religions, some divine beings are male, others female; some are animals; some are other natural forms such as the sun and moon or the wind.

In *dualistic deism*, the Divine and the world are relatively separate from each other, though the Divine is ultimately the creator, or in some manner the source or sustainer, of the universe. Aristotle's concept of God, discussed in the previous unit, is an expression of dualistic deism. For Aristotle, God does not create the universe, but it is totally dependent on God. A Christian form of dualistic deism became very influential in seventeenth- and eighteenth-century Europe in response to the highly successful scientific work of Isaac Newton. According to this version of deism, God created the universe and allows it to operate in accordance with the laws of nature God has established for it. God does not intervene in the natural order by means of miracles or a direct presence, but does guarantee reward for the good and punishment for the evil in a future life. Many outstanding intellectual figures of eighteenth-century Europe and North America accepted this form of deism, among them Thomas Jefferson, author of the Declaration of Independence and third president of the United States.

Dualistic deism is always *monotheistic*. Many forms of dualistic deism have spoken of the Divine in masculine terms, but this probably was the result of cultural influences since in the strict sense the Divine would be neither male nor female.

PANTHEISTIC POSITIONS

According to pantheistic positions, the Divine is the *one and only* reality. For *dualistic pantheism*, everything is a manifestation of the Divine, but moral, religious, and philosophical discipline and insight are required before this can be apprehended by individuals (in the form of enlightenment). For philosophical Hinduism, Brahman is the sole reality. The many gods of Hinduism are merely manifestations of the one Divine Being, which is neither male nor female. The texts in the previous unit from Śankara and Nakamura, concerning the concept of the Void in Buddhism, illustrate this position. It is also exemplified in philosophical Taoism and in the classical Greco-Roman philosophical school known as Stoicism, according to which the Divine Reason or Fire is the source and inner reality of all things.

According to *materialistic pantheism* (sometimes called scientific or philosophical materialism or naturalism), only the physical universe—whether conceived of as matter, mass, or energy—is real. The Greco-Roman school of philosophy known as Epicureanism (founded by Epicurus, 341–270 B.C.E.), based on the conception of the nature of reality of the earlier Greek philosopher Democritus (460–360 B.C.E.), held that all reality is composed of atoms moving in space. The atoms are eternal. They join by chance collisions to form objects, which endure only for a time; then their atoms separate to become temporary components of other objects. The human soul is composed of atoms and is not immortal. Even the gods are composed of atoms and endure only for a time. Epicureanism was powerfully expressed in the Latin poem *On the Nature of Things* by Lucretius (d. 54 B.C.E.). During the nineteenth and twentieth centuries, scientific materialism was widely accepted by educated Europeans. Marxism is one of its many transformations.

TRANSCENDENT-IMMANENT POSITIONS

According to *transcendent-immanent* positions, God is viewed as an individual being both beyond and within the world. This form of theism is found preeminently in Judaism and Christianity and in some schools of philosophical thought. It is monotheistic. Although culturally it has spoken of God primarily in masculine terms, it generally holds that God is neither male nor female but is the ground, or creator, of sexuality and may at times be symbolized by either, or by neither, masculine or feminine characterizations. (Judaism's long opposition to the polytheistic fertility cults of its neighbors in Palestine, which usually had both a male and a female deity who were consorts, may account for the heavily patriarchal language used to describe God in the Jewish scriptures.) According to transcendent-immanent positions,

1. God is understood to be the Creator or Source of the created world who transcends it in an ultimate way (as seen in the passage from Aquinas in Unit 39). If this had been the only characterization of God by Aquinas, the Divine would have been understood in a dualistic pantheistic sense.
2. According to transcendent-immanent positions, however, God in one aspect is fully present and manifest in the created world. For Judaism, God's wisdom is fully expressed in the *Torah*, the same wisdom, made explicit, that was or is expressed in the creation and ordering of the created realm. For Christianity, God's wisdom (the second Person of the Trinity, the Wisdom of God in accordance with which the world was and is created) is fully present in the human Jesus. (See the *New Testament*, Gospel of John, Chapter 1.)
3. In transcendent-immanent views the Divine is also continuously active in the created world. The Voice or Spirit of God in Judaism makes God's will known to the prophets and to others. For Christians, God as the Holy Spirit (not another Divine Being, but a genuine aspect of the one God) is understood to be present and active in the world, especially within the Christian community, making God's power and purposes known and effective. Various philosophical schools, including Platonism and Neoplatonism and the twentieth-century philosopher A. N. Whitehead's process philosophy, approximate this view, though Neoplatonism is perhaps closer in some ways to dualistic pantheism.

The preceding chart and discussion are, to some extent, oversimplification. The native Japanese religious tradition, Shinto, for instance, can be claimed to belong to the polytheistic deistic type. But with its emphasis on the sacredness and interrelatedness of *all* beings, and with the many centuries of Shinto traditions blending with those of Buddhism and Taoism and even Christianity, it might be called pantheistic or it may be said not to "fit" the chart at all. Nevertheless, the chart may prove useful in considering both the texts concerning the Divine given in Unit 39 and earlier and later discussions of the Divine—for instance in the chapter on religious traditions (Chapter 2).

Unit 41   Spirit

The human experience of a transcendent reality is not easily expressed, as noted in other units. It may take many forms, and any conceptualization of it is inadequate and circumscribed by the limitations of human existence and language. Typologies, analogies, and metaphors that attempt to express personal awareness of an encounter with a transcendent reality often do not retain the dynamic vitality of these experiences.

However, most human cultures have attempted to conceptualize these dynamic, transient elements. In Western societies the word *spirit* has been traditionally used to refer to this reality. Drawn from the Latin *spiritus*, which originally referred to human breath, it designates the vitality empowering and activating all of life. The Hindu Sanskrit word *atman*, the Hebrew *ruah*, and the Greek πνευμα carried similar meanings. In early civilizations breath was understood to be the essential element of life; when breath was no longer present, life ceased. One's spirit, breath, was the activator of life.

The word *spirit* has through the centuries taken on other meanings. When we speak of someone's spirit we may be speaking of vigor or zest. For example, if we ask, "Will you do it?" and the reply is "I will try!" we might well respond, "That's the *spirit!*" We are referring to the vitality, the energetic action, or strong intent that motivates and empowers someone. In a similar way, spirit has sometimes come to include such nonmaterial aspects of human experience as awareness, intellect, understanding, judgment, and will, although the emphasis has remained on its designation of the vital, empowering reality of life.

When used in connection with the Divine, *spirit* usually refers to the divine agency that enlivens or empowers life itself. As such it is seen as the power or force, the vitality that is at the center of all existence. This *Divine Spirit* also often serves as the dynamic interconnection between the transcendent realities of life and the finite world in which these experiences take place.

Whether *spirit* is used to refer to a divine presence or to the life force present in humanity and in the natural world (neither of the meanings necessarily excludes the other), it points to that which gives vitality or power to life. This is its primary meaning. As the following examples suggest, however, the word *spirit* carries many additional nuances.

ANCIENT AND PRELITERATE THOUGHT

Each culture seeks to express the reality of spiritual encounter from its own perspective and experience. Ancient societies, and many present-day societies that do not depend extensively on writing for communication, live in a world alive, a world in which all objects, events, and people have inherent power. The inner mysterious power that impels, dominates, and directs the thought and action of a person is his or her *spirit*. The spirit is understood to transcend the physical body and may come to us from outside ourselves. It may be either good or evil, as in many of these societies gods may be either good or evil. Chinua Achebe, writing about the African Igbo people in his novel *Things Fall Apart*, captures this sense of personal spiritual reality: Any reader of the novel is well acquainted with the *chi*, or personal god, of each character in the story.[11]

Since spirits often come from without, they are not understood to be physically limited and are seen as supernatural and often divine. Because for these societies spirits enliven every aspect of nature, all reality is dependent on their power and influence. The particular form of such "spirit power" varies greatly from culture to culture, but its presence is seldom doubted. In its varied forms, *spirit* is the vitality empowering and activating all of life.

JAPANESE PATTERNS

The early views of spirit carry over into most contemporary religions in some form. Shinto, the native Japanese religion grounded in nature and ancestor worship, continues to focus all understanding of life on the presence and role of spirits, known as *kami*.

[11] Chinua Achebe, *Things Fall Apart* (Greenwich, CT: Fawcett, 1959).

Without a concept of a particular deity or Divine Being, all reality is thought to be spiritual and therefore spirit driven. Generally understood as benevolent, these spirits are seen by the Japanese as protective, gracious, and helpful. The *kami* assure harmony and blessings in life. Sokyo Ono describes the general pattern:

> Among the objects or phenomena designated from ancient times as kami are the qualities of growth, fertility, and production; natural phenomena, such as wind and thunder; natural objects, such as the sun, mountains, rivers, trees and rocks; some animals; and ancestral spirits. In the last-named category are the spirits of the Imperial ancestors, the ancestors of noble families, and in a sense all ancestral spirits. Also regarded as kami are the guardian spirits of the land, occupations, and skills; the spirits of national heroes, men of outstanding deeds or virtues, and those who have contributed to civilization, culture, and human welfare; those who have died for the state or the community; and the pitiable dead. Not only spirits superior to man, but even some that are regarded as pitiable and weak have nonetheless been considered to be kami.
>
> It is true that in many instances there are kami which apparently cannot be distinguished from the deities or spirits of animism or animatism, but in modern Shinto all kami are conceived in a refined sense to be spirits with nobility and authority. The kami-concept today includes the idea of justice, order, and divine favor (blessing), and implies the basic principle that the kami function harmoniously in cooperation with one another and rejoice in the evidence of harmony and cooperation in this world.[12]

JEWISH CONCEPTS

Among Jews the image of breath and wind are prominent metaphors for *spirit*. Using the metaphor of breath, the Hebrew tradition vividly expresses this interconnection:

> Then the Lord God formed man from dust from the ground, and breathed into his nostrils the breath of life, and man became a living being. (Genesis 2:7, RSV)

Spirit, in this passage, enters the body and imparts identity and the capacity to act. In this tradition, the term *spirit* also signifies the "soul" or "heart" of a human, that is, something that gives people their identity and psychic strength. Even though Judaism is a monotheistic faith, its earliest beliefs allowed for supernatural beings (angels and devils), which, although ultimately subservient to God, were influential in human life. Jewish thinkers refined and altered these elemental understandings of spirit by elaborating their conception of the Lord's spirit. Molded by their vision of one God, the *Spirit of God* came to signify the force or power that issues from God and is sent into the created order among humans. The individual human spirit responds and interacts with God's Spirit. In this tradition God's Spirit has many modes: It is the creative and sustaining force within the universe; provides extraordinary endowments of leadership to Jewish priests and kings; grants wisdom and discernment; and serves as the agent of communication with humans, particularly through the prophets. The prophets of Israel presumed they were speaking for God, that they were agents of God's Spirit. Through such manifestations the transcendent God is immanently present in human life (see Unit 40). The imagery is clearly that of the human spirit centered in and directed by one all-powerful, Divine Spirit overarching and influencing all of life.

[12] Sokyo Ono, *Shinto: The Kami Way* (Rutland, VT and Tokyo: Charles E. Tuttle, 1962), p. 7.

ISLAMIC PATTERNS

Among Muslims prophesy is a central feature of the faith, and in prophesy they understand the Divine Spirit to reveal itself. Muhammad is understood by Muslims to be the channel or vessel through whom the *spirit of Allah* speaks to humanity. The Qur'an, the Islamic Scripture, is a "recitation" by Allah's "spirit," represented by the angel Gabriel through his prophet Muhammad. Human spirit resides in the soul and has personal contact with Allah, but the emphasis is on the Divine Spirit and its gracious love for and instruction of humanity—a love that, nonetheless, requires submission of the human spirit to the Divine Spirit. Muslims who follow Sufi patterns of thought suggest that a believer's direct personal contact with the Divine Spirit can be much more interactive than simple submission (see Units 16 and 19).

CHRISTIAN THOUGHT

Christian thought on the spirit is grounded in the Jewish precepts described earlier. Many of the nuances and dimensions of the phrase *Spirit of God* in Jewish usage were appropriated by early Christians to talk about God's action in human life. Like Judaism, wind and fire are prominent metaphors for the mystery of the spirit, as illustrated in the following Christian Scripture:

> When the day of Pentecost had come, they were all together in one place. And suddenly from heaven there came a sound like the rush of a violent wind, and it filled the entire house where they were sitting. Divided tongues, as of fire, appeared among them and a tongue rested on each of them. And they were all filled with the Holy Spirit and began to speak in other tongues, as the Spirit gave them ability. (Acts 2:1–4, NRSV)

The experience of personal contact with God is also understood to bestow on believers new possibilities, as seen in these passages. "You shall receive power when the Holy Spirit has come upon you" (Acts 1:8). "For the law of the Spirit of life in Christ Jesus has set me free from the law of sin and death" (Romans 8:2).

Two other elements, however, became important in Christian thinking. First, while Christian writers used traditional attributes of spirit to characterize the forceful, impressive ministry of Jesus, Jesus' power and authority were identified with the Divine Spirit itself; consequently, Jesus is understood to be the very presence of God on earth.

> And when Jesus had been baptized, just as he came up from the water, suddenly the heavens were opened to him and he saw the Spirit of God descending like a dove, and alighting on him. (Matthew 3:16, NRSV)

The second element of Christian understanding of the spirit arose from Jesus' teachings concerning the Divine Spirit. In John's gospel, Jesus promises that a "Counselor . . . even the Spirit of Truth" will be sent by the Father (God) to dwell in his disciples when Jesus is physically gone from their midst (John 14:15–17). The experience of the early church convinced Jesus' disciples that God was uniquely with them, guiding and fulfilling their ministry. Remembering this teaching of Jesus, they began to speak of the presence of the *Holy Spirit*. For the church, the Holy Spirit came to be understood as the unique presence of the Divine Spirit of Jesus. Irenaeus, a second-century church father, stated the concept this way:

> Know thou that every man is either empty or full. For if he has not the Holy Spirit, he has no knowledge of the Creator; he has not received Jesus Christ the Life; he knows not the Father who is in heaven.[13]

Here the Spirit's role is given prominence equal to that of the Father and the Son and is made the channel by which humans may come to know God.

In the main, Christians have taken the Spirit for the "whole nature of God." The name *spirit* defines the nature of God by gathering together in one name the leading attributes of God: power, purity, invisibility, vitality, freedom, love, and so forth. Spirit means God as all-sufficient, almighty, infinite, perfect, the mover of all things. The spirit for Christians indicates the living action of God in history. That action or movement is understood to take place in a dynamic relationship between God and one's own vitality—one's own spirit.

◆◆◆

Think of the different ways you and your acquaintances use the concept of spirit.

In what ways might the word be used in addition to the definitions given in this unit?

In what context do you most often use the word spirit?

How does the kami understanding of the Japanese differ from that of the Jewish or Christian traditions?

Are there similarities between some of the ideas found in Unit 34 and those discussed in this unit?

---

[13] Irenaeus, Fragments XXVI, quoted in *Handbook of Christian Theology*, Marvin Haverson and Arthur A. Cohen, eds. (New York: Meridian Books, 1958), p. 170.

◆◆◆ 8 ◆◆◆

EVIL: ITS REALITY AND MEANING

The last two chapters have shown that reflection on the Divine has historically led humans to confidence in a spiritual reality that transcends ordinary human existence. However, one is confronted daily with experiences that negate the values found in human life and threaten its very reality. We are reflecting on ordinary life when we ask questions such as: "Why do bad things happen to good people?" "Why do natural disasters threaten innocent people?" "How could a mother bludgeon her children to death?" "Why would one racial group attempt to exterminate another?" "How can a drug dealer justify profiting from contributing to the addiction of another person?" In raising such questions we are attempting to understand the experience of a destructive force (or forces) encountered by human beings—a phenomenon of human life most often referred to in religious traditions as evil.

The awareness of evil is a common reality, but careful examination of the topic is often avoided; hence, evil remains a mystery, perhaps because we are too frightened to discuss it. Amazingly, however, it is the subject of a vast number of modern films, books, music, and dramas. Young people seem to be particularly attracted to media presentations of the phenomenon. Why? Numerous sociological, psychological, philosophical, and religious studies seek insights into the issue—seeking answers to what leads humans to be attracted to the topic and why evil is acted out in common life. We examine here some of its features, concentrating on the issue as it is dealt with in religious contexts.

Consciousness of evil arises in various ways. For some, evil is encountered in interpersonal relationships—situations where relationships become so all-consuming that they assume transcendent significance. For others, evil is often equated with the suffering that humans experience in the normal course of daily living, whether it arises from natural disasters, disease, or psychotic behavior. Unit 42 suggests ways in which this reality has been understood in several religious and philosophical traditions. For some, evil is perceived as an autonomous force either within or outside the individual and is often personalized in the form of one or more demonic figures. Evil in this form is explored in Unit

43. Finally, Unit 44 discusses the evil that humans may experience as the unrecognized effects of humanly created societal systems—institutionalized or corporate evil. Before investigating the interpretations of evil found in this chapter, the reader may want to review the concepts of the Divine discussed in the previous chapter in order to compare them with the concepts of evil.

Unit 42   WHY SUFFERING?

The title of this unit poses a question (as do those that introduce the chapter) that perplexes humans whenever they reflect that life, for all its good, is often torn in what seem to be unreasonable and sometimes undeserved ways—containing much pain and sorrow. Attempts to understand and perhaps explain this phenomenon are as ancient and varied as human society itself. Religious traditions and philosophical schools have offered many. These fall into several patterns:

1. Cultures closely related to the natural world, both ancient and modern, usually understand humans to be dependent on "earth gods or spirits" and "sky gods" for all good and evil. As civilizations developed, city and national gods were added to nature gods making a large pantheon of deities.
2. Greek philosophers unsatisfied with the polytheism that accompanied nature and city cult religion offer several explanations:
    a. Plato, who suggested that the Divine was perfectly good, suggested that evil was the privation or corruption of the good. It arose when the ideal good was corrupted or ignored.
    b. Stoic philosophers, understanding that all reality was reasonable, thought evil resulted from "unreason and lack of self control."
    c. Epicureans, convinced that chance controlled all reality, viewed suffering as simply a part of the unknowable nature of the universe.
3. Hinduism, with belief in reincarnation, understands present evil to be the consequence of "bad karma" in a previous existence.
4. Buddhism defines suffering as being an inherent result of self-centered human desire.

What solutions did these traditions propose to the problem of suffering? Nature and city religions tried to outwit the careless and capricious gods. Platonists proposed a "real" realm of perfection "above" the physical world to which one might mystically escape. Stoics believed that reason could order power and thereby conquer evil. Epicureans suggested that since suffering was part of the "blind way of the world" the wise man withdraws from it "as far as possible" and develops a serene indifference to the complications of evil. Hindus rely on "good karma" overcoming the "bad karma" leading to better future lives. Buddhists insist that the cure for suffering is the extinction of self-interested, self-regarding, self-centered desire. The end of suffering is to be reached by extinction of the limited personal self. Most of these responses to suffering tend, in the words of Albert Outler, "to disengage the divine from the hurlyburly of ordinary life." [1]

[1] Albert Outler, *Who Trusts in God, Musings on the Meaning of Providence* (New York: Oxford University Press, 1968), p. 84.

Figure 8.1   Drawing by Jacques Bakke

The question of evil becomes a particularly daunting issue for monotheistic religions such as Judaism, Christianity, and Islam. Each of these religions presents God as sovereign over all creation, a Divine Reality not removed from its creation but intimately involved with it, including whatever is good *and* what is evil. Many see this affirmation as a problem for these religions—how can a good and benevolent God allow evil in the created world?

Each of these religions has affirmed that evil and its suffering have a purpose under God, whether penal (punishment for sins) or pedagogical (disciplinary correction). Early Judaism taught that God sends suffering as punishment for sin or humanity's self-centeredness. The sinfulness of Israel was seen to be the cause of several national disasters because sin evoked God's wrath. The evil that arose out of sin brought suffering both to individuals and to the community (Deuteronomy 31,32). Similarly, Islam has traditionally insisted on the strict following of the Qur'an commandments (Surah 39, 49). Moral and penal codes have for centuries been built on these instructions and have affirmed that evil or sin demands exemplary punishment.

In both religions evil has also been understood pedagogically, or as providing opportunities for humans to learn that sin and disobedience result in evil. Modification of behavior and individual as well as corporate discipline is the intent of such understanding.

These interpretations were not, however, without their difficulties. The biblical character known as Job (along with several Psalmists) protested against the view that suffering was a divinely decreed penalty for sin. Tradition had pointed to suffering as just punishment for the ungodly. Job focuses on the central theological question regarding suffering: Is God just to permit sinners prosperity while the faithful suffer? Job claims innocence before God for he had been a righteous man but finds himself to be in great anguish and pain since many disasters have befallen him. He is visited by several so-called comforters who offer the usual reasons for evil befalling him—suffering is caused by transgressions but such events provide a context for renewal; suffering is simply part of God's plan for human existence used to instruct, so it is ultimately justified. None of these answers adequately dealt with his situation or question. Job's faith is ultimately tested by direct confrontation with God, where he is offered no explanation for evil but is assured that God enters into his sufferings as well as his blessings. Affirmation then comes in his renewed faithfulness to the God present in all of his life (Job 1–42).

Although most old testament writers of the Scriptures of Judaism see suffering as a penalty for transgression, as had Job's friends, other writers suggest that suffering can best be understood by its redeeming purpose (disciplinary, purificatory), as the psalmist indicates: "It was good for me that I was afflicted, that I might learn thy statutes" (Psalm 119:71). Especially in the servant songs of Deutero-Isaiah we find suffering to be vicarious and redemptive. The Servant, whether corporate or individual, is shown as despised, rejected, "a man of sorrows and acquainted with grief," even though he is sinless and does not deserve to suffer (Isaiah 53:3). The Servant suffers for humanity's sins. His "suffering is neither the result of his own sin nor the chastisement that might lead to his own perfection. . . . The suffering apparently gains for itself a merit that is transferable."[2] In these passages Isaiah moved beyond the traditional affirmation of a disciplinary purpose in evil to suffering being an avenue of service to and for others.

Christian writers in the New Testament, like their Jewish predecessors, include punitive theories of suffering, but emphasize the pedagogical and redemptive interpretations seen in the latter Jewish prophets. Christ's redemptive actions in overcoming evil become the focus in Christianity. Also, in the New Testament, God is presented more as a parent than as judge or king, and from the paternal perspective suffering becomes chiefly pedagogical, corrective, or redemptive. Not only does the parental image lend itself to a redemptive view of suffering, but also belief in a redeemed future for the faithful fosters courage and hope among the suffering. Paul's affirmation that "all things work together for good for those who love God" corresponds to his belief that "the sufferings of this present time are not worth comparing with the glory about to be revealed to us" (Romans 8:28,18). Both statements express assurance that suffering will be overcome. This redemptive meaning of suffering focuses on Jesus, who, though sinless, gives himself for others to bring deliverance for sufferers through his atoning death. "For the Son of Man came not to be served but to serve and to give his life as a ransom for many" (Mark 10:45). Christians claim that the paradox and power of the New Testament faith is that God works through suffering to redeem those who suffer.

---

[2] Alan Richardson, A Theological Word Book of the Bible (New York: Macmillan, 1959), p. 251.

Human suffering wrought through natural disasters (earthquakes, hurricanes, and tornadoes) and disease often found explanation in many religions by use of the penal understanding of evil—these events were seen as punishment for either personal or collective sin. Such explanations, however, do not answer questions about the justice of a universe that incorporates such events. Another explanation offered by the Judeo-Christian traditions suggests that human sufferings that arise from natural events are simply a *consequence* of the functioning of nature itself, they are not punishment for sin but a consequence of the natural order. Similarly, in such an understanding death can be seen as a part of life itself, a natural event, which reduces the fear of death so often experienced among humans.

◆◆◆

We have considered several answers to the question "Why suffering?" Which of these answers do you think is most viable?

Can you think of others?

Unit 43   CONCEPTS OF EVIL

In the mid-1970s a film called *Star Wars*, written and directed by George Lucas, played to full houses; it was soon followed by *The Empire Strikes Back*, also a great box-office success. These were followed by equally successful sequels (see Unit 29). These hugely popular films soon acquired a cult following and their stories were told in novels written by Lucas. Since then, there has been a proliferation of further novels authorized but not authored by Lucas and tellings and new-tellings of the *Star Wars* stories in animated TV series, radio programs, comic books, role-playing manuals, and an outpouring of other forms. Recently, the original films returned to theatres with huge audiences and acclaim. In all later elaborations, the *Star Wars* story has continued the same themes and transformations (see Unit 25 on *transformation* as an essential element of myths) found in the original trilogy.

There are several reasons for the popularity of these films. They were well acted and well directed. Photography was strikingly effective. There was suspense and dramatic action. Fascinating special effects abounded: futuristic space vehicles, intelligent machines (robots) with computer intelligence but humanlike dispositions were attractive and humorous. Possibly the most appealing feature of the films was that they dealt with clear-cut opposition between good and evil, between apparently outnumbered and out-weaponed attractive rebels fighting for freedom and justice and fair play against powerful, hideous forces of oppression.

Star Wars seemed to offer a clear choice between good and evil and came at a time when American society was shocked by the Watergate scandal. Americans had just learned of illegal and devious plots concocted by an American president and his top advisors and of their attempt to cover them up. The president had been threatened with impeachment and forced to resign. Many of his advisors were sentenced to prison.

The *Star Wars* story line was simple. A well-governed intergalactic Republic had decayed and fallen into the control of evil rulers. Pushed beyond endurance, good citizens, aided by wise beings who were masters of ancient wisdom and by some benevolent robots, fought to restore justice and freedom. The evil Empire found its clearest embodiment in the hideous Darth Vader—masked, sinister, huge, and malevolent. According to the *Star Wars* worldview, there is a mysterious Force generated by all living beings that holds the galaxy together. This Force has both a light and a dark side and can be used for good or for evil. One must be taught to use the force for good. Too impatient to learn to use the Force for good, Darth Vader turned to its dark side. The agents of evil are shown to be ugly and repulsive. The agents of good are represented by a clean-cut young man, Luke Skywalker, and by a beautiful princess, Leia. At one point in *The Empire Strikes Back* the spacecraft of the rebels was stalled and the evil enemy was bearing down on them. Desperation was vividly portrayed and audiences were taken over the edge of suspense. But at the last possible instant, the rebel spacecraft functioned correctly, accelerated, and zoomed off across the galaxy, leaving their malevolent pursuers far behind. At that moment, in theatres across America, audiences broke into the kind of cheering usually heard from the hometown football crowd whose team has scored the winning touchdown in the last few seconds of a game.

Even in the melodramatic clash between good and evil, ambiguity is allowed to creep in. Late in the series it was revealed that the hideous Darth Vader is father of the clean-cut Luke Skywalker and the beautiful Princess Leia. This leads to even more conflict as Darth Vader tries to persuade his son to convert to the dark side and rule with him; Luke tries to appeal to the innate goodness he believes is buried within his father. There is deadly, bloody conflict between them but finally the father gives his life to save his son and tells him he was right to choose the good.

Although the series ends with the triumph of good over evil, the film suggests that the contrast between them may not be absolute, that even the most evil may have some seeds of goodness and redemption within them.

To many Christians, the existence of evil is a painful mystery. If God is good and the world he has created is good and doing good is rewarding and satisfying, why do so many people commit horrible acts of evil? Certainly that question arises again with brute force in the recent attacks on the World Trade Center and the Pentagon.

Asian religious thinkers have not dealt with the problem of evil in the same way as have many in the West, who have struggled through the centuries with the philosophical issue of good and evil in conflict. Major religions of the East are, for the most part, monistic, reflecting a view of the cosmos as a unity, a oneness of everything rooted in a primal goodness. Hinduism, in Western ways of thinking, is a pantheistic monism; the One, all-inclusive spiritual reality is everything and everyone and yet is greater than all that is, whether experienced by humans as good or evil. Although we may live in a world where wickedness and misery exist, Hinduism claims that even the evil itself, which is at most illusory in the monistic scheme of things, has a divine and good purpose.[3]

Buddhism, as a reform movement in Hinduism, did not include speculations on the Divine but it did focus on ways to become liberated from self-centered desire so that

[3] See Ward J. Fellows, *Religious East and West* (New York: Holt, Rinehart & Winston, 1979), pp. 199–265.

even an evil person, one in bondage to the worst expressions of self-centeredness, will reach purity. In becoming enlightened the Buddhist reaches the freedom of knowing that good and evil are not two realities but "are simply one."[4]

In Chinese Taoism and Confucianism, the forces of *yin* and *yang* may appear to be dualistic, but they are derived from and point toward an all-unifying Power or Principle, designated as the *Tao* in Taoism and *Heaven* in Confucianism. In Taoism the ultimate Power is experienced mystically by intuition, whereas in Confucianism the emphasis is given to reason and learning as ways to understand the moral goodness of Heaven, and thus be enabled to live ethically. Although Confucianists may talk about evil and sins, they can also affirm religious tenets that stress the goodness of Heaven and essential human goodness. Taoism and Confucianism seem to deal with evil as the intuited impropriety that creates disharmony in living and is to be corrected by being in harmony with the ultimate Governing Power. For them, persistent evil is impossible.[5]

Many Christians struggling with the logical problem of how evil can exist when everything has been created by a good and all-powerful God have accepted the position that evil comes from a real but inferior power created by God. By recognizing evil as real, Christianity differs from Eastern strategies that deny the basic reality of evil, reducing it to the status of "illusion, mirage, *maya*, giving it only a deceptive appearance of reality within a great all-encompassing monism. . . .[6] By viewing evil as inferior to God, Christians seek to reject any idea of evil as one all-powerful facet of a dual reality vying on equal terms with God. "Thus the Christian maintains neither the monist nor the dualist solution of the problem of evil while holding it [evil] as both subordinate [to God] and perverse."[7]

Roland Frye, an interpreter of theology in literature, presents his understanding of the normative Christian view of evil as follows:

> Christianity summarizes the source of evil under the symbol of the demonic, and the essence of the demonic is the aspiration to godhead, the attempt to usurp the place of the Creator, followed by assault upon creation in a frenzy of hate which irrevocably dedicates itself to a continuous destruction of life. Satan is thus the continuous source of evil. . . . He is not an independent evil being set opposite an equally independent good being, and his fall from heaven comes precisely from his false claim to be just that. . . . In the Christian conception, then, evil is totally subordinate to God: it is good in its created intention, but perverted from its normative goals. In poetic terms, Satan is a perversion of the great, but subordinate, good, which was Lucifer. . . . It is thus basically a lie, carrying at the core of its existence a falsification of its own nature.[8]

According to Frye, in seeking to elevate himself above God, Satan became the symbol of the fall of all humans and the participation in evil of all humanity.

[4] See Tannisho, *A Primer: A Record of the Words of Shinran Set Down in Lamentation over Departures from His Teaching*, trans. Dennis Hirota (Kyoto: Ryukoku University Translation Center, 1982), p. 81.

[5] Fellows, *Religious East and West*, pp. 70, 91–96, 104–107.

[6] Roland Mushat Frye, *God, Man and Satan: Patterns of Christian Thought and Life in Paradise Lost, Pilgrim's Progress and the Great Theologians* (Princeton, NJ: Princeton University Press, 1960), p. 2.

[7] Ibid.

[8] Ibid., pp. 22–23.

Figure 8.2 M. Gustave Dore, illustration for Milton's *Paradise Lost,* Book IX, Ins. 99,100.

Some Christians have interpreted Satan or the devil as merely a symbol for the sources of evil within humans that cause them to turn from God and to inflict harm on themselves, the world, and other humans through selfishness, greed, cruelty, and anger. Others have interpreted Satan as a symbol for the power of collective movements, such as extreme nationalism (as in German Nazism) or powerful institutions (as in a cruel system of punishment of criminals or the recently repealed racist laws and practices of South Africa's apartheid). Traditionally, most Christians have probably believed in the transhuman objective reality of Satan—a being originally good, created by God for goodness, but who through misuse of freedom became evil and, as stated by Frye, the major source of evil in the universe.

Interpreters have warned about a tendency among some brought up in Christian traditions to romanticize Satan. Figure 8.2 is a good illustration of this tendency. Some have said that John Milton, in his great epic poem *Paradise Lost,* gave Satan such strong characteristics that he became the hero of the poem. In contrast, the twentieth-century Protestant theologian Karl Barth, reflecting on the characteristics Christians attribute to God—unity, goodness, wisdom, and power—[apparently] concluded that Satan is the opposite—dispersed, disorganized, ignorant, and weak—having power only when it is loaned to him by ignorant and foolish creatures. The Devil is, Barth maintained, a "boiling ocean of discontent."[9]

During sixteenth-century religious conflicts in Europe, not only some Protestant and Catholic leaders but also some in opposing Protestant groups accused their opponents of being instruments of Satan. Other Christians cautioned that no matter how intense differences of belief and opinion may be, attributing opponents' motives and conduct to the devil's influence is not compatible with the New Testament commandment for Christians to love one another.

Since the emergence of modern psychotherapy, there has been a tendency to understand "demonic possession" as a prescientific age's way of describing emotional or behavioral ("mental") disturbances. However, in a study called *People of the Lie*, M. Scott Peck, a psychoanalyst and lay Christian, has argued that there are genuine instances of people falling under the influence of demonic—objective and external transhuman—powers distinct from ordinary emotional disturbances, such as neuroses and psychoses that can be medically treated. According to Peck, there are people who actually become evil by allowing themselves to become possessed by evil powers. Peck is cautious rather than sensational in the development of his theory and warns against the tendency to understand "demonic" forces as they are often represented in anthropomorphically popular art, classical art, literature, or in cartoons and comic strips.[10]

Some have cautioned that a view such as Peck's may play into the human tendency to "demonize" one's opponents and warn that even those who seem most evil (demonic) to opponents may see themselves as good. Timothy McVeigh, for example, responsible for the deaths of almost 200 people when he bombed the federal building in Oklahoma City, claimed to be fighting for freedom and justice and avenging wrongs he thought the government had committed. These interpreters are not arguing that what McVeigh (or Hitler) did was justified just because McVeigh (or Hitler) may have thought or said so. They are not saying that all people are equally evil. However, they are insisting (as the theologian Reinhold Niebuhr did) that distinctions between good and evil often contain more ambiguity than the media and talk show hosts will admit.[11]

In an influential work called *On the Free Choice of the Will*, the fourth-century North African bishop Augustine argued that free will is a part of human nature since humans are created by God. But Augustine was convinced that all humans misuse free will because humans have fallen from their created goodness and, to defend themselves against real and imagined threats from others, have become evil—selfish and self-centered. Thus, for Augustine, the problem of the existence of evil—how and why there is evil in a world created good by a good and all-powerful God—ceases to be a logical problem and becomes practical: How can humans regain their capacity to use free choice in ways that will bring good rather than evil?

[9] See Karl Barth, *Prayer* (Philadelphia: Westminster Press, 1952), pp. 72–74.
[10] M. Scott Peck, *People of the Lie: The Hope for Healing Human Evil* (New York: Simon & Schuster, 1983).
[11] See, for example, Reinhold Niebuhr, *The Irony of American History* (New York: Charles Scribner's Sons, 1952).

Figure 8.3 *Calvin and Hobbes,* copyright by Waterson. (Reprinted with permission of Universal Press Syndicate. All rights reserved.)

In recent years, large numbers of novels, sometimes referred to as "Christian fiction" that depict apocalyptic struggles between demonic beings invading parts of human society have become popular. They are often graphic and, according to their critics, lacking subtlety. The widely selling novels by Frank E. Peretti are good examples of the genre. The mid-twentieth-century British writer Charles Williams dealt with similar subjects in a more sophisticated way.[12]

❖❖❖

Having reviewed Units 42 and 43, distinguish between evil and suffering, and compare the explanations given by and within the various religious traditions of why there is evil and why there is suffering in the world and what individuals and societies can do about them.

According to what Augustine said about the origins and sources of evil in humans, do you think it would make sense to him that people we consider very evil, such as serial killers Hitler and Timothy McVeigh, may have been, in very misguided, twisted ways, seeking something they considered good?

[12] A good example of Peretti's work is *Piercing the Darkness* (Westchester, IL: Crossway Books, a Division of Good News Publishers, 1989). One of the best of Charles William's novels is *All Hallows Eve* (New York: The Noonday Press, a Division of Farrar, Straus and Giroux, 1971).

Do you think people are happier when they can believe what Star Wars seemed to suggest at the beginning of the series—that there is an absolute distinction between the good and the evil or if they accept what is suggested later, that the distinction between good and evil may be harder to make, or that even in the very evil, some good may be buried and possibly capable of being encouraged?

How might this apply to ideas and practices related to the criminal justice system in our society?

Unit 44 INSTITUTIONALIZED FORMS OF EVIL

Many people look upon evil as something done by individuals. However, the prophets of ancient Israel and Judah often looked at organized entities—nations or empires such as Assyria—as embodiments of evil. The first-century Christian who wrote the biblical book *Revelation* condemned the Roman Empire as an organized instrument of Satan and the Antichrist. At the height of the cold war between the United States and the Soviet Union, President Ronald Reagan condemned the U.S.S.R. as an "evil empire." Most persons would characterize the German Nazi dictator Adolf Hitler as a supremely evil individual but would also insist that most of the organizations of his government—the political and legal systems, even labor unions and universities—were reorganized as forms of institutionalized evil.

Subtle and often difficult forms of evil to discern, however, are those imbedded in institutions and captured in corporate policy and practice, often uncritically affirmed as normal and necessary. In the eighteenth century, chattel slavery was institutionalized as a part of American history when black field workers became indispensable to the rise of cotton as the major crop of the South. As cotton, dependent on forced labor, became an essential component in America's industrial revolution, it fed the rise of racism that, after the Civil War had freed the slaves, was perpetuated by laws segregating and oppressing black people.

The evils of racism and classism have been present at every turn in American society. When children of color are killed by racists who bomb their churches or homes, we can treat the criminals, if captured and tried, as individuals who broke the law. When children die of malnutrition in a barrio due to an economic system that alienates their parents from work because they are Hispanic—poor with no resources to gain a foothold—then the evil can be interpreted as a systemic and institutionalized component of our society.

Cornel West discusses the systemic evils of racism as forms of Nihilism.

The proper starting point for the crucial debate about the prospects for black America is an examination of the nihilism that increasingly pervades black communities. Nihilism is to be understood here not as a philosophic doctrine that there are no rational grounds for legitimate standards or authority; it is, far more, the lived experience of coping with a life of horrifying meaninglessness, hopelessness, and (most important) lovelessness. The frightening result is a numbing detachment from others and a self-destructive disposition toward the world. Life without meaning, hope, and love breeds a cold-hearted, mean-spirited outlook that destroys both the individual and others.

Nihilism is not new in black America. The first African encounter with the New World was an encounter with a distinctive form of the Absurd. The initial black struggle against degradation and devaluation in the enslaved circumstances of the New World was, in part, a struggle against nihilism. In fact, the major enemy of black survival in America has been and is neither oppression nor exploitation but rather the nihilistic threat—that is, loss of hope and absence of meaning. For as long as hope remains and meaning is preserved, the possibility of overcoming oppression stays alive. The self-fulfilling prophecy of the nihilistic threat is that without hope there can be no future, that without meaning there can be no struggle."[13]

Decaying ghettos and barrios of American cities give credence to West's interpretation of the way classism and racism erode society. Urban riots express rage suppressed for too long. Drive-by shootings, drugs, desperate crimes, violence against the weak and vulnerable, fear, confusion, and hate are everyday realities for those victimized by such chaos. West's portrayal of nihilism as it applies to the American black community may well explain the same phenomenon present among many in the American Hispanic community, among the Palestinian Arab community, and among others in societies around the world. When hope and meaning are not present, then a nihilism in which life holds little value responds in violence—evil producing evil.

The prophet Amos pronounced judgment against the nation Israel at the religious shrine at Bethel where he believed the evils of lives of self-indulgent pleasure by the nation and its wealthy ruling class were given institutional blessing while the poor were being enslaved and oppressed (Amos 4:1–2). West's rhetorical question sharpens the issue for our day. "But why is this shattering of black civil society occurring?" His answer: ". . . corporate market institutions . . . that complex set of interlocking enterprises that have a disproportionate amount of capital, power, and exercise a disproportionate influence on how our society is run and how our culture is shaped."[14] West sees the profit motive as the impetus for these institutions. A culture of consumption is the result; pleasure is the goal. "Like all Americans, African Americans are greatly influenced by the images of comfort, convenience, machismo, femininity, violence, and sexual stimulation that bombard consumers. These seductive images. . . . edge out nonmarket values—love, care, service to others—handed down by preceding generations."[15] West refers to this condition as "a kind of clinical depression"—an "eclipse of hope" . . . linked to corporate economy in America and "the accumulative effect of black wounds" begun in slavery and continued till the present. The emotional symptoms of this historical evil erupting among us are "anger, rage, pessimism" about any possible justice in American life.[16]

West sets this stark analysis of collective evil in relief by noting that there is always a glint of hope, with a chance for change. It lies not in analysis of these social ero-

---

[13] Cornel West *Race Matters* (Boston: Beacon Press, 1993), pp. 14–15.

[14] Ibid, p. 16.

[15] Ibid., p. 17.

[16] Ibid., p. 18.

sions, important as this is, but in a renewed religious ethic. "Nihilism is not overcome by arguments or analysis; it is tamed by love and care."[17]

◆◆◆

Do you agree or disagree with West's analysis of black America? Explain why.

Can you identify other institutionalized forms of evil in contemporary society, including those that victimize members of other ethnic social groups?

Is it possible to examine adequately the realities of corporate evil apart from a concept of religiously based ethics? If so, how would you propose to do it?

Not all religious people would agree with West's analysis of what is wrong with contemporary America. Can you think of some of their reasons for disagreement?

[17] Ibid., p. 19.

✦✦✦ 9 ✦✦✦

UNDERSTANDING THE SELF

In the preceding chapters we explored the varieties of human religious experience and conceptions of the Divine or Ultimate Reality. We now move to an examination that may be more familiar to many: What does it mean to be human, and how does that humanness relate to the Divine? Few persons reach maturity without asking *Who am I?*, *What is the purpose of my life?*, and *What do I or can I contribute to life?* Calvin's comments in the accompanying cartoon (Figure 9.1) sum up such questions, adding the realization of life's limited nature! As the cartoon suggests, such questions are ongoing—in many senses they are lifelong and perhaps never answered fully. Without attempting to "find" complete answers, the next two chapters explore how such questions have been dealt with in various traditions. Chapter 9 investigates the nature of human existence and the meaning of individual selfhood as viewed from different religious and cultural points of view. In Chapter 10, we examine the social dimension of human existence—the interrelationship of the self with other selves, the social solidarity of human existence.

Figure 9.1 *Calvin and Hobbes*, copyright by Waterson. (Reprinted with permission of Universal Press Syndicate. All rights reserved.)

Human beings are, as Aristotle and other social philosophers have suggested, social animals. In a very direct and literal sense, we have to learn to be human, and each society develops its own models and images of what human beings should be like. Nevertheless, human beings, at least in most societies, tend to develop a sense of individuality. In some societies—including Western societies during the modern period—great emphasis has been placed on the uniqueness, the irreplaceable value, of each individual. Even in societies in which the individual's sense of unique identity is muted (as in most societies until the modern period and as in the kibbutzim of contemporary Israel, where the individual tries to see everything through the eyes of the group), the importance of the individual, even if only as a part of the group, is recognized.

What does it mean to be a person, to be (or have) a self? This question has been raised throughout the history of human civilization. In myths of origin, from those of Babylon and Assyria to those of Japan or the Navajo; in philosophical and scientific speculation from Gautama Buddha and Socrates to a twentieth-century existentialist such as Martin Heidegger or the behaviorist B. F. Skinner; and in religious literature, questions about the nature and characteristics of human existence have been posed. In our own time, as in many others, these questions are of deep concern, sometimes painfully so, to individuals searching for meaning in life.

Attitudes and ideas about the meaning of human existence—what it means to be human, what it means to be a self in isolation from or in relation to other selves—have frequently become ingrained in a society and its religions. These attitudes and ideas are transmitted to the young through cultural practices and institutions, often without conscious intent. They become such a pervasive feature of the culture that people are scarcely aware of them; they seem as natural a part of the lifescape as the air or the topography. In times of cultural crisis, people become aware of them in especially sharp ways, when critical attention is directed at their possible inadequacies or biases. One characteristic of our own time is that social unrest and expanding contacts of many different cultural traditions with one another have caused many people to question traditional assumptions about the nature of human existence and the meaning of individuality.

Unit 45   The Nature of Humanity

A hauntingly recurrent theme in human history has been the inquiry into humanity's nature, essence, and uniqueness. The modern behavioral sciences of sociology and psychology often provide astounding insights into elements of human nature yet, many believe, fail to give a complete definition. Perhaps this only suggests that the complexity and variety of human nature may not always accommodate themselves to complete rational definition. Even if this is true, human beings continue to seek explanations.

Definitions of humanity offered through history are myriad. Erich Fromm and Ramon Xirau provide a convenient set of categories describing human attributes: "reason, the capacity for production, the creation of social organization, and the capacity for symbol making."[1] To these attributes may be added others, such as moral systems; propensity

---

[1] Erich Fromm and Ramon Xirau, *The Nature of Man* (New York: Macmillan, 1968), p. 6. Copyright © 1968 by Macmillan, Inc. Used by permission.

for religious affirmations; and, as the insights of modern philosophy and psychology have taught us, the fact that humanity is constantly becoming, modifying, changing. Following is a progression of representative statements concerning the nature of humanity. Each in its own way, and the sequence as a whole, expresses a particular understanding of what it means to be human.

THE REASONING SELF

Blaise Pascal's often-quoted characterization of a human being as a "thinking reed" exemplifies the Western philosophical tradition that defines human nature by the ability to reason.

> Man is but a reed, the most feeble thing in nature; but he is a thinking reed. The entire universe need not arm itself to crush him. A vapour, a drop of water suffices to kill him. But, if the universe were to crush him, man would still be more noble than that which killed him, because he knows that he dies and the advantage which the universe has over him; the universe knows nothing of this. All our dignity consists, then, in thought. By it we must elevate ourselves, and not by space and time which we cannot fill. Let us endeavour, then, to think well; this is the principle of morality.[2]

SELF-AWARENESS

Fromm and Xirau, summarizing variant positions, maintain that human self-awareness incorporates, yet transcends, reason, becoming one's essential nature—a position hinted at in Pascal's statement.

> It can be stated that there is a significant consensus among those who have examined the nature of man (sic). It is believed that man has to be looked upon in all his concreteness as a physical being placed in a specific physical and social world with all the limitations and weaknesses that follow from this aspect of his existence. At the same time he is the only creature in whom life has become aware of itself, who has an ever-increasing awareness of himself and the world around him, and who has the possibilities for the development of new capacities, material and spiritual, which make his life an open road with a determinable end. As Pascal said, if man is the weakest of all beings, if he is nothing but a "reed," he is also the center of the universe, because he is a "thinking reed."[3]

SELF-TRANSCENDENCE

Erich Fromm, working from modern psychological and philosophical insights, also suggests that the ability to transcend one's animal nature creates conflicts and questions that constantly lead to the search for answers. The essence of human nature, then, is to be always becoming: Life is a never-ending process of better answers to old and new questions caused by our unique situation of not being merely animals.

> He [Fromm] sees the essence, or nature, of man in certain contradictions in human—as against animal—existence. Man is an animal, but without having sufficient instincts to

---

[2]Blaise Pascal, *Pensées* (New York: E. P. Dutton, n. d.), para. 347. Pascal was a seventeenth-century mathematician, physicist, and theologian whose influence on French Catholicism was considerable.

[3] Fromm and Xirau, *The Nature of Man*, p. 6.

direct his actions. He not only has intelligence—as has the animal—but also self-awareness; yet he has not the power to escape the dictates of his nature. He is a "freak of
nature," being in nature and at the same time transcending it. These contradictions create conflict and fright, a disequilibrium which man must try to solve in order to achieve
a better equilibrium. But having reached this, new contradictions emerge and thus again
necessitate the search for a new equilibrium, and so forth. In other words, the questions,
not the answers, are man's "essence." The answers, trying to solve the dichotomies, lead
to various manifestations of human nature. The dichotomies and the resulting disequilibrium are an ineradicable part of man *qua* man; the various kinds of solutions of these contradictions depend on socio-economic, cultural and psychic factors; however, they are by
no means arbitrary and indefinite. There is a limited number of answers which have either
been reached or anticipated in human history. These answers, while determined by historical circumstances, differ at the same time in terms of solutions, differ in terms of their
adequacy to enhance human vitality, strength, joy, and courage. The fact that the solutions depend on many factors does not exclude that human insight and will can work
towards attempting to reach better rather than worse solutions.[4]

One can draw the conclusion from the discussion by Fromm and Xirau and their quota-
tion from Pascal that, no matter what differences or similarities may hold between people
in different societies, there is one structural factor that characterizes all human existence
This has been recognized not only by Pascal and earlier Christian thinkers including
Augustine, Martin Luther, and John Calvin but by Buddhist and Hindu thinkers as well.
It has been given clearest expression by the nineteenth-century Danish thinker Søren
Kierkegaard, often called the founder of modern existentialism, in his *The Sickness Unto
Death*.

Kierkegaard stressed that humans are both finite (embodied, with their present
existence defined by their past, located in a specific historical, geographical, space-time
setting) and transcendent, (with consciousness and self-awareness allowing them to transcend, at least in thought, every concrete, finite situation and be open for a yet undeter-
mined future about which they must make decisions). This capacity for transcendence,
according to Pascal, Kierkegaard, and others, allows humans to *think* the infinite and thus
to evaluate critically and make choices concerning every existing state of affairs.

The following two examples emphasize different ways major religious traditions
have thought about the tension between finitude and transcendence (or awareness of the
infinite) as aspects of human existence.

THE SELF AS THE DIVINE

The following Hindu affirmation stresses the dependence on and identity of humans with
the Divine found within the Self. To discover Self in all its essential meaning is to discover the Divine.

> Lords! Inspiration of sacrifice! May our ears hear the good. May we serve Him with the
> whole strength of our body. May we, all our life, carry out His will.
>   Peace, peace, and peace be everywhere.
>   Welcome to the Lord! . . .

[4] Ibid., pp. 8-9.

There is nothing that is not Spirit. The personal Self is the impersonal Spirit. It has four conditions.

First comes the material condition—common to all—perception turned outward, seven agents, nineteen agencies, wherein the Self enjoys coarse matter. This is known as the waking condition.

The second is the mental condition, perception turned inward, seven agents, nineteen agencies, wherein the Self enjoys subtle matter. This is known as the dreaming condition.

In deep sleep man feels no desire, creates no dream. This undreaming sleep is the third condition, the intellectual condition.

Because of his union with the Self and his unbroken knowledge of it, he is filled with joy, he knows his joy; his mind is illuminated.

The Self is the lord of all: inhabitant of the hearts of all. He is the source of all, creator and dissolver of beings. There is nothing He does not know.

He is not knowable by perception, turned inward or outward, nor by both combined.

He is neither that which is known nor that which is not known, nor is He the sum of all that might be known. He cannot be seen, grasped, bargained with. He is undefinable, unthinkable, indescribable.

The only proof of His existence is union with Him. The world disappears in Him.

He is the peaceful, the good, the one without a second. This is the fourth condition of the Self—the most worthy of all. . . . He is whole; beyond bargain. The world disappears in Him. He is the good; the one without a second. (*Mandookya Upanishad*)[5]

THE SELF AS THE IMAGE OF GOD

The following Hebrew psalm indicates wonder at the ability and place of humanity but sees this as the *gift* of God, on whom humanity is totally dependent. Humanity is "next to" God but not God and only because God so wills it.

> O Lord, our Sovereign,
>> how majestic is your name in all the earth!
>
> You have set your glory above the heavens.
>> Out of the mouths of babes and infants,
> You have founded a bulwark
>> because of your foes to silence the enemy
>> and the avenger.
>
> When I look at your heavens, the
>> work of your fingers, the moon
>> and the stars that you have established;
> What are human beings that you are mindful
>> of them, mortals that you care for them?
> Yet you have made them a little
>> lower than God,
>> and crowned them with glory and honor.
> You have given them dominion
>> over the works of your hands;
> You have put all things under
>> their feet, all sheep and oxen, and also
>> the beasts of the field, the birds of the air,

[5] Shree Purohit Swami and W. B. Yeats, trans., *The Ten Principle Upanishads* (London: Faber & Faber, 1937). Reprinted by permission of M. B. Yeats, Benares University, Faber & Faber, and Macmillan, Inc.

and the fish of the sea, whatever passes
along the paths of the sea.

O Lord, our Sovereign,
how majestic is your name in
all the earth!

(Psalm 8, NRSV)

The idea that human uniqueness and meaning are found through creation in the *image of God* characterizes the Hebrew-Christian tradition. Even here, however, the image may be expressed through various emphases. Pascal, Kierkegaard, and Christian existentialists taught that ability to transcend the Self's finitude is the source of both good and evil in the Self. Some Christians have emphasized the tendency of the Self, in its misplaced pride (willfulness, *hubris*) to become morally and spiritually corrupt, fallen. Others have stressed the possibilities of self-aware finite beings to respond positively to God's creation and redemption. Some have stressed both. These dimensions of the Self play large roles in Christian "psychologies."

All religions have, to one degree or another, developed "psychologies" based on their understandings of selfhood. These include concepts of the relation of the self to the Divine, one's ownself, other humans, other living things, and the universe. In the modern period, some of the world's religions, at least in some of their settings, have encountered powerful trends of "secular" European-American medical (therapeutic) and academic psychologies. These encounters often constitute challenges to the religious psychologies.

Secular psychologies have frequently been reductionist in approach, ruling out or ignoring elements of transcendence and stressing the determining role of genetic endowment, of environment, of social or chemical factors in human behavior. Freudian and other forms of psychoanalysis emphasize unconscious fears and prerational wishes as powerful determining forces. This has sometimes seemed to threaten religious or personal responsibility but to some Christians reenforces the concept of human original sin or fallenness.

Twentieth-century behaviorism undermined not only belief in unconscious motivation but denied that consciousness exists. For behaviorists the self is the result of conditioning in and by past and present social environments. This view may threaten some religious orientations but may be compatible with Buddhist concepts of the no-self or non-self.

Similar considerations apply to some postmodernist views (compare Unit 76) that see a network of linguistic (social) conditioning as the origin and meaning of the person, which, when deconstructed (explained in terms of society's power relations and ideological biases) makes the self "empty," a nothing. Even here, Buddhism, Judaism, Islam, Hinduism, and Christianity may see this deconstruction as not negative but positive, seeing the self, when no longer bound by things or events, as freed for new life in encounter with God or the Real.

Possibly more problematic are theoretical or practical (therapeutic) approaches that reduce the self to computer models of brain functioning or to body chemistry. The latter seems implicit in many contemporary therapies aimed at helping disturbed individuals.[6]

◆◆◆

Why is the nature of humanity and human selfhood an essential religious topic?

Recently a talented young philosopher who was trying to explain human behavior and selfhood by constructing models of ways computers function, being unable to simulate spontaneity or unpredictable actions, built into her computer programs elements of random behavior. Discuss and respond to this.

Discuss changes that have occurred in our society concerning gender terms in language ("Man . . . " "Mankind . . . " or "He" to " A person" or "Someone") since the Fromm-Xirau readings were authored. What does this say about how selves or persons were and are being perceived in our society?

How do you define humanity?

Unit 46   ON THE MEANING OF PERSON

The preceding unit inquired into the nature of humanity—what it means to be human. The present unit continues that inquiry by investigating personhood—what it means to be a particular person.

We are constantly reminded by our personal differences that we, and all people we encounter, are unique beings. We are very complex, amazing mixtures of parental genes, ethnic backgrounds, social contexts, education, and many other influences. Even those of us who are identical twins or triplets develop differently and so are unique beings. Each of us develops from birth our own particular personhood.

In this unit as we reflect on this uniqueness, we become aware that personhood has several distinctive dimensions. Every person is not only unique at this moment but is in a constant state of becoming, an ever-developing flux of growth and change. We may experience occasions when development seems to be arrested or suspended, experiences that may temporarily inhibit or thwart growth, but the process of change continues. Gordon W. Allport, in *Becoming, Foundations for a Psychology of Personality*, suggests that the continuing process of becoming a person means that personality is normally ever in flux.

Erik Erikson, another notable student of human development, suggested that our developing identities are continually being modified as we progress through the various stages of life. Each stage helps shape the continuing personality. Because new elements

---

[6] The following publications provide stimulating discussions of several of the issues discussed in the present unit: Charles Taylor, *Sources of the Self*, (Cambridge: Harvard University Press, 1989), an impressive constructive effort to account for and interpret selfhood; Daniel C. Dennett, *Kinds of Minds* (New York: Basic Books, a division of Harper Collins Publishers, 1996), an attempt by a leading philosopher to understand consciousness; Douglas R. Hofstadter, *Godel, Escher, Bach* (New York: Basic Books, Inc., Publishers, 1979), discussion of minds and thinking, using a multitude of sources, from art and music to computers and brain functioning.

enter continually into our living, each stage of our lives presents new crises of identity. In successful maturation these crises are resolved through our daily experience, thus our developing personality experiences ever new and more complex levels. Progress may not be steady or smooth since negative resolutions of identity crises or failure to move into a new and invigorating stage can stand in the way of the full attainment of one's human potential. Erikson, along with Allport, asserts that growth, development, and learning continue until the moment of death, consequently our personhood is never static. In Erikson's model, achieving an acceptance of ourselves and our wholeness as opposed to embracing despair in old age is one of the most important possibilities for personality potential.

In addition to recognizing the continuing process of personal development, models of human personality also suggest that there is some implicit or explicit goal or highest potential for an individual. One may say that most human beings seek the attainment of some form of mature personhood or, as Sigmund Freud put it, seek to achieve their own *ego ideal*. These goals may come from many sources. One source of such goals is religion. Religions and their teachings provide content for personhood—for religion often defines or contributes to the goals we accept, establish, hope for, and seek.

The following examples suggest what it means to be a person—to find a personal identity in one's life experiences. We begin by examining two very different poems that reflect how the authors experience what it means to be a person of African descent in modern America. We could easily find similar examples from many ethnic groups within our society. Through these illustrations see if you can identify factors, other than the ones we suggest, that contributed to each author's process of becoming a person.

The first, by Langston Hughes, exhibits depth of experience and identification with the earth, which became a part of the perspective of many black persons who worked the land in the old American South. The poet expresses an abiding sense of being a part of the flow of history. Notice how in this poem the key to one's identity, one's personal sense of who one is, is found in the history of one's group; in the history of geographical and cultural change and tradition; in one's life space, work history; in ethnic and culturally shared struggle, endurance, and triumph.

I've known rivers:
I've known rivers ancient as the world and older than the flow of human
    blood in human veins.

My soul has grown deep like the rivers.

I bathed in the Euphrates when dawns were young.
I built my hut near the Congo and it lulled me to sleep.
I looked upon the Nile and raised the pyramids above it.

I heard the singing of the Mississippi when Abe Lincoln went down to
    New Orleans, and I've seen its muddy bosom turn all golden in the sunset.

I've known rivers:
Ancient, dusky rivers.

My soul has grown deep like the rivers.[7]

In her poem "Status Symbol," Mari Evans speaks of the personal identification in a modern urban world that came for her during the social revolution of the 1950s and 1960s that helped change race relations. Notice how her personal identity also comes from group history, from struggle and travail and triumph; but it is expressed in symbols of social and economic roles, higher-status roles from which members of her racial group had been excluded.

                    i
          Have Arrived
                    i
                am the
            New Negro
                    i
          am the result of
          President Lincoln
          World War I
          and Paris
          the Red Ball Express
          white drinking fountains
          sitdowns and
          sit-ins
          Federal Troops
          Marches on Washington
                    and
          prayer meetings . . .
          today
          They hired me
          it
          is a status
          job . . .
          along
          with my papers
          They
          gave me my
          Status Symbol
          the
          key
          to the
          White . . . Locked . . .
          John[8]

As noted, personal crises contribute significantly to our developing personhood, as our next example suggests. During World War II in Germany, Dietrich Bonhoeffer, a leader of the underground church movement, was arrested and eventually killed because he participated in a plot to stop Hitler. While he was in prison, he wrote this questing poem. Notice how Bonhoeffer gives three possible answers to the question of where our identity comes from. First, he asks whether he is the self that others see. Then he asks whether he is the self he sees and feels himself to be. Rejecting both as being at most par-

[8] Mari Evans, "Status Symbol," in *I Am a Black Woman* (New York: William Morrow, 1970). Used by permission of the author.

tial explanations of who we are and from where we receive our identity, Bonhoeffer affirms that wherever we receive partial impressions of our identity, our selfness and self-worth, ultimately come from the fact that we belong to God.

> Who am I? They often tell me
> I stepped from my cell's confinement
> calmly, cheerfully, firmly,
> like a Squire from his country house.
>
> Who am I? They often tell me
> I used to speak to my warders
> freely and friendly and clearly,
> as though it were mine to command.
>
> Who am I? They also tell me
> I bore the days of misfortune
> equably, smilingly, proudly,
> like one accustomed to win.
>
> Am I then really that which other men tell of?
> Or am I only what I know of myself?
>
> Restless and longing and sick, like a bird in a cage,
> struggling for breath, as though hands were compressing my throat,
> yearning for colours, for flowers, for the voices of birds,
>
> thirsting for words of kindness, for neighbourliness,
> tossing in expectation of great events,
> powerlessly trembling for friends at an infinite distance,
> weary and empty at praying, at thinking, at making,
> faint, and ready to say farewell to it all.
>
> Who am I? This or the Other?
> Am I one person to-day and tomorrow another?
> Am I both at once? A hypocrite before others,
> and before myself a contemptible woebegone weakling?
> Or is something within me still like a beaten army
> fleeing in disorder from victory already achieved?
>
> Who am I? They mock me, these lonely questions of mine.
> Whoever I am, Thou knowest, O God, I am thine![9]

Our contemporary scene is full of examples of the human search for identity, for the establishment of personhood. Popular culture repeatedly presents us with books and films seeking to help us answer questions such as: What does it mean to be a person? What is a mature person? How should one use religion, psychology, or the economy to contribute to and shape the nature of individuality? We are instructed in how to be healthy, successful, and happy through many practices since we seem to seek continual improvement in our lives. Clearly, it is a universal need.

In our final example, embracing the continuing need for a person to change, Paul

---

[9] Dietrich Bonhoeffer, *The Cost of Discipleship*, trans. J. B. Leishman (New York: Macmillan, 1959), p.18. Reprinted by permission of Macmillan, Inc., and SCM Press Ltd.

Tournier, a French theologian, elaborates on the subject. He suggests that not only is there a self that acquires identity through constructive experience and personal growth but that this growth leads to an "expanding self," or at least a developing self, a self that becomes more mature, creative, and better related to others by expanding its capacities. (See also Carl R. Rogers, *On Becoming a Person*.) For Tournier this expanding self is a mystery unexplained by simple accumulation of experiences—it is a mystery that presupposes a religious context for developing personhood.

> A completely satisfied man would be a fossil. Dissatisfaction maintains the constant movement of life, like an unending search. . . . What is a child? You cannot describe him without thinking of the whole life of the man, with all its unknowns, for which he is preparing. . . .
>
> We must resist the temptation to give a doctrinaire answer to the question . . . "Who am I?" We must give up the idea that knowing the person means compiling a precise and exhaustive inventory of it. There is always some mystery remaining, arising from the very fact that the person is alive. We can never know what new upsurge of life may transfigure it tomorrow. . . .
>
> It is a mysterious spiritual reality, mysteriously linked to God, mysteriously linked with our fellows. We are aware of these links at those privileged moments when there springs up a fresh current of life, bursting the fatal fetters of the personage, asserting its freedom and breaking out into love.[10]

While these examples suggest the many ways we can understand human identity there are other perspectives on the significance and development of personhood. Perhaps because Western cultures, through recent centuries, have concentrated on the significance of the individual in social structures, personhood and its nature has taken on increased significance and called for the identifications (and many others) we see in the previous examples. However, there are many societies, particularly in Asia and Africa, where social structures do not depend so much on the individual but on the family and community (see Unit 47). In such societies personhood is most often defined only as it relates a person to larger social groups, such as family, clan, tribe, or nation.

Buddhism, the most widely spread of Asian religious traditions, in some of its forms reverses this group pattern to embrace the ideal of a contracting or diminishing self. In this teaching, true reality comes through achieving "nonidentity" by breaking ties to external objects, other selves, and the world. Breaking such ties allows the elimination of the (false or superficial) personality or character traits—traits that one has acquired as defensive reactions to past *misguided* attempts to become and to be! One experiences enlightenment when self is no longer of any consequence—when one achieves the state of "no-self" (see Unit 11). While such an idea may seem unusual to many, particularly in the West, it points to a religious idea found in many Eastern *and* Western religious traditions—nonattachment to the present world. Interestingly, it also involves a "process." By advancing through stages of meditation and moving beyond everyday commonsense reason, one comes to resolution or fulfillment of one's own being (personhood) by moving beyond self.

---

[10] Paul Tournier, *The Meaning of Persons*, trans. Edwin Hudson (New York: Harper & Row, 1957), pp. 230–232, 232–234.

◆◆◆

Reflecting on your own personality development, what cultural elements, events, or presuppositions can you identify as molding your own personhood?

Is Tournier correct that we can never be totally satisfied? How may that affect your looking toward the future?

Compare and contrast the insights of Erikson with those of Bonhoeffer.

What is your response to the Buddhist's and postmodernism's suggestion of a "no-self?"

Unit 47   VIEWS OF BEING HUMAN, EAST AND WEST

Just as one's religious experience is shaped by the life experiences, religious traditions, patterns, and models encountered daily, so is it molded by one's cultural understanding of humanity. Eastern and Western cultures view humanity in distinctively different perspectives. As a result, their views of the value and place of humanity in the scheme of the universe contrast rather dramatically, as the following selections indicate.

EAST: HUMAN BEINGS AS ONE SPECIES AMONG MANY NATURAL BEINGS

Chinese and Japanese visual art (see Figure 9.2) illustrate the Eastern predisposition to see human beings as blending into the vastness of the natural universe, as small interdependent parts of a much larger whole. This view reveals an Eastern religious bias toward monism and pantheism arising out of the strong Taoist, Confucian, Buddhist, and Shinto emphasis on the interrelatedness of all things.

> Before assuming brush and silk painters would go out to nature, lose themselves in it, and become the bamboo that they would paint. They would sit for half a day or fourteen years before making a stroke. The Chinese word for landscape painting is composed of the radicals for mountain and water, one of which suggests vastness and solitude, the other pliability, endurance, and continuous movement. The human part in that vastness is small, so we have to look closely for him in the paintings if we find him at all.[11]

> We love natural truth; our philosophers were convinced that human desire has grown beyond bounds; man's eagerness to grasp the object of his desire gives rise to much unnatural and untruthful behaviour. Man, we think, is no higher in the scale of things than any other kind of matter that comes into being; rather, he has tended to falsify his original nature, and for that reason we prefer those things that live by instinct or natural compulsion; they are at least true to the purpose for which they were created. We paint figures occasionally, but not so much as you do in the West.[12]

[11] Huston Smith, *The Religions of Man* (New York: Harper Collins, 1991, 1958), p. 213.

[12] Chiang Yee, *The Chinese Eye: An Interpretation of Chinese Painting* (Bloomington: Indiana University Press, 1964), pp. 9–10.

Figure 9.2 Landscape by K'un-ts'an. (Reproduced with the permission of the Museum fuer Ostasiatische Kunst Berlin, Staatliche Museen Preussicher Kulturbesitz.)

WEST: HUMAN BEINGS AS GOD'S CREATION, AN EXALTED VIEW OF HUMANITY

In the West, human beings are usually seen as standing out against, or even apart from, the natural universe. Although this view became pronounced during the European Renaissance of the fourteenth and fifteenth centuries and has highly influenced modern culture, it is apparent even in earlier religious and artistic traditions. The following examples from the Hebrew Scriptures and classical (Greek and Roman) visual art (see Figure 9.3) illustrate the concept.

> When I look at your heavens, the work of your fingers,
>   the moon and the stars that you have established:
> what are human beings that you are mindful of them,
>   mortals that you care for them?
>
> Yet you have made them a little lower than God,
>   and crowned them with glory and honor.
> You have given them dominion over the works of your hands;
>   You have put all things under their feet, all sheep and oxen,
>   and also the beasts of the field,
> the birds of the air, and the fish of the sea,
>   whatever passes along the paths of the sea.
>   (Psalms 8:3–8, NRSV)

Figure 9.3 Frans Hals, *Marriage Portrait of Isaac Massa en Beatrix van der Laen*, oil on canvas, c. 1622, Rijksmuseum, Amsterdam (Photo by K. Lawrence.)

◆◆◆

Examine carefully the photographs of the Oriental painting and the Western sculpture.

What does comparison of these symbolic, artistic representations show about the differences between Eastern and Western views of humanity?

✦✦✦ 10 ✦✦✦

FREEDOM AND THE SELF

Each day in human life brings the opportunity and responsibility to make numerous decisions, decisions about the most mundane aspects of living (Where and what shall we eat?) and occasionally life changing decisions (Should I ask her/him to marry me?). Many philosophers, psychologists, and religious leaders say that humanity is unique—that human beings are distinguished from other animals because of their freedom to make these everyday choices. For some this means humanity is altogether unfettered by the circumstances of life that seemingly limit individual and personal freedom—in other words, one is free to be and do what one chooses. Others, often called determinists, believe that humans have little personal freedom because many biological, environmental, social, and cultural factors circumscribe life and consequently shape every decision and action. If total freedom is seen as one pole on a continuum of thought and determinism is the other pole, in the center are those who maintain that freedom lies in what one is able to do with the determinants that have been bequeathed to each individual human.

In our modern technological world the issues surrounding an adequate understanding of human freedom are complicated by the ever-increasing pace of ordinary human life, in which the urgency and complexity of decision making threatens the traditional concepts of freedom just listed.

> Many individuals trapped in dull or slowly changing environments yearn to break out into new jobs or roles that require them to make faster and more complex decisions. But among the people of the future, the problem is reversed. "Decisions, decisions. . . ." they mutter as they race anxiously from task to task. The reason they feel harried and upset is that transience, novelty and diversity pose contradictory demands and thus place them in an excruciating double bind. . . .
>
> The rapid injection of novelty into the environment upsets the delicate balance of "programmed" and "non-programmed" decisions in our organizations and our private lives.[1]

[1] Alvin Toffler, *Future Shock* (New York: Random House, 1970) p. 3.

In the thirty years since Alvin Toffler wrote these words, his predictions have become reality. With the explosion of information at our command, we find ourselves making more and more decisions that would have been determined for us in earlier times. Day-traders on the stock market now have the tools to do the research previously supplied by stockbrokers, but as a consequence they must make decisions without the suggestion and perhaps the wisdom of years of stock trading provided by these brokers. Similarly, information on medications is now available to laypersons, persons who may find themselves making suggestions about treatment of illness to their medical doctors. Illustrations need not be extended to suggest that modern decision-making has become much more complex and demanding of our attention. Toffler helps us understand some of the pressures of the present and the future that are upon us, pressures that demand countless decisions, often without the cushion of background information or an opportunity for reflection on the consequences. This complexity causes us to reexamine the traditional understandings of human freedom.

Most religions have dealt with issues of human freedom, and some of these are discussed here: the definition of freedom, freedom and decision making, responsibility and freedom, and various understandings of human nature as they affect conceptions of freedom. Indeed, we can immediately see that how a particular religion answers these important questions determines its outlook on a wide range of religious issues.

Unit 48   HUMAN FREEDOM

Responsibility assumes that each person enjoys intellectual and moral freedom, the nature of which has been described differently by the world's religions.

In Eastern religions the Divine is generally understood as an all-pervasive, immanent reality that permeates the physical as well as the spiritual universe. Seldom understood as distinct from everyday life, whatever particular deities may be present essentially represent this impersonal Divine Reality. Often humans are seen to contain within themselves this Divine Reality, so human responsibility includes the discovery and uncovering of the Divine within. In fact, true humanity must identify and cooperate with the Divine to be *freed* from the impermanence and irrelevancies of everyday physical existence. In Hinduism, *moksha* frees or releases an individual to identify completely with the Divine so that all other realities become meaningless. To be truly free is to lose all personal desires and to be delivered from the endless round of physical reincarnations. Obviously, to move toward this state, a person must have the ability to make the choice for the Divine, to have freedom to choose; yet the goal of freedom *from* the world in some sense gives a very different emphasis to the concept of human freedom. The emphasis is not on the human ability to decide but on the ultimate goal, where one will be *free*. In a corollary belief, Hindus also believe that actions always have consequences, so decisions based on one's personal desires lead to blessing or curse—*law of karma*. To be freed through *moksha* is to be released from the determinism of *karma* (see Unit 10).

Similarly, in all forms of Buddhism there is an emphasis on an individual's responsibility both to recognize the situation of humanity (the Four Noble Truths) and to choose the method taught by the Buddha to overcome selfish human desires (the

Eightfold Path). Although the Buddha's teachings are variously interpreted in the several branches of Buddhism, the ultimate goal is the same, enlightenment (*Nirvana*), wherein one's everyday existence is, as in Hinduism, freed from the traps of self-centered desires and the endless round of *karma* (see Unit 11). In Buddhism, however, the emphasis is not really on escape from the daily round as much as on freedom to live that daily round without allowing its demands to overcome the true reality—the spiritual life unbound by daily physical existence. Again, one must be able to choose, but the ultimate freedom is *freedom from life's entrapments.*

In contrast, the understanding of the Divine in Western religions raises different issues for the definition of human freedom. Since humans are understood to be creatures of a particular Divine Being, freedom of the will must always be defined within a context that includes Divine Will. For example, the Muslim definition of the relationship between the Divine and the human assumes that human beings must be able to choose between the will of Allah and their own self-directed, most often sinful, will. The proper Muslim response in this context is to submit to the will of Allah. Symbolizing this reality, the word *Islam* means "submission" (a *Muslim* is one who submits). The most complete and true life is one lived within the perimeters laid down by Allah in the Qur'an and the inspired example of Muhammad, known from *hadith*, the law defining everyday life. Once one submits to Allah's will, human choice, although still present, is molded by the Divine Will (see Unit 16).

Judaism, like Islam, also emphasizes the greatness of God, the holiness, wisdom, goodness, and power of God, the Creator of all things, beside whom there are no other gods. Judaism joins to this perception of God the dignity and potential greatness of humanity. Human beings are dependent on God, receiving their being and life and all things necessary to life as gifts from God. However, humans are potentially co-creators with God. They should show reverence to God but not sacrifice their own talents or lose their creative initiative in blind submission: It is God's will that people develop their creative potential to the fullest in accordance with the commandments of God.

This double aspect of the human relationship to God in Judaism is well illustrated in the Jewish Scriptures. In the book of Genesis, for instance, Abraham (the patriarch of Judaism) is praised because of his faithful obedience to God. Certainly there is no lack of reverence for God on Abraham's part. Nevertheless, it is shown as entirely proper that Abraham should attempt to persuade God to change his mind about destroying the wicked cities of Sodom and Gomorrah. Abraham succeeds in getting God to agree to spare the wicked cities, provided some good people can be found in them (see Unit 82). In the same way, Moses persuades God to change his mind about destroying the Hebrews who have worshipped a golden calf, thereby showing their lack of faith in God after God has just delivered them from slavery in Egypt (Exodus 32). In both cases, God takes counsel and accepts the suggestions of his faithful servants, his obedient and loyal friends (see Unit 14). The same point is made in story form in the Talmud:[2]

---

[2] The Talmud is a collection, or collection of collections, of commentaries on the body of law revealed in the Jewish Scriptures. It developed over a period of centuries and was handed down as oral tradition before being put in written form.

Rabbi Eliezer disagreed with some other rabbis about a point of law and, unable to convince them, said, "If the law is as I think it is, then this tree shall let me know." Immediately the tree jumped a hundred yards, but the other rabbis said: "One does not prove anything from a tree." Rabbi Eliezer then appealed to a brook, which immediately began to flow upstream, but his colleagues replied: "One does not prove anything from a brook." Rabbi Eliezer said: "If the law is as I think, then the walls of this house will tell." And the walls began to fall. Rabbi Joshua reprimanded the walls: "If scholars argue a point of law, what business have you to fall?" Then the walls stopped midway: to show their respect for Rabbi Joshua, they did not fall further; and in deference to Rabbi Eliezer they did not straighten up. Then Rabbi Eliezer appealed to heaven, and a voice said: "What have you against Rabbi Eliezer? The law is as he says." Rabbi Joshua, however, replied: "It is written in the Bible (Deuteronomy 30:12): It is not in heaven. What does this mean?" Rabbi Jirmijahu said: "The Torah has been given on Mount Sinai, so we no longer pay attention to voices, for on Mount Sinai already thou hast written into the Torah to decide according to the majority." Some time after this dispute, Rabbi Nathan met Elijah, the prophet, and asked him what the Holy One, blessed be His Name, had done in that hour. And Elijah replied: "God smiled and said: My children have won against me, my children have won."[3]

According to Judaism, a full illumination of true humanity can be attained when humans gain this perspective of their relationship to the one God. In the light of this distinctive Jewish understanding of freedom—an interaction with the sovereign God, even to the point of questioning and influencing God's actions—Jewish imagery of the value and place of humanity is greatly enhanced and has significantly affected Western understandings of humanity.

The reduction of moral, economic, and social restraints in modern society means for many that human freedom is not only an innate right but provides an unfettered license to do as one pleases without attention to traditional restraints. The usual consideration of how one's actions may affect others appears to have often been lost in the erosion of boundaries on behavior. Such freedom raises significant questions concerning the traditional definitions of human will, but is not without consequences. How one's actions affect others often limits personal choice and creates new patterns determining the parameters of freedom. Freedom may not then provide the complete freedom it seemed to allow.

The accompanying cartoon in Figure 10.1 suggests that human freedom doesn't allow one the freedom not to decide—to fail to decide is to choose—whether it is recognized or not.

◆◆◆

Stated in your own words, what are the central differences between Eastern and Western religious concepts of freedom?

How does the Jewish concept of freedom differ from that of Muslims?

---

[3] An adaptation of a story from the *Talmud*, Baba Mezia 596, cited by Erich Fromm, *Psychoanalysis and Religion* (New Haven, CT: Yale University Press, 1950), p. 45.

"My motto was 'Go with the Flow,' but I had no idea the flow would end up here."

Figure 10.1 (© The New Yorker Collection 1983 Dana Fradon from cartoonbank.com. All Rights Reserved.)

Are there significant contrasts in the Jewish and Christian explanations of human freedom?

Why is freedom of the will considered an essential human attribute?

Unit 49   CONCEPTS OF CHRISTIAN CHOOSING: GRACE, PREDESTINATION, AND ACCOUNTABILITY

Like Judaism and Islam, Christianity also emphasizes the majesty and greatness of God and at the same time highlights human responsibility. One of its central tenets proclaims that humanity is totally dependent on God's grace for salvation. If that is true, what is the nature of human freedom among Christians? Here we consider how some Christian theologians, ancient and modern, have interpreted freedom and what it means to decide.

CONCERNING FREE WILL

Pelagius, a British monk who taught in Rome late in the fourth and early in the fifth century, maintained that people are created free to choose good or evil and that they always have that freedom. Pelagius asked: How can humans be held responsible for the choices they make unless they can freely make those choices?

We have implanted in us by God a possibility for acting in both directions. It resembles, as I may say, a root which is most abundant in its produce of fruit. It yields and produces diversely according to man's will; and is capable, at the cultivator's own choice, of either shedding a beautiful bloom of virtues, or of bristling with the thorny thicket of vices. . . . But that we really do a good thing, or speak a good word, or think a good thought, proceeds from our own selves. . . . Nothing good, nothing evil, on account of which we are deemed either laudable or blameworthy, is born with us, but is done by us; for we are born not fully developed, but with a capacity for either conduct; we are formed naturally without either virtue or vice. . . .[4]

CONCERNING THE "UNFREE" WILL

Augustine, a contemporary of Pelagius and a North African bishop, responded to Pelagius's teachings. He asked: How can God be all-powerful and not be the ultimate determiner of everything that happens? How can human beings, once they have become sinful (he thought humans were born sinful) ever choose, without an act of God's grace, to do good? Augustine vehemently rejected Pelagius's position, for he felt that Pelagius neglected the grace of God in human actions; although humanity (Adam representing all persons) originally had freedom to sin or not to sin, because of their pride people sinned by choosing themselves over God and therefore lost their freedom to choose between the alternatives of good and evil. Since this original choice, according to Augustine, individuals have no freedom of their own to choose good or evil; they choose only the evil. Humanity's only hope of freedom to choose goodness depends on God's grace—God's willingness to restore human ability to do good. This restoration emphasizes humanity's dependence on God for any ability to do good. John Calvin, the sixteenth-century Protestant reformer, agreed with Augustine, as the following statement indicates:

The will, therefore, is so bound by the slavery of sin, that it cannot excite itself, much less devote itself to any thing good. . . . We must . . . observe this point of distinction, that man, having been corrupted by his fall, sins voluntarily, not with reluctance or constraint; with the strongest propensity of disposition, not with violent coercion; with the bias of his own passions, and not with external compulsion: yet such is the pravity of his nature, that he cannot be excited and biased to any thing but what is evil. If this be true, there is no impropriety in affirming, that he is under a necessity of sinning. . . . Man is so enslaved by sin, as to be of his own nature incapable of an effort, or even an inspiration, toward that which is good.[5]

Martin Luther, another Protestant Reformer of the sixteenth century, also affirmed that human lives are completely determined by God's predestining will. By the seventeenth century, a Dutch Calvinist theologian, Jacob Arminius, although insisting on the necessity of God's predestining grace to set sinful humans free of sin, insisted that God had given humans enough freedom to choose to respond positively to God's grace. Those God foresaw as responding positively were then predestined by God to salvation.

[4] Paul Lehmann, "The Anti-Pelagian Writings," in *A Companion to the Study of St. Augustine*, ed. Roy Battenhouse (New York: Oxford University Press, 1955), p. 208.

[5] John Calvin, *A Compend of the Institutes of Christian Religion*, ed. Hugh Thomson Kerr, Jr. (Philadelphia: Presbyterian Board of Education, 1939), pp. 49, 51.

The argument between Calvinists and Arminians about free choice grew heated among eighteenth-century Protestants both on the continent of Europe and in Britain and America.

The position of the Catholic Church on free will was between positions of Pelagius and Augustine, though Pelagius was regarded as a heretic and Augustine a saint. From the early Middle Ages, the Catholic Church affirmed, against Pelagius, that humans cannot choose goodness and God without God's grace, but held against Augustine that God has given humans enough grace to respond positively to God and goodness.

These arguments may seem antiquated. However, we should remember that at the very time Calvinist predestinarians and Arminians were arguing about predestination and free will, many secular thinkers in Europe and America, scientists and philosophers, believed that the New Science, established by Isaac Newton, was showing that humans live in a deterministic and completely determined universe.

Some twenty-first century scientists and philosophers argue that today's New Science, an updated version of Darwin's evolution (according to which humans have been decisively shaped by environment) and microbiology (emphasizing how genetic makeup shapes human life) can be used to make a case for determinism. For instance, there are genes that predispose some people to be violent and genes that influence one's sexual orientation. Many caution that these merely influence and do not determine or necessitate violent behavior or sexual orientation, but how much influence they have and how much room is left for human free choice may be an open question.

At the same time, the arguments continue among theologians and clergy. Some American Southern Baptists are insisting that Baptists are Calvinists. Others assert that they should be Arminians.

Many religious traditions show the same tensions. In the Jewish Scriptures, persons are held accountable for their wrongdoing, but sometimes are said to have had their hearts "hardened" by God, as in Exodus Chapters 7–12, where Egypt's ruler apparently was made to choose against God. Buddhism affirms a strict law of cause and effect involving *karma*, a law that governs human destiny, yet adherents are told to seek enlightenment (Hinduism affirms a similar position). And Islam, though holding humans accountable for doing wrong, stresses that the overwhelming power of Allah governs all existence.

◆◆◆

In the light of these interpretations, what does it mean to decide?

Do you agree or disagree with Pelagius that we are born without either virtue or vice and can choose between the alternatives of doing good or evil? Why?

Do you agree or disagree with Augustine's understanding that we have no real freedom in doing good or evil? Why?

If there are elements of truth in both positions, what resolution would you propose to rectify the seeming contradictions found between the two positions?

✦✦✦ 11 ✦✦✦

SIN AND GUILT

It starts early in life—a consciousness that we have done something "wrong" and we feel guilty about failing to act as we "should." The development of *conscience* is a lifelong process that begins when a baby learns one of his or her first words—no. The process by which we acquire an active conscience begins early and is so pervasive that we are seldom aware of its development or its continuing maturation. When there are big decisions to be made or clear temptations to go against our moral training, we may be very aware that our conscience is reminding us of our commitments and principles. Generally, however, the conscience operates within us without much notice in our daily lives. We live by the values and principles that have come throughout life to inform our consciences.

How we develop a conscience and how it operates is continually discussed among philosophers, ethicists, behavioral scientists, and theologians, but it is generally agreed that a major contributing factor to its development is one's faith commitment made to a religion and the ethical/moral values taught by that tradition. The values arising from basic beliefs concerning the nature of the Divine, the universe, and humanity are the foundation for ethical/moral instructions integral to every religion.

To transgress the moral values of one's social community normally leads to guilt and if the guilt is intense enough, it may lead to some action to rectify the transgression. For example, one gasoline service station operator offered refunds to persons he had overcharged in the emotional crisis immediately following the destruction of the World Trade Center. His conscience had obviously come to bother him once the emotion of the moment and his chance to "make a buck" passed—he felt guilty, ashamed, and wanted to redress his injury to others. To transgress the moral values of one's faith certainly carries this same guilt, but moves beyond it to what Western religions call "sin"—the transgression of the faith commitment one has made with the Divine. To transgress this commitment is to remove oneself from values embraced through the Divine and consequently from the Divine itself.

While shame and guilt arise out of transgression, they differ according to the

195

religious beliefs and experiences that produce these emotions. Attention is also given here to the concept of sin as developed within the Judeo-Christian heritage.

Unit 50   ROLES OF SHAME AND GUILT

A pompously, pretentiously dressed individual, through no fault of his own, slips on a banana peel and careens into a mud puddle. He looks quickly and furtively around and is relieved that no one has seen his fall.

A woman sends a large check to a bank, explaining that years ago a teller had given her twenty dollars too much. Though no one else has ever known about it, she explains that over the years she has come to feel increasingly guilty and is now returning the original sum with the correctly calculated interest.

These two incidents illustrate the contrasting attitudes of shame and guilt as discussed by Ruth Benedict in the passage that follows. A person who would have been ashamed if others had seen his disgrace, since no one did see, felt relief, not shame. The woman was burdened by guilt, even though no one else knew she had accepted the overpayment. Her guilt could be relieved only by confession (even if she remained anonymous) and restitution.

At the time of writing *The Chrysanthemum and the Sword*, Ruth Benedict believed that Western societies relied heavily on guilt, perhaps as a part of their Puritan heritage, and much less on the sense of shame to regulate behavior. Some recent observers have suggested that perhaps a shift has occurred, that there is more likelihood now than formerly for many in Western societies to be shame oriented rather than guilt oriented. As you read Benedict's discussion, ask yourself whether the distinction between the two attitudes and the corresponding contrast between Western and Eastern orientations are as clear today in your own personal experience as this passage suggests.

> In anthropological studies of different cultures the distinction between those which rely heavily on shame and those that rely heavily on guilt is an important one. A society that inculcates absolute standards of morality and relies on men's developing a conscience is a guilt culture by definition, but a man in such a society may, as in the United States, suffer in addition from shame when he accuses himself of gaucheries which are in no way sins. He may be exceedingly chagrined about not dressing appropriately for the occasion or about a slip of the tongue. In a culture where shame is a major sanction, people are chagrined about acts which we [in the West] expect people to feel guilty about. This chagrin can be very intense and it cannot be relieved, as guilt can be, by confession and atonement. A man who has sinned can get relief by unburdening himself. This device of confession is used in our secular therapy and by many religious groups which have otherwise little in common. We know it brings relief. Where shame is the major sanction, a man does not experience relief when he makes his fault public even to a confessor. So long as his bad behavior does not "get out into the world" he need not be troubled and confession appears to him merely a way of courting trouble. Shame cultures therefore do not provide for confessions, even to the gods. They have ceremonies for good luck rather than for expiation.
>
> True shame cultures rely on external sanctions for good behavior, not, as true guilt cultures do, on an internalized conviction of sin. Shame is a reaction to other people's

criticism. A man is shamed either by being openly ridiculed and rejected or by fantasying to himself that he has been made ridiculous. In either case it is a potent sanction. But it requires an audience or at least a man's fantasy of an audience. Guilt does not. In a nation where honor means living up to one's own picture of oneself, a man may suffer from guilt though no man knows of his misdeed and a man's feeling of guilt may actually be relieved by confessing his sin.

The early Puritans who settled in the United States tried to base their whole morality on guilt and all psychiatrists know what trouble contemporary Americans have with their consciences. But shame is an increasingly heavy burden in the United States and guilt is less extremely felt than in earlier generations. In the United States this is interpreted as a relaxation of morals. There is much truth in this, but that is because we do not expect shame to do the heavy work of morality. We do not harness the acute personal chagrin which accompanies shame to our fundamental system of morality.

The Japanese do. A failure to follow their explicit signposts of good behavior, a failure to balance obligations or to foresee contingencies is a shame (*hajj*). Shame, they say, is the root of virtue. A man who is sensitive to it will carry out all the rules of good behavior. "A man who knows shame" is sometimes translated "virtuous man," sometimes "man of honor." Shame has the same place of authority in Japanese ethics that "a clear conscience," "being right with God," and the avoidance of sin have in Western ethics. Logically enough, therefore, a man will not be punished in the afterlife. The Japanese—except for priests who know the Indian sutras—are quite unacquainted with the idea of reincarnation dependent upon one's merit in this life, and—except for some well-instructed Christian converts—they do not recognize post-death reward and punishment or a heaven and a hell.[1]

◆◆◆

Reflecting on the changes taking place in Western society as you can observe it, what illustrations do you find that we may be moving from a guilt-oriented society to a shame-oriented one? What effects might that have for the traditional nature of the society?

Unit 51   GUILT AND RELIGIOUS EXPERIENCE

When we say that humans are "ethical animals," we refer to the reality that humans know right from wrong and are able to choose between good and evil. The personal responsibility that arises out of this freedom to choose is part of what it means to be human and to act ethically. In religious language, *righteousness* denotes proper ethical actions and *guilt* is associated with actions that do not conform to the ethical principles of the religion. Guilt, arising from improper or evil action, is therefore one expression of the personal ethical principles operative through an individual's conscience. Guilt may lead to contrition, confession, and restitution, as one seeks to make amends for improper action.

Although guilt may be examined and at least partially explained through an intellectual process, its foundation is in the feelings: It is a part of the subconscious that

---

[1] Ruth Benedict, *The Chrysanthemum and the Sword: Patterns of Japanese Culture* (Boston: Houghton Mifflin, 1946), pp. 222–224. Used by permission of the publisher.

activates our daily lives, a powerful psychological phenomenon. Because of its power and usefulness, it is a significant element in the religious experience of many cultures, particularly in Western religious traditions.

Among the early Jews, the nature of an offense defined the degree of guilt, making it possible for some forms of guilt to become an objective contamination. Johannes Pedersen, a biblical scholar, describes this ancient Jewish understanding:

> It follows from the psychological conception of the Israelites that a man is responsible for all his actions. Every action must exercise its effect, also in the soul of the person who acts. . . . The decisive thing is what is the relation of the action to the acting soul: does it arise in the central will of the soul, or does it merely lie in the periphery of the soul? If the latter is the case, then it can be wiped out and be removed before it gains ground. . . . But if an infringement upon the law of righteousness is more deeply seated in the soul, then it is not to be removed.[2]

In other words, one may remove the guilt of minor acts through confession and restitution; however, in more serious offenses a person is not necessarily able to remove the guilt; it becomes an objective reality. For example, in the case of murder, the guilt is so intense that it not only shapes the reality of the murderer but also becomes attached to his or her family. It also demands reciprocal action, which may not take place for generations. This is the basis of the teaching that "the sins of the fathers shall set the teeth of the children on edge" and "an eye for an eye" and "a tooth for a tooth." In early Judaism this presumption of objective guilt was sometimes used by a violated family to destroy the offending party and/or their family. More often guilt became a consuming poison to the offender, recompensing the violated family by destroying the unregenerate soul and thereby ridding the Jewish community of a danger. This understanding is in accordance with the fundamental Jewish law of the soul. In Israel's conception of the psychic life, guilt produces misfortune, just as righteousness undergirds happiness.

> But the wicked are like the tossing sea
>   that cannot keep still;
>   its waters toss up mire and mud.
> There is no peace, says my God
>   for the wicked. (Isaiah 57:20–21 NRSV)

In Judaism's prophetic period (from 750 B.C.E.), the emphasis began to shift from objective guilt to the more subjective or psychological elements of guilt. Such guilt results from and expresses itself in wrong or rebellious attitudes rather than objective acts of revenge that arise from such attitudes. The prophets taught that such attitudes had to be changed. The emphasis was no longer on the contagion of an objective guilt that could not be removed (as in early Judaism) or on a debt that could be paid or canceled only by God (as in medieval Christian teaching).

These psychological and subjective aspects of guilt have been emphasized in Christianity from the New Testament period to the present. Guilt, and the human respon-

---

[2] Johannes Pedersen, *Israel, Its Life and Culture* (London: Oxford University Press, 1926), Vols I-II, p. 419.

sibility it incorporates, became a central issue for Saint Augustine of Hippo (354–430 C.E.) and the Danish Christian philosopher Søren Kierkegaard (1819–1855 C.E.). Without guilt individuals cannot recognize or appropriate true responsibility for their actions, they remain totally selfish—unable to accept God's grace offered in forgiveness.

Modern theological study of the role of guilt and conscience in personality development draws on the traditions within Judaism and Christianity that have emphasized the subjective and psychological character of guilt, as well as on recent psychological models of personality development. John G. McKenzie, an English psychotherapist and adherent of Christianity, distinguishes between a socially created and immature conscience (Freud's concept of the *superego*), which often functions on the level of taboos and neurotic (false) guilt, and a mature conscience able to be self-governing in accordance with the authentic needs of (and duties to) the self and others. McKenzie suggests that a child's morality begins when he or she becomes conscious of approval and disapproval from those surrounding the child, usually parents and teachers. Since parents and teachers are not always with the child, he or she internalizes their teachings and prohibitions, and these become the basis of moral action; however, they are still adopted from others.

> Now, many people never outgrow this infantile Super-ego. Unconsciously they strive to obey the prohibitions and conform to the commands. Inwardly they rebel against its rigidity and compulsions; and they may develop . . . a perfectionist character-trend, or a dynamic trend to restrict their lives within narrow limits. The least deviation from perfection and they are full of guilty-feelings, recriminations, and yet at the same time a raging hostility has to be kept repressed, or projected.
>
> Thus we come, again, up against the ambivalence which lies at the root of the origin of guilt-feelings. I would not say that the child or the adult wants to comply with the Super-ego, but he or she fears the guilt-feelings. He or she is afraid of freedom; they are afraid lest the impulses prove too strong for the Ego to control. Hence unconsciously they cling to the authoritative conscience. . . .
>
> The problem of moral growth is simply the problem of growing up. . . . We have to pass from Super-ego control to conscience-control. . . . It is doubtful whether the Super-ego ever withers away entirely; but with the development of the adult or positive conscience it performs a different role. Instead of repressing through the guilt-sense an offending line of behaviour, it pulls us up, compels us to reflect upon what we are tempted to do; and then exercises control through reason rather than through feeling. If we cross the "barrier" and fall then there is a consciousness of objective guilt, but instead of morbid guilt-feelings with all their threats there is sincere contrition . . . that is to say, there is sorrow for the guilty behaviour and a turning away from such behaviour. . . . It is the passing from the "borrowed morality" of the Super-ego to the free morality of conscience where oughts, commands and prohibitions have become moral guides and not moral policemen. We accept these not in virtue of external authority, but because we see they are true. . . .[3]

Similarly, in religious traditions a mature believer not only accepts responsibility for his or her actions but also develops a "mature morality" based on the ethical teachings of the tradition, not as something imposed from outside by religious teachers but because such teachings are true and lead to a fruitful and joyous life. Transgression of the religious

---

[3] John G. McKenzie, *Guilt: Its Meaning and Significance* (Nashville, TN: Abingdon Press, 1962), pp. 40–49.

teachings may lead to guilt, but in a mature believer these become avenues for returning to responsible action, often through contrition and restitution.

◆◆◆

Do you distinguish between types of guilt, for example, healthy and unhealthy guilt?

Do religions play a constructive role in society by providing some content for the conscience?

Do you agree with McKenzie that "appropriate" or "healthy" guilt experiences are necessary for people to live in a social context?

In your judgment, have contemporary changes in family structures and educational patterns modified the role of guilt in the development of ethical behavior?

Unit 52   JUDEO-CHRISTIAN CONCEPTS OF SIN

Non-Western religions generally stress right living that incorporates clear consequences for transgressions of moral and ethical codes; but none of these consequences is separation from the Divine or the created order. In Hinduism and Buddhism, for example, bad karma may lead to a lesser reincarnation but one is never "outside" a relationship with universal life.

In contrast, a central emphasis in the Judeo-Christian tradition has been the broken relationship between God and humankind, denoted by the word *sin*. Most Christians have connected the concept of sin with disobedience to the commandments or laws of God. The Ten Commandments given by God to the descendants of Israel (see Exodus 20) have often been taken as a prototype of God's commandments, in that they contain an indication of the conduct God desires or forbids. Primarily, God's will has been interpreted to include the exclusive devotion to God and justice and love toward one's fellow humans. Christianity, departing from Judaism, has laid great stress on original sin, an attitude involving self-will and self-indulgence held to be characteristic of all humanity that precedes and causes specific acts of sinfulness. Thus, medieval Christianity stressed as deadly sins seven dispositions, or character traits—pride, covetousness, lust, envy, gluttony, anger, and sloth. As particular manifestations of the underlying original sin (an attitude or disposition rather than an act), these attitudes are motivating causes of sinful acts both in the unredeemed and in Christians who have fallen away from the restored innocence given them by baptism.

The following passage from Genesis gives an account of the fall of Adam and Eve, a symbol to many Christians and Jews of how all humans turn toward their own will rather than God's will for them.

> Now the serpent was more crafty than any other wild creature that the Lord God had made. He said to the woman, "Did God say, 'You shall not eat of any tree of the garden'?" The woman said to the serpent, "We may eat of the fruit of the trees of the garden; but God said, 'You shall not eat of the fruit of the tree that is in the middle of the garden, nor shall you touch it, or you shall die.' " But the serpent said to the woman, "You will not die; for God knows that when you eat of it your eyes will be opened, and you will be like

God, knowing good and evil." So when the woman saw that the tree was good for food, and that it was a delight to the eyes, and that the tree was to be desired to make one wise, she took of its fruit and ate; and she also gave some to her husband, and he ate. Then the eyes of both were opened, and they knew that they were naked; and they sewed fig leaves together and made loincloths for themselves.

They heard the sound of the Lord God walking in the garden at the time of the evening breeze, and the man and his wife hid themselves from the presence of the Lord God among the trees of the garden. But the Lord God called to the man, and said to him, "Where are you?" He said, "I heard the sound of you in the garden, and I was afraid, because I was naked; and I hid myself." He said, "Who told you that you were naked? Have you eaten of the tree of which I commanded you not to eat?" The man said, "The woman whom you gave to be with me, she gave me fruit from the tree, and I ate." Then the Lord God said to the woman, "What is this that you have done?" The woman said, "The serpent tricked me, and I ate." (Genesis 3:1–13 NRSV)

This passage describes actual disobedience but also—and more important—the desire to be like God or to be God, a wish that separates humanity from God.

Reinhold Niebuhr, a well-known theologian, expands on this interpretation.

> Since Augustine it has been the consistent view of Christian orthodoxy that the basic sin of man was his pride. In this view Christian thought agreed with the conception of the Greek tragedies, which regarded hybris as man's most flagrant fault and one which was invariably followed by punishment or nemesis. The basic sign of pride does not mean some conscious bit of exaggerated self-esteem, but the general inclination of all men to overestimate their virtues, powers, and achievements. Augustine defined sin as the "perverse desire of height," or as man's regarding himself as his own end, instead of realizing that he is but a part of a total scheme of means and ends.[4]

Although Niebuhr stresses sin as pride, he also finds another basic mode of human sinfulness in sloth or self-indulgence.

Harvey Cox offers yet another explanation of sin—one that contrasts with the broadly accepted concept of sin as pride but to some extent resembles Niebuhr's concept of sin as sloth.

> Man-as-sinner has usually been pictured by religious writers as man-the-insurrectionary, the proud heaven-storming rebel who has not learned to be content with his lot. Refined and escalated in literature, this image blossoms in the heroic Satans and Lucifers of Goethe and Milton. No wonder we find sin so interesting and sinners more attractive than saints. No wonder we secretly admire Lucifer while our orthodox doctrine condemns him to the lake of fire. This misleading view of sin as pride and rebelliousness has given the very word sin an intriguing lustre: a naked Eve with moist bedroom eyes guiltily tasting the forbidden apple; a slithery, clearly phallic, serpent; man defying the petty conventions imposed on him by small-minded people. In these terms why shouldn't we be in favor of sin? The only trouble is this mish-mash of sex and self-affirmation images has almost nothing to do with the biblical idea of sin. It is basically a Greek, or more precisely, promethean notion larded with remnants of medieval folk piety, Victorian antisexuality, and the bourgeois obsession with orderliness.[5]

[4] Reinhold Niebuhr, "Sin" in *A Handbook of Christian Theology*, ed. Marvin Halverson and Arthur A. Cohen (New York: World Publishing Company, 1958), p. 348.

[5] Harvey Cox, *On Not Leaving It to the Snake* (New York: Macmillan, 1964), pp. xi- xiii. Copyright © 1964, 1965, 1967 by Harvey G. Cox. Used by permission.

. . . Apathy is the key form of sin in today's world. . . . For Adam and Eve, apathy meant letting a snake tell them what to do. It meant abdicating what the theologians have called *gubernatio mundi*, the exercise of dominion and control over the world. For us it means allowing others to dictate the identities with which we live out our lives.[6]

. . . I believe a careful examination of the biblical sources will indicate that man's most debilitating proclivity is not his pride. It is not his attempt to be more than man . . . it is his sloth, his unwillingness to be everything man was intended to be.[7]

◆ ◆ ◆

Is it necessary to have a concept of sin or wrongdoing in a religion? If so, why is it necessary? If not, how can broken human relationships be explained?

What does Niebuhr mean by sin as pride?

Which of the explanations of sin presented here do you find most appropriate?

[6] Ibid., p. xviii.
[7] Ibid., p. xi.

✦✦✦ 12 ✦✦✦

DEATH AND THE SELF

In every society, in every period of human history, people have struggled to understand the experience and meaning of death. The inevitability of death has often been referred to as the one clear fact of life. All other realities of one's existence may change or be modified but death is a given fact that cannot be escaped. Consequently, it is a custom among some Christian groups for individuals to remind each other on Ash Wednesday each year, "Recall, O man, thou art mortal. Dust thou art, and to dust thou shalt return." Throughout human history death, its meaning, its mystery, and the uncertainty or promise of what may come after, has been the subject of wide-ranging speculation and deepest interest.

A student wrote in a journal entry,

> Why are some people so sure they will find the answers to life when they die? I asked one person why she was sure. She said, "Because Jesus said so in the Bible." Faith is their answer. Faith is not my answer. I have heard people witness of God's part in their lives, and how they could feel his presence. But I haven't felt Him directly in my life. I have experienced the love of people. I guess that's how He works. God is very vague to me. I guess that is why I'm not sure I'll find the "whys" of life when I die. I don't have any idea of what is after death, as some people think they do. Perhaps that is why death scares me. I talked to a girl one time who believes there is nothing after death. I can't believe that either. I can't imagine a nothing. I can't feature a complete end to everything.

The ambiguity of feelings toward life and death expressed in this statement is not an uncommon human experience. The reality of death is recognized and for this person there seems little assurance of an afterlife; nevertheless, there is still the hope and anticipation of continuance. This anticipation of some persistence after death is a common trait among humans. Why is it that humans generally cannot conceive of life ending at physical death? Why, particularly in Western societies, is death so feared, if it indeed is a given fact of life? Philosophers, behavioral scientists, and religious communities have suggested answers to such questions but death still remains a mystery because we have so little insight into what follows life.

All religious traditions have interpreted the meaning of death—usually embracing a more positive stance toward death and its consequences than just expressed. Most have contained teachings about the meaning of existence beyond the present one, in the continuity of future generations; in an afterlife; in a succession of rebirths; or in a restored or resurrected, totally renewed existence. This chapter explores several facets of the phenomenon of death as a fundamental human experience and gives examples of various religious interpretations of death and an afterlife.

Unit 53   ATTITUDES TOWARD DEATH

Life in all its aspects has been greatly modified by the scientific and technological developments of the past century, particularly in the West. This is most obvious in the health care field, where startling innovations have greatly lengthened our life span and increased our control over disease. Such advances are seldom without their price, however. One has been the need to modify and change the behavioral patterns by which we deal with death. In America until the mid-twentieth century, death normally took place in the home where one might be surrounded by family, friends, and known caregivers. With the changes in medical technology and services, death nowadays more often occurs in a hospital or nursing home, often in limited visitation intensive-care units. Family, patients, and friends are consequently often cut off from the personal care previously available for the dying person. Such changes contribute to a cultural "distancing" of persons from the reality and experience of death. Consequently, traditional grief processes for both patient and family are in many cases interrupted and sometimes eliminated. The medical community has in recent decades struggled to overcome its own traditional attitude that viewed death as a sign of failure, but that has proved difficult since a primary goal of medicine is to sustain life.

Other aspects of cultural change also contribute to attitudes that modify our perception of death. The ability of medical science to lengthen life often allows many persons to simply avoid the inevitability of death throughout much of their lives. Confidence that science will be able to continue to lengthen life or even overcome death may also play a part in developing such attitudes. The influence of TV, violent movie presentations, and video and computer games in desensitizing viewers to the "real life" consequences of death is debated among sociologists, psychologists, and religious leaders, but there seems little question that such media presentations contribute to changing attitudes toward death, particularly among the youth of the society. The growing availability of Eastern religious thought patterns in the West may be seen as another factor in changing concepts. The popularity of reincarnation beliefs and identification of all of life with the natural order perhaps reduces the fear of death often found in Western society.

In recent decades people working with the dying have come to recognize that these changing patterns have turned us into a society that avoids and sometimes denies the reality and consequences of death, creating numerous psychological, emotional, and religious problems. This recognition led to an immense amount of academic investigation and writing on death, many popular books, and plentiful workshops and seminars for

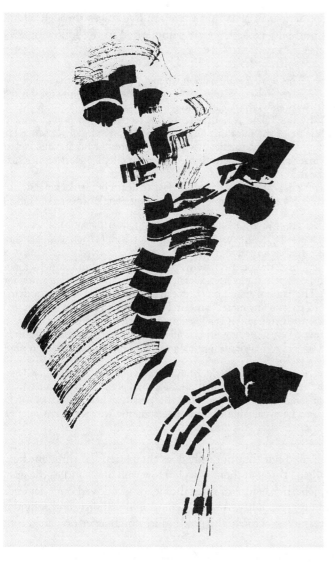

Figure 12.1 *Death* by Jacques Bakke

health professionals, social workers, chaplains, pastors, and laity. There has arisen among some of the professionals who work with the dying a renewed consciousness that the whole society needs to admit the reality of death and to accept it as a part of life. Awareness of death may indeed mean the growth and expansion of meaning for life as it is lived each day. This recognition among many who deal with the dying contributed to the rise in the medical community of "hospice" care. This nursing and volunteer care program provided within homes or hospitals recognizes not only the need for more personal care for the dying but also the limits of medicine to sustain life.

Renewed concern for the dying among many in the society produced significant information about societal attitudes and patterns of behavior. Dr. Elisabeth Kübler-Ross, after extensive study of dying patients, suggests that there are five stages through which dying patients and loved ones normally pass. They are summarized in the following passage by Hans Mauksch:

1. Denial—"No, not me." This is a typical reaction when a patient learns that he or she is terminally ill. Denial, says Dr. Ross, is important and necessary. It helps cushion the impact of the patient's awareness that death is inevitable.
2. Rage and anger—"Why me?" The patient resents the fact that others will remain healthy and alive while he or she must die. God is a special target for anger, since He is regarded as imposing, arbitrarily, the death sentence. To those who are shocked at her claim that such anger is not only permissible but inevitable, Dr. Ross replies succinctly, "God can take it."
3. Bargaining—"Yes me, but. . . ." Patients accept the fact of death but strike bargains for more time. Mostly they bargain with God—"even among people who never talked with God before."
    They promise to be good or to do something in exchange for another week or month or year of life. Notes Dr. Ross: "What they promise is totally irrelevant, because they don't keep their promises anyway."
4. Depression—"Yes, me." First, the person mourns past losses, things not done, wrongs committed. But then he or she enters a state of "preparatory grief," getting ready for the arrival of death. The patient grows quiet, doesn't want visitors. "When a dying patient doesn't want to see you any more," says Dr. Ross, "this is a sign he has finished his unfinished business with you, and it is a blessing. He can now let go peacefully."
5. Acceptance—"My time is very close now and it's all right." Dr. Ross describes this final stage as "not a happy stage, but neither is it unhappy. It's devoid of feelings but it's not resignation, it's really a victory."

These stages provide a very useful guide to understanding the different phases that dying patients may go through. They are not absolute; not everyone goes through every stage, in this exact sequence, at some predictable pace. But this paradigm can, if used in a flexible, insight-producing way, be a valuable tool in understanding why a patient may be behaving as he does.[1]

Dr. Kübler-Ross additionally pointed out that not only does the patient go through these stages, but the bereaved normally go through them as well. How well one handles the grief work inherent in these stages, whether before or after the death of a loved one, depends on a number of factors, including personality, training, emotional stability, and religious faith. Healthy grief work is necessary to achieve the position in which a person can accept and find meaning in death.

The title of one of Dr. Kübler-Ross's books, *Death: The Final Stage of Growth*, expresses her conviction that the acceptance of our own death and that of loved ones is ultimately a growing experience wherein we come to recognize the importance of each day of our lives. Growth here means awareness of ourselves and our situation, acceptance of ourselves and others, embracing our own value structures and not merely those of other people, and willingness to share ourselves and our insights with others. Out of this growth, life becomes meaningful just when it seems to have lost all meaning.

---

[1] Summarized by Hans O. Mauksch, "The Organizational Context of Dying," in Elisabeth Kübler-Ross, *Death: The Final Stage of Growth* (Englewood Cliffs, NJ: Prentice-Hall, 1975), p. 10. Used by permission.

Dying is something we human beings do continuously, not just at the end of our physical lives on this earth. The stages of dying that I have described apply equally to any significant change (e.g., retirement, moving to a new city, changing jobs, divorce) in a person's life, and change is a regular occurrence in human existence. If you can face and understand your ultimate death, perhaps you can learn to face and deal productively with each change that presents itself in your life. Through a willingness to risk the unknown, to venture forth into unfamiliar territory, you can undertake the search for your own self—the ultimate goal of growth. Through reaching out and committing yourself to dialogue with fellow human beings, you can begin to transcend your individual existence, becoming at one with yourself and others. And through a lifetime of such commitment, you can face your final end with peace and joy, knowing that you have lived your life well.[2]

It is the denial of death that is partially responsible for people living empty, purposeless lives; for when you live as if you'll live forever, it becomes too easy to postpone the things you know that you must do. You live your life in preparation for tomorrow or in remembrance of yesterday, and meanwhile, each today is lost. In contrast, when you fully understand that each day you awaken could be the last you have, you take the time that day to grow, to become more of who you really are, to reach out to other human beings.[3]

Insights such as these into the meaning of everyday life and the function of death in life have historically been taught by the various religious traditions. As modern society has placed less emphasis on religion for meaning and purpose in life, these insights and the patterns of behavior they cultivate have often been abandoned—now to be rediscovered by psychologists and others who deal with the difficulties that abandonment creates.

The phenomenon of detachment from death and the inability to deal constructively with it is not limited to modern industrial societies. Yet it seems to be most acute in the societies in which medical advances, insensitivity to death's consequences, and death patterns have removed family members and friends from the actual death event.

✦✦✦

What is your attitude toward death? How have your experiences with death shaped that understanding?

Do you think that the death of the person closest to you could bring growth to your life?

Is Kübler-Ross correct when she says that acceptance of death can mean acceptance of life, making it more meaningful?

Unit 54   HOW IT MAY FEEL TO DIE

The reality of death has always been intriguing, and the event itself has been surrounded in all cultures by ritual preparation, elaborate burial practices, and stylized grief formulas. Accounts of death and an anticipated afterlife have been numerous throughout history; for example, the fourteenth-century Tibetan *Book of the Dead* contains elaborate

---

[2] Kübler-Ross, *Death*, p. 145.
[3] Ibid., p. 164.

descriptions of the patterns of death and methods for contacting the dead. Preliterate/ prehistorical societies often developed elaborate ceremonies and rituals to assure persons of a good passage from physical life to life beyond death. The Egyptian pyramids and the Tomb of Qin Shi Luang in Xian, China, and other such elaborate burial sites stand as visual physical evidence of belief in life after death.

From ancient times another phenomenon relative to death and its meaning has been the recounting in myths and legends of what today we call "near-death" experiences —experiences in which persons are conscious of beginning a journey toward a different state of existence but then returning to present life. Plato, the fourth-century B.C.E. Greek philosopher, in his *Republic* (Book X), recounts the experiences of a soldier, killed on the battlefield, reviving on his funeral pyre and recounting a journey out of his body to tell others about the afterlife as a place of judgment and preparation for a return to life. Plato's *Phaedo* and *Gorgais* contain similar accounts and speculations about life after death.

As the advances of modern medicine have made the phenomenon of "clinical death" more common, a number of studies have focused on the nature of near-death experiences encountered in a substantial number of these cases. Accounts of such experiences have become popular reading, and the frequency of the phenomenon has opened discussions among psychologists and medical professionals of life after death in ways unanticipated a few years ago. These accounts and others usually arising from nonmedical crisis events in life inevitably raise anew images and questions that have been an integral part of religious traditions throughout human history. Raymond Moody, a philosopher and physician, compiled accounts of such experiences in a 1973 book entitled *Life after Life*. Moody's study, the first in a number of modern investigations of the phenomenon, identified distinctive and defining features in such experiences that have been confirmed in later investigations.[4] Every incident investigated is unique, so while similar features or characteristics may be found in any number of the events all were not reported to occur in any particular experience.

The following accounts illustrate such near-death episodes and contain many features found by researchers. The first example is an unsolicited account given to Peter Fenwick, a British psychiatrist, by one of his long-term patients.

> Then I was aware I was losing consciousness and of people rushing around me, knocking things over in their efforts to get emergency equipment set up. Then there was nothing— no pain at all. And I was up there on a level with the ceiling—I say 'I was up there,' because that's how it was. It wasn't a dream, it wasn't imagination. It was as real as me sitting here talking to you. I could actually see myself; me, my body, down there on the bed. Doctors scurrying round it, a general air of panic, but it didn't worry me at all. I suppose it should have done—I knew it was me down there but it didn't seem to be *me* if that makes any sense. The me that was really me was up there, out of it all.
>
> Then I was floating in what seemed to be a tunnel; dark, but not frightening at all. I could see a light at the end and I felt as though I was being pulled towards it. I had to go—

[4] Raymond A. Moody, Jr., *Life after Life and Reflections on Life After Life* (Atlanta, GA: Mockingbird Books, 1975). See also Craig R. Lundahl, *A Collection of Near-Death Research Readings* (Chicago: Nelson-Hall Publishers, 1982); Elisabeth Kübler-Ross, *On Death and Dying* (New York: Macmillan, 1969). These works themselves have been analyzed and discussed in such works as Hans Küng's *Eternal Life?* (Garden City, NY: Doubleday, 1984).

there was no alternative. But I wasn't frightened. Rather the reverse—I had the most wonderful feeling of peace, more than I've ever felt before, at any time in my life, as though everything that was happening was right. And you know me—this isn't anything like my usual self. The light at the end got brighter and brighter, but it didn't hurt my eyes. Although it was brilliant, it wasn't dazzling. I felt I was being drawn into it and the feeling was well, the only way I can describe it is pure bliss and love. There was someone there in the light, waiting for me. And then suddenly I was pulled back, away from it, back, slammed into my body again, back into pain, and I didn't want to go. I just wanted that peace.[5]

The out-of-body feeling of detachment from events occurring around the body, the sense of peace, a tunnel leading to a brilliant light, the presence of someone, and the reluctance to return are features of this experience that seem to be common in near-death experiences. Other aspects include enhanced awareness, a barrier not crossed; pastoral scenes; meeting relatives or friends, a life review, and a point of decision.[6]

The second example displays many of the same features but also notes two other aspects—the witnessing of the event by another person and a reluctance to tell of this experience for fear of being thought odd, a reluctance to share because of the unusual nature of the events:

It's very hard to put my experience into words, initially I felt very frightened. I was only fifteen and knew I was dying. Gradually I relaxed and felt very calm, an acceptance of what was going to happen. My fear vanished. I saw a distant light that was friendly and warm, and felt myself drawn towards it. There was just a feeling of tremendous peace. I felt I was floating, weightless, I appeared to see only a tunnel. I think I looked down on myself in bed, but this was very brief. There was a light or glow at the end of the tunnel, a beautiful gold like the sun rising. I felt it was warm and pleasant. It made me feel very secure and loved. I saw someone, but no one I knew. He held out his arms to me, he was smiling and calling my name. I seemed to know what he was saying but he didn't appear to talk to me. It was more a sort of telepathy. I felt very comfortable and secure. At the time I felt it was Christ. There was no evil, nothing frightening. I reached out to touch his hands, but he told me I was not ready to join him and I must go back and I would recover. I knew I only had to touch his hands and I would join him. There was definitely some threshold I had to cross. At the time I thought it was betwixt Heaven and Earth. I felt reluctant to go.

I felt I had experienced something wonderful. My mother certainly thinks I experienced something that night as she witnessed it all. According to her, I sat up in bed. Minutes before I had been delirious and throwing myself around the bed. My temperature had gone and I improved rapidly from that night. The doctor was amazed at such a dramatic recovery. I have told my fiance and one or two close friends – most people, I fear, would brand me a nutcase, or say I dreamed it.[7]

Reluctance to share the experience because of its oddity and unusual nature is common among persons who have participated in such incidents. For many persons the near-death experience is also credited with having a profound affect on their subsequent lives.

---

[5] From *The Truth in the Light* by Peter Fenwick and Elizabeth Fenwick, copyright © 1995 by Peter and Elizabeth Fenwick. Used by permission of Viking Penguin, a division of Penguin Putnam, Inc., pp. 5–6.

[6] Ibid., pp. 9–11.

[7] Ibid., p. 28.

I suppose this experience molded something in my life. I was only a child when it happened, only ten, but now, my entire life through, I am thoroughly convinced that there is life after death, without a shadow of a doubt, and I am not afraid to die. I am not. Some people I have known are so afraid, so scared. I always smile to myself when I hear people doubt that there is an afterlife, or say "When you're dead, you're gone." I think to myself, "They really don't know."

I've had many things happen to me in my life. In business, I've had a gun pulled on me and put to my temple. And it didn't frighten me very much, because I thought, "Well, if I really die, if they really kill me, I know I'll still live somewhere."[8]

That such events modified attitudes toward life and death is perhaps not surprising since for most persons the experience takes on particular and unique significance. The confidence expressed in this last passage about an afterlife was not necessarily shared by all persons whose experiences have been studied, but many found the events to be life changing.

Raymond Moody and others who have studied the phenomenon do not claim that the phenomena of near-death experiences "prove" in any scientific way that there is life after death. What is clear from this research is that many people unknown to each other and most often without knowledge of research into this topic or the accounts of other persons have similar experiences that point beyond present life that cannot be easily explained by our present psychological and scientific knowledge.[9] Many religious persons have welcomed research into the near-death experience as confirmation of ancient religious beliefs in an afterlife although others see such belief as a matter of faith needing

[8] Moody, *Life*, p. 71.
[9] Ibid., pp. 129–131; Fenwick, *The Truth*, pp. 249ff.

"Apparently there is life after death."

Figure 12.2   (© The New Yorker Collection 1997 Leo Cullum from cartoonbank.com. All Rights Reserved.)

no other confirmation. The following unit presents understandings of death found in differing cultures grounded primarily in religious traditions and worldviews.

◆◆◆

Have you or someone you know had such experiences?

What is your reaction to such descriptions? Do you think the content of the experiences was real or the product of hallucination, dreams, etc.?

To what extent, if any, might one's beliefs about life and death influence the nature of such an event?

If one were willing to embrace concepts of spirituality not related to death, would near-death experiences confirm spiritual reality? Why? Why not?

Compare the experiences of a light or figures recounted here with (1) Gautama's comments concerning Nirvana, Unit 18; (2) Zen enlightenment, Unit 28; and (3) mystical experience of God, Unit 28.

Unit 55   DEATH AND THE AFTERLIFE: CULTURAL PERSPECTIVES

Cultural understandings of death most often embrace the religious understandings of their dominant religions. India, China, Japan, and many other Asian cultures view death from Hindu, Buddhist, and Taoist/Confucian worldviews. Consequently, death may have many meanings unfamiliar to many in the West. Hindu and Buddhist acceptance of reincarnation or a continuum of life through eons makes death a part of an ongoing, unending process. While life beyond this physical existence may be influenced by current actions, death, not being the end of existence, does not carry the threat it may have for many Western cultures. Similarly, in Native-American religion, many African religions, and those arising out of a Taoist/Confucian tradition, death is to be reunited with the natural world or the melding of one form of nature into another.

With worldviews that differ so dramatically it is not surprising to find a great variety of responses to and treatment of death among diverse cultures, as the following descriptions illustrate. Although the following examples are drawn from the religious traditions of several cultures, it should be noted that philosophical systems that incorporate monism and pantheism also display belief in forms of immortality.

JUDAISM

As Judaism firmly believes in the God-given soul, bestowed pure on every man, it also maintains a firm faith in *Olam Haba*, the world to come. This is not the same as the time of the Messiah, or the Resurrection. It is the sheltering of souls in God's eternal dwelling forever. There they will share the joys of their closeness to the divine glory.

Again, Maimonides [a Jewish philosopher] warns against the formulation of any picture. As we do not know God, we know not what He has in store for us. But Judaism does not devote excessive thought to the question of the "salvation" of souls. "All of Israel will have a share in the world to come." "All the righteous of the peoples of the world have a share in it."[10]

As Leo Trepp suggests, the expectation of a Messiah who would right the evils of the world and of a resurrected state in which good would be triumphant have historically been prominent features of Jewish belief (see Unit 56). Yet many modern Jews reject concepts of an afterlife, believing that the present life is a sufficient field of encounter with God and there is no necessity for continuation. Jewish tradition does not stress doctrinal agreement over such questions.

CHRISTIANITY

In the light of the Christian gospel death appears both as the penalty of sin and as the means of salvation. As the penalty of sin it brings estrangement from God. Not spatial separation from Him . . . but spiritual and moral remoteness from God which makes the sinner's inability to escape from God a torment. . . .

The death of Christ, the second Adam, transforms death, sin's penalty, into a means of deliverance from its guilt and power. Because Christ "has tasted death for every man," He has made death the gateway into eternal life. The crucified Son of God has drawn the sting of death—which is sin. The believer must still undergo "natural" death, but he has been delivered from "the second death" of final estrangement from God. He lives in newness of life, because by the saving grace of God in Christ he has learned how to die.[11]

HINDUISM

The Hindu believes in *samsara*, that the present life is the result of previous existences bound by the law of *karma*. The law is based on the causal relationship in which what one does in the present form of existence determines what one will be in the next form of existence (see Figure 12.3). This cycle of birth, growth, decay, and death will not be broken until one experiences *moksha*—release from *samsara*. Thus, to one who believes in reincarnation, death is just another phase in the cycle of rebirths. "Death is the separation of the soul [*Atman*] from the physical body; it becomes a starting point for a new life with fresh opportunities. It opens the door for higher forms of life; it is a gateway to fuller life."[12] (See also Unit 10.)

TAOISM

Since man is an aspect of Tao, death is but another incident in the eternal movements of nature. It is told of Chuang Tzu that he sang and beat time on a wooden bowl, when his wife lay dead. Reproached for this apparent callousness, he replied that her death was but a change into a new aspect, as fall merges into winter, as a leaf drops from a tree to become leaf mold. For him to grieve over her death would be to show himself ignorant of Tao. In

---

[10] Leo Trepp, *Judaism: Development and Life* (Belmont, CA: Dickenson Publishing Co., 1966), p. 135.

[11] H. F. Lovell Cocks, "Death" in *A Handbook of Christian Theology*, eds. Marvin Halverson and Arthur A. Cohen (New York: World Publishing Co., 1958), p. 73.

[12] Frederick H. Holck, ed., *Death and Eastern Thought* (Nashville, TN: Abingdon Press, 1974), p. 194.

Figure 12.3   The wheel is one of the symbols used in Hindu religion and represents the cyclical nature of existence. This is one of a number on the temple of Surya, Konarak, India. (Reproduced with permission of the Hamlyn Group.)

original Taoism, therefore, there is no positive view of life after death, but only the idea of changing into a new aspect of the monistic principle of Tao.[13]

SHINTOISM

> Since one's kami nature will survive death, a man desires to be worthy of being remembered with approbation by his descendants. Therefore it is preferable to die than to fail in duty to one's family or nation. The famous kamikaze pilots of World War II acted on this principle. . . . A kamikaze pilot, by his brave but suicidal action in the national cause, exemplified the height of loyalty to the emperor and his people. He then became an illustrious ancestor, joining the eight hundred myriads of kami beings in the spirit world.[14]

Other religious traditions have similar or unique concepts of rebirth and afterlife. In the various forms of Buddhism, for example, there is a generalized sense that (in a way similar to Hinduism) what one is in one life is transmitted to succeeding lives. With the Buddhist concept of the no-self or nonself, successive rebirths present a series of challenges and tasks since what is transmitted from life to life tends to be the pattern of false and superficial characteristics of the (false) self. The task is to work through, untangle, and eliminate them until the self becomes what it truly is, the nonself. However, there is great diversity within the different varieties of Buddhism, ranging from the teachings of

[13] D.G. Bradley, *Guide to the World's Religions* (Englewood Cliffs, NJ: Prentice Hall, 1982), p. 138 (see also Unit 12).

[14] Ibid., p. 154. *Kami* is a Shinto word denoting the spiritual force in all things (see Unit 40).

the Japanese Pure Land sect—that there is life after life in the Great Western Paradise—to the more austere no-self and Nirvana of traditional Buddhism to the esoteric (to most Westerners) teachings of the Tibetan *Book of the Dead*.

✦✦✦

Reflecting on the differing understandings of the ultimate significance of death outlined in this unit, comment on how such differences may influence the future of a world growing ever more interdependent economically, socially, and intellectually.

Unit 56   RESURRECTION AND MONOTHEISTIC FAITH

In Western cultures the reality of death and the emphasis on hope have often been accompanied by the belief in the resurrection of the dead. Resurrection is an ancient concept shared by several Near Eastern religions—among them Judaism and Christianity. In Egypt, Mesopotamia, and Canaan, the seasonal cycle of nature became the basis for religious affirmations of an interconnection between the annual dying and rising of the gods and the natural productivity of the land. The idea of rising from the dead was then part of the common culture that surrounded Israel from its earliest days. It is not surprising to find Hebrew Scriptures, depending on an utter confidence in the sovereignty of God, referring to dying and rising by God's power (I Samuel 2:6; Deuteronomy 32:39). The story of Elijah's restoration of the life of a widow's son goes further to imply a conception of resurrection, although it is not very clearly developed (I Kings 17:17–24).

The Hebrew idea of resurrection and restoration is most vividly portrayed in the writings of the prophets. Grounding their ideas on God's covenantal promises to sustain and not desert Israel—especially the promise made to uphold David's household—the prophets saw the only hope of their fulfillment in a great day of restoration and renewal. "On that day I will raise up the booth of David that is fallen and repair its breaches, and raise up its ruins, and rebuild it as in the days of old" (Amos 9:11, NRSV). Ezekiel's valley of dry bones (Ezekiel 31:1–14) carries the symbolism to the point of restoring dead Israel. From the threat of death and complete extinction, the prophet constantly looks to the day of restoration. In the prophetic treatment, the concept generally remains that of anticipated communal resurrection of Israel as a faithful and blessed community of God.

After the Israelite exile to Babylon, the concept of resurrection began to change in that the communal restitution was now joined to a belief in the resurrection of the individual. The books of Daniel and the Maccabees, written during a national crisis, when extinction of the community was a clear possibility, contain affirmations of individual resurrection within a communal hope. Here also the concept of a great day of renewal, when all Israel's enemies would be overcome and Israel would be restored, was joined with the idea of a last day of judgment, when each individual would be judged on the basis of his or her faithfulness or unfaithfulness to God. How much this latter concept can be credited to the influence of Persian religion is debatable. It is clear that Persian Zoroastrianism did contain the basic concept of a final great battle of good and evil wherein good would triumph and there would be a general resurrection of the dead. Israelite elaboration on similar concepts came to full fruition in the period after the exile and lengthy contact with the Persian community.

> At that moment Michael shall appear,
> Michael the great captain,
> who stands guard over your fellow-countrymen;
> and there will be a time of distress
> such as has never been ...
> But at that moment your people will be delivered,
> every one who is written in the book:
> many of those who sleep in the dust of the earth will wake,
> some to everlasting life
> and some to the reproach of eternal abhorrence.
> The wise leaders shall shine
> like the bright vault of heaven,
> and those who have guided the people in the true path
> shall be like the stars for ever and ever.
>
> (Daniel 12:1–3, NEB)

By the New Testament period, resurrection of both the individual and the community was accepted broadly in the Hebrew community, although not necessarily embraced by all Jews. The attempt of the Sadducees (one of the religious parties that rejected resurrection) to trap Jesus over a question about resurrection illustrates that the concept was disputed during the time of Jesus (Mark 12:18–27).

In Hebrew thought, the body meant the whole person, for no distinction was made between the physical body and the spiritual soul. Resurrection, then, was a resurrection of the entire person. Unlike the Greek concept of an immortal soul, which continued after the death of the physical body, the Hebrew understanding envisioned a renewal—a new beginning—for the person. Immortality was, therefore, not a part of original Hebrew belief. Resurrection did not represent a continuation of life but a renewal made possible only through the grace of God and dependent on his initiation and his sovereignty.

Christianity, arising in the Hebrew milieu, appropriated this belief in both individual and communal resurrection. In Christianity it formed the background for the early church emphasis on the second coming of Christ and became a prominent part of Christian eschatology, as expressed, for example, in the Revelation to John.

However, Christianity did not simply adopt the ancient ideas. The Christian testimony and affirmation that the man Jesus had been resurrected carried the concept to a new and unique dimension. Christianity did not apply resurrection to the distant future but declared that it was now present in history itself. God's sovereignty over life and death was evident within historical life as a dynamically different testimony to God's love. The death and then the resurrection became the climactic act in the drama of Jesus' revelation of God's love and power. It served as the central sign of God's power over human sin and over the demons and powers of the universe. Jesus' exaltation, through resurrection, as the Lord of life came to symbolize the new life of a Christian believer. "So you must consider yourselves dead to sin and alive to God in Christ Jesus" (Romans 6:11, NRSV). In this central act the Christian saw God's ultimate sovereignty, his gracious love of humankind, and humanity's dependence on his grace. Belief in this unique act carried a new realization of one's own relationship to God and dependence on the love revealed in Jesus' life, death, and resurrection. For the Christian, the concept of resurrection was no longer limited to that which had been accepted by the Jews but was significantly and decisively expanded. It now constituted a new revelation of God's love and therefore became a unique event. Resurrection of Jesus, then, was and is a central precept of ancient and modern Christian belief; it gave new understanding of God and became the basis of Christian trust (faith) in him.

Christianity has also conceptualized Jesus' resurrection as testimony to the reality of the more ancient concepts of resurrection. Jesus' resurrection—an example of God's might, power, and inexhaustible love—has become the touchstone of belief in personal and communal resurrection appropriated from the Jewish culture. (It is interesting that modern Judaism has, to a large degree, rejected the belief in individual resurrection, although the messianic expectation of communal renewal is still widely accepted.) The ancient concepts and the new understanding of resurrection as revealed in Jesus, though distinguishable in Christianity, are closely related. They have occasionally been confused with each other, causing variant understandings to arise.

◆◆◆

Why do Christians insist that belief in resurrection is necessary to Christian faith?

For further comments on resurrection, see Paul's commentary in I Corinthians 15 and I Thessalonians 4.

✦✦✦ 13 ✦✦✦

Salvation and Redemption

Heaven, Nirvana, enlightenment, wholeness, self-actualization, absorption into the Ultimate, concord, reconciliation between humans and God—these and many other terms refer to the ultimate goal, or destiny, of human beings as proclaimed in the various religious traditions. Every religion has a concept of wholeness and fulfillment, and most religions stress the need to arrive at this state from one of brokenness or lack or separation. The term *salvation* itself is closely identified with the Christian religious tradition: it connotes a process, event, state of healing, health, fulfillment, and wholeness.

In this chapter, we examine the concepts of salvation and redemption. They take on rich meaning and variety of use not only among different religious traditions but also within the same tradition. Some aspects of this richness and diversity are explored in the units that follow:

1. The meaning of the concept salvation;
2. A concept of salvation that is identified with God's grace or divine action;
3. Varied expressions, both religious and secular, of the transition from the present "broken" age or world to a new and transformed age or world, a vision that often expresses most fully what *salvation* means.

Unit 57   Salvation

Salvation is a key term in Christian religious traditions. It has a variety of meanings, which partly depend on particular theological perspectives and specific historical settings. Because of its key role in dominantly Christian societies, it has sometimes been transferred to secular or nonreligious contexts. Whatever the interpretation, however, the concept signifies movement from one state or condition of being—a bad, deficient, inadequate, or "lost" state—to another—a good, fulfilled, adequate, or "saved" state. This movement may be seen either as something that is suddenly grasped or as an unfolding and developing process, a growth into the new life through new insight or change of character. Whatever the process, *salvation* implies the belief that something is wrong in the present natural state of human life; that existence has gone askew. Human beings are in a "fallen" or "sinful" state and need restoration to a redeemed or God-centered, or reality-centered, state.

Redemption, or restoration, depends on some activity, process, event, or agent that can reorient one's existence. For the Christian, the agent is God's love in Jesus Christ, and the process or event of salvation involves belief and faith (trust) in God's mercy given in Christ. Salvation, in this case, means being saved from a destructive self-centeredness through repentance and faith in Jesus Christ.

> It [the gift of Jesus] is the saving power of God for everyone who has faith . . . because here is revealed God's way of righting the wrong, a way that starts from faith and ends in faith. (Romans 1:16–17, NEB)

The *religious* concept of salvation depends generally on action on behalf of an individual or society by God (or the gods). In the Christian tradition this action is denoted by the word *grace*, a central concept of the tradition. The basic idea is also found in other, but not all, religions. For some in the Christian community, God's grace (God's free, unmerited love given to lost and needy humans), which bestows salvation, is understood in an objective sense, primarily signifying the beneficence of God toward the natural order—including humanity—that God has created. This view has been preserved and transmitted within the Roman Catholic tradition, where *grace* has often referred to a supernatural substance bestowed on the believer to supplement and complete his or her natural being.

However, some Christians understand *grace* in a subjective sense. As Hegel points out, a new awareness and concern arose in Europe, and especially Germany, in the late medieval period—the internalization both of guilt and of grace. This development set the stage for the modern Protestant exploration of the meaning of grace. Paul Tillich, in one of the most quoted Christian sermons of the twentieth century, explored the idea of grace as inner experience. To Tillich the essential experience of God's grace is its presence, experienced by an individual—even if the recipient feels totally unworthy, unacceptable, unbelieving, and powerless—recognizing that she or he is accepted.

> You are accepted. *You are accepted*, accepted by that which is greater than you, and the name of which you do not know. Do not ask for the name now; perhaps you will find it later. Do not try to do anything now, perhaps later you will do much. Do not seek for anything, do not perform anything, do not intend anything. *Simply accept the fact that you are accepted.*[1]

For Tillich the inner experience of grasping one's acceptance by the Divine provides the basis of all other actions and experiences.

---

[1] Paul Tillich, *The Shaking of the Foundations* (New York: Charles Scribner's Sons, 1948), p.162.

Many Protestants, such as Martin Luther, John Calvin, and Tillich himself, insist that an objective experience of grace accompanies the subjective experience; but for Luther and Tillich the subjective experience is crucial. Many Protestants also stress, in contrast to Tillich, a need to strive actively for the subjective sense of grace, the assurance of salvation, as John Wesley did. Wesley, however, taught that one should perform objective "good works" (even though they did not bring either the assurance or the reality of salvation) while seeking the subjective experience of an "assurance of grace."

Objective and subjective understandings of what God's grace is and how it brings salvation are usually combined in Christian traditions. Some Christian traditions (Roman Catholic, for example, and some Protestant) have stressed the need for a cooperative response to God's grace (even if God has in some sense previously provided grace to enable the response). Others (especially Lutheran and Calvinist traditions) have insisted that God's grace *and* a human response to it are entirely a gift from God and that it is misleading to speak of the cooperation of those who can only passively receive. Whatever a particular Christian's definition of grace, it represents the power of God acting within life, transforming the life of the believer.

As we have seen, the term salvation as a process or event of being made whole is stressed in Christianity. However, the concept itself is not limited to Christianity but is found in one form or another in other religions, as the following example illustrates.

> The transcendental vibration established by the chanting of Hare Krishna, Hare Krishna, Krishna Krishna, Hare Hare/Hare Rāma, Hare Rāma, Rāma Rāma, Hare Hare is the sublime method for reviving our transcendental consciousness. As living spiritual souls, we are all originally Krishna conscious entities, but due to our association with matter from time immemorial, our consciousness is now adulterated by the material atmosphere. The material atmosphere, in which we are now living, is called *māyā* or illusion. *Māyā* means that which is not. And what is this illusion? The illusion is that we are all trying to be lords of material nature, while actually we are under the grip of her stringent laws. . . . We are trying to exploit the resources of material nature, but actually we are becoming more and more entangled in her complexities. Therefore, although we are engaged in a hard struggle to conquer nature, we are ever more dependent on her. This illusory struggle against nature can be stopped at once by revival of our eternal Krishna consciousness. Hare Krishna, Hare Krishna, Krishna Krishna, Hare Hare is the transcendental process for reviving this original pure consciousness. By chanting this transcendental vibration, we can cleanse away all misgivings within our hearts. The basic principle of all such misgivings is the false consciousness that I am the lord of all I survey.[2]

As the example explains, for the Hindu salvation, or fulfillment, comes through movement from *maya* (illusion) to *moksha* (release from the cycle of rebirths). Similarly, for the Buddhist one moves from a state of bondage to destructive self-centered desire to *Nirvana*.

In both these religions and others one also finds a concept similar to the Christian understanding of Divine grace. The graciousness of the Divine is expressed in some forms of Hinduism that teach that an individual may rely on the gods *Vishnu* and *Shiva* for assistance in attaining release from reincarnation. For the Mahayana Buddhist, the role of

---

[2] A. C. Bhaktvedanta Swami Prabhupada, *On Chanting the Hare Krishna Mantra* (Boston, MA: Iskcon Press, n.d.), p. 5.

the *Bodhisattva* also suggests a form of gracious love benefiting the believer in the journey toward Nirvana. Muslim and Jewish traditions incorporate similar concepts whereby salvation is dependent on God's gracious love given through prophets and other religious leaders. Even in polytheistic religions, there is frequently a concept of grace as the special unbidden, unmerited state bestowed on some individual or group by a god or goddess. A kind of grace, or healing and restoring power, may be conferred by the impersonal (Divine) nature of things. This is exemplified in some of the Greek tragedies: Oedipus, after terrible suffering in expiation of a fate-ordained violation of the order of nature (by murdering his father and marrying his mother), became a source of blessing (grace) to those among whom he resided.

Concepts of salvation, such as those discussed in this unit, are not limited to traditional religious expression. They also appear in secular movements and ideologies. The Marxist concept of a classless society in which there will be no oppression and in which there will be equality, material plenty, and freedom for all is an example (see Units 4 and 58). In Nazi Germany the concept of the thousand-year reich in which the Aryan master race would rule the world is another.

◆◆◆

What elements of Western religions lead them to stress personal salvation, whereas this has been stressed relatively less in Eastern religions?

Does the definition of religion that incorporates "pivotal value" as a central element require or suggest an emphasis on salvation?

Unit 58   Eschatology: The Coming Fulfillment

The supreme vision of what salvation—health, wholeness, fulfillment, well-being—means in a religious or secular tradition may often be seen in its *eschatology*, literally "a study of last things." In Christian tradition it includes doctrines dealing with the end of history—both the termination and transformation of history as we know it—as well as such concepts as the second coming of Christ, resurrection of the dead, immortality of the soul, final judgment, and Heaven and Hell.

For some, Christian eschatology may be focused primarily on the destiny of individuals (the soul, what happens after death). Ordinarily, however, eschatology is centered not only on the ultimate fate of individuals in relation to good and evil and God's ultimate power but also on the ultimate destiny of the whole human race and of the cosmos. Thus, Christian eschatology reflects the earlier Jewish apocalyptic tradition, which, especially from about 170 B.C.E. until the second destruction of Jerusalem by the Romans in 135 C.E., was expressed in apocalyptic works. *Apocalypse* means "revelation," and apocalyptic writings of Judaism depict, in highly symbolic form, a particular moment in time when the dominant forces of evil will be defeated by the power of God. The struggle is foreseen as bitter and intense, frequently involving terrible suffering of humans, both the evil and the good (those who remained faithful to God in spite of terrible persecution). The result of the struggle would be a complete, decisive, and final triumph of God and the forces of good, a cosmological victory that would end in the transition from the old, evil order of things in our world to a new and perfect realm under God's justice. Salvation would be finally real: The faithful would be vindicated and the evil judged and rendered powerless and ineffectual.

Although such an understanding of eschatology is familiar in Christian, Jewish, and Islamic traditions, it is only one pattern of eschatological thought. The following sections present religious as well as secular eschatological concepts and beliefs about human and cosmic salvation.

A NEW SOCIETY

Throughout history there have arisen both religious and secular groups whose dissatisfaction with what they believe to be an unjust society has led them to anticipate its dissolution and its replacement by a new, more just arrangement of social opportunities. In the nineteenth century, many American and English "communitarians" formed separated communities, often anticipating the millennium when Jesus would return to earth to establish a just and perfect society: the Shakers (so called for their incorporation of sacred dance in their worship services), German pietist groups such as the Ephrata Community in Pennsylvania, and the Church of Latter Day Saints (Mormons). Similar groups espousing various patterns of socialism, sometimes undergirded by religious principles, organized communalistic utopian groups, the most famous of which were New Harmony in Indiana, the Oneida Community in central New York, and Brook Farm in Massachusetts. Much of the philosophical base for these groups and their advertisement of themselves included evangelistic eschatological statements; each group offered salvation from an evil world.

Such associations generally sought transformation only for those who joined their group. The general societies that surrounded them were considered beyond transformation, so they formed idealized and separated communities. In this same period, however, others were also envisioning fundamental societal change.

Although maintaining that their work was scientific rather than utopian and rejecting religion, Karl Marx and Friedrich Engels, writing in mid-nineteenth-century England, used many eschatological images and patterns to define communism. According to Marx, a vigorous struggle was underway between the forces of the workers and those of the capitalists, a struggle he expected to be soon completed. The success of the struggle against "the capitalist yoke" and the "world ruled by violence" was for Communists already apparent, with final victory on the horizon. The vision of the "new world, a world of freedom" in which "those who have nothing will inherit the earth," was a bright hope that the adherents of this view looked toward with eager longing. Similar eschatological perspectives are found in the writings of Mao Tse-Tung, a founding leader of Chinese communism:

> People of the world, unite and defeat the ... aggressors and all their running dogs! People of the world, be courageous, dare to fight, defy difficulties and advance wave upon wave. Then the world will belong to the people. Monsters of all kinds shall be destroyed.[3]

[3] Mao Tse-Tung, *Quotations from Chairman Mao Tse-Tung* (New York: Bantam Books, 1967), p. 44.

Figure 13.1   Drawing by Jacques Bakke

The failure of Russian communism to achieve a classless society and the dissolution of communism as a political alternative in the Soviet Union have not meant the complete rejection of many of the eschatological teachings of Marx or Mao. Although Chinese communism is rapidly changing as it responds to international market forces, the eschatological visions of Mao still play an important role in the organization and future goals of the society. The Marxist critique of an elitist capitalism and the vision, often stated in eschatological terms, of an equitable economic distribution of scarce natural resources among all peoples has become part of much Christian liberation theology, especially in Latin America.

PROTEST

The civil rights movement in the United States drew on three powerful sources for its strength and impetus: the affirmations of the Constitution, insights of the Jewish and Christian faiths concerning the rights and dignity of individuals, and the Gandhian-Tolstoyan teaching of nonviolence (see Unit 22). Martin Luther King, committed to nonviolent love, was aware that he was involved in a life-and-death struggle. The sense of imminent victory and the vision of a day of fulfillment implicit in the eschatological perspective are apparent in the statement that follows. This sense of approaching triumph was even more intense when the speech was delivered at the civil rights march on Washington in August 1963. Approximately 200,000 persons gathered on the Mall between the Washington Monument and the Lincoln Memorial to demonstrate peacefully in support of pending civil rights legislation. To the outside observer, it seemed that there were many people involved, but the event was nothing extraordinary. To the person inside the civil rights movement, however, it was a tremendous sign of the strength of the movement and its fast-approaching victory.

> I say to you today, my friends, even though we face the difficulties of today and tomorrow, I still have a dream. It is a dream deeply rooted in the American dream.
>
> I have a dream that one day this nation will rise up and live out the true meaning of its creed: "We hold these truths to be self-evident; that all men are created equal."
>
> I have a dream that one day on the red hills of Georgia the sons of former slaves and the sons of former slaveowners will be able to sit down together at the table of brotherhood.
>
> I have a dream that one day even the state of Mississippi, a state sweltering with the heat of injustice, sweltering with the heat of oppression, will be transformed into an oasis of freedom and justice.
>
> I have a dream that my four little children will one day live in a nation where they will not be judged by the color of their skin but by the content of their character.
>
> I have a dream today.
>
> I have a dream that one day, down in Alabama, with its vicious racists, with its Governor having his lips dripping with the words of interposition and nullification, one day right there in Alabama little black boys and little black girls will be able to join hands with little white boys and white girls as sisters and brothers.
>
> I have a dream today.
>
> I have a dream that one day every valley shall be exalted, every hill and mountain shall be made low, the rough places will be made plain, and the crooked places will be made straight, and the glory of the Lord shall be revealed, and all flesh shall see it together.
>
> This is our hope. This is the faith with which I return to the South. With this faith we will be able to hew out of this mountain of despair a stone of hope. With this faith we will be able to transform the jangling discords of our nation into a beautiful symphony of brotherhood. With this faith we will be able to work together, to pray together, to struggle together, to go to jail together, to stand up for freedom together, knowing that we will be free one day. . . .
>
> Let freedom ring from every hill and molehill of Mississippi. From every mountainside, let freedom ring. And when this happens—when we let freedom ring, when we let it ring from every village and every hamlet, from every state and every city, we will be able to speed up that day when all of God's children, black men and white men, Jews and Gentiles, Protestants and Catholics, will be able to join hands and sing in the words of the old Negro spiritual, "Free at last! free at last! thank God almighty, we are free at last!"[4]

[4] Martin Luther King, Jr., "I Have a Dream." Reprinted by arrangement with the Estate of Martin Luther King, Jr., c/o Writers House as agent for the proprietor. Copyright 1963 by Martin Luther King, Jr., Copyright renewed 1991 by Coretta Scott King.

TRANSFORMATION OF CONSCIOUSNESS

During the 1960s, many Americans, especially the young, became convinced that their society was dominated by oppressive political and economic power. They protested America's participation in the war in Vietnam; the continued denial of equal rights to all Americans, especially blacks; and attitudes of thoughtless greed on the part of large corporations, greed they understood to result in pollution of the environment. Some became convinced that America could be saved by a transformation of consciousness, changing attitudes of selfishness, aggression, and greed to those of peacefulness and love. This notion was expressed in a book that quickly became a best-seller, *The Greening of America*, written by a Yale law school professor.[5] It probably found its most popular and effective expression in the words and music of a successful folk-rock musical called *Hair*, which was later made into a powerful film, dramatizing protest against the Vietnam war; racial discrimination; and subordination of the individual, especially the young, to harsh and puritanical moral and economic restrictions by an uncaring, older establishment. The song "Aquarius" captures what many of the young involved in "the movement" of the 1960s believed and shows how, often indiscriminately, sources of salvation were sought— in reinterpretations of traditional religious figures (Jesus, Gautama) and their teachings, in sources of spiritual insight often rejected in the general society (astrology), in drugs and rock music and free sexual expression as sources of consciousness transformation. In the eyes of many of the younger and some of the older generation of that time, institutionalized religion, especially Christianity and Judaism, had failed to protest the wrongs of society, indeed frequently had given moral support to war and racial injustice. "Aquarius" thus brought to bear a semireligious worldview—astrology—in support of longed-for social and individual experiences.

> When the moon is in the seventh house,
>   and Jupiter aligns with Mars,
> Then peace will guide the planets
>   and love will steer the stars.
>
> This is the dawning of the Age of Aquarius,
> The Age of Aquarius, Aquarius, Aquarius
>   Aquarius, Aquarius, Aquarius.[6]

JEWISH PROPHECY

For Jeremiah, like the prophets before him and the apocalyptic thinkers who came afterward, history was the arena in which God was at work. The purpose of his activity was the creation of a redeemed, responsive people. Yet Jeremiah believed that the history of the Hebrew nation had become the history of a continuing conflict between God and many of the people. This could not continue. Jeremiah had spent his life delivering, though reluctantly and sometimes almost bitterly, the word from God concerning God's

---

[5] Charles A. Reich, *The Greening of America* (New York: Random House, 1970).

[6] "Aquarius" © 1966, 1967, 1968 James Rado, Gerome Ragni, Galt MacDermot, Nat Shapiro, and United Artists Music Co., Inc. All rights administered by United Artists Music Co. Inc. Used by permission.

judgment. He told the people of Judah that God's judgment was against them. He prophesied an invasion of Judah from the north. Few believed him because the King of Judah had surrounded himself with false prophets of optimism who said that all was well with God's people.

Suddenly, after the destruction of Jerusalem in 598 B.C.E. and before its devastation in 587 B.C.E. by the Babylonians, everybody believed him. And just as suddenly the word of God changed from doom to hope. Jeremiah announced God's decision to fulfill God's ancient purpose in the times to come. The "old" covenant would be perfected by a "new" covenant written within the heart, and God's purpose behind the old would become a reality in the new—"I will be their God, and they shall be my people." The struggle between faithful God and unfaithful people, which had infected the life of humankind and nature, would be resolved, and the Jewish nation would fully become that which God had intended: the faithful wife of a compassionate "husband."

> The days are surely coming, says the Lord, when I will sow the house of Israel and the house of Judah with the seed of humans and the seed of animals. And just as I have watched over them to pluck up and break down, to overthrow, destroy, and bring evil, so I will watch over them to build and to plant, says the Lord. In those days they shall no longer say:
> > "The parents have eaten sour grapes,
> > and the children's teeth are set on edge."
> But all shall die for their own sins; the teeth of everyone who eats sour grapes shall be set on edge.
> The days are surely coming, says the Lord, when I will make a new covenant with the house of Israel and the house of Judah. It will not be like the covenant I made with their ancestors when I took them by the hand to bring them out of the land of Egypt—a covenant that they broke, though I was their husband, says the Lord. But this is the covenant that I will make with the house of Israel after those days, says the Lord: I will put my law within them, and I will write it upon their hearts; and I will be their God, and they shall be my people. No longer shall they teach one another or say to each other, "Know the Lord," for they shall all know me, from the least of them to the greatest, says the Lord; for I will forgive their iniquity, and remember their sin no more. (Jeremiah 31:27–34, NRSV)

ISLAMIC VISION

The following passage from the Qur'an is an example of one of the most common types of eschatology, one that looks for an end to the present existence and something totally new in the times to come.

Muhammad clearly announced the coming of a day of judgment by Allah, when the earth and all creation would be shaken and Allah would sit on his throne. The judgment would follow, each person being rewarded or punished in accord with his or her actions in this world.

Muhammad declared in pronouncements found elsewhere in Muslim Scriptures that this life is a time of testing, when people must choose between submission to Allah and the doing of his will and following the way of Satan, the rebel against the All-Merciful. This struggle between the forces of good and evil, of righteousness and sin, inevitably and unalterably will end with the assertion of Allah's sovereignty and power.

The wise person chooses and lives by the will of Allah and lives this life in awareness of the new life to come.

> So, when the Trumpet is blown with a single blast
> and the earth and the mountains are lifted up and crushed with a single blow,
> then, on that day, the Terror shall come to pass,
> and heaven shall split, for upon that day it shall be very frail,
> and the angels shall stand upon its borders,
> and upon that day eight shall carry above them
> the Throne of the Lord.
> On that day you shall be exposed, not one secret of yours concealed.
> Then as for him who is given his book in his right hand,
> he shall say, "Here, take and read my book!
> Certainly I thought that I should encounter my reckoning." So he
>   shall be in a pleasing life
>   in a lofty Garden,
>   its clusters nigh to gather.
> "Eat and drink with wholesome appetite for that
> you did long ago, in the days gone by."
>
> But as for him who is given his book in his left hand,
> he shall say, "Would that I had not been given my book
> and not known my reckoning! Would it had been the end!
>   My wealth has not availed me,
>   my authority is gone from me."
> Take him, and fetter him, and then roast him
> in Hell, then in a chain of seventy cubits' length
> insert him! Behold, he never believed in God
> the All-mighty, and he never urged the feeding
> of the needy; therefore he today has not here
> one loyal friend, neither any food saving foul pus,
> that none excepting the sinners eat.[7]

EARLY CHRISTIAN ESCHATOLOGY

Written some 500 years before the time of Muhammad, the following passage also looks forward to the complete and final end of this world and the coming of a new, splendid creation. Although Muhammad may have envisioned a complete reordering of this creation, the author of the New Testament book, *Revelation to John*, thought it beyond renovation. This work articulates apocalyptic eschatology at its fullest. The author saw in the historical events just before and during his time the implementation in human experience of the cosmic, age-old plan and purpose of God. People and nations were caught up in the pervasive struggle between God and Satan, Christ and Anti-Christ, the saints and the wicked. Convinced that God had revealed to him the secrets of his purpose and activity, he interpreted for his fellow Christians the hidden, "real" meaning of what appeared to be ordinary, worldly events. And then would come the end—very shortly.

---

[7] Reprinted with permission of Scribner, a Division of Simon & Schuster., from *The Koran Interpreted* by Arthur J. Arberry, Sura LXIX, verses 13–37. Copyright © 1955 by George Allen & Unwin, Ltd.

The portrayal of the end of the present heaven and earth is bluntly stated, followed by the resurrection and the judgment. But the author quickly passes to his real interest—the glorious new existence that is to come. In the new heaven and the new earth, the "sea"—which in Jewish literature had come to stand for all that threatens human life—would be no more. The covenant promise to ancient Israel would be fulfilled, not within but beyond history. God—the beginning and the end of all things—would make it so.

> Then I saw a great white throne and the one who sat upon it;
> The earth and the heaven fled from his presence,
>   and no place was found for them.
> And I saw the dead, great and small, standing before the throne,
>   and books were opened.
> Also another book was opened, the book of life.
> And the dead were judged according to their works, as recorded in
>   the books.
> And the sea gave up the dead that were in it, Death and Hades gave up the
>   dead in them, and all were judged according to what they had done.
> Then Death and Hades were thrown into the lake of fire.
> This is the second death, the lake of fire; and anyone whose name was
>   not found written in the book of life was thrown into the lake of fire.
> Then I saw a new heaven and a new earth; for the first heaven and the first
> earth had passed away, and the sea was no more.
> And I saw the holy city, the new Jerusalem, coming down out of heaven
> from God, prepared as a bride adorned for her husband;
> and I heard a loud voice from the throne saying,
>   "See, the home of God is among mortals.
>   He will dwell with them as their God,
>   they will be his peoples,
>   and God himself will be with them;
>   he will wipe away every tear from their eyes,
>   Death will be no more;
>   mourning and crying and pain will be no more,
>   for the first things have passed away."
>   (The Revelation to John 20:11-21:4, NRSV)

DISAPPOINTED EXPECTATIONS: CHRISTIAN MILLENNIALISM IN THE NINETEENTH AND TWENTIETH CENTURIES

What happens when hopes for extraordinary fulfillment of religious or quasi-religious visions of the future are disappointed? Many have asked this question with the collapse of Communist governments and political parties in the former Soviet Union and in Eastern European countries during the late 1980s and early 1990s. Many former Communists have abandoned their faith in and their work toward a coming Communist triumph. Still, some maintain the belief that, no matter how long delayed, there will eventually dawn a perfect Communist order on this earth. Several years ago, at a conference of scholars studying Marxism as a branch of the international socialist movements, one of the coauthors of *Exploring Religious Meaning* heard an outstanding Marxist scholar and leader in a splinter Marxist (Trotskyite) movement answer the question: "How can anyone continue to believe in Marxism since Marx's prediction of a classless society has not happened?" The Marxist leader replied: "The classless society will come. Marx was so far ahead of his time that it may take five hundred years for his prediction to come true. But the classless society is based on Marx's scientific knowledge of the future and it will occur."

In 1956 a group of behavioral scientists led by Leon Festinger published a book called *When Prophecy Fails*.[8] It gives an account of their study of a small cult in a Midwestern American city who believed that the earth was soon to be destroyed. The cult's leader claimed to be in contact with a group from outer space who would rescue them, saving them just before the destruction of the earth's population. At various times, the cult leadership announced public dates on which these events were to occur. Festinger and his colleagues found that each time the predictions failed to materialize, some members left the group, feeling that they had been fooled and made to look ridiculous. However, other members remained with the group, intensifying their beliefs in the group's teachings.

During the nineteenth century in the United States, several large Christian offshoots of established Protestant groups arose as the result of a similar set of experiences. A preacher named William Miller announced a date on which Jesus was supposed to return to earth. Many people became his followers, sold their possessions, and waited for the coming of the Lord. When Jesus did not come on the date and in the way Miller had predicted, Miller chose a second date about a year in the future. Even more people became his followers, sold their property, and awaited the Lord's coming. When Miller's prediction failed to be fulfilled on this second date, many of his followers left him. The date became known as "The Great Disappointment." Still, many of his followers remained, and many who had been his followers contributed to the rise of a large variety of Adventist groups—groups of Christians expecting the imminent return of Jesus to the earth. Miller's former followers and others influenced by him or by other Adventist teachers in England and America became heavily involved in Christian pre-millennial movements, groups of Christians who interpret the New Testament in such a way as to believe that very shortly Jesus will return to the earth and rule for a thousand years before he finally defeats the powers of evil. Many individuals and many groups of modern Christians, including some Baptists, some Pentecostals, Seventh Day Adventists, and Jehovah's Witnesses hold to some type of Christian millennialist beliefs.

Some scholars have noted that after the first millennium (1,000-year period) of Europe's acceptance of Christianity (roughly from the time of the Roman Emperor Constantine 313 C.E. until the fourteenth century) European religious movements arose with expectations that in some way (either through the return of Christ or the coming of an "Age of the Holy Spirit") God's Kingdom would soon be fully realized on earth.

At the present time, there is continuing interest by Christians in interpreting biblical apocalyptic or eschatological writings. Many New Testament scholars and theologians interpret the historical references in the *Revelation to John* (the Apocalypse) as being specifically and literally about events during the late first century C.E. and the Roman government's persecution of early Christianity. A good recent source for this

---

[8] Leon Festinger, et. al., *When Prophecy Fails* (New York: Harper Torchbooks, 1956).

interpretation by a distinguished biblical scholar is Bruce Metzger's *Breaking the Code: Understanding the Book of Revelation*.

There are many other contemporary Christian biblical interpretations, however, that see *Revelation* or the *Apocalypse* as referring to contemporary or very soon to be expected events, such as a Second Coming of Christ. Timothy LaHaye has published many books interpreting the Bible in this way. Much recent attention is focused on the concept of a *Rapture*, an event based on readings of *Revelation* and Paul's first letter to the Thessalonians (I Thessalonians 4: 13–18). According to LaHaye's teaching, the Rapture will be a literal event in which faithful Christians will be snatched into the heavens to safety while the horrendous punishments described in *Revelation* are inflicted on followers of Satan and the Anti-Christ. A film called *Left Behind*, based on LaHaye's writings, has received wide distribution. One may consult, among LaHaye's many books, one he wrote with Jerry B. Jenkins, *Are We Living in the End Times?*[9] As noted, numerous biblical scholars see events like the Rapture and the Millennium as having validity for faith but intended by the biblical authors as symbolic in nature.

CONTEMPORARY SCIENTIFIC APOCALYPSE

The latest scientific cosmology has its own apocalyptic visions. In the early 1960s, two very different theories about the origin and nature of the universe competed. Each had been created to account for the expansion of the universe. They were postulated because of a shift of light coming from distant clusters of galaxies to the red end of the light spectrum. One of these was the steady state theory. It hypothesized a universe with no beginning but with just enough new hydrogen coming into existence to prevent the density of matter from thinning to almost nothing because of the expansion. The other theory, called the "Big Bang," projected a date, eventually settled on as from 16 billion to 14 billion years ago, at which all of the matter in the universe was packed in an area or point without dimensions but with infinite mass. At the first instant of time there was an explosion and the universe's expansion began.

In 1960 the odds on these theories were even. Since then evidence has mounted overwhelmingly in favor of the Big Bang. The state of the universe at a point in time after the Big Bang marked by a decimal point followed by thirty-two zeroes and a one is now thought to be known. With the triumph of the Big Bang hypothesis, theories were developed concerning the possible fate of the expanding universe. One possibility is that gravity will eventually overcome the expansion and cause the universe to contract to an infinitely dense point like the primordial point. A second theory suggests that the universe might forever expand and contract like a beating heart. A third group of theories speculate on a universe that will forever expand but with different scenarios, depending on whether space is curved or flat. A presently favored view, reported in *TIME* magazine for June 25, 2001, is that space *is* flat and that the universe will forever continue expanding, with matter becoming less and less dense and less and less interactive until in a few

---

[9] Compare Bruce Metzger, *Breaking the Code: Understanding the Book of Revelation* (Nashville, TN: Abingdon Press, 1993) with Timothy LaHaye and Jerry B. Jenkins, *Are We Living in the End Times?* (Wheaton, IL: Tyndale House Publishers, 1999).

billion years it will seem almost empty. Several letters to *Time's* editors in response to the coverage of this prediction reported that the authors of the letters were dismayed and distressed at the thought that the universe might come to such an end. Several religious thinkers have not found the prospect dismaying. Alfred North Whitehead wrote nearly eighty years ago: "The universe shows us two aspects: on one side it is physically wasting, on the other side it is spiritually ascending."[10] Much more recently, Pope John Paul II has asserted that the Big Bang is an acceptable theory for Christians to hold, but he reasserted that Christians believe that God is ultimately Creator and Redeemer of the universe.

◆◆◆

How might persons of various religious traditions—Hindus, Buddhists, Muslims, Jews, fundamentalist Christians and others—respond to contemporary scientific cosmology and the Big Bang theory?

Some Christian religious groups have almost completely ignored eschatological elements in the earlier Christian traditions; other groups—for instance, the Jehovah's Witnesses—have made them their dominant concern. Why do some religious traditions emphasize eschatological salvation as a universal, cosmic event and others do not?

In traditions emphasizing mystical religion, eschatology often takes the form of inner subjective fulfillment, union, or communion with the Divine rather than looking to a fulfilling future historical state. What forms of eschatology—visions of a fulfilled or perfected state of being involving all or most humans and the future world—different from those presented here—can you think of?

In this unit the term premillennialism has been briefly described. There are other varieties of Christian millennialism, also based on ways of interpreting the Bible. Find the meanings of the following terms as they represent types of Christian positions regarding "the coming fulfillment": postmillenialism, amillennialism.

Are you familiar with any increase of groups or individuals proclaiming the end or fulfillment of time as an imminent reality?

---

[10] A. N. Whitehead, *Religion in the Making*, (Cleveland and New York: The World Publishing Company, a Meridian Book, 1960), p.153.

✦✦✦ 14 ✦✦✦

THE RELIGIOUS MATRIX
OF INTERPERSONAL RELATIONS

In the preceding section, we have examined the self and the dimensions of religion that affect its sense of identity—its selfhood. Now we move to a discussion of the sociocultural setting that profoundly affects the way people define what selfhood means. Our concern in this chapter is to explore the context in which the self relates to other selves. Every self finds itself defined in interpersonal relationships with other selves. One is neither born nor lives in a vacuum. Whether a person speaks to a neighbor in a classroom or to the person who lives next door, they are involved with each other simply by their common location and what that entails. Most of daily living consists, however, of complex interpersonal relationships with others, so the interaction among individuals is a significant element in our understanding of ourselves as well as our society. Humans are social beings and are constantly responding to and defining their social interaction and context.

The social setting of the self is important both for the sense of personal identity and for the religious dimensions of the self's experiences. Competing codes of morality and definitions of competing scientific systems, along with competing systems of religious beliefs and practices, will be offered to the individual by the culture that the individual participates in, inherits, belongs to, or presently inhabits.

Religion—every religion, even the religion of a tiny minority—is a social phenomenon, and the culture in which it exists is a social product. Religion is a constitutive element of culture. The phrase religious matrix in the title of this chapter refers to the creative power of religion to give meaning to relationships between the self and others.

Some anthropologists have defined culture as "the social heritage . . . the sum of the historical achievements of human social life transmitted in the form of a tradition."[1] According to this definition, the term *culture* refers to the things a society teaches the individuals who are members of that society. Culture, then, is something already existing that individuals absorb or passively acquire.

---

[1] David Bidney, *Theoretical Anthropology* (New York: Columbia University Press, 1953), p. 25.

Other students of human behavior have questioned this definition of culture. The anthropologist David Bidney holds that humans are active creators and transformers of culture.[2] Sociologists Peter Berger and Thomas Luckmann write, "Society is a human product. Society is an objective reality. Man is a social product."[3] Berger and Luckmann emphasize here that humans are created by their societies and the cultures of those societies but that ultimately the societies and cultures are created by actual, specific, individual human beings interacting with other human beings. According to this view, culture is not just something handed down from generation to generation: Each person, in interaction with other people—in interaction with the whole of society during that person's life's span—creates culture by acquiring and transforming it.

To see the connectedness of selves in society is not sufficient. We need to analyze various ways in which religious commitment enters the process of individual and group interaction. In this chapter, we consider general dimensions of individual and group, and of group and group, interaction, as well as ethical dimensions. Also, we examine the role of religion in promoting social stability, as an agent of social change, and as affected by social change.

The ethical issues focused on in this chapter arise as a person relates to others—primarily the way the individual relates to other individuals. The discussion of ethical issues involving relationships between groups will be considered in the next chapter.

The first unit deals with the tension or dynamic interplay that exists between an individual and his or her community. We then turn to an exploration of love and duty as two approaches to personal involvement in a community. Finally, we examine the connection between particular actions and the motivations for those actions.

UNIT 59   THE INDIVIDUAL AND THE COMMUNITY

In the modern world the desire to preserve individual identity is seldom exactly and delicately balanced with the concurrent necessity to participate in corporate life. Each changing moment tilts the balance one way or the other, and many feel that life results in a frightening and often disorienting seesaw as we try to be ourselves in an increasingly complex world. Historically, humans seeking to escape such disorientation have emphasized one aspect of identity over the other. An emphasis on either pole reflects a particular understanding of the human role in the natural order. These interpretations of humanity in turn reflect religious beliefs or perceptions that are often illustrated in both religious and secular literature.

William Ernest Henley, writing in the late nineteenth century, reflects the extreme individualism of the period, the roots of which reach back at least into the eighteenth century.

---

[2] Ibid.

[3] Peter L. Berger and Thomas Luckmann, *The Social Construction of Reality* (Garden City, NY: Doubleday, 1966), p. 58.

Out of the night that covers me,
   Black as the Pit from pole to pole,
I thank whatever gods may be
   For my unconquerable soul.

In the fell clutch of circumstance
   I have not winced nor cried aloud.
Under the bludgeonings of chance
   My head is bloody, but unbowed.

Beyond this place of wrath and tears
   Looms but the Horror of the shade,
And yet the menace of the years
   Finds, and shall find, me unafraid.

It matters not how strait the gate,
   How charged with punishments the scroll,
I am the master of my fate;
   I am the captain of my soul.[4]

Henley's poem emphasizes the individual's capability to determine his or her life. Little room is left for the influence of other persons and society, or for any Divine influence. For Henley, the "gods," if there be any, clearly have no final or pervasive control over life or the future: It is the individual who determines his or her own fate. Timothy McVeigh, whose bomb destroyed the federal building in Oklahoma City, quoted Henley's poem before his execution.

Some thirty inches from my nose
The frontier of my Person goes,
And all the untilled air between
Is private pagus or demesne.
Stranger, unless with bedroom eyes,
I beckon you to fraternize,
Beware of rudely crossing it:
I have no gun, but I can spit.[5]

In this brief poem, W. H. Auden also stresses the need to be an individual—everyone must have one's own space, one's own being. Yet he recognizes the concurrent reality: No individual is alone, is an island unto herself or himself; an individual is always part of some community. Although one may be responsible for maintaining personal identity in a community, one can never escape the reality of the social character of human existence.

Because of this social nature of humanity, many people put the interests, goals, and purposes of the community over those of the individual. Personal fulfillment in life does not necessarily depend on what one acquires but rather on one's contribution to the

---

[4] William Ernest Henley, "Invictus," *Poems* (New York: Scribner, 1919), p. 119.

[5] W. H. Auden, "Thanksgiving for a Habitat," *About the House* (New York: Random House, 1963), p. 4. Copyright © 1965. Reprinted by permission of Random House, Inc.

community. This interpretation led Mo-ti, an early Chinese moral philosopher, to insist that the needs of a community overarch and encompass those of an individual:

> Mo-ti said: The purpose of the magnanimous is to be found in procuring benefits for the world and eliminating its calamities.
>
> But what are the benefits of the world and what its calamities?
>
> Mo-ti said: Mutual attacks among states, mutual usurpation among houses, mutual injuries among individuals; the lack of grace and loyalty between ruler and ruled, the lack of affection and filial piety between father and son, the lack of harmony between elder and younger brothers—these are the major calamities in the world.
>
> But whence did these calamities arise, out of mutual love?
>
> Mo-ti said: They arise out of want of mutual love. At present feudal lords have learned only to love their own states and not those of others. Therefore they do not scruple about attacking other states. The heads of houses have learned only to love their own houses and not those of others. Therefore they do not scruple about usurping other houses. And individuals have learned only to love themselves and not others. . . . Therefore all the calamities, strifes, complaints, and hatred in the world have arisen out of the want of mutual love. . . .
>
> But what is the way of universal love and mutual aid?
>
> Mo-ti said: It is to regard the state of others as one's own, the houses of others as one's own, the persons of others as one's self. When feudal lords love one another there will be no more war; when heads of houses love one another there will be no more mutual usurpation; when individuals love one another there will be no more mutual injury.[6]

The ideal of social responsibility noted in Mo-ti's comments incorporates a consciousness of the self that in reality becomes the basis for relationships in the community. One does not lose one's identity in the community, but the needs of others are as important as or more important than one's own. Reinhold Niebuhr, a twentieth-century American Christian theologian, goes a step further when he maintains that love of one's fellow humans is a basic law of humanity demanded by the social character of human existence

> [Another] source of religious vitality is derived from the social character of human existence; from the fact that men cannot be themselves or fulfill themselves within themselves, but only in an affectionate and responsible relation to their fellows. It is this fact, rather than the fiat of any scripture, which makes the law of love the basic law for man. The law is not of purely religious origin, and indeed it is not necessary to be religious to ascertain its validity.[7]

Niebuhr's suggestion assumes that an individual only lives purposefully and completely in interaction with others.

The contrast between positions as diverse as those of Henley and Niebuhr is obvious. Most major religious traditions agree with the insights of Mo-ti and Niebuhr that the needs of others (the community) take precedence over the wants and needs of the individual and that an individual cannot find fulfillment solely in the self.

[6] Mo-ti, "Universal Love II," *The Wisdom of China and India*, trans. Y. P. Mie, ed. Lin Yutang (New York: Random House, 1942), pp. 794–795.

[7] Reinhold Niebuhr, "The Religious Situation in America," in *Religion and Contemporary Society*, ed. Harold Stahmer (New York: Macmillan, 1963), p. 146.

❖❖❖

Is it possible to achieve a meaningful balance between the individual and society? Is it necessary to achieve such a balance? Why?

Which of the positions is closer to your own understanding? Why?

What value is there in each of the positions?

UNIT 60   LOVE AND DUTY

Although there are people whose self-image is uniquely individualistic and perhaps anti-social, most people find genuine fulfillment in their social relationships. The forms of involvement with others are multitudinous, but there are discernible patterns of response that tell us much about basic life attitudes and assumptions (both conscious and unconscious).

Among the many ways people relate to others and to society, two patterns are central: *love* and *duty*. In every culture, affection (love) and a sense of responsibility (duty) motivate responses to others. Love and duty often complement and support each other in daily life, but they may also be a cause of anxiety and conflict. Many times one must balance their demands, occasionally selecting one over the other. This process is often unconscious, yet it reflects basic personal assumptions about the nature of life.

Love by its very nature expresses the content of a relationship between two individuals; consequently, it is often understood to express a social attitude that begins with the individual. Although it may not be limited to one individual and may incorporate many people or a group, it usually begins with the concern of one person for another. In love one begins with the self and moves toward the other—love bridges the gap between. In this movement, one's individual will and its encounter, assessment, and acceptance or rejection of another is primary to all other considerations.

Duty, in contrast, begins with the sense of responsibility for or to the other. It is the other, often the corporate group itself, which defines one's duties or responsibilities. By performing one's duties, one finds fulfillment as a part of the larger whole; therefore society—expressed in the family, village, caste, or modern industrial society—is the central focus of life. People achieve significance as they perform their duties within the larger community.

The contrast between the approach of love based on individual affection and that of duty based on social responsibility is obvious. They are both present in daily personal life and in all cultures. Sometimes they are delicately balanced and sometimes one dominates the other. Preliterate and Eastern cultures, with their emphasis on society and the family as the primary units of human life, often stress duty to the society before personal affection. In contrast, modern Western culture, based on a belief in a personal God and God's relationship to individuals, puts personal relationships and accomplishments first and tends to idealize love as the central pattern of human relationships. Illustrations of both positions and their interconnection abound in the literature of both East and West.

LOVE

Charlie Brown's incredulous response to a love that continues to offer itself even to the unloving suggests an insight into the unlimited nature of love (see Figure 14.1). Christian teachings about the nature of love are found in the following comments of Jesus:

> Just then a lawyer stood up to test Jesus. "Teacher," he said, "what must I do to inherit eternal life?" He said to him, "What is written in the law? What do you read there?" He answered, "You shall love the Lord your God with all your heart, and with all your soul, and with all your strength, and with all your mind; and your neighbor as yourself." And he said to him, "You have given the right answer; do this, and you will live." (Luke 10:25–28, NRSV)

> But I say to you that listen, Love your enemies, do good to those who hate you, bless those who curse you, pray for those who abuse you. If anyone strikes you on the cheek, offer the other also; and from anyone who takes away your coat do not withhold even your shirt. Give to everyone who begs from you; and if anyone takes away your goods, do not ask for them again. Do to others as you would have them do to you. (Luke 6:27–31, NRSV)

In Mahayana Buddhism (see Unit 11), the ideal human is a *Bodhisattva*—one who has come close to Nirvana yet delays entrance into that state to lead others compassionately (lovingly) toward it. This compassion is overwhelming and all-consuming.

Figure 14.1   (PEANUTS reprinted by the permission of United Features Syndicate, Inc.)

A Bodhisattva resolves: *I take upon myself the burden of suffering,* I am resolved to do so, I will endure it. . . . *I have made the vow to save all beings.* All beings I must set free. The whole world of living beings I must rescue, from the terrors of birth, of old age, of sickness, of death and rebirth, of all kinds of moral offence, of all states of woe, of the whole cycle of birth-and-death, of the jungle of false views, of the loss of wholesome dharmas, of the concomitants of ignorance—from all these terrors I must rescue all beings. . . . And I must not cheat all beings out of my store of merit. I am resolved to abide in each single state of woe for numberless aeons; and so I will help all beings to freedom, in all the states of woe that may be found in any world system whatsoever. (Sikshasamuccaya, 280–81, *Vajradhvaja Sutra*)

DUTY

India's ancient caste system was founded on the principle that each person finds a productive place in society by performing the proper duties of one's caste. To break caste is to destroy self and society. (Modern developments have modified the rigidity of the caste system somewhat, but ancient concepts are slow to change and it is still highly influential.) The following passage is taken from the *Puranas* (c. 350 C.E.):

He best worships Vishnu who observes the duties laid down by scripture for every caste and condition of life; there is no other mode. . . .

The Brahmana [member of priestly caste] must advance the well-being of all and do injury to none—for the greatest wealth of a Brahmana consists in cherishing kind feelings towards all. He must consider with an equal eye the jewel and stone belonging to another. . . .

The duties of the Kshatriya [member of warrior caste] consist in making gifts to the Brahmanas at pleasure, in worshiping Vishnu with various sacrifices and receiving instruction from the preceptor. His principal sources of maintenance are arms and protection of the earth. But his greatest duty consists in guarding the earth. By protecting the earth a king attains his objects, for he gets a share of the merit of all sacrifices. If a king, by maintaining the order of caste, represses the wicked, supports the pious, he proceeds to whatever region he desires.

The Father of Creation has assigned to the Vaisyas [members of the merchant caste], for their maintenance, the feeding of the cattle, commerce, and agriculture. Study, sacrifice, and gift are also within the duties of the Vaisyas: besides these, they may also observe the other fixed and occasional rites.

The Sudra [member of the servant caste] must maintain himself by attending upon the three higher castes, or by the profits of trade, or the earnings of mechanical labour. He may also make gifts, offer the sacrifices in which food is presented, and he may also make obsequial offerings.

Besides these, the four castes have their other duties, namely—the acquisition of wealth for the support of servants, cohabitation with their wives for the sake of children, kindness towards all creatures, patience, humility, truth, purity, contentment, decorum of manners, gentleness of speech, friendliness, freedom from envy or avarice and the habit of vilifying. These also constitute the duties of every condition of life.[8]

Traditional Chinese culture has been built on the principle of "filial piety" (respect, honor, and obedience to one's family and ancestors). One lives fully and com-

---

[8] Excerpts from *The Vishnu Purana*, trans. H. H. Wilson, ed. M. N. Dutt (Calcutta, 1894), as cited in Lewis Browne, *The World's Great Scriptures* (New York: Macmillan, 1946), pp. 121–122.

pletely by performing all of one's proper duties to family and society. The principle of *shu*, or reciprocity, spelled out by Confucius, forms the basis of these proper relationships.

> Tzu-kung asked, saying, "Is there one word which may serve as a rule of practice for all one's life?" The Master said, "Is not Reciprocity [shu] such a word? What you do not want done to yourself, do not do to others."[9]

Confucius made this principle the basis of the widely known Five Relationships. In each set of relationships, one's duty or responsibility to the other is central to a proper and ful-filling life.

> Kindness in the father, filial piety in the son
> Gentility in the eldest brother, humility and respect in the younger
> Righteous behavior in the husband, obedience in the wife
> Humane consideration in elders, deference in juniors
> Benevolence in ruler, loyalty in ministers and subjects.[10]

The same sense of duty to family and society carried over from China to Japan, where it became incorporated in the ethical code of the Japanese warrior-knight. Known as the Bushido Code, it incorporates many virtues, all derivative of the proper perform-ance of duty. The following is an analysis of the code by a Christian missionary:

1. Loyalty.
   This was due first of all to the Emperor and under him to the lord whom one more immediately serves. One of the most familiar proverbs says, "A loyal retainer does not serve two lords."
2. Gratitude.
   It may surprise some to hear that this is a Japanese characteristic, but the Christian doctrine that the spring of a right life is not duty, but gratitude, is one that is readily appreciated by the Japanese.
3. Courage.
   Life itself is to be surrendered gladly in the service of the lord. An American cannot fail to be touched by the noble words of a young warrior of ancient times to the effect that he wanted to die in battle for his lord and feared nothing so much as dying in bed before he had a chance to sacrifice his life for the object of his devotion.
4. Justice.
   This means not allowing any selfishness to stand in the way of one's duty.
5. Truthfulness.
   A knight scorns to tell a lie in order to avoid harm or hurt to himself.
6. Politeness.
   It is the mark of a strong man to be polite in all circumstances, even to an enemy.

---

[9] Robert Ballou, *The Bible of the World* (New York: Viking Press, 1939), p. 413.

[10] John Noss and David Noss, *A History of the World's Religions*, 9th ed. (Upper Saddle River, NJ: Prentice-Hall, Inc., 1994), p. 323. Reprinted by permission of Pearson Education, Inc.

7. Reserve.

No matter how deeply one is moved, feeling should not be shown.

8. Honor.

Death is preferable to disgrace. The knight always carried two swords, a long one to fight his foes, a short one to turn upon his own body in case of blunder or defeat.[11]

◆◆◆

Is it correct to say that love essentially emphasizes an individual approach to one's understanding of life and its meaning? Conversely, is it correct to assume that duty stresses a community or social approach?

Which of the examples best expresses your own ideal interpretation of life?

Is it necessary to balance love and duty? Are they exclusive of one another? If one must dominate, which do you think it should be?

If the concerns of the individual or the society cannot be perfectly balanced, which should dominate? What does your answer say of love and duty?

UNIT 61   ACT AND MOTIVE

The social context in which individuals live requires the development of interpersonal relationships, which are expressed through particular acts and attitudes, positive or negative. The interaction between particular acts (such as doing some service for a neighbor) and the motivations (love, duty, and so on) for them is the topic of the following discussion.

As they develop, societies create codes of moral conduct, a set of prescribed actions that people, depending on their social status (the various roles occupied in society—husband, wife, father, mother, uncle, warrior, and so forth), must perform as well as a set of taboos (acts forbidden to all or some). In less complex societies, the role of the taboo is very significant, as it regulates a person's actions. The following passage, for example, describes some of the taboos in Navajo society.

A very high portion of all the acts which arise out of convictions about beings and powers are negative in character. Thus lightning-struck trees must be avoided. Coyotes, bears, snakes, and some kinds of birds must never be killed. The eating of fish and of most water birds and animals is forbidden, and raw meat is taboo. Navahos will never cut a melon with the point of a knife. They never comb their hair at night. No matter how crowded a hogan may be with sleeping figures, no Navaho may step over the recumbent body of another. Mother-in-law and son-in-law must never look into each other's eyes. Any kind of sexual contact (even walking down the street or dancing together) with members of the opposite sex of one's own or one's father's clan is prohibited. Most technical processes are hedged about with restrictions: the tanner dare not leave the pole on which he scrapes hide standing upright; the porter and the basket-maker work in isolation, observing a

[11] Christopher Noss, *Tohoku, The Scotland of Japan* (Philadelphia: Board of Foreign Missions of the Reformed Church in the United States, 1918), pp. 87–88, as cited in Noss and Noss, *A History*, p. 375.

bewildering variety of taboos; the weaver shares one of these, the dread of final completion, so that a "spirit outlet" must always be left in the design.[12]

Although taboos, often unconsciously appropriated, continue to be operative in more complex societies, they tend to be replaced in importance by elaborated sets of rationally formulated, often written, moral rules. In Judaism, the simplest set of rules, the Ten Commandments, is embedded in a much larger set of over 600 rules regulating every aspect of daily life. Similarly, Islamic Law, based on the Qur'an supplemented by the hadith reports, regulates the everyday life of the Muslims down to the smallest detail, and the Eightfold Path of the Buddha is embellished in complex Buddhist scriptural commentaries as they relate these teachings to daily living.

Sets of rules inherently raise the problem of motivation and intention, however. If one simply follows the rules without understanding the motivation or the reason for a particular act required by the rules, the regulations often degenerate into a legalism readily compromised or avoided. Therefore, with the elaboration of rules defining most actions in life, many societies also experienced a developing interest in the motivation and intention for following the rules.

In Judaism, for instance, it is not enough to fulfill the duties, moral or cultic, that the law prescribes: One must fulfill them with a right heart or a right spirit—for the right reasons and with the right intention. One should fulfill the law because of gratitude and love toward God. The following passage, an abridgment of and commentary on a *halakhic* discourse from the *Talmud*, shows how Jewish ethical reflection attempted to clarify the relation of motive (or intention) and action.[13]

> The Mishna states "If someone blows the *shofar*[a] in a cistern, in a cellar, or in a barrel, if one heard the sound of the *shofar*, he has fulfilled his obligation; but if he heard the echo he has not fulfilled his obligation." Then it adds: "And also, if one was passing behind a synagogue, and he heard the sound of the *shofar* or the reading of the *megillah*,[b] if one set his mind to it, he fulfilled his obligation; if one has not, he has not fulfilled his obligation—even though the one heard and the other heard, the one set his mind to it, but the other did not set his mind to it."
>
> The subject to be explored, then, is "intention" or to be exact, whether in the carrying out of a religious duty it is necessary to intend to carry out the duty or not.[14]
>
> [a]The ram's horn sounded in the services on Rosh Hashana, the New Year. On the requirement to hear the sound of the shofar, see Leviticus 23:24 and Numbers 29:1.
> [b]The Book of Esther, read on the festival of Purim.

Clearly, the Jews understood that one's motivation for particular acts could be as important as the act itself.

---

[12] Reprinted by permission of the publisher from *The Navajo* by Clyde Kluckholm. Cambridge, Mass.: Harvard University Press, copyright © 1974 by Florence Kluckhohn Taylor and Dorthea Leighton, pp. 139–40.

[13] The *Talmud* contains both *Halakha*—reflections on the requirements of the Jewish law carried on in a characteristically legal style of reasoning—and *Hagada* (or *Agada*)—non-legal material including folklore, philosophical and theological speculation, parables, prayers, historical and legendary tales, and so forth.

[14] Judah Golden, trans., *The Living Talmud* (New York: New American Library, 1957), p. 30.

Christian theologians and philosophers such as Augustine (353–430 C.E.) and Abelard (1079–1142 C.E.) raised the same concerns. Although both insisted that right actions are important, the intention or motivation behind the act is even more important. According to Augustine, the traits of character—habits or dispositions—that Greek philosophy held to be the highest virtues—temperance, fortitude, justice, and prudence—are empty of value, are "splendid vices," unless they flow out of and are motivated by proper love of God and neighbor. The emphasis on motive—inner attitude or disposition—determining the value of acts and patterns of life had been present in Christianity from the beginning, as the following words of Jesus show:

> "Listen to me, all of you, and understand: there is nothing outside a person that by going in can defile, but the things that come out are what defile."
> When he had left the crowd and entered the house, his disciples asked him about the parable. He said to them, "Then do you also fail to understand? Do you not see that whatever goes into a person from outside cannot defile, since it enters, not the heart but the stomach, and goes out into the sewer?" (Thus he declared all food clean.) And he said, "It is what comes out of a person that defiles. For it is from within, from the human heart, that evil intentions come: fornication, theft, murder, adultery, avarice, wickedness, deceit, licentiousness, envy, slander, pride, folly. All these evil things come from within, and they defile a person." (Mark 7:14b–23, NRSV)

Compare the following Zen Buddhist story, "Muddy Road," with the preceding examples:

> Tanzan and Ekido were once travelling together down a muddy road. A heavy rain was still falling. Coming around a bend, they met a lovely girl in a silk kimono and sash, unable to cross the intersection. "Come on girl," said Tanzan at once. Lifting her up in his arms, he carried her over the mud. Ekido did not speak again until that night when they reached a lodging temple. Then he could no longer restrain himself. "We monks don't go near females," he told Tanzan, "especially not young and lovely ones. It is dangerous. Why did you do that?" "I left the girl there," said Tanzan. "Are you still carrying her?"[15]

Also consider the words of Archbishop Thomas Becket in T. S. Eliot's "Murder in the Cathedral":

> The last temptation is the greatest treason:
> To do the right deed for the wrong reason.[16]

❖ ❖ ❖

In everyday decision making, are people normally more aware of acts or of the motives for them?

---

[15] Paul Reps, ed., *Zen Flesh, Zen Bones* (Tokyo: Charles E. Tuttle Co., 1960), p. 18.

[16] T. S. Eliot, "Murder in the Cathedral," in *The Complete Poems and Plays of T. S. Eliot*, Part I. (New York: Harcourt, Brace and Company, 1952), p. 196. Used by permission of Harcourt Brace Jovanovich, Inc., publishers, and Faber and Faber Ltd.

Why are many religious moral thinkers more concerned with motivation than with particular moral acts?

Why is it that moral instruction is often reduced to a series of prescriptions relative to particular acts?

How often do you consider your motivations for particular acts? If not often, why not?

✦✦✦ 15 ✦✦✦

CORPORATE EXPRESSIONS
OF ETHICAL CONCERNS

When persons are confronted with moral situations in which they must choose between right and wrong, good and evil, they find that they apply ethical principles that have been acquired from a variety of sources and their own life experiences. College and university students faced with the opportunity of disregarding family and traditional community wisdom often experiment with new or different ethical norms. In doing so they are testing tradition and at the same time continuing to build their own set of norms, but this always takes place within a structure that has been previously established. In a university setting actions taken outside accepted norms may lead to expulsion from the community. Individuals always live within social structures that identify ethical norms, whether those be family, local community, university, or the society as a whole. This chapter investigates how these community norms or principles relate to the broad ethical concerns that face humans in the current world situation. We will be examining the sources of ethical principles and how they are applied to specific issues as well as the relationship of these issues to religion.

When considering a society and its ethical relationships, attention must be given not only to broad principles of right and wrong but also to the ethical norms of particular subgroups. These groups have many organizing principles including political, economic, and religious factors. Each group develops a "corporate identity," which influences the individuals within it. As such, it applies norms of ethical behavior to the social issues it confronts. In determining the norms for any such group or the society as a whole, many questions arise, the answers to which determine how individuals and groups respond to particular issues.

Is the ethical character of a group the simple sum of the character of its members?
Does each member of the group exercise equal influence on the decision-making process, good or bad, of the group itself?
Does the group have needs and goals that transcend the individual members?

Is the process of corporate identification the same regardless of whether the group is religious, political, cultural, social, or economic?

How does a group maintain its integrity in the face of conflicting claims?

In the following units, several ethical and social issues are examined in the light of social and religious norms. Most of the examples are drawn from Western sources, but many of the issues reflect universal concerns, particularly as the world's cultures are drawn closer. The questions raised by these issues do not lend themselves to simple religious answers for they often involve multiple political, economic, and cultural differences that add to their complexity. The necessity of careful and considered response in applying religious principles and norms is equally obvious.

The first two units are concerned with the relationships among humans such as justice, love, conflict, and peace on the collective—social and international—level. The next two units are concerned with an issue present in every society, though not always recognized—the status of women. The last two units deal with racial and ethnic differences as sources of conflict or creative opportunity in contemporary societies. With each of these issues, the major focus will be on their interaction with the religious perspectives of a society's pivotal value.

UNIT 62   LIBERATION THEOLOGY AND JUSTICE

Jewish and Christian Scriptures demand love of neighbors and justice for all, including the poor, the powerless, the oppressed, strangers, and foreigners. Prophets of eighth-century B.C.E. Israel and Judah insisted on mercy and compassion for the poor and justice for the oppressed. Incorporating these prophetic insights, Christian teachers, including Jesus, taught love for all, including enemies.

Sometimes there is felt to be tension between love and justice as goals for individual and group life. Reinhold Niebuhr, an eminent Protestant theologian, taught in an early phase of his ethical writings that some individuals can rise to fulfill the command to love but that all that can be expected of societies and other groups is justice.[1] Three decades later Niebuhr's fellow ethicist, Joseph Fletcher, argued that justice is simply love distributed and that love and justice are the same.[2]

An illustration of how to distribute love justly has been sharply focused in recent decades by "liberation theologians." Struggling with the vast inequities between wealthy and poor nations as well as class and economic differences within particular nations, liberation theologies seek new ways to apply justly the insights of love in modern societies. Liberation theologies have received impetus especially among Latin Americans and ethnic minorities of the United States who call for theology to start from a nontraditional starting point: the poor.[3] While utilizing the tools of the social sciences in analyzing the

---

[1] See Reinhold Niebuhr, *Moral Man and Immoral Society* (New York: Charles Scribner's Sons, 1932).

[2] See Joseph Fletcher, *Situation Ethics: The New Morality* (Philadelphia, PA: Westminster Press, 1966).

[3] Robert McAfee Brown, *Theology in a New Key: Responding to Liberation Themes* (Philadelphia, PA: Westminster Press, 1978), p. 60.

reality of conflict between the oppressed poor and the oppressors in a society in which the very structure of society is unjust and evil, liberation thinkers call for the engagement of *praxis*, a method of action and reflection by the community in the light of Scripture. Just love is action demanding reflective interpretation by Christians in group discussion that then compels even more just acts of love, which in turn call for reflection again, and so on in a continuous circle.

Injustices must be viewed through the eyes of the poor, who have often been disenfranchised and voiceless in society, for God is to be found among the poor and marginalized. Liberation theologies claim that God is calling and can empower the poor of the world to exercise responsibility for the future and modify and eliminate social and economic structures that presently enslave them in poverty.

The justice that comes with liberation will be a transformation not only of individuals in bondage to inward and personal sin but also of the evil structures and institutions of society that dehumanize and perpetuate poverty and corporate injustice. Further, it should be emphasized that the God in Christ revealed through the struggle of the poor is the force to liberate not only the oppressed but also the oppressors, who perhaps unknowingly are also enslaved to the unjust structures of power.

Whereas Latin American liberation theologians emphasized that the starting point for theological reflection should be "the poor," James Cone, a black American theologian writing in the 1960s, focused his thinking on "oppressed black people" as the place to begin Christian theology. Along with other black theologians, Cone wanted to move beyond a narrowly interpreted economic interpretation of oppression toward a heightened sensitivity to issues of racism.

Cone's position is as follows:

> Black Theology is a theology of liberation because it is a theology which arises from an identification with the oppressed blacks of America, seeking to interpret the gospel of Christ in the light of the black condition. It believes that the liberation of black people is God's liberation.
>
> The task of Black Theology then is to analyze the nature of the gospel of Jesus Christ in the light of oppressed black people so they will see the gospel as inseparable from their humiliated condition, bestowing on them the necessary power to break the chains of oppression. This means that it is a theology of and for the black community, seeking to interpret the religious dimensions of the forces of liberation in that community.[4]

Cone expressed this theology in terms that were congruent with the 1960s black power movement that may be defined as "complete emancipation of black power from white oppression by whatever means black people deem necessary. The methods may include selective buying, boycotting, marching, or even rebellion."[5] Cone's view was considered too radical by many whites and some African Americans who followed Martin Luther King, Jr. toward nonviolent integration rather than assertion of black power as the ideal solution to the societal inequalities.[6]

---

[4] James H. Cone, *Liberation: A Black Theology of Liberation* (Philadelphia and New York: JB Lippincott Company, 1970), p. 23.

[5] James A. Cone, *Black Theology and Black Power* (New York: Seabery Press, 1969), p. 6.

[6] Phillip Berryman, *Liberation Theology* (New York: Pantheon Books, 1987), p. 168.

As the 1970s unfolded, Cone's writings moved beyond his narrow attack on white theology's neglect of oppressed black people to broadened expressions that affirmed black cultural contributions in music (spirituals and blues), sermons, folk tales, and stories as valid sources for theological reflection. Furthermore, he expanded his attack on white racism to include also a focus on "United States capitalism as a major enemy of black people."[7] In his view the profit motive of capitalism exploited black humanity in particular as well as humankind in general. He further charged "social, economic, media and political power systems" with preventing black people from participating fully in the reality of daily living.

In his critique of American capitalism Cone "initiated a dialogue between black prophetic theologians and progressive Marxist thinkers," calling into question the class inequality suffered especially by black people.[8] While most African-American theologians are suspicious of Marxism as the scheme under which to subsume racism, some black theologians have continued the conversation with Marxism, especially Cornel West.[9] Thus, whereas the earliest stirrings of a black theology of liberation focused on white racism (oppression of blacks) rather than on classism (oppression of the poor), more recent expressions of liberation thought in African-American theology have included the economic analysis of society as crucial for understanding what it will take for Christian equality to be realized.

Recent Christian feminist theology, arising from gender inequalities, has often identified itself with liberation theology as it has shared images of oppression, insights into systemic sources of subjugation, and critique of limiting social structures (see Units 64 and 65). These various patterns of liberation movements seeking to free humanity from racism, sexism, and poverty have found common ground and sustentation. In doing so they have contributed to substantial changes in social patterns in the past quarter century.

◆◆◆

How do you respond to Cone's focus on "oppressed black people" or liberation theologians' focus on the "poor" as the place to begin Christian theology?

What "pivotal value" may be found in capitalism that would lead Latin American and black theologians to be so highly critical of the economic system?

What applications of love and justice can you envision that might alleviate the inequalities of modern society noted by liberation theologies?

Unit 63   Peace or Justice?

Historically, religious traditions and religious groups have taken a variety of positions regarding justice in society and the need at times to use force to secure peace and a just social order. Within the Hindu and Buddhist traditions there have been major strands

[7] Cornel West "Black Theology of Liberation as Critique of Capitalist Civilization," in *Black Theology. A Documentary History*, Vol II 1980–1992, eds. James H. Cone and Gayraud S. Wilmore (Maryknoll, NY: Orbis Books, 1996), p. 414.

[8] Ibid., p. 415.

[9] Berryman, *Liberation Theology*, p. 169.

that support pacifism and nonviolence. The twentieth-century Hindu leader Mohandas Gandhi, who led the struggle for India's freedom from British colonial domination, appealed to ancient Hindu sources, including the *Bhagavad-Gita*, to advocate complete nonviolence in attitude and action toward his opponents. He even suggested during Hitler's persecution of German Jews that they should mount a campaign of massive nonviolent public protest against their Nazi persecutors.

The same *Bhagavad-Gita* that Gandhi appealed to for support of total nonviolence was originally written to show that from the Hindu perspective of the caste system, it is appropriate for those in the military or princely caste to function as warriors when their situation imposes this as a necessity for maintaining order and justice. The rise of Islam was partly accomplished by military conquest, but the teachings of Muhammad and the Qur'an insist that all wars must be a response to injustice and that peace should be sought and treasured.

Roland Bainton has pointed out that traditionally there have been three Christian positions about war.[10] One has been the *pacifist* position of such groups as the Society of Friends and the Church of the Brethren and of such individuals as Leo Tolstoy and Muriel Lester. Included are a number of Catholics and traditionally Protestant Christians including Martin Luther King, Jr., and the German World War I submarine commander, Pastor Martin Niemoeller, later imprisoned by the Hitler government for resistance to the Nazi attempt to take over the churches.

A second position identified by Bainton, that of a *crusade*, was introduced by Christian leaders to account for some wars (mostly those of the ancient Israelites against their Canaanite enemies) believed to have been directly commanded by God. Later Christian leaders sometimes called for crusades against the Muslims during the Middle Ages, against the Germans during World War I, or against the "atheistic" Russian Communists during the cold war.

The dominant Christian position concerning war, however, has been adherence to the criteria of the *just war*, as set forth by ancient stoic or eclectic philosophers such as Cicero, Roman theories of the Natural Law, and Christian thinkers from the time of Augustine (354–430 C.E.) to Aquinas (1225–1274 C.E.) to the present. According to such theorists, these criteria are or should be recognized by all civilized nations since they are derived from universal human reason. In a war the following conditions must be met before it can be considered just or justifiable:

1. War must be authorized and waged under the authority of a legitimately established government. It cannot be initiated by private citizens.
2. War can be undertaken only if there is a just cause, a grave and unjustifiable injury done to the people of a country by the government or citizens of another country.
3. War must be waged with right intention—the intention of seeking a better, more just peace than would exist if the unjust situation were left uncorrected. The war should also be fought with a proper motive, aiming at doing good to all who will be affected, including the enemy.
4. War must be waged with proper means. Especially, the lives and safety of noncombatants must be protected from direct attack or harm.
5. War must be undertaken as a last resort only after all possibilities of peaceful settlement have been exhausted.

---

[10] Roland Bainton, *Christian Attitudes Toward War and Peace* (New York: Abingdon Press, 1960).

6. War can be undertaken only when there is a reasonable expectation that the just side will prevail; otherwise great harm would be done without a correction of the original evil.
7. War can be undertaken only when the good (to all affected parties) that will result from correcting the unjust situation will be greater than the destruction that the war will produce.

Past discussions of the moral problem of war have focused on several issues:

1. How can one be even reasonably sure that the cause for which a war is undertaken or risked is just?
2. Can any war between independent nation-states in a world where any international conflict might lead to nuclear war be justified?
3. Under what conditions is a revolutionary uprising (civil war) against an aggressive or tyrannical government justified?
4. Can a counterrevolutionary war, aided by outside powers, fought to preserve a stable international balance of power, be justified, even if it means keeping an oppressive government in power against the wishes of a large part of the population in the country involved?

Religious groups and leaders are closely examining these issues. A pastoral letter of American Catholic Bishops that many observers considered epochal urged the reconsideration of just-war arguments that favor retention of a defense based on nuclear weapons. The continued reliance on a nuclear arsenal for deterrence can be justified, the bishops suggest, only if governments and individuals make it a matter of first priority to move away from the nuclear balance of terror through negotiation and disarmament.[11]

During the 1980s, the stability of the international system during the cold war confrontation between the two opposing superpowers, the United States and the U.S.S.R., was thought by many to depend on the nuclear standoff policy of mutually assured destruction (MAD). Since the perceived end of the Cold War, the question of a justified use of force, nuclear or conventional, has not gone away. The dissolution of the Soviet Union and its block of supporting nations in Eastern Europe has in many places produced turbulence, civil war, and anarchy (for example, the former Yugoslavia and the former U.S.S.R. itself). Tensions in the Middle East, including decades or centuries-old conflicts, continue to erupt into violence, including Operation Desert Storm; and its continuing uneasy, militarily composed peace. There are many areas of continuous conflict in other parts of the world. During Desert Storm in 1991, President George Bush, in a speech to a convention of evangelical Protestant leaders, cited all of the traditional just-war criteria in support of the United States and its allies, whose soldiers were under the authority of the United Nations. President Clinton, using the same rationale, used military force in response to what were considered acts of terrorism and deployed troops to act as peacekeeping forces providing a source of stability in many parts of the world. The questions listed earlier are still operative and are being confronted almost daily by the world's reli-

---

[11] The National Conference of Catholic Bishops, *The Challenge of Peace: God's Promise and Our Response, A Pastoral Letter on War and Peace*, May 3, 1983 (Washington, DC: United States Catholic Conference, 1983).

Figure 15.1 *Sally Forth* (Reprinted with special permission of King Features Syndicate.)

gious leaders (as well as by secular leaders and ordinary citizens) as well as in the consciences of faithful adherents of the world's religions.

As the sixth edition of *Exploring Religious Meaning* is being prepared, there is
renewed violence in many areas, including in the Middle East between citizens of Israel
and the Palestinians; in Eastern European countries, formerly under Communist governments; between ethnic and other dissident groups, and in Ireland. Much of this violence
takes the form of "terrorist" acts.

Terrorism is the systematic indiscriminate use of violence against a population or
group by a state or some group in order to intimidate, repress resistance, and deter cooperation with the opponents of the state or group. A state may use terrorism against its own
population. This was done in Nazi Germany and in Stalinist Russia. It can also use terrorism against citizens or groups within other states. Revolutionary groups can use terrorism
against supporters of the established government or against populations in other territories.
As the criteria of justified war just outlined, traditional ethics condemns all acts and policies of terrorism because they are indiscriminate. They violate the rule of right means.

Some theorists have justified terrorism either of a government to repress internal
resistance or of a revolutionary group to topple a repressive regime. The Marxist revolutionary Trotsky justified terrorism by Marxist regimes against recalcitrant populations. He
argued that the Marxist cause was just; therefore Marxist terrorism to weaken counterrevolutionary movements was justified.[12] The French philosopher Jean-Paul Sartre justified terrorism by revolutionaries in Africa attempting to overthrow oppressive European
imperialist governments. Sartre thought terrorism was justified not only because it
allowed relatively "weak" revolutionary movements the chance of overcoming highly
armed, technologically superior forces, but also because acts of terrorism against the
oppressor are therapeutic for the oppressed.[13] Some behavioral scientists argue that far
from being therapeutic, terrorism is the expression of suicidal self-hatred of the terrorists

---

[12] See Leon Trotsky, *Terrorism and Communism* (Ann Arbor: The University of Michigan Press, 1961).

[13] See Jean-Paul Sartre, *Critique of Dialectical Reason* (London: Verso, 1976) and *The Communists and the Peace* (New York: George Braziller, 1968).

projected onto their victims. Although some terrorists engage in suicide attacks after being told they will be martyrs and receive rewards in heaven, these behavioral scientists say that such a belief is only a "screen" for feelings of weakness, worthlessness, and self-rejection.

On September 11, 2001, a possible point of decision occurred in the encounter of global civilization and terrorism. Suicidal terrorists representing an extremist movement commandeered four U.S. commercial airliners, crashing two of them into New York City's World Trade Center, destroying it and killing thousands of persons from many different countries who were working or visiting in the destroyed buildings. A third airplane was crashed into the Pentagon in Washington, DC. The fourth crashed in a rural area of Pennsylvania, killing all aboard but harming no one else when a group of passengers attempted to overthrow the highjackers. These terrorist acts, while expressing political and economic motivations, were ostensibly done for religious reasons. They were directed at driving U.S. economic, cultural, and military influence out of the Middle East. Some Muslims disapprove of the U.S. presence because they see the United States as sustaining Israel's right to exist, supporting moderate Muslim regimes in Muslim countries that the terrorists would like to overthrow, and having a corrupting "Westernizing" effect on Muslim culture (see the remarks on *fundamentalism* in Unit 77). Many interpreters of Islamic religion and Muslim governments repudiated these actions as contrary to the spirit and teachings of Islam. Almost every government in the world condemned the attacks. Many governments pledged to join with the United States in what was predicted to be a long overdue multifaceted campaign to end terrorism, some predicting that terrorism and the struggle against it on economic, political, and military fronts will be the form that war will take in the twenty-first century.

After World War II an international tribunal tried leaders of Hitler's Nazi government and military for war crimes and crimes (atrocities) committed against humanity. At present, leaders, including a former president of Serbia, have been indicted and ordered to stand trial for violating international law by allowing such crimes against humanity as ethnic cleansing during war waged between ethnic groups in the former Yugoslavia. The principles justifying war through the centuries lie behind these trials.

In the past, wars between sovereign nations have often been thought to be rational means of seeking rational goals—defense against aggression, justified defense or expansion of territory or populations or economic power. Uprisings within a society by dissident groups were often condemned as unjustified because they were unsanctioned by legal authority. In the modern world this distinction has been blurred by philosophies such as that of John Locke, a seventeenth-century Englishman, and by the American *Declaration of Independence*. Both justify the right to revolt against a tyrannical or unjust sovereign (government). But in many ways the rationality of both forms of war—between sovereign nations and in civil rebellions—is at present called into question. Some argue that weapons and strategies of destruction have become too extreme to justify war between nation states. Examples of civil war based on generations or centuries of ethnic or religious hatreds and carried on by indiscriminate terrorism are questioned as to their being rationally justifiable. These issues lead to the concerns of religious leaders and adherents to move toward peaceful solutions to conflict.

One further factor involving violence in contemporary societies is the increase of deadly violence in modernized, postindustrial societies. "Road rage" is often blamed for numerous brutal attacks on public streets, expressways, and highways by individuals infuriated by some stranger's inept or discourteous driving of an automobile. Also, the numerous attacks with high-powered weaponry by disaffected public school students on teachers and fellow students or by employees on fellow employees and supervisors have raised questions about underlying causes of alienation, frustration, and despair in contemporary society. Religious persons have insisted that new or renewed sources of support for group and personal development rather than stricter laws and larger prisons are needed. They have pointed to new and old teachings concerning opportunities for acceptance and belonging that may promote growth toward responsible maturity in community.

❖❖❖

> Can you give instances of cases where religion held either by groups or by individuals has been a source of peace and reconciliation? A source of conflict?

> Can war ever be considered reasonable in our modern world? When? How?

Unit 64   Religion and the Social Status of Women

TRADITIONAL VIEW

One of the first books of poetry by a North American writer—and the first published work by a North American poet whose works are still recognized as having literary merit—was published in England in 1650. The writer was Anne Bradstreet, daughter of Thomas Dudley, the second governor of the Massachusetts Bay Colony, and wife of a man who, after her death, also served as governor of the colony. Anne Bradstreet was the mother of eight children; devoutly Puritan in her religious outlook; and well read in religion, history, and science.

Anne Bradstreet did not think of herself as a poet. She wrote poetry for recreation and for the edification of herself and her friends and family. The manuscript of her book *The Tenth Muse* apparently was taken to England by her brother-in-law, John Woodbridge, without her knowledge and given to a publisher. In his "Epistle to the Reader," published as a foreword to the book, Woodbridge wrote,

> I might trim this book with quaint expressions . . . but I fear 'twill be a shame for a man that can speak so little, to be seen in the title-page of this woman's book, lest by comparing the one with the other, the reader should pass his sentence that it is the gift of women not only to speak most but to speak best.

Woodbridge then goes on to suggest that male readers will not be envious of the "excellency of the inferior sex" unless "men turn more peevish than women." It would be interesting to know what Anne Bradstreet's reaction was to this half-derogatory—"women speak most"—half-self-effacing mock compliment from her brother-in-law.

Another Massachusetts poet, Nathaniel Ward, had written these lines, again without Anne's knowledge, in his introductory verse published at the beginning of *The Tenth Muse*:

> I muse whither at length these girls will go;
> It half-revives my chill frostbitten blood,
> To see a woman once do ought that's good.

Anne often wrote as if she did in fact accept the belief, recommended for good Christian women of her time—and other times—that women are "the inferior sex." But Anne seems to have accepted this belief with irony, and in at least one poem, her poem on Queen Elizabeth, she wrote,

> Nay say, have women worth? or have they none?
> Or had they some, but with our Queen is't gone? . . .
> Let such as say our sex is void of reason
> Know tis a slander now, but once was treason.

Apparently Anne Bradstreet was not entirely convinced that women really were the inferior sex, who only occasionally—or once—could come up to the high standards of the male sex.[14]

Anne Bradstreet's subtle questioning of a cultural assumption—female inferiority—was perhaps unusual in seventeenth-century America. Yet the assumption that females are inferior and subservient to males is an ancient tradition in many cultures of the world. All of the societies from which Western civilization grew—Greek, Roman, Mesopotamian, Israelite, Egyptian—accepted such distinctions between the sexes. Even though women who were Roman citizens could hold property and seek divorce, the superior/inferior distinction was the accepted perception in the Roman Empire.

Plato, in his *Republic*, is one of the few, perhaps the only figure in the ancient Western world, who argued for complete equality of women in society. The Greek philosopher Aristotle, however, wrote,

> A husband and a father . . . rules over wife and children, both free, but the rule differs, the rule over his children being a royal, over his wife a constitutional rule. For although there may be exceptions to the order of nature, the male is by nature fitter for command than the female, just as the elder and full-grown is superior to the younger and more immature. . . . The inequality is permanent.[15]

The subordination of women continued throughout Western history until modern times, only occasionally being questioned when strong women monarchs such as Britain's Queen Elizabeth and Spain's Isabella rose to power in the sixteenth and seventeenth centuries. The changing vocational roles of women in industrialized nations during the eighteenth and nineteenth centuries brought attention to social inequalities between the sexes. By the mid-nineteenth century, Christian women in both Britain and America began to organize to achieve moral reforms within the societies (temperance and the closing of brothels being significant objectives). To achieve these goals they created a

---

[14] The materials in this unit dealing with Anne Bradstreet are partly based on Adrienne Rich, "Anne Bradstreet and Her Poetry," and Jeannine Hensley, "Anne Bradstreet's Wreath of Thyme," in *The Works of Anne Bradstreet*, ed. Jeannine Hensley (Cambridge, MA: Harvard University Press, 1967), pp. ix–xxxv.

[15] Aristotle, *Politics*, Book I, Ch. 12 (1259a–1259b), trans. Benjamin Jowett, The Modern Library (New York: Random House, 1943).

"women's movement," which soon sought greater equality for women in society and the privilege of political power as voting citizens.[16]

As more women enter the workforce than at any other time in history, the time-honored tradition of female inferiority has been vociferously denied by a rising feminist movement. One of its facets has been "consciousness development"—the overcoming by women of negative attitudes about their identity that derive from traditional stereotypes and practices based on social discrimination. The movement has attracted substantial male support and has become a major agent for change in society. The most obvious evidence of such change is seen in the participation in and rising position of women in almost all occupations. The academic community has recognized changing attitudes toward women by creation of "women's studies" as a separate field of study. This many-faceted discipline includes extensive critiquing of past attitudes toward women, recovery of the lost history of women, and a revision of the very understanding of women and their nature.[17] Political organization among women has brought pressure on all governing bodies to rethink their positions and policies relative to a number of educational, social, economic, and moral issues. The past half-century has witnessed substantial advancement for women in every area.

As these changes have taken place, redefinitions of the "role" of both men and women in society, the workplace, and the home have become much more complex. Consciousness of sexual harassment, based on the traditional ideas of male independence/superiority and female dependence/inferiority, has produced charges of misconduct from the lowest to the highest levels of society. The prominence of government and philanthropic support for local "women's shelters" in most American cities is only one testimony to the adverse social consequences of superiority/inferiority attitudes. Recent charges of sexual harassment involving the President of the United States, Supreme Court justices, and military commanders at all ranks, as well as in most other fields of employment, testify to the pervasiveness of such misconduct throughout the society.

While redefinitions of women's societal place and position have been most prominent in Europe and America, extensive cultural interaction, brought about by worldwide democratization and capitalization in the second half of the twentieth century, has also called for the reevaluation of the role and place of women in most non-Western societies. Even the most conservative countries have experienced stress over the issue: Witness the rise of women to positions of political leadership in India and Pakistan and a recent "revolt" of Turkish women when their prime minister sought to reinstate traditional Islamic practices that limit women's public participation in the society.

WOMEN IN THE CHRISTIAN TRADITION

Some historians of Christianity have claimed that the position of women—in contrast to their position in the Roman Empire of the first century—was significantly elevated in Christian teaching and practice. One text cited is Paul's saying that in Christ there is "neither male nor female" (Galatians 3:27–28). But Paul also had an elevated conception

[16] See Olive Banks, *Faces of Feminism: A Study of Feminism as a Social Movement* (New York: St. Martin's Press, 1981).

[17] Ann E. Carr, *Transforming Grace* (New York: Continuum Publishing Co., 1996), pp. 7–9.

of male responsibility in the marriage relationship: He assumed that the male would be dominant. His teachings about the role that women should play in the life and worship of the church reflect a conservative spirit (see I Corinthians 11:2–16; 14:33–35).

With the rise in the second and third centuries of asceticism as a major factor in the life of the church, the conservative view of the role and status of women became more pronounced. From the standpoint of the Christian ascetic, who had withdrawn to the desert to flee the wickedness of the world, women were sources of temptation; after all, Eve had been responsible for Adam's fall, for the entry of evil into the world.

Clement of Alexandria (150–215 C.E.), however, argued that by nature there was (and ought to be) complete equality between the sexes. (He did believe that there should be some differences in vocation.) Nevertheless, for the majority of early Christian writers, for example, John Chrysostom and Ambrose, women were blamed for being immature and ignorant, conditions that where they existed are easily explained by the educational neglect of, and social discrimination against, women characteristic of the period. This social position was largely unaffected by the spread of Christianity in the Roman Empire. In the Eastern part of the empire (and perhaps also in the West), there was regular ordination of deaconesses. Deaconesses were allowed, however, to minister only to women, and they were not allowed to perform ecclesiastical functions thought to be proper to the male, such as teaching or praying aloud in worship services or approaching the altar. This is in stark contrast to the practice of many of the heretical sects of the period, such as Montanism, in which women were allowed more active roles. With the onset of feudalism in the seventh and eighth centuries, women lost many of the rights they had had in the earlier urban setting of the Roman Empire.[18] When monastic houses for women were formed in the early Middle Ages, they were attached to and subordinate to male monastic orders.

Modern changes in the societal perception of women have caused intense scrutiny of traditional Christian and Jewish organizational attitudes and practices. Criticism has been broad. The tendency of Judaism and Christianity to represent and describe God in only masculine terms has been repeatedly questioned.[19] Rosemary Ruether suggests that a further difficulty lies in a fundamental dualism assumed by Western culture:

> Christianity, as the heir of both classical Neo-Platonism and apocalyptic Judaism, combines the image of a male, warrior God with the exaltation of the intellect over the body. The Classical doctrine of Christ, which fused the vision of the heavenly messianic king with the transcendent logos of immutable Being, was a synthesis of the religious impulses of late antique religious consciousness, but precisely in their alienated state of development. These world-negating religions carried a set of dualities that still profoundly condition the modern worldview.
>
> All the basic dualities—the alienation of the mind from the body, the alienation of the subjective self from the objective world; the subjective retreat of the individual, alienated from the social community; the domination or rejection of nature by spirit—these all have roots in the apocalyptic-Platonic religious heritage of classical Christianity. But the alienation of the masculine from the feminine is the primary sexual symbolism that sums up all these alienations. The psychic traits of intellectuality, transcendent spirit, and autonomous will that were identified with the male left the woman with the contrary

[18] Based on D. S. Bailey, *Sexual Relation in Christian Thought* (New York: Harper and Brothers, 1959).

[19] See Rosemary Radford Ruether, *Sexism and God-Talk* (Boston, MA: Beacon Press, 1983).

traits of bodiliness, sensuality and subjugation. Society, through the centuries, has in every way profoundly conditioned men and women to play out their lives and find their capacities within this basic antithesis.[20]

Ruether, among others, also suggests that this same duality contributes to our present-day ecological crisis where the natural world, seen through a male superiority image, is subjected to human exploitation.

Feminist arguments such as these call on Christianity and other major world religions to rethink traditional images of the Divine, understanding of relationships of men with women, and traditional structures of worship, moral order, and religious institutions.[21] Christian feminist theologians and Bible scholars carry the discussion into every aspect of traditional hermeneutics, theological systems that fail to be holistic, and all practices of the faith.[22] In modern America and Europe this call for reformulation of Christian women's roles has often focused on the historic exclusion of women from the priesthood and ministry, the denial of their full participation in decision making by religious organizations, and the explicit and implicit assumption of male superiority in the church. As changes in the role of women have occurred throughout the world, Christian women theologians are recognizing the cultural differences among women and their perceptions of themselves. Such recognition calls for a broadening discussion of how women should conceive of themselves, males, and the Divine. Western reimaging, which has dominated discussion to this point, may not be sufficiently broad.[23]

In response to such feminist critiques of women's place in Christianity, conservative Protestant denominations continue to assert Biblical sanction for the authenticity of traditional views. On the issue of ordination of women to the ministry their arguments are several. They sometimes repeat the historical assertion that woman, having been created from man, must by nature be subservient to man (Genesis 2:18–24). Some suggest women, following in the lineage of Eve, who committed the first sin (Genesis 3:1–13), are not worthy of the ministerial role. Others point to New Testament passages to assert that as a tainted gender, women cannot render a pure ministry (I Timothy 2:11–15). On issues of church leadership the Apostle Paul's description of women's place in the church as subservient to that of men continues to be cited to justify limitation of women's participation in positions of church leadership (I Corinthians 14:33–35). Roman Catholics and some Anglican communities also refuse to ordain women because of Biblically based (Matthew 16:17–19; 28:16–20) and historically established church principles; according to these

[20] Rosemary Radford Ruether, "Motherearth and the Megamachine," *Christianity and Crisis* (December 13, 1971).

[21] For discussions of a rising feminist consciousness and activity in the world's religions, see Paula Cooey, William Eakin, and J. McDaniel, *After Patriarchy: Feminist Transformation of the World's Religions* (New York: Orbis, 1996). See also Units 69 and 70 for comment on the status of women in preliterate and ancient cultures.

[22] See Letty M. Russell, ed., *Feminist Interpretation of the Bible* (Philadelphia: Westminster Press, 1985); Elizabeth A. Johnson, *She Who Is: The Mystery of God in Feminist Theological Discourse* (New York: Crossword Publishing, 1992); Judith Plaskow and Carol P. Chris, eds. *Womenspirit Rising* (New York: Harper and Row, 1979).

[23] Rosemary Radford Ruether, *Women and Redemption: A Theological History* (Minneapolis, MN: Fortress Press, 1998) pp. 200–201.

"It seems to me that ordination of women might brighten the place up a bit."

Figure 15.2   (© The New Yorker Collection 2000 Ed Fisher from cartoonbank.com. All Rights Reserved.)

concepts, apostolic succession, understood to be essential to ordination, is limited to men. In the eyes of feminists, these assertions overlook the significant role of women as Jesus' disciples and throughout the history of the church.[24]

Nevertheless, some conservative communities, recognizing the significance of several critiques of traditional patterns, have begun to reconsider their understandings. While continuing to exclude women from ordination and rights of leadership in worship services, they have begun to include women in their governance structures and publicly recognize their historically significant teaching and mission roles with the church. Roman Catholics have similarly given larger roles to women in local church administration and some lay patterns of worship.

More moderate, liberal Christian denominations, appropriating some of the feminists' insights, point to the incompatibility of much of Jesus' teachings with the historical inequities between the sexes and recognize the effective ministries women have rendered in the churches through the ages. Consequently, they see little justification for barring women from any role in their churches. As a result, female participation in the governance of many Protestant denominations is now common. Educational instruction on the rights and equality of women in the church is broadly practiced. Women are now regularly ordained to ministerial service in the United Methodist, Presbyterian, and Episcopal churches as well as other mainline American denominations. United Methodists have also elected women to their highest ministerial office—that of bishop. Seminaries of

[24] See Elisabeth Schussler Fiorenza, "Women in the Early Christian Movement," Judith Plaskow and Carol P. Christ, eds., *Womenspirit Rising* and Amy Oden, *In Her Words: Women's Writings in the History of Christian Thought* (Nashville, TN: Abingdon Press, 1994).

these denominations often find women constituting 40 percent to 50 percent of their students and a significant percentage of their faculties.

Although unwilling to ordain women, in 1970 the Roman Catholic Church named two of its female saints, Teresa of Avila and Catherine of Siena, to a very small, select group of theologians—fewer than forty from the whole history of Catholic theology—who have been given the distinguished title of *Doctors of the Church*. No other women had ever been given this title in the Roman church.

These modifications of the role of women in many Christian churches reflect major changes in attitude toward the role of women during the past several decades. The rising number of women in Protestant seminaries and among pastors serving local congregations, as well as those in positions of general church leadership, suggests that such modifications will continue to reshape Christian churches and their ministries within society.

◆◆◆

> *What roles are regarded by our society as really "first class"—as conferring maximum prestige and dignity on the individuals who fill them?*
>
> *How many women, in comparison with men, are in these roles?*
>
> *Are there some roles of maximum prestige value in our society that have never been filled by women?*
>
> *What factors—social, psychological, economic, ideological—have contributed to the bias?*
>
> *How may changes in the role of women affect images and understanding of the Divine and humanity's relationship to the Divine?*

UNIT 65   SEXUALITY AND HUMAN LIBERATION

Sally's conversation with her husband in Figure 15.3 offers a view of the most obvious change in perception of the sexual roles in modern society. As Ted serves her a very late dinner Sally recounts her day at the office reflecting issues that would in a traditional

Figure 15.3 *Sally Forth* (Reprinted with special permission of King Features Syndicate.)

setting have been the domain of the husband rather than the wife. The modifications of male and female roles in the workplace certainly has contributed, along with many other factors, to new social structures in schools, churches, families, and most other group relations. The modern feminist movement began partly as a response to the changes in women's roles during World War II. Consequently, the longstanding subservience of women to men, while not eliminated in Western societies, has been restructured, and the feminist protest against having an identity only in relation to one's husband or parents has been appreciatively heard in many sections of the society. However, the issues surrounding these changes and arguments relative to the issue continue.

A student in a philosophy course recently proposed the following thesis: "Human sexuality is likely to be the most enduring of all philosophical topics." His line of reasoning was as follows: In the past, differences of race, nationality, language community, educational attainment, and religion have been the basis for fundamental differences in status and treatment. We know now that these differences are not essential and that human beings can and should be treated on a basis of equality in spite of these differences, in line with one of the major moral and political goals of our time—equal opportunity and equal treatment. But one major and apparently irreducible difference between human beings does exist and seems to pose irreducible problems for the goal of equality, the difference between the sexes.

Many contemporary speakers and writers would challenge the last statement, insisting that the basic differences between the sexes, insofar as they bear on social roles, are socially created by a patriarchal society rather than natural or inevitable. According to traditional concepts of "natural law" (Unit 79) the biological differences between men and women indicate their proper role in society. According to this understanding women are physically and morally best fitted to be mothers, supervisors of the home, protectors, comforters, and healers of husband and children. Against this view, many in recent years have argued that the traditional roles assigned to women, and the traditional characteristics considered feminine, are not the result of biological differences but are cultural creations, cultural stereotypes.

Adrienne Rich, a poet and a contemporary feminist, has written,

> The patriarchy looks to its women to embody and impersonate the qualities lacking in its institutions—concern for the quality of life, for means rather than for pure goal, a connection with the natural and the extrasensory order. These attributes have been classified as "female" in part because the patriarchy relegates them to women and tends to deny them—with a certain fatalism—to men. The encouragement of such qualities as intuition, sympathy, and access to feeling by a mother in her sons is deplored because this is supposed to make them unfit for the struggle that awaits them in a masculine world. Thus the "masculinity" of the world is perpetuated.
>
> The "liberated" woman encounters male hostility in the form of psychic rape, often masked as psychic or physical seduction. It occurs overtly in the classroom where a male teacher denigrates female intellect; more subtly in the committee where she sits as token woman and where her intelligence is treated with benign neglect; in the magnanimous assumption that she is "not like other women" and for this reason is so desirable a colleague, figurehead, or adornment to the establishment (the pitting of woman against woman, woman against herself). At the same time that she is told about her "specialness" she is expected to be flattered, like all women, by flirtation. She is also expected to be flattered by man's sexual self-hatred and sexual confusion, his avowal "I can talk to women,

but not to men," his romanticizing of his sexual dishonesty "I can't talk to my wife, but I can talk to you.". . .

One of the devastating effects of technological capitalism has been its numbing of the powers of the imagination—specifically, the power to envision new human and communal relationships. I am a feminist because I feel endangered, psychically and physically, by this society, and because I believe that the women's movement is saying that we have come to an edge of history when men—in so far as they are embodiments of the patriarchal idea—have become dangerous to children and other living things, themselves included; and that we can no longer afford to keep the female principle—the mother in all women and the woman in many men—straitened within the tight little postindustrial family, or within any male-induced notion of where the female principle is valid and where it is not.[25]

◆◆◆

What do you think Adrienne Rich is saying about the relation of men and women in contemporary society?

In what ways does her discussion relate to the student's suggestion that there are "irreducible" differences between the sexes?

◆◆◆

It is difficult to be objective in discussing these issues. Behavioral scientists are often heavily influenced by the assumptions or presuppositions they bring to research on the topic. Behaviorism, an influential trend in American behavioral research during the past fifty years, has emphasized the role of social conditioning in shaping what is often thought of as "human nature." Thus, behaviorists have tended to see human nature as relatively open and changeable. In contrast, Freudian psychotherapists have often assumed that there are innate psychological differences between men and women that predispose them toward different personality structures and social roles. Recently a behavioral approach called "sociobiology" has emphasized genetic, biological factors that some have held fit men and women for different roles in society. These three approaches to the issue not only color the conclusions that may be reached but show the multiple possibilities of interpretation among present-day researchers.

Christian leaders and theologians similarly have taken several different positions on the issue. Conservatives sometimes appeal to the Genesis story of creation, according to which Eve was created to be a helper for Adam so that Adam would not be alone, arguing for a basis in God's will for male superiority. In contrast, more moderate and liberal interpreters have stressed Jesus' refusal to distinguish between men and women in his moral and ethical teachings and his own social relations. In an interesting (and difficult to interpret) New Testament passage, I Corinthians 11:8–12, Paul seems to argue that according to the original creation, woman was created for the sake of man and subject to man's authority, but in the new creation that has come through Christ, there is to be complete mutuality between woman and man. They are to be not independent of each other but mutually dependent.

Some feminists have stressed that as long as women are oppressed in our society no one is fully free. They thus see the feminist movement as working for complete human

[25] *New York Review of Books*, 19, no. 9 (November 30, 1972), 35–40.

liberation. Elizabeth Johnson, a Catholic theologian, offers a feminist's ethic grounded in mutuality that suggests that equality and interdependence lead to such liberation and overcome traditional antitheses:

> The particular pattern of relationship consistently promoted in feminist ethical discourse is mutuality. This signifies a relation marked by equivalence between persons, a concomitant valuing of each other, a common regard marked by trust, respect, and affection in contrast to competition, domination, or assertions of superiority. It is a relationship on the analogy of friendship, an experience often used as metaphor to characterize the reciprocity/independence dialectic at the heart of all caring relationships. Women's moral development and psychology; women's ways of knowing; women's ways of loving; women's ways of living bodily—all are marked, upon reflection, by an intrinsic connectedness quite different from the male ideal in classic and contemporary culture. . . . The centrality of relation ensures that feminist ethics presses ultimately toward the flourishing of all people, children as well as men, and the earth and all its creatures. In the realm of theory, if the self is not defined by opposition but by the dialectic of friendly, constitutive relation, then it begins to be possible to hold together in a rich synthesis all manner of previously dichotomous elements: not just self and other, but matter and spirit, passions and intellect, embodiedness and self-transcendence, nurturing and questing, altruism and self-affirmation, receptivity and activity, love and power, being and doing, private and public domains, humanity and the earth. Oppositional, either-or thinking, which is endemic to the androcentric construction of reality, dissolves in a new paradigm of both-and.[26]

◆◆◆

How do you feel about the changing roles of men and women in our society?

Do you agree that in most societies women have been oppressed and are denied the opportunity to fulfill their human potential?

What are some of the differences that Johnson's concept of mutuality might make in personal and social relations?

◆◆◆

The role of sexuality in human life and in human personality as understood traditionally by religions has become a matter of intense concern and often a cause of conflict. In the United States since the late 1960s, changes in traditional attitudes toward variations of expected gender roles have been the subject of intense debate. As explained, some Catholics have suggested that the accepted view that priests should be male, unmarried, and celibate not only is demeaning to women but suggests a negative attitude toward human sexuality. The leadership of the Catholic Church has denied holding a negative view of women or of sexuality but has maintained that Jesus set the example of male, unmarried, celibate clergy and that example should continue to be followed. Mainline Protestant churches have been much more willing to ordain women and place them in roles of authority (see Unit 64).

Both Catholics and Protestants have debated the issue of whether homosexual sex can be acceptable from a Christian point of view. Catholics have generally argued that a person who has ("is born with") erotic orientation toward persons of the same gender is not to be blamed for this orientation, but that homosexual acts in response to this orientation are wrong. Many Protestant churches also accept this position. Additionally,

[26] Elizabeth Johnson, *She Who Is*, pp. 68–69.

Protestant groups have argued (as have Catholics) that Christians should have compassion for persons who are homosexual and for their families, should minister to them in love, and should insist that they receive full civil rights as citizens and persons. In the past two decades the issue of how one should respond to homosexuals has become a critical discussion among the largest Protestant denominations. Many conservative Protestants in different denominations have agreed that homosexuals should be ministered to in love, but have argued that if a homosexually oriented person is converted to Christianity, the person can be healed or freed of his or her homosexual orientation. Others, including many in mainline Protestant groups and Catholics, are skeptical of this possibility.

Some Protestant religious thinkers have argued that sexual orientation, whether heterosexual or homosexual, is a gift from God; promiscuous sexual experiences would be wrong, but a monogamous, faithful, loving sexual relation between two people will be blessed by God. This has not become a majority position in mainline Christian groups. Much argument has arisen about whether self-acknowledged "practicing" homosexuals can be ordained to or serve in Christian ministry. The United Church of Christ, a mainline liberal Protestant denomination, has accepted the ordination of such self-acknowledged homosexuals while the General Assembly of the Presbyterian Church U.S.A. in the spring of 2001 recommended that local presbyteries (the groups responsible for ordination of ministers) be given the option of ordaining gay and lesbian clergy. This recommendation requires approval by the local presbyteries to become church policy, but such a recommendation shows that attitudes are changing among many Christians.

Most mainline churches have continually debated the issue in recent legislative sessions but retained their positions that legitimate sex for Christians can be expressed only in faithful, monogamous unions between a woman and a man; therefore, practicing homosexuals cannot be ordained to ministry. Many persons in variant denominations, nevertheless, find themselves questioning the position of their churches. Many persuasive moral teachings accept homosexual sex as sometimes legitimate. They also recognize that the large number of heterosexual divorces and remarriages in the society have led to a much more lenient attitude toward divorce in most churches. Similarly, while generally disapproved, the largely socially accepted practice of unmarried heterosexual couples living together signals major attitudinal changes among Christians. Consequently, many wonder whether most Christian groups have not in effect changed, broadened, or relaxed their views concerning sex and sexuality whether or not that may be recognized in church polity.

Some have also argued that the traditional view that marriage should be only between individuals of opposite gender is based on religious tradition and should not be held to by the secular government. According to this view, marriage should be a matter of consent or covenant between two adults regardless of gender, but should be recognized by government to secure equality in such matters as pension, medical benefits, and protection for children.

◆◆◆

What have religions traditionally taught about sexual identity and sexual experience as components of the human person, personality, or self?

Can you identify methods that Christians who sincerely differ over issues of sexual identity might use to come to an acceptable consensus on the issue?

UNIT 66   POVERTY AND RACE

Common today are homeless and hungry people seeking shelter, food, and work—mostly people of color. Statistics confirm what we see. According to the Census Bureau, in 2000 22.1 percent of African Americans were below the government-defined poverty line of $17,603.00 (for a family of four). Next were Hispanics, at 21.2 percent. Asians and Pacific Islanders fared better, at 10.8 percent, as did whites, at 7.7 percent.[27] Although Native Americans are not ranked in this account, many have suffered dire poverty since they were forced onto reservations in the last century. While there has been a definite reduction in the percentages of persons living in poverty since the early 1990s, the ratios between ethnic groups have not changed substantially. Since 1970, African Americans have experienced poverty at a ratio to whites of three to one, and Hispanics currently share that rate. The concentration of minorities in deteriorating urban centers often abandoned by middle-class citizens signifies deep wounds in our social structure.

Why such inequality in U.S. economic life? Racism is certainly part of the answer. Racial ideologies really did not emerge until the nineteenth century, when biological imagery began to supersede religious reasons for Anglo-Saxon ethnocentrism (exalting a particular group of people based on a common history, culture, and language without reference to racial traits based on skin color). The rise of the new "science of man" augmented misguided ethnocentric beliefs by the English to beliefs in the innate superiority of the white race. In the New World these racial ideologies became convenient justifications for the dominance of white colonists over people of color. Although blacks were enslaved at first for economic reasons, in time racial prejudice took on a life of its own as subsequent generations were socialized to claim white superiority over all nonwhites. It was generally believed that God was smiling on the Anglo-Saxon people and that it was the "white man's burden" to "Anglo-Saxonize" and Christianize other races. In short, it was the "Manifest Destiny" of white Americans to evangelize the world.[28] In the spirit of this religious justification for white superiority, the racist rubrics of European colonialism motivated the rise of what has been characterized as "internal colonialism" in America.[29] White colonialists established dominance economically and otherwise over "Indians, Negroes and Mexicans" as well as the immigrant Chinese workers and others from Asia and the Pacific Islands.

Although overt racism has been outlawed at certain levels since the 1960s Civil Rights Act, the continued ill effects of covert, institutionalized racism perpetuate the racial inequalities that are so difficult to correct. A brief reminder of the economic backgrounds of African Americans and Hispanics, the two largest populations of nonwhites in the United States, will help us draw connections between poverty and race.

The African-American story, of course, recounts slavery and its horrors as an

[27] U.S. Government Statistics from www.census.gov.
[28] E. C. Orosco, *Republican Protestantism in Aztlan* (Glendale, CA: Peterins Press, 1980), pp. 138–141.
[29] See Mario Barrera, *Race and Class in the Southwest: A Theory of Racial Inequality* (Notre Dame, IN: University of Notre Dame Press, 1979), pp. 188–219.

economic reality in U.S. history. Although slavery's shackles were broken by the Civil War, African Americans are frequently held down by disadvantages of the past: capital deficits that often limit their qualifications as workers and give them less access to opportunities because of continuing inequalities in education, job opportunities often limited to the lower-paying service segment of the economy, and enduring discrimination. David H. Swinton, a specialist in racial economics, writes, "Because blacks experienced such pervasive inequality in the past, they have not inherited the wealth, business ownership and human capital that make it possible for them to obtain current equal incomes."[30] In other words, in a society where those who "have" gain the greater advantage for "having more," those who "have not" are perpetually disadvantaged and thus continue to "have less" so the economic gap widens between the groups.

The story of Hispanics in the Southwest concerns a conquered people and their losses. In 1848 when the United States defeated Mexico and annexed territories from California to Texas and from Colorado to Nevada, the Treaty of Guadalupe Hidalgo supposedly guaranteed freedom of life and religion for Mexican residents of the Southwest as well as protection of their properties. Since then, most of those Mexican Americans have lost their lands to Anglos through economic exploitation, armed confrontation, and swindles regarding property rights under the guise of legality. "Within decades those Hispanics who once controlled the Southwest became the laborers who enabled the Anglos to become even more powerful expressions of the racist doctrine of Manifest Destiny."[31] As the fastest-growing ethnic population in the United States, Hispanics continue to suffer both large disadvantages in job opportunities and the resultant economic disadvantages as well as racist structures that demean them as a people.

While religious justification was often given in an earlier day for slavery and economic exploitation by citing the biblical instances of slavery and inequality, racism in the United States is predominantly the result of white prejudice against nonwhites, a prejudice that has been displayed through economic control. Modern religious interpreters see this as a "sin because it violates God's will" that everyone obey "the law of love."[32] The law of love calls for justice and fairness in all relationships, whether person-to-person or collective societal expressions. Nevertheless, neither religious condemnation of the pattern nor enactment of laws requiring equality have succeeded in eliminating racism and its resulting poverty.

How can society be moved toward economic equality? Education at all levels about the past and present realities of racism can help change racist attitudes—to know, for example, that the biological designations for the three races (Caucasian, Negroid, and Mongoloid) merely refer to skin pigmentation, nature's way of protecting people from the sun's rays. Those living nearest the equator thus developed the darkest skins. In the past two centuries, with the intermixing of these races, however, a pure race cannot be easily

[30] David H. Swinton, "The Economic Status of Black Americans During the 1980's: A Decade of Limited Progress," *The State of Black America* (New York: The Urban League, 1990), p. 52.

[31] Bert Affleck, "Cross-Cultural Evangelism: A Case Study in New Mexico," *Journal of the Academy for Evangelism in Theological Education*, Vol. 2, ed. David Lowes Watson (Nashville, TN: General Board of Discipleship, United Methodist Church, 1986–87), p. 62.

[32] William B. McClain, *Traveling Light: Christian Perspectives on Pilgrimage and Pluralism* (New York: Friendship Press, 1981), p. 75.

designated. Religious proclamations that challenge everyone to treat others with love and respect can inspire harder work for justice. Calls for inclusiveness in religion and society counter religious dogmatisms that exclude any race. Political power distributed more equally among people of all backgrounds allows more varied voices to be heard and to be served more fairly. However, educational, religious, and political efforts to attain equality may not address the economic inequalities so often tied to racism—an area churches and religious bodies in the United States have tended to overlook.

Some recent advocates for equality focus on economic needs. Many have advocated a program of reparations,[33] monetary investments, and gifts to help the "have nots" gain momentum in a society of competitive economics in order to eliminate the inherited economic gaps that have been perpetuated through the years. Swinton suggests that "in a free market 'lassez faire' economy . . . those who advocate free markets and 'laissez faire' and who also support the elimination of racial inequality in economic life must support reparations for the elimination of the inherited differences in wealth and ownership."[34]

Cain H. Felder, biblical scholar at Howard University, cites Jesus' strong advocacy for compensatory justice in "inaugurating the Kingdom of God, not the least for marginalized socioeconomic groups. . . ." as a basis for reparations.[35] He refers to Jesus' central concern for the poor in Luke 4:16–30, Luke 7:22–23, and Matthew 11:4–6. Such New Testament teaching by Jesus exhibits the power and value of the prophetic vision (Isaiah 56:6, 61:1) and the Jubilee ideal (Leviticus 25:10) found in Jewish Scriptures. The Levitical teaching of Jubilee stresses that God, not any human, owns all the land and that every fiftieth year debts will be forgiven; thus everyone can begin anew as stewards of the land God provides.

The concept of the Jubilee became popular among many church bodies and other groups at the turn of the century (2000) as they called for monetary debt relief for Third World countries with very large debts that threaten to subvert their economies and send more persons into poverty throughout the world. Some relief of these debts has recently been forthcoming, but little real progress has been achieved within the United States in affecting or eliminating poverty. Its basic causes remain. Welfare reform has returned many to the workplace but whether fuller employment of the traditionally poor can be sustained in a weak economy remains to be seen.

Even though President George W. Bush has identified Jesus as the political philosopher who has influenced him most, many people would call Jesus' teaching unrealistic and unworkable for our society. Many people are unwilling to give up any of their economic possessions to help create economic equality. Others continue to hold to a racist idea that people of color are inherently deficient and thus are ordained to fill subsidiary roles in a white world. Some would look to a future kingdom, in which God alone will bring justice, and thus they would not take any action to change our economic system as they wait for God's future salvation. Some might excuse poverty in the United

---

[33] Reparation in this context means providing payment to blacks and other racial groups for the systematic economic disadvantages they have historically suffered because of race or ethnic origin.

[34] Swinton, "Economic Status of Black Americans," p. 52.

[35] Cain Hope Felder, *Troubling Biblical Waters: Race, Class, and the Family* (Maryknoll, NY: Orbis Books, 1989), p. 73.

States by rationalizing that racial and economic inequalities are worse in other countries such as South Africa, where blacks have been systemically oppressed, or in Latin America, where Indians of darker hue are discriminated against by those of lighter skin, most often richer power brokers. Others are just plain apathetic and do not care to think about or do anything about racial economic inequality.

The issues pertaining to poverty and race are indeed complex, as we have indicated all too briefly. Clearly racism and its accompanying poverty is not simply an American problem but is present in many societies today. To deal with these issues will require careful thought and unselfish action.

◆◆◆

Does the radical call for compensatory justice, based on Judeo-Christian literature, offer viable solutions pertaining to poverty and racism?

The idea of paying reparations to those whose ancestors experienced injustice in the past is presently controversial. Can you give arguments for and against reparations?

How do non-Judeo-Christian religions consider the issues of race and poverty?

What do you think about these problems?

Unit 67   Ethnic Pluralism and Contemporary American Religion

The history of the so-called mainline churches in the United States reveals patterns of exclusivism in which Anglo-American culture has dominated other cultures within the structures and activities of the churches. Segregation in the United States has been reflected in the churches, separating people of color—especially Asians, blacks, Hispanics, and Native Americans—into congregations apart from whites. In most cases the ethnic-minority churches have been composed of those struggling to move beyond poverty. The larger, more affluent, white churches have usually been paternalistic toward Christians of color, extending charity but without being truly inclusive.

New efforts to be inclusive began to emerge after the civil rights movement of the 1950s and 1960s. Since the 1954 Supreme Court decision striking down inequality in education, a number of denominations have adopted a policy of integration. This policy, however, has been applied for the most part from the vantage point of the more powerful white churches. Altruistic as they may have been, white Christians have tended to reflect the idea of the American melting pot, but with a racist proviso—that the melding of races in America would still turn out white. "Whiteness" as a value indicating supposed superiority has been maintained throughout the history of Western civilization and, of course, has been a tragic theme in the Christian religion. "White is used to express the pure, while black expresses the diabolical."[36]

---

[36] Roger Bastide, "Color, Racism, and Christianity," in *Color and Race*, ed. John Hope Franklin (Boston, MA: Beacon Press, 1968), p. 34.

Even though minorities received invitations to join white churches, they still felt excluded. In various subtle ways, they were made aware of how difficult it is to cross cultural barriers and become integrated. Too often they felt that if they were to become equal in integrated white churches, they would have to be absorbed and abandon their own cultural roots.

In recent years the idea of integration has been reevaluated. Mainline denominations in America have begun to propose pluralism as preferable to integration. Pluralism connotes "diversity-in-unity and unity-in-diversity"—that is, fostering diverse cultural contributions while seeking unity in the church. Some believe that ethnic minorities represent vibrant cultures through which God is renewing the total life of the church. They support and seek to nurture cultural uniqueness, although in a context that affirms equally the positive contributions of all cultures.

In an address delivered in El Paso, Texas, Woody White, Bishop of the United Methodist Church, proposed another image to replace the melting pot—that of the "stewpot." The melting-pot metaphor signifies a melding of different races and cultures into one in which each loses its original identity. The stewpot, however, suggests that just as various vegetables and meats contribute to a delicious stew without losing their identities, so can ethnic minorities unite in "oneness" with one another and with the dominant culture while at the same time retaining their highly valuable cultural differences.

A factor that has strengthened pluralism as a significant way of viewing interethnic Christianity is the rapid growth of ethnic minorities in both numbers and influence in the United States. This has prompted mainline churches to reexamine church growth strategies, with an eye toward evangelizing ethnic minorities. Asian and Pacific Americans as well as Hispanics are expanding in numbers too quickly to enable them to be counted accurately. Although blacks are the largest ethnic minority group (which is still growing) in the United States, demographic projections indicate that Hispanics will soon become the largest minority in the United States. Asian and Pacific Americans are immigrating by the thousands to the United States and have formed numerous new churches. Native Americans have asserted themselves throughout recent decades in search of ways to redress historical injustices and recapture elements of their native worship within the context of Christian belief, thereby pricking the consciences of some Christians.

Those advocating ethnic pluralism argue for not only inclusive worship but also interethnic cooperation in all areas of church life. This is no easy task and demands that Christians of every ethnic background learn how to listen and learn from one another without racist bias but with ears tuned to the authentic sounds of every culture. In a time when several mainline congregations have settled into traditional modes of institutional existence and have experienced significant declines in membership, it may well be that the influx of more people of color into various denominations will offer new life, variety, and enriched cultural perspectives through which the meaning of Christian commitment can be empowered. In recent years increasing numbers of white congregations have experienced this cross-cultural ferment as they have intentionally made contact with ethnic minority churches for crosscultural worship, interethnic education, and the more difficult task of discussing and debating the church's mission to a suffering world.

It has become clear that the future profile of at least some of the Christian churches in the United States will be pluralistic. This can provide both participants and observers a creative opportunity to examine the interaction between changing patterns of culture and the norms and values of Christian religious groups as they interact in society.

Ethnic pluralism challenges Christianity in other ways as well. Since the settlement of North America, its dominant religious image has been Christianity. However, ever increasing immigration from Asian, Pacific, Indian, and Near Eastern countries has meant large-scale importation of various religions from these areas. Any major American city now offers worshippers Buddhist and Hindu temples, Muslim mosques, Shinto Gardens, and worship houses of a host of "new" religions based on aspects of these ancient faiths. Many white Americans, introduced to the tenets of these religions, find them attractive. Participants often represent the pluralism now found in society and not simply the ethnic groups who brought the religions to America. Christianity, while still dominant, has become one among many religious alternatives in society.

In addition to this religious development, ethnic pluralism also represents only one dimension of the larger phenomenon of pluralism and its increasing range in modern and postmodern societies (see Units 75 and 77). In addition to ethnic pluralism, there is increasing pluralism in lifestyles; culture; national, linguistic, and religious backgrounds; gender; and sexual orientation. In this unit the term *white* has been used to refer to a single ethnic grouping, but many whites would question whether they have much in common with other whites of differing national, cultural, or religious backgrounds. Understanding the problems and opportunities that the many kinds of pluralism represent for contemporary societies is possibly the greatest challenge facing contemporary societies and the world as a whole.

◆◆◆

What evidences of religious pluralism have you experienced?

Is the "stewpot" image for Christianity really a viable possibility among your family and friends?

With the American Christian emphasis on evangelism, can religious pluralism be achieved in American society?

What American religious patterns foster pluralism?

✦✦✦ 16 ✦✦✦

RELIGIOUS TRADITIONS AND SOCIAL STABILITY

Religious traditions often function as integrative and stabilizing forces in society (as in individual life). We sometimes characterize or define a particular society by referring to the religious tradition that empowers and shapes its cultural attitudes, understandings, and mores. To identify Saudi Arabia or Iran as Muslim is to help understand the unity of daily life as well as political commitments of these countries. Similarly, religious traditions may also function as agents of change or even of conflict in society (and in individual life). The attempt of the Muslim Taliban to purge Afghanistan of all religions except a rigorously interpreted Islam was a movement of change that caused major conflicts among its people and with neighboring countries as well as the international community. In this chapter we will be concerned with the role of religion as a unifying, integrative force in society, and in the next chapter with religion as a factor in social change.

We have defined religion as "reliance on a pivotal value in which the individual finds wholeness as an individual and as a person in community." The term *religious tradition* as used in this chapter refers to any complex pattern of behavior, attitudes, and beliefs that express reliance on, or adherence to, a pivotal value (or values) by a group of people maintained and transmitted with some degree of continuity during a period of time.

In many cases a religious tradition coincides with the value system of a whole society. In some cases it may be in tension with other value systems in the society, but still provide some elements of unity. Oftentimes a religious tradition, even that of a minority group within a larger society, endorses the dominant cultural values. Conservative Christian churches may be very critical of many social trends such as the loosening of sexual mores but be staunch supporters of the cultural values fostered in a capitalistic state. Social change may also come about by the adoption in the larger society of specifically religious values or attitudes belonging to what was originally a minority group; for example, the changes brought about for African-American citizens through the 1960s civil rights movement. In other cases, a religious minority's system may be modified by the adoption into it of attitudes and values prevalent in the larger society. While religious traditions encourage cultural and social stability and in that sense are conservative, they may also encourage progressive social change without causing major conflict within the society.

The units in this chapter deal with (1) the nature of religious community and some of its roles; (2) the role of religion in a highly unified, traditionally oriented, simply organized Brazilian tribal society; (3) the unity of the various facets of life in classical Greek culture; and (4) one of the major integrating themes or elements of Japanese society, the theme of simplicity.

UNIT 68   COMMUNITY OF FAITH

The experience of religion is often uniquely individual. But even in those religions that most encourage individual beliefs, attitudes, and practices, there is a communal side to the nurturing of these attitudes and to the preservation and continuity of tradition. This is true even if the tradition being handed on is one that emphasizes and promotes change. Belief in shared objects of faith, participation in shared rituals or practices, adherence to the same pivotal value—all these create community. Again, this is true even in the traditions in which the religious hermit is seen as the highest ideal of human life (as in Christianity in Egypt during the early centuries of the Christian era or among the holy men of Hinduism). Whatever the religious tradition, the community of faith, dependent itself on individual commitment and participation, provides support and guidance for individual believers and gives them a sense of belonging that helps to define individual identity and supports them in times of personal crisis.

Buddhism in many of its forms is highly individualistic. Theravada Buddhism, especially, teaches that the individual must achieve Nirvana (complete enlightenment, fulfillment, salvation) by individual effort alone. Nevertheless, as the Buddhist monk's vow vividly shows, membership in the monastic community is indispensable as a source of discipline, sustaining order, and guidance.

> I take refuge in the *Buddha* (the Ideal)
> I take refuge in the *Dharma* (the Law or the Truth)
> I take refuge in the *Sangha* (the Order of Monks)

Hebrew thought and experience is replete with this sense of community. One of the most ancient creeds, repeated individually through the centuries, is a striking example of the corporate nature of religion:

> A wandering Aramean was my ancestor; and he went down into Egypt and lived there as an alien, few in number; and there he became a great nation, mighty, and populous. When the Egyptians treated us harshly and afflicted us, by imposing hard labor upon us, we cried to the Lord, the God of our ancestors; and the Lord heard our voice and saw our affliction, our toil, and our oppression. The Lord brought us out of Egypt with a mighty hand and an outstretched arm, with a terrifying display of power, and with signs and wonders; and he brought us into this place and gave us this land, a land flowing with milk and honey. (Deuteronomy 26:5b–9, NRSV)

In the change from a third person recounting of the story in the first sentence of the creed to a first person "we," the Jewish believer who recites this creed joins personal present participation with historical precedents. In it the past and the present become one reality, one unity.

Malcolm X, a leader of the American black consciousness movement in the early 1960s, found a sense of community that he had not experienced before when he converted to Islam. Traveling to Mecca to participate in the *hadj* (the sacred pilgrimage), he came into contact with a unity of the faithful described in the Qur'an:

> The believers indeed are brothers; so set things right between your two brothers, and fear God; haply so you will find mercy.[1]

Impressed, as a black man, with the oneness of the brotherhood, Malcolm X commented extensively on how common belief breaks down all lines of distinction—especially that of color. Having been asked what most impressed him in the *hadj*, he replied,

> I said, "The brotherhood! The people of all races, colors, from all over the world coming together as one! It has proved to me the power of the One God. . . ."
>
> Never have I witnessed such sincere hospitality and the overwhelming spirit of true brotherhood as is practiced by people of all colors and races here in this Ancient Holy Land, the home of Abraham, Muhammad, and all the other prophets of the Holy Scriptures. For the past week, I have been utterly speechless and spellbound by the graciousness I see displayed all around me by the people of all colors. . . .
>
> America needs to understand Islam, because this is the one religion that erases from its society the race problem. Throughout my travels in the Muslim world, I have met, talked to, and even eaten with people who in America would have been considered "white"—but the "white" attitude was removed from their minds by the religion of Islam. I have never before seen sincere and true brotherhood practiced by all colors together, irrespective of their color. . . .
>
> During the past eleven days here in the Muslim world, I have eaten from the same plate, drunk from the same glass, and slept in the same bed (or on the same rug)—while praying to the same God—with fellow Muslims, whose eyes were the bluest of blue, whose hair was the blondest of blond, and whose skin was the whitest of white. And in the words and in the actions and in the deeds of the "white" Muslims, I felt the same sincerity that I felt among the black African Muslims of Nigeria, Sudan, and Ghana.
>
> We were truly all the same (brothers)—because their belief in one God had removed the "white" from their minds, the "white" from their behavior, and the "white" from their attitude.
>
> I could see from this, that perhaps if white Americans could accept the Oneness of God, then perhaps, too, they could accept in reality the Oneness of Man—and cease to measure, and hinder, and harm others in terms of their "differences" in color. . . .
>
> All praise is due to Allah, the Lord of all Worlds.[2]

Unity is here defined in terms of hospitality and brotherhood that transcends any distinctions of race or color but that same sense of unity may be found in other aspects of religion such as belief, ritual, and moral codes.

---

[1]Arthur J. Arberry, *The Koran Interpreted*, Sura XLIX, verse 10 (New York: Macmillan, 1955).

[2]Malcolm X, *The Autobiography of Malcolm X*, with the assistance of Alex Haley, pp. 338–342. Reprinted by permission of Grove Press Inc. Copyright © 1964 by Alex Haley and Malcolm X. Copyright © 1965 by Alex Haley and Betty Shabazz.

❖❖❖

Is it possible to have religion without some community of faith?

Is there a central affirmation that holds the community together in the preceding examples?

UNIT 69   WHOLENESS OF LIFE IN A SIMPLY STRUCTURED SOCIETY

The role of religion as a unifying element within society may be illustrated by a preliterate and simply structured society. In a book called *Tristes Tropiques*, the French anthropologist Claude Lévi-Strauss records observations made during his stay in a Bororo village in the interior of Brazil. The village, with a population of about 150, was a self-contained society, and at the time of Lévi-Strauss's observations it had been relatively little affected by the outside influences of European or Brazilian cultures.

One of the centers of Bororo life was the "men's house," a large building in the middle of the village. The young, unmarried males of the Bororo tribe lived there; married males often took their meals and spent much of their leisure time in the men's house. It was also the place where preparations for the religious activities of the village went on: Religious chants were sung, and the closely guarded religious implements of the community (women were not allowed to see them) were made and stored. Married women were not allowed to enter the men's house; an unmarried woman was supposed to enter the building only once, when she came to propose marriage to her future husband.

Lévi-Strauss contrasts the Bororo attitude toward the "religious" dimension of life as he observed it in the men's house with the attitude he believed to be more characteristic of contemporary European society.

> For the European observer, the apparently incompatible activities carried out in the men's house seem to harmonize in an almost shocking way. Few peoples are as deeply religious as the Bororo, and few have such a complex metaphysical system. But spiritual beliefs and everyday habits are closely intermingled, and the natives do not appear to be conscious of moving from one system to another. I found the same easy-going religiosity in Buddhist temples along the Burmese frontier, where the priests live and sleep in the same hall as is used for worship, arrange their jars of ointment and personal collections of medicines on the ground in front of the altar. . . .
>
> This casual attitude to the supernatural was . . . surprising to me . . . I lived during the First World War with my grandfather, who was Rabbi of Versailles. The house was attached to the synagogue by a long inner passage, along which it was difficult to venture without a feeling of anguish, and which in itself formed an impassable frontier between the profane world and that other. . . . Except when services were in progress, the synagogue remained empty. . . . Apart from my grandfather's silent prayer at the beginning of each meal, we children had no means of knowing that we were living under the egis of a superior order. . . .
>
> Not that religion was treated with greater reverence among the Bororo; on the contrary, it was taken for granted. In the men's house, ritualistic gestures were performed with the same casualness as all others, as if they were utilitarian actions intended to achieve a particular result, and did not require that respectful attitude which even the [European or Western] non-believer feels compelled to adopt on entering a place of

worship. On a particular afternoon there would be singing in the men's house in preparation for the evening's public ritual. In one corner, boys would be snoring or chatting; two
or three men would be humming and shaking rattles, but if one of them wanted to light
a cigarette or if it were his turn to dip into the maize gruel, he would hand the instrument
to a neighbour who carried on, or sometimes he would continue with one hand, while
scratching himself with the other. When a dancer paraded up and down to allow his latest creation to be admired, everybody would stop and comment upon it; the service might
seem to be forgotten until, in some other corner, the incantation was resumed at the point
where it had been interrupted.[3]

In another passage, Lévi-Strauss describes one part of an elaborate funeral ceremony in the Bororo village:

Towards evening two groups, each consisting of five or six men, set out, one to the west,
the other to the east. I followed the first group, and saw them making their preparations
about fifty metres from the village, behind a screen of trees which concealed them from
the other villagers. They covered themselves with leaves, like the dancers, and fixed their
crowns in position. But this time, the secrecy of their preparations could be explained by
the part they were playing: like the other group, they represented the souls of the dead
which had come from their villages in the east and the west to welcome the deceased.
When all was ready, they moved towards the dancing area, whistling as they went. The
eastern group had already preceded them there (one group was, symbolically, going
upstream, the other downstream, and the latter therefore moved faster).
    Their timid and hesitant gait admirably conveyed their ghostly nature; I was reminded
of Homer—of Ulysses struggling to prevent the flight of the ghosts repelled by blood. But
all at once, the ceremony burst into life: men seized one or other of the two mariddo [sym-
bolic male and female rope disks covered with fresh vegetation], . . . lifted it high in the
air and, thus encumbered, danced until they were exhausted and had to allow a rival to
take it from them. The scene no longer had any mystic character; it had turned into a fair,
where the young men were showing off their physical prowess in an atmosphere characterized by sweat, thumpings and gibes. And yet this sport, which exists in secular forms
among neighbouring communities—for instance, in the log races practiced by the Ge
tribes of the Brazilian plateau—retains its full religious significance with the Bororo: in
this mood of gay abandon, the natives feel they are playing with the dead and wresting
from them the right to remain alive.[4]

For Bororo society, "the religious" is not, then, one aspect or activity of life, distinct from other aspects. There is not a specifically religious attitude different from the
attitude toward everyday or secular activities and events; the religious dimension of life
thoroughly penetrates and is penetrated by the nonreligious dimensions; in fact, speaking
of the religious and the nonreligious or secular as two different dimensions of life would
probably be foreign to the Bororo way of thinking. Nevertheless, Lévi-Strauss points out
that there is a social division of labor in religious matters. "The women were excluded
from the [religious] rites and deceived as to their true nature—doubtless to sanction the

---

[3] Adapted from *Tristes Tropiques* by Claude Lévi-Strauss. Copyright © 1973 by Jonathan Cape Limited. Originally appeared in French copyright © 1955 by Librarie Plon. Reprinted by permission of Georges
Borchardt, Inc. for the author.
    [4] Ibid., pp. 227–228.

division of rights by which [women] take priority, where housing and birth rites are in question, leaving the mysteries of religion to their men."[5]

◆◆◆

Why does Levi-Strauss find the lack of distinction among the Bororo between the sacred and the ordinary so striking?

Do Western religions teach that religion should be evident in all of life as is evident in the Bororo culture? If so, why is it not practiced?

How does the Bororo attitude toward religion as a dimension of life compare with the attitude of classical Greek society as described in the next unit?

Unit 70   Wholeness of Life in Classical Greece

Unit 69 describes the unifying effect of religion in a simple society. This same function of unification may also be observed in more complex societies such as that of the ancient Greeks. According to H. D. F. Kitto, in a study on the classical period of Greek culture (especially the sixth and fifth centuries B.C.E.), the Greeks did not see different dimensions of life (like the religious and the secular, the moral and the aesthetic, the intellectual and the physical, the private and the social) as separated from one another. Many civilizations have made rather sharp distinctions among these areas. The wholeness, or integration, of the various areas of life in Greek civilization can be seen, Kitto thinks, if we examine some Greek terms. The word *kalos* is usually translated as "beautiful," but *kalos* is used to describe actions that we would consider heroic or noble, traits of character we would consider morally good, and instruments that are well made or useful. In fact the word means something like "worthy of warm admiration" and may be used to refer to goodness or beauty or appropriateness—anything that we might want to classify under one of the following categories: moral, intellectual, aesthetic, or practical. Kitto thinks that most civilizations, including our own, have made distinctions among these categories, but the Greeks did not. In the same way, the Greek word *aischros*, usually translated as "ugly," can be used to describe morally bad actions, physical ugliness, baseness (in the sense of lack of worth or merit), uselessness (in the practical sense) and badness of character. To look at two other terms, Kitto notes that

> The word "hamartia" means "error," "fault," "crime" or even "sin"; literally, it means "missing the mark," "a bad shot." We exclaim, "How intellectualist these Greeks were! Sin is just 'missing the mark'; better luck next time!" Again we seem to find confirmation when we find that some of the Greek virtues seem to be as much intellectual as moral—a fact that makes them untranslatable, since our own vocabulary must distinguish. There is "Sôphrosynê," literally "whole-mindedness" or "unimpaired-mindedness." According to the context it will mean "wisdom," "prudence," "temperateness," "chastity," "sobriety," "modesty," or "self-control," that is, something entirely intellectual, something entirely

[5] Ibid., pp. 229–30.

moral, or something intermediate. Our difficulty with the word, as with hamartia, is that we think more in departments. Hamartia, "a bad shot," does not mean "better luck next time"; it means rather that a mental error is as blameworthy, and may be as deadly, as a moral one.[6]

Kitto finds the classical Greek understanding of life's wholeness clearly present in the Greek attitude toward athletic contests:

The sharp distinction which the Christian and the Oriental world has normally drawn between the body and the soul, the physical and the spiritual, was foreign to the Greek— at least until the time of Socrates and Plato. To him there was simply the whole man. That the body is the tomb of the soul is indeed an idea which we meet in certain Greek mystery-religions, and Plato, with his doctrine of immortality, necessarily distinguished sharply between body and soul; but for all that, it is not a typical Greek idea. The Greek made physical training an important part of education, not because he said to himself, "Look here, we mustn't forget the body," but because it could never occur to him to train anything but the whole man. It was as natural for the polis to have gymnasia as to have a theatre or warships, and they were constantly used by men of all ages, not only for physical but also for mental exercise. . . .

But it is the Games, local and international, which most clearly illustrate this side of the Greek mind. Among us it is sometimes made a reproach that a man "makes a religion of games." The Greek did not do this, but he did something perhaps more surprising: he made games part of his religion. To be quite explicit, the Olympian games, the greatest of the four international festivals, were held in honor of Zeus of Olympia, the Pythian Games in honour of Apollo, the Panathenaic Games in honor of Athena. Moreover, they were held in the sacred precinct. The feeling that prompted this was a perfectly natural one. The contest was a means of stimulating and displaying human *aretê*, and this was a worthy offering to the god. . . . But since *aretê* is of the mind as well as of the body, there was not the slightest incongruity or affectation in combining musical contests with athletic: a contest in flute-playing was an original fixture in the Pythian Games—for was not Apollo himself "Lord of the Lyre"?

[The Greek word aretê is usually translated to mean "virtue," but "excellence" is probably better since in modern English, "virtue" usually means only "moral goodness."]

It was *aretê* that the games were designed to test—the *aretê* of the whole man, not a merely specialized skill. The usual events were a sprint, of about 200 yards, the long race (1 1/2 miles), the race in armour, throwing the discus, and the javelin, the long jump, wrestling, boxing (of a very dangerous kind), and chariot-racing. The great event was the pentathlon: a race, a jump, throwing the discus, and the javelin, and wrestling. If you won this, you were a man. Needless to say, the Marathon race was never heard of until modern times: the Greeks would have regarded it as a monstrosity. As for the skill shown by modern champions in games like golf or billiards, the Greeks would certainly have admired it intensely, and thought it an admirable thing—in a slave, supposing that one had no better use for a slave than to train him in this way. Impossible, he would say, to acquire skill like this and at the same time to live the proper life of a man and a citizen. It is this feeling that underlies Aristotle's remark that a gentleman should be able to play the flute—but not too well.[7]

This stress on the unity of language and on athletic competence in many sports illustrates the integration of all of one's abilities in Greek culture. Religion was an inte-

---

[6] H. D. F. Kitto, *The Greeks*. Copyright © H. D. F. Kitto, 1951, 1957, pp. 170–171. Used by permission of Penguin Books, Ltd.

[7] Ibid., pp. 173–174.

gral part of all activities and so unified or supported these and other elements of life, both social and individual.

◆◆◆

Does the fact of vocational specialization in complex, modern societies—the fact that there are religious professionals (ministers, priests, rabbis), professional athletes, military professionals, professional critics of art and literature, and so forth—necessarily lead to a division of life, a loss of the wholeness or integration of its different parts or dimensions?

Do you find that people in modern society tend to see religious and secular activities as separate or different from each other?

Is Kitto right in saying that Western culture has "normally drawn" a "sharp distinction" between body and soul, the physical and the spiritual? If so, why has Western culture lost the sense of unity of all life found in the classical Greek culture?

Do Oriental or Eastern religions—for instance, Hinduism or Zen Buddhism—make as sharp a distinction between the physical and the spiritual as Kitto suggests?

Unit 71   Japanese Fondness for Simplicity

The Japanese cherish simplicity, which has been a characteristic unifying element in Japanese culture. It has helped the Japanese adapt foreign ideas, forms of expression, and practices to Japanese life, integrating them into Japanese culture and giving them a distinctively Japanese flavor. It has also helped integrate religious traditions so that both the native religions and those imported have a particular Japanese form and character.

Fondness for simplicity is seen in most areas of Japanese life and expression. For each of the examples cited in the following discussion by Hajime Nakamura, compare Western attitudes toward simplicity or the lack of it in the corresponding areas of life.

Traditionally, the Japanese have been inclined to dislike fanciful, complicated expressions and to take to simple and naive expressions. The Japanese language . . . is deficient in words expressing prolix and abstract conceptions. Consequently, even to this day, they use Chinese words, in most cases, to express abstract ideas.

In art, also, this tendency can be discerned clearly. The Japanese are very fond of the impromptu short verse, like the haiku and tanka. In the history of Japanese poetry, the long verse . . . is reduced to a short one (tanka), and then to a still shorter one (haiku). The extremely short form of artistic expression is characteristically Japanese and the like of it cannot be found elsewhere. . . . In Japanese literature, lyric poems and scenery sketches have been highly developed, but poems of grand style, with dramatic plots full of twists and turns, have made only a poor start.

Tanka—a thirty-one-syllable poem
Haiku—a seventeen-syllable poem

The *haiku* is extraordinarily simple, but it is highly symbolic and suggestive. Here is an example by the poet Matsuo Bashō (1644–1694):

> Breaking the surface
> of a still pond a frog jumps—
> The silence echoes.

Not only in poetry but also in architecture, we can recognize the characteristic love of simplicity. The Japanese imported various formative arts from Indian Buddhism, indirectly through the hands of Chinese and Koreans. As seen in the magnificent splendor of golden Buddhist altars and mural paintings of temples, the complicated sculptures of transoms, the fantastic statue of the Goddess of Mercy . . . all of them had, in general, a very elaborate structure. But such an art could hardly penetrate into the life of the common people. The Japanese could not abandon the simple and unpainted wooden architecture of ancient style, in many shrines as well as in the Great Shrine of Ise. [See Figure 16.1.] And, even in the architecture of Buddhist temples, the various sects of the Kamakura period [1185–1333] turned to a rather simple style. Also, in the Zen-influenced taste of the tea-ceremony house, we can discern a naive simplicity.... In some cases, especially under the influence of the Zen cult, the Japanese endeavored to infuse unlimited complexity into this simplicity. This tendency emerged especially in such arts as architecture, drawing, and poetry. For example, the void of empty spaces or of silent pauses is often not devoid, in fact, of important meaning. Even in the etiquette and conversation of everyday life, silence can be a very positive expression at times. This ideal fusion of the complex and the simple was realized by the Chinese people, who loved complicated thinking

Figure 16.1   The Ise Shrine, in Japan, is the national shrine of Japanese Shintoism. (Courtesy Ministry of Foreign Affairs, Government of Japan)

and whose spiritual life was greatly influenced by the Zen cult. When introduced into Japan, however, this, too, was altered by greater simplification. . . .

The Japanese, in assimilating Buddhism, did not depend upon its philosophical doctrines. Of course, the clergymen of large temples were engaged in philosophical debates and wrote a great number of books. The common people, however, demanded concrete and empirical clues rather than philosophical theories. . . .

The tendency to fondness for simple symbols appeared in the process of adoption of Buddhist ideas by Japanese Shintoists in ancient and medieval times. . . . Shintō, in the process of its development as religion, advanced from the cleanness of the body to the idea of cleanness of spirit. This "internal cleanness" was expressed by moral virtues of "sincerity" and "honesty." The virtues of gods of Shintō were admired through these virtues . . . it is not too much to say that almost all of the terms of the central virtues of medieval Shintō were derived from Buddhist sutras. It must be pointed out, however, that Shintoists never adopted the doctrines of Buddhism indiscriminately. Only the virtues, which had originally existed as germs in Shintō, were brought to definite consciousness and expression by the help of Buddhist philosophy. The Shintoists did not take in the speculative, schematized, and generalized classifications of virtues of the Indian Buddhism. . . . ["Virtues of the Indian Buddhism" refers to such teachings as those contained in the Four Noble Truths and the Eightfold Path. See Unit 11] They took in directly those virtues which happened to appear congenial to Shintō. Consequently, they hardly endeavored to interpret the relations among these virtues systematically and speculatively.

We have tried to demonstrate that through the process of assimilation of Buddhism many Japanese people are inclined to give direction to their practice through very simple symbols. . . .

We may say that religion is always simplified when it is popularized. . . . If we look back to the trend of Japanese thought in recent years, we can realize that the complete reliance upon simple symbols has been one of the most deep-rooted attitudes of the Japanese people.[8]

The ability of the Japanese to take religious ideas and practices from many cultures and integrate them with their native Shinto religion allows them to participate in several religious traditions without any sense of conflict or dissonance. Variant traditions have been unified into one whole.

◆◆◆

Why do Western persons find the idea of integrating various religions into one unity surprising?

Do you find any comparison between the Japanese tending to simplify religious belief and practice and the belief systems and practices of ordinary Western people?

---

[8] Hajime Nakamura, *Ways of Thinking of Eastern Peoples: India-China-Tibet-Japan* (Honolulu, HA: East-West Center Press, 1964), pp. 564–565, 572–573. By permission of the University Press of Hawaii.

✦✦✦ 17 ✦✦✦

RELIGIOUS TRADITIONS
AND SOCIAL CHANGE

As society becomes more open, urbanized, and heterogeneous, social stability becomes more difficult to maintain. At the same time, religious institutions themselves cannot remain unaffected. They respond to change either positively or negatively—that is, either by coming to terms with the problems created by societal change or by resisting or withdrawing from them.

In this chapter we present aspects of the response religious institutions may make to the problems relating to social change. The first unit is centered on population growth and the resultant mass hunger. In Unit 73 we consider the rapid increase in the growth of technology, and in Unit 74 the process of secularization. The stress between forces of change and the reluctance of some in every society to identify with change is the focus of Unit 75. The patterns and character of modernization and the alienation it creates are the topics of Unit 76. In Unit 77 consideration is given to the rise of new religious movements.

UNIT 72   POPULATION GROWTH AND WORLD HUNGER

In 1950 the world's population stood at 2.5 billion people. By 2000 it was 6 billion. This figure is expected to double during the next two to three decades. If population continues to grow at present rates, within a century there will not only be inadequate food for the earth's humans, there will not be enough standing room. Some have suggested seriously that the answer is to colonize the moon and Mars, but technological problems associated with building and maintaining artificial environments make this seem impractical. The only viable option seems to be to reduce population growth and make food production and distribution more efficient.

Figure 17.1   Drawing by Jacques Bakke

Different religious groups respond differently to issues involving population reduction. Because of strong opposition to any forms of abortion by the Catholic Church, the U.S. government has at times banned funding efforts to limit population growth in countries that support abortion as one method of population control, even when that funding would not be for abortions. China, which has the largest human population, has used the most drastic methods to try to limit population growth: encouraging postponment of marriages, abortion, and legally limiting to one the number of children per family.

Most Third World nations, because of traditional patterns of family size, lack of information, and lack of technology and economic infrastructure to shift their economies from the old large family production base, have not been very successful in reducing population growth. The Third World has been devastated by wars and pestilence, but this has only aggravated problems associated with population growth. The problem of hunger is acute and promises to become more so with each passing year. Concerned people throughout the world ponder the complexities of the food crisis, what has led to its more rapid development, and what solutions may be found.

WHAT IS HUNGER[1]

Hunger is a weakened condition brought about by the prolonged lack of food. There are four basic types of hunger.

Chronic Undernutrition

Undernutrition results when people do not consume sufficient calories and protein over a prolonged period of time. This is the most widespread but least recognized form of hunger. It is invisible, persistent, and debilitating. The headlines capture dramatic images of acute starvation, but the vast majority of the hungry suffer in quiet obscurity through chronic undernutrition. The effects include

Decreased mental attentiveness
Permanent mental retardation
Increased susceptibility to disease
Listlessness
Decreased productivity
Emotional stress

Malnutrition

Malnutrition results from specific deficiencies in essential vitamins and minerals vital to good health. Malnutrition is closely related to undernutrition, but the physical manifestations are more obvious. Common effects include

Blindness: Hundreds of thousands of children become blind each year because of insufficient vitamin A.
Anemia: In developing countries, hundreds of millions of women are anemic because of a lack of iron in their diets.
Death: Starvation resulting in death is the ultimate consequence of extreme malnutrition.

Famine

Famine is the widespread, extreme scarcity of food, affecting an entire region. Often it is closely associated with disasters such as drought, flood, and war, which disrupt the availability of food to an area. Without social institutions able to handle the crisis, famine results. No more than 10 percent of hunger-related deaths are due to famine. Food may exist in an area struck by famine, but because of the deep poverty of the people, it is available only to the wealthy. Modern economic patterns that emphasize the global marketing of food and general agricultural products have meant a major shift in many developing countries to cash crops in areas where previously crops supported only the local economy. Consequently, decreased acreage is planted in foodstuffs for local consumption. Sometimes such changes have caused a widespread loss of productivity, and local famine

---

[1] Much of the material in this unit is drawn from *The Hunger Primer*, a publication of Food for the Hungry, a Christian hunger-relief organization. Used by permission.

now occurs even in countries where food is exported. In Africa, inappropriate agricultural technologies combined with drought have caused vast areas of productive land to become desert. Presently, the desert in some places is expanding at a rate of some 6 miles per year, threatening famine to those who live in the area.

Seasonal Undernutrition

Seasonal undernutrition occurs annually, as harvests stored from the previous year are depleted before the new crops can be harvested. Families may go hungry for weeks or even months at a time.

WHAT IS THE MAGNITUDE OF HUNGER?

One out of every eight people is hungry most of the time.

Four hundred fifty million people, one-fourth of the developing world, suffer from undernutrition.

Every year, almost thirteen million people die as a result of hunger and starvation—the equivalent of all the children under five in the United States. This means more people have died from hunger in the past 10 years than have been killed in all wars, revolutions, and murders in the past 150 years.

One billion people have various degrees of brain damage because of inadequate consumption.

WHO ARE THE HUNGRY?

Children

One-third of all the children in developing countries die of malnourishment before age five.

Of the twenty-four people that die from hunger each minute, eighteen are children.

One out of every four children in the developing world dies by the age of five from hunger and hunger-related causes.

Rural Poor

Three-quarters of the hungry live in rural areas.

Over 600 million people live in rural households that are either completely landless or near landless.

In Latin America, 7 percent of the farmers own 93 percent of the land, and more than 60 percent of the rural poor are landless altogether. Eight out of ten farmers in central America cannot grow crops for themselves.

Urban Poor

One-fourth of the hungry live in burgeoning urban slums.

Slums form up to 75 percent or more of the cities in some developing countries, with as many as twenty people living in one room.

Millions of rural landless have moved to cities in the hope of finding work but discover that jobs are not available.

Refugees

A refugee is a person who flees home to escape invasion, oppression, persecution, or natural disasters such as drought and famine.

Currently, according to the U.N. High Commission for Refugees, 20 million people are classified as refugees.

At least one million people a year are added to the list of refugees in the world.

More than a million and a half refugees have resettled in the United States.

Recent turmoil created by war and ethnic strife in eastern Europe and Africa has greatly added to the refugee population.

WHAT ARE THE CAUSES OF HUNGER?

It is difficult to attribute hunger to a single cause. Much of it today arises from economic, social, technological, and demographic changes that have accompanied the development of modern civilization. A major result of these changes is a vastly increasing population and the stress it puts on food supply and distribution. Arthur Simon offers the following insights:

Almost two centuries ago, in 1798, an Englishman named Thomas Malthus warned that the population would race ahead of the food supply. It would do so, he argued, because we can only add to the food supply, while the population multiplies. At that time the world's population of less than one billion was growing at a rate of about one-half of 1 percent annually. Now the growth rate is about 2 percent for the world and 2.5 percent for poor countries as a whole. These percentages may seem small, but the increase makes a dramatic difference.

Consider the evidence, however:

Lower death rates, not higher birth rates, are responsible for today's population growth. Poor countries as a whole have actually lowered their birth rates slightly over the past several decades—but death rates have dropped more sharply, and that achievement has touched off the population boom. Advances in medicine and public health, along with increases in food production, account for most gains against early death.

The population explosion began in Europe. Not the "inconsiderate poor" of Asia, Africa and Latin America, but our own ancestors touched it off. A few simple statistics show this. In 1800 about 22 percent of the human race was Caucasian; but by 1930 (only five or six generations later) that percentage had jumped to 35. This happened because the new technologies that pushed back the death rate occurred in the West. During that time the white, European peoples had two enormous advantages:

1. *Industrial growth kept ahead of population increases.* Because gains in public health occurred gradually, population growth rates also increased gradually. The Industrial Revolution had begun earlier, so the population increase was usually needed in the cities by industries, which depended upon a growing supply of unskilled workers.

2. *New lands opened up for colonization.* New lands, including North America, offered an important outlet to population stresses that did develop. For example after the potato famine ravaged Ireland in the 1840s, almost a million Irish came to our shores within five years.

Poor nations face a sharply different situation today. Two centuries of public health gains were made available to them more rapidly, so their populations began to soar almost without warning. Their people now pour into the cities long before industries can possibly supply them with jobs; and for all but a few there simply is no frontier, no new lands to colonize, no safety valve.[2]

[2] Arthur Simon, *Bread for the World* (New York: Paulist Press, 1975), pp. 28–31.

Figure 17.2   (**FRANK AND ERNEST** reprinted by permission of Newspaper Enterprise Association, Inc.)

RELIGION AND HUNGER

Because of their differing attitudes toward humanity and nature itself, religions vary greatly in their assessment of individual and corporate religious responsibility for social and economic conditions. Judaism, Christianity, and Islam have insisted that religion is a relevant force in all social organization—so the economy and its impact is of great moral concern. The preceding quotation on the moral dimensions of poverty and hunger reflects the type of concern raised by these traditions.

Similarly, Chinese religions and those of other nations influenced by Chinese civilization, particularly Japan and Korea, have understood religion to influence significantly the social context. In the modern world, economic issues and their consequences have been an important part of their religious concern.

Hinduism and Buddhism, with their traditional emphases on spirituality, have not usually concentrated on social issues, so modern difficulties raised by economic developments do not typically attract significant attention among adherents of these religions. However, in recent years religious leaders of these traditions, particularly Buddhism, have begun to apply their moral teachings to the social setting, including those where economic injustice produces poverty.

In addition to the severe threat of world hunger as the earth's population increases, the world is facing a rising threat from deadly epidemics. Not only are there threats from such diseases as AIDS, which destroys the human immune system, but there are increasing threats from more virulent strains of "traditional" diseases, which have multiplied because of their greater tolerance to antibiotics that have been effective in destroying weaker varieties of the organisms that spread diseases. Such threats of disease are affecting the entire world, not just Third-World countries.

In the past, some religious teachers have taught that famine and disease are simply a part of life that must be tolerated. Others, like Gautama, taught that by changing our attitude toward suffering, humans can become immune to the fear of famine and disease and the sufferings they cause the unenlightened. Other religious interpreters have taught that famine and disease are ways God punishes human beings for their sinfulness. Still others have seen them as challenges to put faith into practice to improve the world, to bring it into harmony with a vision of the goodness of its Creator.

✦✦✦

> *What do you find contemporary religious interpreters saying about the causes and the meaning of famine and disease and the proper human response to them?*
>
> *Have you or anyone you are acquainted with been exposed to hunger? What difference does it make or might it make in your attitude toward social causes of hunger?*

UNIT 73   RELIGION, HUMANITY, AND TECHNOLOGY

How do different religious traditions look at technology? The answer to this question can be found by asking how different religious traditions view humanity and its relation to nature and history. How do different religious traditions view historical change? Will human beings have a role in shaping the future? If they do, is this a way of fulfilling their destiny or is it a kind of impiety, a way of disrupting the divinely or naturally ordained patterns of life?

The Protestant theologian Harvey Cox has argued that the Judeo-Christian tradition has been inconsistent or ambivalent in answering these questions. He finds three different positions about the role of humanity in shaping the future among religious traditions. In the Jewish or Christian tradition some people have held an "apocalyptic" view that foresees an imminent catastrophe brought about by direct divine intervention. This view carries a negative evaluation of the present world, of humans' ability to shape the future through their own efforts and therefore through their own technology. A second view is the "teleological." It sees the future as the certain unfolding of fixed purposes built into the structure of the universe. Present technological efforts, as a part of the inevitable movement of life into the future, may be valued highly. But human responsibility to exercise critical judgment about which technological possibilities to develop and how to use them often is ignored so technology, while a blessing, may also be a threat. Finally, some people have held a position described by Cox as "prophetic." The prophetic tradition, he believes, has emphasized that the future is open and that it will become what the human race makes of it. Thus, both human technology and the responsibility to use it wisely, with concern for its effects on the whole human community, are stressed.[3]

Cox's analysis gives us a typology defining how Protestant Christianity has responded to the problem. Two popes of the Roman Catholic Church in recent years have issued encyclicals that present a particular Christian position regarding human technology in relation to God's will and purposes.

> Peace on earth, which men of every era have most eagerly yearned for, can be firmly established only if the order laid down by God is dutifully observed.
>
> The progress of learning and the inventions of technology clearly show that, both in living things and in the forces of nature, an astonishing order reigns, and they also bear witness to the greatness of man, who can understand that order and create suitable instruments to harness those forces of nature and use them to his benefit.
>
> But the progress of science and the inventions of technology show above all the infinite greatness of God, who created the universe and man himself. God also created man in his own image and likeness, endowed him with intelligence and freedom, and made him lord of creation, as the psalmist declares in the words: You have made him little less than the angels, and crowned him with glory and honor. You have given him rule over the works of your hands, putting all things under his feet.
>
> Nevertheless, in order to imbue civilization with sound principles and enliven it with the spirit of the gospel, it is not enough to be illumined with the gift of faith and enkindled with the desire of forwarding a good cause; it is also necessary to take an active part in the various organizations and influence them from within.
>
> And since our present age is one of outstanding scientific and technical progress, one cannot enter these organizations and work effectively from within unless he is scientifically competent, technically capable and skilled in the practice of his own profession. . . .
>
> In other words, it is necessary that human beings, in the intimacy of their own consciences, should so live and act in their temporal lives as to create a synthesis between scientific, technical and professional elements on the one hand, and spiritual values on the other.[4]

> All of you who have heard the appeal of suffering peoples, all of you who are working to answer their cries, you are the apostles of a development which is good and genuine, which is not wealth that is self-centered and sought for its own sake, but rather an economy which is put at the service of man, the bread which is daily distributed to all, as a source of brotherhood and a sign of Providence.
>
> With a full heart We bless you, and We appeal to all men of good will to join you in a spirit of brotherhood. For, if the new name for peace is development, who would not wish to labour for it with all his powers? Yes, We ask you, all of you, to heed Our cry of anguish in the name of the Lord.[5]

[3] Harvey Cox, "Tradition and the Future," Parts I & II, in *Christianity and Crisis*, 27, nos. 16–17 (1967).

[4] Pope John XXIII, *Pacem in Terris* (Peace on Earth) (New York: American Press, 1963), pp. 3–4, 46–47.

[5] Pope Paul VI, *Populorum Progressio* (On the Development of Peoples) (Boston, MA: St. Paul Editions, 1967), pp. 50–51.

Each of these encyclicals calls for active involvement in the changes wrought through technology by people committed to a religious perspective.

C. P. Snow, a twentieth-century novelist who was trained as a physicist, expressed concern about what he understood to be a dangerous gulf between the scientific-technological world and the rest of human experience (in academic terminology, the humanities). Discussing the complicated question of how we can best utilize scientific-technological-industrial developments in a social and human world, he wrote,

> Industrialization is the only hope of the poor. I use the word "hope" in a crude and prosaic sense. I have not much use for the moral sensibility of anyone who is too refined to use it so. It is all very well for us, sitting pretty, to think that material standards of living don't matter all that much. It is all very well for one, as a personal choice, to reject industrialization—do a modern Walden, if you like, and if you go without much food, see most of your children die in infancy, despise the comforts of literacy, accept twenty years off your own life, then I respect you for the strength of your aesthetic revulsion. But I don't respect you in the slightest if, even passively, you try to impose the same choice on others who are not free to choose
>
> The industrial revolution looked very different according to whether one saw it from above or below. It looks very different today according to whether one sees it from Chelsea or from a village in Asia. To people like my grandfather, there was no question that the industrial revolution was less bad than what had gone before. The only question was, how to make it better.
>
> In a more sophisticated sense, that is still the question. In the advanced countries, we have realized in a rough and ready way what the old industrial revolution brought with it. A great increase of population, because applied science went hand in hand with medical science and medical care. Enough to eat, for a similar reason. Everyone able to read and write, because an industrial society can't work without. Health, food, education; nothing but the industrial revolution could have spread them right down to the very poor. Those are primarily gains—there are losses too, of course, one of which is that organizing a society for industry makes it easy to organize it for all-out war. But the gains remain. They are the base of our social hope.[6]

One can argue that scientific and technological advances are themselves based on values. They are expressions of human goals for the individual and society. As such, they improve humanity's condition. Nevertheless, they also disrupt and modify our patterns of living. Inevitably, these changes cause conflict between traditional religious and moral values and the possibilities offered by technology. The amazing medical technological advances of recent decades illustrate the advantages of technical research and practice as they at the same time raise innumerable questions concerning their use.

◆◆◆

Should our technology determine our future as a society? To what extent should it shape the direction of our lives? Who should make these decisions?

[6] C. P. Snow, *The Two Cultures: And A Second Look* (New York: Cambridge University Press, 1959, 1963), pp. 30–32.

Does the use of technology need to be regulated? By whom?

Should religious and moral values regulate the use of findings of scientific investigation?

Should technological changes be made merely because they are possible?

Can we expect societies to have the knowledge and commitment to resolve these questions according to democratic decision-making procedures?

In what ways have religious, political, economic and scientific interests intersected in recent controversies concerning cloning and embryonic stem-cell research?

Unit 74   Secularization

Changes and modifications in the relationship of religion to modern society are often referred to as *secularization*. Depending on one's perspective, this word takes on varied meanings. To some, it may mean the fragmentation or breakup of the religious values that undergirded past experience. To others, it may mean progress in religious understanding, the movement beyond antiquated and irrelevant values.

Paul Ricoeur, a contemporary French philosopher and Christian layman, commented on secularization as follows:

> We mean by secularization an institutional phenomenon: the emancipation of most human activities from the influence of ecclesiastical institutions. In this first sense, secularization is synonymous with laicization: the community no longer coincides with the parish, political authority dissociates itself from religious authority. This transfer of power from the churchman to the civil servant and politician has been marked by a series of crises in which communities, hospitals, and schools have been successively affected.
>
> In a second sense secularization is characterized by the erasing of the distinction between the spheres of the sacred and the profane. This distinction, applying to time (religious and non-religious holidays), space (holy places and public buildings), social roles (the priest and the layman), the world-view (the heavens and the earth), the emotions (piety and justice), has tended to disappear for modern man. Its disappearance characterizes modernity as such. To this loss of distinction is connected the dissolution of peculiarly religious traditions, which today have become merely cultural provincialisms resistant to the universal industrial society.[7]

Harvey Cox, another contemporary Christian thinker, in his book *The Secular City* commented on this sense of secularization in a similar way:

> Recently, *secularization* has been used to describe a process on the cultural level, which is parallel to the political one. It denotes the disappearance of religious determination of the symbols of cultural integration. Cultural secularization is an inevitable concomitant of a political and social secularization. Sometimes the one precedes the other, depending

[7] Paul Ricoeur, *Political and Social Essays*, David Stewart and Joseph Bien, eds., (Athens, GA: Ohio University Press, 1974), pp. 182–183.

on the historical circumstances, but a wide imbalance between social and cultural secularization will not persist very long. In the United States there has been a considerable degree of political secularization for many years. The public schools are officially secular in the sense of being free from church control. At the same time, the cultural secularization of America has come about more slowly. The Supreme Court decisions in the early 1960s outlawing required prayers pointed up a disparity, which had continued for some years.[8]

There have been debates among religious thinkers about whether secularization is a good thing or a bad thing from the religious point of view. Some have lamented the legally required removal of religious practices and symbols (such as prayer in schools or manger scenes in city parks) from American public life as a deterioration of the traditional moral and religious values that undergird our society.

In the nineteenth-century United States, there were many efforts to effect a legal, constitutional connection between religion and the state. One proposal would have made the United States officially a "Christian Commonwealth," with the right to vote restricted to "genuine Christians" (defined as Presbyterians, Congregationalists, Episcopalians, Methodists, and Baptists). In Massachusetts, Catholic children who had been told by their parish priests not to participate in reading aloud from the King James version of the Bible (regarded as a Protestant translation) were ordered by public school officials to be beaten until they agreed to take part. In response to a controversy concerning Bible reading in the public schools in Cincinnati, Ohio, Judge Alfonso Taft in 1870 ruled as follows:

> Legal Christianity is . . . a contradiction of terms. When Christianity asks the aid of government beyond mere impartial protection, it denies itself. Its laws are divine and not human. Its essential interests lie beyond the reach and range of human governments. United with government, religion never rises above the merest superstition; united with religion, government never rises above the merest despotism, and all history shows us that the more widely and completely they are separated, the better it is for both. [9]

Historically, some people have favored secularization because they believe that legally established religion has a harmful effect on government and violates the liberties of individuals and groups within society. Judge Taft obviously believed that both government and religion benefit from the separation that results from secularization. Many then, and probably many now, questioned this ruling. In the United States today, some Catholics and Protestants, including but not limited to those sympathetic to the new Protestant fundamentalism, the Moral Majority, and the prolife (antiabortion) movement, have argued that divine and human law cannot be separated in an absolute or final way. They have argued that some legally permitted rights of religious expression (such as

---

[8] Reprinted with permission of Macmillan, Inc., from *The Secular City*, rev. ed. by Harvey Cox. Copyright © Harvey Cox 1965, 1966.

[9] Quoted in Perry Deane Young, *God's Bullies: Power, Politics, and Religious Tyranny* (New York: Holt, Rinehart & Winston, 1982), p. 170.

limited times of prayer in public schools that do not require participation) should be recognized when they are wanted by a majority of citizens.

In contrast, the religious thinkers Paul Ricoeur and Harvey Cox believe that the secularization process is inevitable. They, like Judge Taft, see value for both religion and government in the resulting separation. Still others have seen both losses and benefits for religion and for modern societies in the secularization process.

The question of church-state relations goes far back in Western history. In ancient societies—ancient Greece, Rome, Egypt, Babylon, and Israel—church and state were one, although as societies became more complex, there was some differentiation between religious and secular officials and institutions. Nevertheless, the "secular" government was generally seen as having a divine foundation, and often kings and other government officials had sacred, priestly roles and functions.

In Western Europe during the Middle Ages, church government and secular governments were separate in theory but nearly always influenced and exerted various degrees of control on each other. By the high Middle Ages (thirteenth century), some theologians, including Thomas Aquinas, argued that in some cases the church—especially in its highest office, the papacy—had the authority from God to exercise control over secular governments when the spiritual welfare of the subjects was at stake. One tendency of the early modern period (fourteenth to seventeenth centuries) was for thinkers, religious (Marsilius of Padua) as well as secular (Thomas Hobbes), to argue that the secular government should have authority over the church. This was part of a trend toward the differentiation of Europe into separate, independent nation-states. In the new situation of national independence, at first nearly everyone thought that a society or nation could not have the necessary unity to survive unless all of its members participated in common religious beliefs and traditions.

It was a very new development when in the seventeenth century a few religious (Roger Williams) and secular (John Locke) thinkers argued that there could be a meaningful separation of church and state, in which the state did not attempt to regulate or control the religious beliefs and practices of its citizens and religious organizations did not attempt to control or gain power from the secular government. At that time several of the American colonies had state-supported churches.

Henry David Thoreau is a nineteenth-century example of the new attitude toward church-state relations and freedom of individual religious practice from state control. Threatened with imprisonment for refusing to pay a tax to support the state-established Congregational church—and Thoreau did go to jail for his refusal to pay taxes that he believed supported the system of slavery and the war of the United States against Mexico—he was finally given the option of signing a declaration that he was not and did not intend to be a member of the church. He signed, remarking that he would gladly sign a statement that he was not a member of any of the other organizations he had never joined if only he knew what they were.

These ideas very much show the new or "modern" attitude toward religious commitment. In most societies, even very recent ones, one was born into membership in a religious organization; there was no question of individual choice. To some extent this is still true for most people, even in modern societies; but the fact that religious participation has increasingly become "privatized" and that societies have become "secularized" has added many new dimensions to the role that religious traditions, organizations, and commitments have in the contemporary world.

In Unit 75, "secularization" is interpreted as being part of, and partly a cause and partly a result of, the more general process called "modernization," which has led us to speak of living in a "postmodern" world.

The phenomenon here called "secularization," which involves separation of private morality and religious belief from government control, has led many in contemporary societies to believe that there has been a decline in morality, moral standards and practices, and religious belief. Some religiously and politically conservative thinkers in contemporary America speak of a "culture war" that is now going on between advocates of traditional Christian morality (involving family values that prescribe the traditional nuclear family as normative for all) and upholders of a "new morality" that abandons traditional values. Such thinkers see much in contemporary sexual practices, entertainment depictions, and media descriptions of sexual promiscuity, divorce, homosexual lifestyles, and the acceptance of abortion as elements in the culture war, indeed, as weapons launched against traditional religion, morality, and values.

✦✦✦

Do religious traditions today, as Paul Ricoeur thought, resist "the universal industrial" (or global) society?

See the discussion in Unit 77 of globalization, a main focus of contemporary protest movements. Are protests of globalization largely, or partly, religiously motivated?

UNIT 75   CHARACTERISTICS OF MODERNIZATION

The inevitability of rapid and comprehensive change differentiates a modern society from a traditional one. This is the basis of the process of secularization. Though change has always been part of any culture, it has become so accelerated that it is now a central feature of modern societies. To change is to modernize. In light of this, the following list indicates some of the factors that sociologists have suggested are characteristic of modern societies.

1. *Urbanization:* Modernization implies not just that people live in cities (people have lived in cities since 3000 B.C.E.) but also that the great majority of the population is not engaged in agricultural (primary) production but in industrial (secondary) and service (tertiary) occupations. Overcoming the necessity for a majority of the population to be engaged in the production of food and basic raw materials for clothing and shelter has been one of the keys to the transition from a traditionally oriented to a modernized society.

2. *Atomization:* Modernization has resulted in a breakdown of traditional family structures and group relationships. This is seen in the shift from extended family (or clan) groupings in traditionally oriented societies to the nuclear family (parents and children). It is more difficult for the nuclear family—two parents or one parent with families of relatively few children and with relatives living geographically far away—to provide

guidance and role models for young children. This affects families at every economic level, often those at middle-class levels more than those at other levels. In the days of the extended family there were usually uncles and aunts, cousins, older brothers and sisters living in close proximity to one another who would care for and associate with younger children and frequently shield them from too strict parental expectations, disappointment, and anger. Atomization is also seen in the tendency of modern society for one's economic role to be separated from family relationships—the family group does not work together as an independent economic unit. Individuals also find themselves more and more independent and capable of determining their own patterns and relationships; thus they become more and more isolated—individual atoms separated from any larger molecular structure.

3. *Rationalization*: Activities of individuals and organizations tend to be coordinated systematically in modern societies, either by semi-automatically functioning mechanisms (the market in the economic sphere in capitalist societies) or by deliberately created agencies (bureaucracies). All activities tend then to be structures in interconnected, interacting relationships that demand rational and systematic responses.

4. *Differentiation*: One of the characteristics of modernizing societies, according to a number of contemporary sociologists—including the Americans Talcott Parsons and H. W. Pfautz and the German Joachim Matthes—is that the basic institutions of the society—political, economic, educational, and religious—must undergo a process of differentiation. According to Parsons, all human institutions and all aspects of human life undergo processes of development in the course of social, cultural, and personal change. There are both internal differentiation (expansion and diversification) and differentiation in relation to (change of relation to) other factors in the system of interaction. Thus, as society evolves, the religious element (the sacred) becomes separated, or differentiated, from the nonreligious elements (the secular). Religion tends to lose some of its earlier functions, for instance, as in Western society, some of its educational, charitable, and political functions. This process is exemplified, Parsons held, in the Protestant Reformation's extension—or transfer—of autonomous responsibility, traditionally lodged in the church, to individual Christians for their activities in their secular roles. According to Parsons, in modernized European and American societies, the Christian church's role is no longer "parental." The ethical principles that had been institutionalized within the church now became the responsibility of the individual. And the present church system typical of America, which Parsons called "denominational pluralism," was interpreted as being a further extension of the "institutionalization of Christian ethics"; each denomination differentiates and establishes its own ethical pattern.

> The denomination . . . shares with the church type the differentiation between religious and secular spheres of interest. . . . Both may be conceived to be subject to Christian values, but to constitute independent foci of responsibility for their implementation. . . . The denomination shares with the sect type its character as a voluntary association where the individual member is bound only by a responsible personal commitment. . . .[10] (Compare to Unit 77)

[10] Talcott Parsons, "Christianity and Modern Industrial Society," in *Sociological Theory and Modern Society* (New York: Free Press, 1967), p. 413.

5. *Institutionalization of innovative attitude*: A further characteristic of modernizing, in contrast to traditionally oriented societies, is that change not only is expected but encouraged. This value underlies the role of science and technology in modernizing and modernized societies. Life is lived with the expectation that newer and better methods of doing things will be invented, that newer and truer knowledge will be discovered. John R. Platt has argued that modern societies are in the process of creating a "steady-state" world, a world of societies in which there will be nothing static: "What will begin to be steady is our acceptance of . . . new ways of creative leisure and interaction as being the most interesting and most satisfying ways of life."[11]

6. *Globalization:* Increasingly modernization is turning the world into a global society. In the nineteenth century, Karl Marx praised capitalism for delivering people in rural areas of economically advanced societies from isolation, from what he called "the idiocy of rural life." Now persons in every area of the world are being incorporated into networks of economic and technological development as suppliers of labor and raw materials and markets for products and services. The emerging global economy is more and more interactive and rationalized.

The implications of this understanding of modernization and change for the world's religions are many. Traditional formulations of religious truths and traditional patterns of ritual are being constantly modified. Technological innovations that change life patterns require new forms of organization, worship, communication, and most important a rethinking of the ethical applications of religious insights.

◆◆◆

What changes in medical technology require the rethinking of religious and ethical definitions and teachings?

What effect does it have on religion to say, "change is a way of life"?

What effect do the changes in military technology have on religious concepts of, and teachings about, war?

What aspects of modernization do you find most attractive or most threatening?

UNIT 76   MODERNISM AND POSTMODERNISM : SOME VARIATIONS

Many interpreters of change in the modern period argue that the processes described in Unit 75 as characteristics of modernization have led to a new condition of the world described as "postmodern." The term *postmodernism* was probably first used to describe differences between the "modern" architecture of the first half of the twentieth century and the newer architecture that began appearing in the 1950s and 1960s. However, *postmodern* has now come to be used to contrast two differing trends that seem to be present in all areas of human life, society, and activity. In this unit the differences between "modernism" and "postmodernism" as contrasting attitudes toward life and truth are briefly described.

[11] John R. Platt, *The Step to Man* (New York: Wiley, 1966), p. 200

According to many interpreters, the *essence of modernism* or *the modern* has been a quest for the Absolute. Artists sought absolute perfection of style and expression in their paintings, novels or poems; scientists and philosophers sought systems of principles and laws that would explain all phenomena of nature and human behavior. The late-eighteenth–early-nineteenth-century German poet Johann Wolfgang von Goethe captured these aspirations in his dramatic poem *Faust*. Faust sells his soul to the Devil in order to have and master every possible human experience.

In Part II of *Faust*, Faust tries to fulfill dreams of the eighteenth-century Enlightenment of using power to benefit humanity, recovering land from the sea. Throughout the work, he exemplifies early-nineteenth-century Romanticism's goal of plumbing the heights and depths of human experience. In one of his adventures, he marries the Greek beauty Helen of Troy, symbolically bringing about a union between Ancient Greece's ideals of rational harmony and order and the modern quest of the Infinite, for perfection of life, knowledge, and art. In *Faust*, Goethe explores the grandeur and potential destructiveness of the modern quest. Faust sometimes enjoys and at times is bored by his many adventures but causes much harm. He does recover land for human use but destroys innocent lives. Goethe's examination of the modernist project in its two forms of Enlightenment and Romanticism is appreciative but critical. At the end of the drama, even though he had sold his soul to the Devil to gain power and experience, Faust is saved because of his infinite, if never fulfilled, striving. If *Faust* had been a postmodernist work, there would have been no possibility of damnation or of salvation. Faust possibly would have ended by advertising women's apparel on television as the French postmodernist Jacques Derrida did.

The modern in literature appeared in the second half of the nineteenth century and the first half of the twentieth. Modernist writers held that the act of writing itself was a matter of life and death, indeed of salvation, for the writer (and for the world). Such seriousness of purpose is manifested in the work and attitude of many writers of the period, including the poets Arthur Rimbaud, Stephane Mallarmé, and Rainer Maria Rilke and the novelists Thomas Mann, Marcel Proust, and James Joyce.

In postmodern literature, writing became much like a game, the writer either despairing of or unconcerned about salvation through literature. Typically, the "lesson" of literature was that there is no salvation through writing or any other avenue. At the extreme, postmodern critics may argue that bad writing is as good as, or even better than, good writing. Postmodern writers include e.e. cummings, Franz Kafka, Donald Barthelme, and Vladimir Nabokov, all of whom practiced "good writing," and many others, some of whom wrote "badly" on purpose.

In painting, modernism was represented by, among others, impressionists and postimpressionists, abstract expressionists, and cubists; postmodernism by surrealists, pop artists, and artists who create many forms of a renewed but ironic realism and naturalism.

In philosophy and the sciences, the modern period began in the seventeenth century with the rise of a new physical science and a new philosophy that attempted to promote and interpret the new ("Newtonian") science. Here the modern attitude was expressed in the desire for and hope of absolute certainty in a system of knowledge and is represented by René Descartes, Isaac Newton, John Locke, Immanuel Kant, Albert Einstein, and a host of others. Although Einstein revolutionized modern physics, he is considered one of the last great scientists of the modernist period, since he sought the same kind of certainty, with different beginning points, that Newtonian science sought. In philosophy, the first phase of the philosophy of Ludwig Wittgenstein was modern; the second, postmodern. In his first phase, Wittgenstein argued that there is an absolute distinction between meaningful and meaningless language, that all meaningful language (such as that of the sciences and everyday life) shares the same logical structure, and any language uses that do not have this structure (such as the language of ethics and religion) is nonsense. (Compare Units 32 and 33.) In his second phase, Wittgenstein argued that there is no underlying structure to language, just a variety of differing "language games," each with its own rules. Postmodernism rejects the idea that humans will ever reach absolute certainty in knowing or belief. In philosophy postmodernism is represented by Friedrich Nietzsche, Jacques Derrida, and C. S. Peirce.

Probably all postmodernist thinkers agree in being antifoundationalists. Foundationalism is the attempt to find absolute beginning points, or an ultimate foundation, for knowledge and belief. Seventeenth-century rationalist thinkers (Descartes, Spinoza, Leibniz) tried to find an absolute foundation in self-evident truths or ideas, such as that every event has a cause or that God necessarily exists. Seventeenth- and eighteenth-century empiricists (Locke, Berkeley, Hume) appealed to simple ideas derived from the elementary components of sense experience (length, width, size, color, taste) as starting points for all knowledge. The great eighteenth-century German philosopher Immanuel Kant attempted to combine rationalist and empiricist elements to provide foundations for all knowledge and belief. Englishman John Locke, who wanted a foundation in sense experience for knowledge and belief, was a foundationalist in religion as well. Locke argued that sense experience provides a foundation for belief in God as the ultimate cause or creator of the natural world, and belief in God provides a foundation for acceptance of the Bible as the revelation of God's will to humanity. In the Bible, Locke found a small number of foundational teachings about the need for humans to repent of their sins and be forgiven by God. Locke used these foundational Christian beliefs to argue for personal liberty, religious toleration, and a (relative) separation of religious matters from government, which must respect the rights of personal conscience in matters of belief. Assumptions such as these defined the modern period.

One can see that in philosophy and science—and in religion—there are at least two kinds of postmodernists. Some argue that the concept of Truth as traditionally believed in science, philosophy, and religion (Truth with a capital "T") was mistaken. There is only truth with a lowercase "t." Or, as one of America's best known postmodernist theorists, Richard Rorty, is often reported to have said: "Truth is what your society will let you get away with saying."

For these postmodernists, there is no objective truth. Another kind of postmodernist, exemplified by the American philosopher C. S. Peirce, doesn't reject the idea of objective truth but does reject the idea that there are absolutely certain starting points ("self-evident") that can be used to build an infallible system. These postmodernists call themselves "fallibilists" and say that all beliefs are always, in principle, subject to reevaluation.

All postmodernists argue that there is an important shaping of beliefs—whether scientific, moral, philosophical, or religious—by the societies in which they are held.

Some scientists argue that at least some of the sciences are purely objective, are not influenced by social pressures, and have an infallible method—that of hypothesis forming and testing—of arriving at objective truth. However, philosophers and historians of science, such as Thomas S. Kuhn, and some scientists themselves have pointed to features in the social context of scientific activity that shape the forms theories take and the design of experiments (see Unit 81).

Though the term *postmodernism* is used in many ways, it signals at least a partial abandonment of Modern Europe and America's quest for totality of comprehension and achievement. Modernism's view of history involved progress toward a meaningful *Goal* in accordance with a *Story* involving values of human life and civilization. (See the examples of Metastories—visions of human history that posit progress to some Ultimate Goal, discussed in Unit 58). The first type of postmodernism gives up on belief in progress or an overall Goal or Story of History and instead sees numerous relatively disconnected stories. It seeks partial or "regional" insights rather than all-embracing Meaning or Metastory. Many religious thinkers identify closely with some forms of postmodernism. Some Christian thinkers find in the early fifth century C.E. theologian Augustine's separation between the City of man and *the heavenly City of God* a downplaying of the idea that there can be any meaning in purely *human* history. Some contemporary Catholic thinkers believe that modernists went wrong by disrupting the unity and wholeness of Medieval Europe with its synthesis of faith and reason. Some contemporary Protestants have argued that modernist conceptions of a deistic God in a supernatural realm beyond the Newtonian clockwork universe created by this powerful but now absent God violated the Christian understanding of God as radically transcendent found in Thomas Aquinas, Martin Luther, and John Calvin.[12] Still, religious thinkers who value aspects of postmodernist criticism of traditional views of human progress may not be willing to accept radical postmodernist perspectives of meaning or of meaninglessness in history. The question can be asked whether most religions do not hold or affirm foundational principles and some Metastory.

◆◆◆

Do you believe that social customs, pressures, and accepted values sometimes, or even always, have an influence on what scientists accept as scientific truth?

What might be some differences between modernist and postmodernist approaches to religion? (Hint: Many postmodernist Christians believe that religious truth may be much more fully grasped through narratives, such as those found in the Book of Genesis or the parables of Jesus, than in abstract theological statements, moral principles, or credal affirmations.)

Using the definitions of modernism and postmodernism given here, how would you classify yourself? Which of these perspectives do you find yourself using in your own thought and action?

[12] See William C. Placher, *The Domestication of Transcendence* (Louisville, KY: Westminster John Knox Press, 1996).

Unit 77   New Religious Movements

The forms and types of organization or structure taken by religious movements often depend on their relation to other religious movements in their society. In the present unit we use the terms "established church," "sect," "denomination," and "cult." Often religious movements do not use these terms to characterize themselves. When we use them, we do not intend to imply that some are good and some are not good. We are not praising or criticizing a religious organization by calling it an established church or a sect or cult or denomination. We are attempting to describe its characteristics, its structure, and its relation to other groups and movements within its society.

The second half of the twentieth century has witnessed the growth and rapid spread of religious movements in many parts of the world. In some instances the movements have been very new, apparently generated spontaneously through the experience and concern of readily identifiable individuals. But even in such cases, the "new" religious movements have usually been offshoots or modifications of existing groups or movements. For instance, the Branch Davidian group led by David Koresh, which was involved in tragic events near Waco, Texas, in the early 1990s, was an offshoot of a Christian Adventist group, which was itself an offshoot of a larger Adventist group whose history is traceable to the millennialist excitement in the mid-Atlantic states of the United States of the 1840s (see Unit 58). Being an offshoot of another group is true not only of the Branch Davidians but also of the Unification Church, an offshoot of Korean Christianity led by Sun Myung Moon, and of many other religious movements of all periods (review Units 5 and 6).

Another sort of relation of the "new" religious movements of our time to older religious groups is simply this: The "new" movement may not be new at all in an absolute sense but new to the society or part of the world where it exists. Often it is really an extension, sometimes spontaneous but more frequently the result of missionary activity by adherents, in a society or societies where it has been long established. Thus, Pentecostal Christian groups have spread rapidly in recent years in traditionally Catholic regions of Latin America, but have existed for more than a hundred years in North America. The same is true of the expansion of the Church of Jesus Christ of Latter Day Saints, which originated as a "new prophecy" movement from traditional nineteenth-century American Protestantism and has existed since then in the United States and parts of Great Britain, but now is growing rapidly in many places in Europe, the Pacific, and elsewhere. The same is true concerning the present rapid growth of Islam in the United States, which, in this case, has grown largely because of immigration of Muslims from other societies and also because of the emergence of black American Muslim groups.

In "modern" or "postmodern" societies such as the United States, there is increasing religious diversity. However, in some parts of the country there is less diversity than might be expected. For instance, in the Deep South, the overwhelming majority of the population consists of mainline—Baptist, Methodist, and Presbyterian—or sectarian—Pentecostal or Fundamentalist—Protestants. Other churches and groups are present but in much smaller numbers.

One useful tool in understanding the formation and spread of new religious movements is a typology suggested by the twentieth-century sociologist Max Weber and his theologian colleague, Ernst Troeltsch. These scholars suggested that Christianity has historically formed itself into two basic forms of religious organization, the church and the sect (Troeltsch also thought there was a third form, mysticism). Since the time of Weber and Troeltsch, the typology has been expanded and modified by many students of religion, criticized by some, and rejected as useless by others. Possibly the most interesting recent treatment or modification of the typology has been given by sociologists Rodney Stark and William Sims Bainbridge.[13]

The following characterization of types of religious organizational or group structures draws to a large extent on the work of Stark and Bainbridge but also differs in significant ways from their treatment, thus they should not be blamed for any shortcomings (that may seem strong points to the authors of *Exploring Religious Meaning*) of our treatment.

For Troeltsch and Weber, a church was a socially and sometimes legally established, highly inclusive religious organization, looked upon by the majority of its society as the most or only legitimate religious organization of the society. Normally, persons were born into it, were guided or disciplined and taught by it, but usually with requirements that showed a large amount of variation in strictness or laxity depending on one's social roles. Thus, in medieval Europe, the Catholic church was held to be the only legitimate religious organization; all belonged to it, but the requirements for those believers called to the monastic life were much more strenuous, involving vows of poverty, celibacy, and obedience, than requirements for those Christians who lived secular lives "in the world." They were expected to be honest, just, and merciful, monogamous, and devoted to family, community duties, and God. Also, as long as the church experienced little or no competition from other religious groups, a fairly wide diversity of ways of expressing religious beliefs was tolerated.

In contrast, the sect type of religious group generally was composed of persons dissatisfied with the major trends of their society, its ruling class, and its religious establishment. Sects tended to be made up of persons from the lower economic strata of society and of educated persons who felt that the society's "church" or "church type" groups had become spiritually and morally lax and had sold out to the economic and political ruling classes of society. Membership in the sect was voluntary, but its requirements for conduct were strict. Members often were not merely disciplined for moral failure or religious deviation but were expelled. A much narrower, more stereotyped expression of religious belief was required. Usually a sect emphasizes a smaller number of crucial beliefs than the established church or denomination does but will make some areas of belief or practice crucial that the church or denomination consider marginal or optional.

Troeltsch also allowed for a third type of religious "organization" or orientation—a relatively unstructured individualistic way he called "mysticism," which might arise within church or sect and as often as not was treated as heretical or dangerous.

[13] See their books, *The Future of Religion* (Berkeley: University of California Press, 1985) and *A Theory of Religion* (New York: Peter Lang, 1987).

In looking at expressions of religion in the contemporary world we find societies, for instance, in many of the traditionally Muslim countries, where there is an established religion, supported by government, established by law and public opinion, with varying degrees of tolerance for human shortcomings, but with the insistence that it is in control of all of society's legitimate religious institutions. We will call a religious organization that is recognized by law or an overwhelming majority of public opinion an "established church."

One can see sectarian religious groups in many societies of the contemporary world. These are the groups that take a stricter interpretation than other adherents of the traditional religion of the society. In contemporary America, examples of sectarian groups are conservative or Pentecostal Protestant groups and possibly some religious groups that began as cults (see following), such as Jehovah's Witnesses.

In contemporary pluralistic, diverse societies, instead of one established church, there is likely to be a number of denominations. Like a church, a denomination is more inclusive in membership and less strict in demands of members than the sect. But unlike church and sect, the denomination recognizes the legitimacy of other religious groups, of other denominations, and frequently of sects, even (for some societies) of established churches, possibly of some cults, and of other world religions. In contemporary America, denominations are often referred to as "the religious mainline" or as "mainline denominations." It is understood by most people that this includes such Protestant groups as Episcopalians, Presbyterians, Lutherans, Methodists, Baptists, Disciples of Christ, and other groups. Increasingly, Protestants and many Catholics have come to regard American (and World) Catholicism as a mainline denomination (in spite of past and present claims to supremacy or primacy) and sometimes to regard branches of Judaism, Islam, Buddhism, and others among the world's religions as mainline "denominations" of that religion.

The sectarian groups in our society are usually offshoots of the denominations. Thus, in the nineteenth century, as American Methodism moved from being a sect to a denomination, there were sectarian offshoots from Methodism, including splinter groups that kept the name Methodist, but also Nazarenes, Holiness churches, and some Pentecostal movements. Many of these groups have become more like denominations than sects. In fact, when a sectarian group grows, if it is not persecuted by government or society, it tends to relax, to become more tolerant, to become a denomination.

During the past several decades, among sectarian religious movements growing in membership or influence (or both) have been groups described as *fundamentalist*. Many behavioral scientists see religious fundamentalism as a negative response to secularizing and modernizing trends in society (see Units 74 and 75). In the United States, Southern Baptists have come close to a split between Moderate and Fundamentalist wings. Although Southern Baptists have always refused to give a closed or defined list of creedal beliefs, the Fundamentalists have formulated a "short list" of essential beliefs. They also share in criticism of trends that they see as corrupting lifestyles: acceptance of equality of women, homosexuality, sexual permissiveness and toleration of non-Christian religions as expressing truth from God. Some Islamic countries have been dominated by Islamic fundamentalists who reject changes in traditional moral codes and toleration of non-Muslim religions and acceptance of Western, particularly American, entertainment and styles of dress. By and large rulers and citizens of Islamic countries have wanted technology that can be imported from the West, but many have feared and hated the secularization and lifestyles that come with it.

Another type of religious organization found in contemporary society is called a "cult." There are two basic ways of characterizing cults; sometimes these principles are shared by one group and sometimes not. Normally a group is called a cult if it is under the close personal leadership of one or a few individuals, usually its founder(s) or their immediate successors. Belief is strictly controlled, and most often the group's lifestyle is also strictly controlled. The cult's leaders are held to have a special relationship to God or a Divine Power or Principle, and thus have the authority to modify traditionally accepted beliefs and practices. Often this means that a cult will be quite small; if it grows beyond the immediate leadership of an individual or small group of individuals or their successors, it may be said to have become a sect, or a denomination, or even an established church. This is not always the case; the Church of Jesus Christ of Latter Day Saints, though very large and growing rapidly, has to a large extent retained its leadership-authority principle, giving very decisive authority to a single designated individual and maintaining rather strict control, at least in matters of belief, over its adherents.

The second way that the term *cult* is used by those studying behavioral patterns and aspects of religion is by recognizing that the teachings and practices of the cult are in many ways alien or foreign to the society's traditional religion(s). Stark and Bainbridge emphasize this feature, noting that in contemporary America, where the mainline denominations (representing an inclusive version of traditional religion that appeals broadly to people who feel "at home" with their society's power structures and values) are strong, so are sectarian groups (giving a stricter interpretation of traditional religion and not feeling at home in the society). Stark and Bainbridge also point out that when both denominations and sects are relatively weaker in a society, as in California and the western United States, cults tend to flourish and grow. A cult may draw its teachings from secular sources rather than from traditional religion. As mentioned in Unit 58, there have been cults whose beliefs derived from modification of beliefs related to contemporary science or pseudoscience. Scientology's founder, L. Ron Hubbard, derived beliefs from some schools of psychology and contemporary natural science to create his cult's beliefs.

In the spring of 1997, many throughout the world were startled to hear of the mass suicide of members of a cult in San Diego, California. The cult was called "Heaven's Gate" and was led by an elderly man named Marshall Applewhite. Cult members, some of whom had belonged to the cult for more than twenty years, had been taught that the earth was soon to be recycled, but that members of the cult could, through committing suicide, ascend to a higher level of existence—bodiless, genderless, spiritual—by being transported from the earth on an Unidentified Flying Object (UFO). When the newly discovered comet Hale-Bopp appeared close to earth, Applewhite and thirty-eight of his followers committed suicide, believing that by leaving their bodies, which Applewhite referred to as material "vehicles," behind, they would be transported by a UFO following the comet to a higher level of existence.

The Heaven's Gate cult shows both aspects of the nature of cults as we have described them: a small group with strong loyalty to an identifiable leader and nontraditional beliefs. Instead of beliefs (Jewish, Christian) common to its society, the cult's beliefs were woven from materials of contemporary science and science fiction (or fantasy) together with elements of Gnostic or Eastern religious concepts of mind-body dualism.

Often a large part of a cult's appeal is to persons who feel "out of place" in their own society—alienated or marginalized. The cult may capitalize on its nontraditional content, appealing to the "prestige" of modern scientific or pseudoscientific elements— the Heaven's Gate cult used the Internet as a recruiting device—or to "exotic" teachings of religions foreign to the society.

The Jonestown group led by Jim Jones in mass suicide in 1978 after some members of the group had killed a U.S. Congressman was much less a cult using nontraditional materials than Heaven's Gate. Jones's group held to fairly traditional Christian sectarian beliefs, though those beliefs were evolving in utopian or apocalyptic ways. However, the strong domination of the hundreds of members of this apocalyptic group by its leader, Jim Jones, qualifies it as a cult.

The new and rapidly growing religious movements in a society are likely to be sects or cults. But, recall, the terms are relative. Catholicism may be a denomination in the United States and an established church in a European country like Spain (where it is relatively strong and often the major or only religious organization). The Church of Jesus Christ of Latter Day Saints may approximate an established church in Utah, a sect in New Mexico, a denomination in California, and a cult in Mississippi. One would expect a rapid growth of cults—especially foreign religious traditions—in countries where sectarian and denominational groups are becoming weaker, and of sectarian groups where cults are weak but denominations are strong though relatively becoming weaker. A group like the Jehovah's Witnesses may be considered a sect (with a stricter than most interpretation of traditional Christianity) or a cult, depending on how its adherents and outsiders interpret it or on its leadership structure (or both).

◆◆◆

Are these processes happening in our society? Where and what kinds of sects and cults are originating or growing?

◆◆◆

Two further issues should be noted. First, it has been pointed out that denominations tend to become more and more convinced that other religious groups are legitimate, so they are less likely to attempt conversion of outsiders to the denomination. The attitude that Christians take or should take toward adherents of non-Christian religions is a live one in American denominations today. In fact, it is evident that within many denominations, some adherents feel that conversion of non-Christians to some form of Christianity is still a central requirement for Christians. Others disagree. This issue has even become a part of the content or subject matter of the "culture war" mentioned in Unit 73.

Conversely, in some societies, those with an established religion, it is illegal to distribute or possess material that might be used to convert someone from the established religion to what would be a "cult" in that society, i.e., from Islam to Christianity in Iran or Saudi Arabia. In the spring of 1997, a law was introduced into the Knesset of Israel that, if passed, would forbid the possession or distribution of materials that might be used in converting persons from Judaism to another religion. In "postmodern" societies, religion tends to be looked upon as a private, personal matter. In more traditionally oriented societies, and in many early modern ones, religion was, and still may be, a matter of one's loyalty to family, society, and state.

❖❖❖

Do you find tensions in our society between personal rights concerning religion (with its associated beliefs and values) and the rights of groups? Consider how freedom of expression or conduct, the right to privacy, or the right to uphold the values of a majority or the law may be affected by personal and group religious attitudes. What conflicts may arise in attempts to convert from one religion to another, for example, or in claims to freedom of expression that some find offensive, pornographic, obscene, racist, or unpatriotic?

Recalling the definition of "religion" given in Chapter 1 of Exploring Religious Meaning, *explain the following:*

"A political party can be a cult, a sect, a denomination or an established church," with reference to Russian history during the twentieth century and especially with reference to the Marxist movements led by Lenin, Trotsky, and Stalin.

✦✦✦ 18 ✦✦✦

HUMAN RESPONSE
TO THE NATURAL PROCESS

The two units in this chapter focus on attitudes and understanding of human beings concerning the natural order. The chapter discusses the contrasting attitudes—feelings, images, concepts—that different societies have taken toward nature and its impingement on and relationship to human life. In some cultures the natural process has been viewed with warmth and acceptance, in others as something impersonal to be used, and in still others as something to be downgraded and dispensed with in the human search for truth. Each of these attitudes finds support and grounding in the religious traditions and teachings that are interwoven in the fabric of a particular society.

We can easily recognize how attitudes toward nature in the West have fostered pollution and other forms of environmental violence. We have not included descriptive material on these problems because of lack of space and the abundance of materials elsewhere. Instead we have sought to penetrate the attitudes prevalent in the West that have produced the disruptive actions toward nature. We have also sought to relate these attitudes to the religious traditions that have transmitted them. The wealth of resources, contemporary and traditional, presently available will enable the reader to go beyond the limited discussion of the chapter.

Neither have we investigated the changing attitudes toward nature and the resultant conflicts caused by the rapid globalization of the modern world. Economic production of goods for Western societies in Eastern nations, along with the corporate culture that accompanies it, inevitably brings contact and sometimes conflict between contrasting views of nature. Again, while we have not considered these issues here they are discussed in other studies because of their importance for understanding some of the confusion and disorientation present in our new "one world."

Unit 78   Humanity and the World

What is the relationship between humanity and the natural process? Different cultures and different individuals have responded to this question in diverse ways. Some responses have been analytical, some descriptive, and still others imitative. Some have emphasized the cognitive dimension, others the affective. Some responses have been given consciously, others unconsciously. We will isolate and tentatively explore three types of responses, each a basic perspective concerning the natural process: (1) symbiosis, (2) apobiosis, and (3) diabiosis.

SYMBIOSIS

The term *symbiosis*, derived from the field of biology—the study of living things—is widely used to stress the interrelatedness of all living things. The prefix *sym-* is a Greek preposition used as part of a compound word and signifies "together, interdependent, mutual, reciprocal." The morpheme *-bios-* in Greek signifies "life in all of its appearances and expressions." Hence the term symbios- literally means "life together, interdependent life, life lived mutually or reciprocally." When used to characterize a type of attitude toward the natural process, symbiosis denotes the accommodation of humanity to the natural process in a relationship of harmony, unity, and organic wholeness. Symbiotic persons regard themselves as one with the natural world, from which they draw their sustenance and meaning with a minimum of disruption and interference. This type of relationship is exemplified by how most animals behave in their natural environment. Few animals kill for the sake of killing. Animals will kill out of hunger, sometimes out of fear, in self-defense, or perhaps as a part of a life ritual such as mating. But few ravage for the sake of ravaging.

Some cultures strongly reflect this type of primary understanding. The cultures of Native Americans are and were symbiotic in relation to the natural process. Likewise, the Chinese and Japanese cultural ethos, the bygone culture of ancient Egypt, and many isolated Western cultures today reflect this mentality. More developed expressions of symbiotic awareness may be found in aspects of popular Hindu religion—veneration of animals, especially the cow; reverence toward rivers and lakes, especially the Ganges; the recognition of the process of life/death, creation/destruction, within the natural process, as mediated through the worship of Shiva; *ahimsa*, nonviolation of living things; and the extremely profound recognition of the continuity and interdependence of human existence, *samsara*, or rebirth/redeath.

This symbiotic attitude is not absent in Western culture: Rod McKuen's 1960s poem *The Earth* and several other poems, much of Robert Frost and Thoreau, and the strain of nature-mysticism within Christianity. Even the preoccupation of many Westerners with sex—including its mutation in advertising—may be only a disguised expression of the ancient, symbiotic nature/human fertility cult. But on the whole, Western culture, unlike the cultures of the East, has not been dominated by the symbiotic consciousness.

This mentality, therefore, is seldom found in pure form. Even in the cultures and for those individuals most shaped by symbiotic awareness, a distinction is noted—in varying degrees—between humanity and the rest of nature. The totem of an Eskimo tribe may be one of community, even as in prehistoric Nile culture a village appears to have identified with a particular animal; but the existence of the totem itself reflects at least an unconscious awareness that the totem animal or plant is distinguishable from the group. Even where the affirmation of the natural process is depicted in religious or divine imagery, the distinction between humanity and the world is preserved. Yet the symbiotic perspective persists as the dominant tone of humanity's sense of relationship to the natural process. This perspective values stability and order and tends to encourage the status quo. Change—when it means interference or manipulation or reordering of the natural process—is resisted. One is encouraged to observe and to adjust to the natural process rather than to manipulate it.

From a religious perspective, this mentality is based on the perception of a Divine Power or force that is immanent in the natural process (see Unit 40), including humanity. This Divine Power may be depicted in many ways: the Japanese veneration of *kami*, the precommunist Chinese reverence for Heaven and the ancestors, *shaktism* in India, the love of natural order and beauty in the West, the experience of the psychic powers of sexuality. These are only a few examples. In any case, nature itself—including humanity—is considered an expression or materialization of the Divine Presence.

> Nature is an indispensable part of me, especially mountains. I am really looking forward to this summer when I can again be in the mountains. It is in the mountains where I find real peace. I can feel life and really be aware of it, and not just take it for granted. I feel closer to God when I am alone in the mountains than any other time. Then I know there is a God who is still active whereas at other times I'm not really sure.[1]

APOBIOSIS

The term *apobiosis*, coined for our purposes, signifies the antithesis of symbiosis. The prefix *apo-* is the Greek preposition meaning "apart, separate from, alienated." Hence the compound apobiosis reflects humanity's apartness, its separation, its lack of oneness with the natural order. Or more positively, people see themselves as detached from the natural process, and not only free from it, but also impelled to oversee, manipulate, and exploit it for their own ends.

This mentality is one of the wellsprings of the technological thrust of European and North American culture and has at least two sources in its history: on the one hand, the affirmation in Greek culture of humanity's capacity to understand and to order phenomena through reason; on the other hand, the conviction drawn from the Jewish tradition and mediated through Christianity that God and humanity stand somewhat apart from the natural process. Examples of this attitude are seen in the "naming" of the animals in the creation story of Genesis 2 and the injunction to humans to "fill . . . subdue . . . have dominion" in Genesis 1. Both of these components issued eventually in the

[1] Unpublished student journal of Beth Utton. Used by permission.

intellectual and artistic rebirth called the Renaissance in fourteenth- and fifteenth-century Europe; in exploration, settlement, and development of new political and social patterns; in the industrial revolution; and in the awesome development of modern science and technology. The *apobiotic* mentality is a requisite for the conquest of space, disease, and all other frontiers.

Yet it is striking that only in Western Europe and North America do we find the sustained advancement of science and technology; only recently, along with expanded interaction with Western culture, have these advances appeared throughout the world. One reason for this may be found in the observation that while other cultures have enjoyed advanced scientific progress they have not generally sustained their technological applications of this knowledge. An explanation may lie in the attitude toward the natural world that developed among the three Western religions. Harvey Cox, in his work *The Secular City*, credits the beginning of the Western image of the human relationship to the natural order to the transcendent understandings of God that dominated first Hebrew and then the Christian and Islamic traditions. These religions share a strong emphasis on transcendent deity, which also gives to humanity a semitranscendent role in the natural order. Embracing such a concept, however, Muslims more often see the natural order as one channeled through submission to the sovereignty of Allah, who has created, controls, and provides for those who abide by his will. On the other hand, European Jews and Christians combined their traditional understandings of human separation from the natural order with the rediscovered Greco/Roman emphasis on reason and practicality when they began to think of the natural order as something to be manipulated and controlled. In doing so they were thinking apobiotically. This generated a mentality that eventually found its fruition in modern Western science and technology, where technology (which means "building knowledge") depends on apobiotic individuals who think of themselves as the builders.

Again, one may not find a pure expression of apobiosis. The contrast with symbiosis lies not in the means but in the objective. Both rely on observation, but symbiotic people observe so that they may participate. Apobiotic people observe so that they may manipulate, although in their apobiotic efforts they are often caught up in the order and beauty they are seeking to understand and then harness. Affective involvement fostering harmony and identification with the natural process has no place in a scientific experiment or technological application. The astronauts of the Apollo series, looking out at the lunar terrain, may have been awestruck by the sight, but this was extracurricular as far as their mission was concerned: They were after rocks, not scenery. Their response to the moonscape was symbiotic, but their mission was apobiotic. As men they combined the two. The apobiotic mentality aims at conquest and change, harnessing the powers (no longer divine) of nature. Exploitation, frustration, disorder, or failure may occur, but only at the price of humanity's creativity, a creativity that transcends the natural order.

Thus the natural process itself does not contain a divine presence. Humanity, by becoming master of nature, shares in the transcendent power of God.

> Presecular man lives in an enchanted forest. Its glens and groves swarm with spirits. Its rocks and streams are alive with friendly or fiendish demons. Reality is charged with a magical power that erupts here and there to threaten or benefit man. Properly managed and utilized, this invisible energy can be supplicated, warded off, or channeled. If real skill

and esoteric knowledge are called into play, the energies of the unseen world can be used against a family foe or an enemy of the tribe. . . .

Many historians of religion believe that this magical world-view, although developed and organized in a very sophisticated way, was never really broken through until the advent of biblical faith. The Sumerian, Egyptian, and Babylonian religious systems, despite their fantastically complicated theologies and their enormously refined symbol systems, remained a form of high magic, relying for their cohesion on the integral relation between man and the cosmos. . . . Both god and man were part of nature.

This is why the Hebrew view of Creation signals such a marked departure. It separates nature from God and distinguishes man from nature. This is the beginning of the disenchantment process. . . . Whereas in the Babylonian accounts, the sun, moon, and stars are semidivine beings, partaking the divinity of the gods themselves, their religious status is totally rejected by the Hebrews. . . . None of the heavenly bodies can claim any right to religious awe or worship.

Nor is man tied to nature by kinship ties. The lines of kinship in the Bible are temporal, not spatial. Instead of reaching out to encompass kangaroos and totem shrubs, they reach back to the sagas of the fathers and forward to the fortunes of the children's children. . . . Just after his creation man is given the crucial responsibility of naming the animals. He is their master and commander. It is his task to subdue the earth. Nature is neither his brother nor his god. As such it offers him no salvation. . . . For the Bible, neither man nor God is defined by his relationship to nature. This not only frees both of them for history, it also makes nature itself available for man's use.[2]

The contrast between symbiosis and apobiosis may be illustrated by the response to the following situation: A certain city was located on a river that received water from a large watershed. At intervals the watershed far above the city would receive large amounts of rainfall, causing the river, without perceptible reason, to overflow, resulting in severe damage to the urban area. The symbiotic inhabitants tried to combat the problem by clearing the channel of underbrush and building their houses on stilts. Yet to a large measure, they remained vulnerable to the threat of the river. The apobiotic inhabitants were not opposed to these measures but in addition sought to build dams upstream to control the flow of water. In so doing, they created an even greater hazard if one of the dams should break. Both had at least one thing in common: Both symbiosis and apobiosis regard the natural process as having reality. The third mentality differs on this point.

DIABIOSIS

The term *diabiosis*, also coined for our purposes, is compounded from the noun *bios* and the prepositional prefix *dia-*. This preposition is used in Greek to signify movement through a place, duration through a time, or the agent or instrument by which something is accomplished. *Diabiosis*, therefore, regards nature as that through which one must move if one is to reach reality. In this view, the natural process is regarded as changing, impermanent, imperfect, and of secondary importance at best. The diabiotic person believes that one must penetrate or survive the natural order to arrive at that which is real and eternal.

[2] Harvey Cox, *The Secular City* (New York: Macmillan, 1965), pp. 21–23. Copyright © Harvey Cox, 1965, 1966.

The culture of India most consistently exhibits diabiosis as the dominant mentality. As Heinrich Zimmer states, the natural process, including human existence itself, is considered "as fugitive and evanescent as cloud and mist." Humanity may be deluded by the seductiveness of *maya*, but in the end, that which is ultimate and real can be known only when the illusion dissolves. This Indian perspective continues in the movement of *Mahavira*, modern Jainism. In this tradition, the natural process is identified with "matter," which attaches itself to the soul through sin and can be purged only through asceticism and the practice of nonviolence toward all living things. Only then can the soul become free. Another child of Indian culture, *Buddhism*, also exhibits this mentality toward the natural process, including humanity's ego and culture: Gautama, the initiator, regarded not matter but destructive craving as that which perpetuated one's egoistic existence and bound him or her to the world of illusion. Later Buddhists held to this position. Yet, unlike Gautama, they returned to the conviction that beyond this illusory existence is cosmic reality, be it compassion or energy, and only by penetrating through maya can this reality be reached. In the philosophical form of Taoism in China we also encounter the conviction of a reality beyond. Yet unlike Indian culture, this reality—or Tao—is also within the natural process. Thus the knowledge of Tao informs and transforms one's relationship to the natural process. Nature, then, is not unreal; rather, it is dependent for its existence and meaning on the Tao inherent in it.

This diabiotic mentality is not absent from Western culture, especially in the Christian tradition. From the very earliest times some Christians have seen the natural process as irretrievably corrupted by human sin. The natural process, therefore, is regarded as temporary, as that which must soon pass away. People, in this view, are at best pilgrims in a strange land, and at worst victims of the natural order. *The Revelation to John* of Patmos is the strongest New Testament example; contemporary examples may be found on the radio, TV, and in the newspapers. Other non-Christian Western expressions of this diabiotic view may be noted in Greco-Roman times in Platonism and neo-Platonism, Stoicism, Gnosticism, and Manicheanism. Modern non-Christian Western expressions may be found in the alcohol and drug cultures, in which one attempts to escape the world as one experiences it.

Diabiotic people seek release from a natural process that is regarded as corrupt, illusory, or secondary. Because they seek reality beyond, they tend to neglect and abandon societal problems and values. The quest is an individual one: One is primarily concerned with saving oneself, and the rest, if necessary, must look out for themselves.

> The *māyā* of the gods is their power to assume diverse shapes by displaying at will various aspects of their subtle essence. But the gods are themselves the productions of a greater *māyā*: the spontaneous self-transformation of an originally undifferentiated, all-generating divine Substance. And this greater *māyā* produces, not the gods alone, but the universe in which they operate. All the universes co-existing in space and succeeding each other in time, the planes of being and the creatures of those planes where natural or supernatural, are manifestations from an inexhaustible, original and eternal well being, and are made manifest by a play of *māyā*. . . .
>
> *Māyā* is Existence: both the world of which we are aware, and ourselves who are contained in the growing and dissolving environment, growing and dissolving in our turn. At the same time, *Māyā* is the supreme power that generates and animates the display: the

dynamic aspect of the universal Substance. Thus it is at once, effect (the cosmic flux), and cause (the creative power). In the latter regard it is known as Shakti, "Cosmic Energy." . . .

Enthralled by ourselves and the effects of our environment, regarding the bafflements of *Māyā* as utterly real, we endure an endless ordeal of blandishments, desire and death; whereas, from a standpoint just beyond our ken (represented in the perennial esoteric tradition and known to the illimited, supraindividual consciousness of ascetic, yogic experience) *Māyā*—the world, the life, the ego, to which we cling—is as fugitive and evanescent as cloud and mist.[3]

It should be noted again that most societies manifest contrasting attitudes toward nature. Perhaps nowhere would one of the three types discussed in this unit be found in an entirely pure form. However, cultures may, over a long period of time, be characterized in a fairly definite way by one of the forms. India, for instance, and the Europe of the Patristic and early Middle Ages were essentially diabiotic in attitude and ideology, if not always in lifestyle. A society like that of contemporary Japan is interesting. With its mixture of Eastern religious traditions—Shinto (symbiotic) and Buddhism (with Zen, especially, characterized by both diabiotic and symbiotic streams)—and the emulation of Western technical-manipulative attitudes (apobiotic), one finds a stimulating, sometimes confusing, and possibly fruitful intermingling of attitudes.

❖❖❖

Do you find one dominant attitude, a conflict of attitudes, or a mixture of attitudes about the relation of human beings to the natural order in contemporary American society?

If you were asked to describe your own attitude toward nature using the descriptions given in this unit, which one would be most appropriate? Why?

Unit 79   Nature and the Natural

There is a profound religious dimension to our concepts of and attitudes toward the natural realm. Even our feelings about nature express this. When we respond to nature—whether we mean the world that the astronomer and physicist present in their highly abstract theories or the concrete experience of a sunset—the way that we *feel* embodies our commitment to and understanding of what seems to us to be of supreme value. In this unit, we attempt to explore some of the ambiguities—the many not always harmonious meanings—of the term *nature* as it is reflected in contrasting religious attitudes.

What do the terms *nature* and *natural* mean? Is nature the world of living things that the biologist studies, or is it the abstract, mathematically stated laws that the physicist gives us as a description of "reality"? Is nature what Romantic poets like Wordsworth wrote about? Is nature the realm of the sounds, scents, and colors that we experience? Or

---

[3] Heinrich Zimmer, *Myths and Symbols in Indian Art and Civilization*, ed. Joseph Campbell, Bollingen Series VI (Copyright © 1946 by Bollingen Foundation), reprinted with permission of Princeton University Press, pp. 24–26.

is it only the motion and interaction of events, waves, and particles—sound waves rather than sounds? Is it the sunsets and mountain peaks that the tourist sees? Is it what the hippie or the hermit who has abandoned the world of suburbia or the industrial centers returns to, a realm of cosmic and personal harmony? Is it the world of the jungle that the explorer seeks to conquer, where animal species struggle for survival?

Does nature include humanity's social institutions: Are civilizations, human societies, "natural"? Or is nature whatever exists independently of, or apart from, human activity? We speak of natural rather than artificial (manufactured) products. But are people a part of nature? Or do they stand over against it, different from it, opposed to it? Are people at war with nature? Or is nature, in people, at war with itself? Some religious traditions speak of humanity as evil by nature. Others speak of humanity as naturally good. One thing is certain: Not only must we ask whether different cultures and different traditions (or the same cultures in different moods or at different periods of time) have a positive or a negative attitude toward nature; we must also ask what they think of as natural and what they think nature includes.

MODERN WESTERN VIEWS OF NATURE

Alfred North Whitehead described a view of nature that arose as Western scientific thought took a new approach to physics and chemistry in the seventeenth century.

> Nature is that which we observe in perception through the senses. In . . . sense-perception we are aware of something which is not thought and which is self-contained for thought. This property of being self-contained for thought lies at the base of natural science. It means that nature can be thought of as a closed system whose . . . relations do not require the expression of the fact that they are thought about.[4]

This rather abstract definition is perhaps typical of what nature, as described by the laws of physics, has meant to many Western thinkers since the seventeenth century.

Describing the view of nature held by such seventeenth-century philosophers and scientists as Galileo, Descartes, Locke, and Newton, Whitehead wrote,

> We then ask in what sense are blueness and noisiness qualities of the body. By analogous reasoning, we also ask in what sense is its scent a quality of the rose.
>
> Galileo considered this question, and at once pointed out that, apart from eyes, ears, or noses, there would be no colours, sounds, or smells. . . . The occurrences of nature are in some way apprehended by minds, which are associated with living bodies. Primarily, the mental apprehension is aroused by the occurrences in certain parts of the correlated body, the occurrences in the brain, for instance. But the mind in apprehending also experiences sensations which, properly speaking, are qualities of the mind alone. These sensations are projected by the mind so as to clothe appropriate bodies in external nature. Thus the bodies are perceived as with qualities which in reality do not belong to them, qualities which in fact are purely the offspring of the mind. Thus nature gets credit which should in truth be reserved for ourselves: the rose for its scent: the nightingale for his song: and the sun for his radiance. The poets are entirely mistaken. They should address their

[4] Alfred North Whitehead, *The Concept of Nature* (Cambridge, MA: Cambridge University Press, 1920), p. 3.

lyrics to themselves, and should turn them into odes of self-congratulation on the excellence of the human mind. Nature is a dull affair, soundless, scentless, colourless; merely the hurrying of material endlessly, meaninglessly.

However you disguise it, this is the practical outcome of the characteristic philosophy which closed the seventeenth century.[5]

The Romantic poets Wordsworth and Coleridge, at the end of the eighteenth century, reacted against this way of conceiving nature, as did Whitehead himself in his philosophical writings. The Romantics and Whitehead conceived of nature as dynamic and alive, as a realm of feeling and meaning and value in which we are involved not first as abstract observers but as sentient participants.

EASTERN UNDERSTANDINGS OF NATURE

In contrast to both these Western approaches, in the Hindu civilization of India nature has been viewed negatively, as illusory or unreal—including the whole of existing reality, the natural and the social spheres. In China, nature has been viewed positively. According to the Confucians, nature is inclusive of the social order and its institutions and relationships: One is living "naturally" (harmoniously, as one ought to live) when one lives according to the rational and traditional precepts that make one a properly and actively functioning member of the social order. However, the Taoists regard the world of social institutions and moral precepts as artificial: Humanity lives naturally when it returns to the passive and harmonious simplicity of communion with mountain, flower, animal, and stream.

JEWISH, CHRISTIAN, ROMANTIC, AND ANTI-ROMANTIC VIEWS OF NATURE

Even before the post-seventeenth-century tendency to look at nature abstractly (see the quotations from Whitehead), there had been an ambivalence toward nature in Western thought. Both Judaism and Christianity emphasize that the created order—including the social order—is (or should be) good.

And God saw all that He had made, and it was very good. (Genesis 1:31, NEB)

This is certainly true of the "natural" world of cosmos and minerals, plants and animals (see Genesis 1). But Christianity especially has been inclined to suggest that nature was involved in the calamity of humanity's historical (individual and social) fall. Thus not only has humanity, through its sin, become alienated from nature (its own and that of the rest of the universe) but also the rest of nature has suffered.

And to the man God said:

"Because you have . . . eaten from the tree which I forbade you, accursed shall be the ground on your account. . . . It will grow thorns and thistles for you, none but wild plants. . . ." (Genesis 3:17–18, NEB)

[5] Alfred North Whitehead, *Science and the Modern World* (New York: Macmillan, 1948), pp. 78–80.

Paul in Romans 8:19–23 writes that the whole of creation, which has been subject to bondage and decay, is longing to be set free. Other Christian thinkers—for instance, John Milton in Adam's speech in the Tenth Book of *Paradise Lost*—develop the idea that nature and its order have been upset as a result of Adam's sin. Both Paul and Milton also suggest that nature is in fact being restored through God's redemptive activity in Christ.

Not only Romantic poets and writers like the American transcendentalist Thoreau but also contemporary poets have suggested that participation in a complex urban and industrialized society represents a fall from a harmonious relationship with nature and have called for a return to "natural simplicity." The American poet James Dickey has said,

> I'm much more interested in a man's relationship to the God-made world, or the universe-made world, than to the man-made world. The natural world seems infinitely more important to me than the man-made world. I remember a statement of D. H. Lawrence's; he said that as a result of our science and industrialization, we have lost the cosmos. The parts of the universe we can investigate by means of machinery and scientific empirical techniques we may understand better than our predecessors did, but we no longer know the universe emotionally. It's a great deal easier to relate to it as a collocation of chemical properties. There's no moon goddess now. But when men believed there was, then the moon was more important, maybe not scientifically, but more important emotionally. It was something a man had a personal relationship to, instead of its being simply a dead stone, a great ruined stone in the sky. The moon has always been very important to me. The astronauts have introduced me to a new kind of mythology about the moon. This may in the end be greater than the old Greek one.[6]

In contrast, according to Enid Starkie, the nineteenth-century French poet Charles Baudelaire believed

> that art existed only by reason of what man added of his own substance, of his own soul, to the raw material of nature. He could not endure the Romantic idealisation of nature, nor the Rousseau myth of the nobility of natural man, uncorrupted by civilisation. He believed, on the contrary, that the only value in man consisted in his spiritual essence, which only self-discipline and self-culture could develop, and that this was of greater price than anything which could be discovered in nature.... Baudelaire ... tried to put nature in her proper place, for he thought that man lost his pride and dignity by being too humble with her. The violence of his opinions is due to his reaction against sentimentality.[7]

How one understands nature profoundly affects how one lives and thinks. Religion and every other aspect of life are influenced by one's understanding of nature.

◆◆◆

> *What does the word* nature *mean to you? Which of the descriptions given above do you find most appealing? Why?*

> *How do your religious commitments relate to your view of nature?*

[6] James Dickey, *From Self-Interviews by James Dickey*, pp. 67–68.
[7] Enid Starkie, *Baudelaire* (New York: New Directions, 1958), p. 293.

✦✦✦ 19 ✦✦✦

ORDER AND ORIGINS

The previous chapter suggested that there are many ways to view the natural order in which we live. Many of the perspectives one may assume toward nature, as that chapter notes, are related to basic religious attitudes and understandings of humanity and its relationship to its universe. Yet, when we speak of *nature*, the natural world, and the universe, we refer not only to the immediate physical, psychosocial, and cultural setting of human activity; in one sense we also refer to the whole of reality that can be comprehended or imagined *by finite rational experimental processes*. Consequently, when we use the term *natural universe*, we may at times mean the realm that we apprehend through the senses. This is the realm normally studied by the various sciences. This realm of description, experimentation, and understanding is also of significant interest to religious traditions as the following units show. Most religious traditions have included among their cognitive features (their beliefs) concepts about the nature, origin, goal, destiny, and significance of the natural universe.

In considering the natural world, religion and science are often viewed as two separate ways of understanding reality; however, we assume that scientific understanding and religious understanding must be considered in a common context, especially since both religious vision and scientific method have influenced the modern view of the natural order.

Several modes of understanding the universe and its relationship to religion are investigated in this chapter. Unit 80 cites diverse creation stories and interpretations of creation drawn from religious traditions. These stories illustrate notable differences among religious traditions and suggest that the meaning of the natural order has significant implications for one's religious understanding. From concepts included in this unit, and the one that follows it, two important considerations emerge. First, as the Eastern and Western views of life come into closer contact, their views concerning the nature of the universe become more relevant in our modern pluralistic and highly interrelated world. Second, the prevailing view of modern science that reality is a *process* may give us tools for appropriating conflicting religious views of the universe.

Unit 81 explores another significant issue as it investigates the relationship of science and religion. Kepler and Copernicus represent giant minds in the modern scientific revolution, yet we must quickly note that although they were scientists, they depended heavily on religious interpretations in spelling out their new view of the universe. In more recent times, thinkers diverse in other ways represent a similar spirit. You may want to consider the following question as you read this unit: Can science and religion work together to lead to richer and deeper understanding of the universes present in our experience—the inner universe that we know in feeling and achieved self-consciousness and the external universe that we know through sense experience and the imaginative constructions of intellect? Both religion and science involve powerful impulses to creative and imaginative expression.

Unit 82 considers the contrast between religious traditions that emphasize time, history, and a personalized concept of the Divine and those that stress a timeless eternal natural order and an impersonal deity.

UNIT 80   RELIGIOUS VIEWS ON THE ORIGIN OF THE UNIVERSE

Although we may sometimes contrast religious approaches to the understanding of the natural universe with scientific or secular (the terms may not be interchangeable) approaches, it is important to realize that there have been and are contrasting religious attitudes toward the nature and origin of the universe.

How the universe, at least in its present configuration, originated; what its present stage of development is; and toward what future states it may be evolving—these questions have fascinated thoughtful and imaginative people in many ages. In contemporary astrophysics, the field of cosmology—the study of the structure and development of the universe—has grown excitingly in the past several decades. Scientists have been fascinated with concepts of an expanding universe. The model known as the "Big Bang" theory—that expansion of the universe began as a result of the explosion of densely packed matter some billions of years ago—currently seems to have won the day, but theorists continue to elaborate on the concept (see Unit 58).

Concepts and images relating to the origin and development of the universe have appeared in the world's religions, too. Integral to the religions has been an interest in understanding, or at least in recognizing, the power(s) or being(s) that activate(s) the process. Such interest often finds expression in images of God(s) as creator(s) and sustainer(s) of the universe. These images are numerous and yet varied in their understanding of the Divine, the process of creation, and humanity's place in it.

EGYPTIAN HYMN TO THE CREATOR (1300 B.C.E.)

Pharaoh Amenhotep IV, in the fourteenth century B.C.E., consolidated ancient Egyptian worship into worship of one God—the sun god, Aton. The following passages praising Aton stress his creativity, which is seen as a continuing process that is constantly renewing itself. (Compare this hymn with the Hebrew Psalm 104.)

Thy dawning is beautiful in the horizon of the sky,
O living Aton, Beginning of life!
When thou risest in the eastern horizon
Thou fillest every land with thy beauty.
Thou art beautiful, great, glittering, high above every land,
Thy rays, they encompass the lands, even all that thou has made. . . .

Creator of the germ in woman,
Maker of seed in man,
Giving life to the son in the body of the mother . . .

How manifold are thy works!
They are hidden from before us,
O sole God, whose powers no other possesseth.
Thou didst create the earth according to thy heart
While thou wast alone:
Men, all cattle large and small,
All that are on high,
That fly with their wings,
The foreign countries, Syria and Kush,
The land of Egypt;
Thou settest every man into his place,
Thou suppliest his necessities,
Everyone has his possessions,
And his days are reckoned.[1]

Arising from a common geographical and cultural matrix around the same time as the preceding Egyptian passage were two well-known stories of creation. The Babylonian *Enuma elish'* epic may be fruitfully compared with the Hebrew story found in Genesis 1. The similarities as well as the differences are striking and attest to the distinctive religious perspectives from which each account is written.

BABYLONIAN STORY OF CREATION (ABOUT 2000 B.C.E.)

The story begins with a picture of the earliest imaginable period of time, when only the divine pair, *Apsu*, the freshwater, and *Tiamat*, the saltwater, existed. Out of their commingling, the younger gods arose. When they began to cause disturbances, Apsu determined to destroy them, but they were able to kill him. Tiamat, the primordial saltwater, set out to avenge him. *Marduk*, one of the younger gods, was chosen to fight her. After extensive preparation, he engaged the primordial mother-god in battle. Marduk, referred to as "Sun of the heavens," succeeded in destroying her. What follows is the description of what he did with her body.

Then the lord [Marduk] paused to view her dead body,
That he might divide the monster and do artful works.
He split her like a shellfish into two parts:
Half of her he set up and ceiled it as sky,
Pulled down the bar and posted guards.

[1] "The Hymn to Aton," trans. J.H. Breasted, in *Development of Religion and Thought in Ancient Egypt* (New York: Scribner, 1912).

He bade them to allow not her waters to escape.
He crossed the heavens and surveyed the regions.
He squared Apsu's quarter, the abode of Nudimmud,
As the lord measured the dimensions of Apsu...

The Great Abode, Esharra, he made as the firmament.
Anu, Enlil, and Ea [gods] he made occupy their places.
He constructed stations for the great gods,
Fixing their astral likeness as constellations,
He determined the year by designating the zones:
He set up three constellations for each of the twelve months . . .

In her belly he established the zenith.
The Moon he caused to shine the night (to him) entrusting.
He appointed him a creature of the night to signify the days . . .
When Marduk hears the words of the gods,
His heart prompts (him) to fashion artful works.
Opening his mouth, he addresses Ea
To impart the plan he had conceived in his heart:
Blood I will mass and cause bones to be.
I will establish a savage, "man" shall be his name.
Verily, savage-man I will create.
He shall be charged with the service of the gods
    That they might be at ease! . . .

The most guilty of the gods is then selected to be killed as material for the creation of humankind.

It was Kingu who contrived the uprising,
And made Tiamat revel, and joined battle.
They bound him, holding him before Ea.
They imposed on him his guilt and severed his blood (vessels)
Out of his blood they fashioned mankind
He imposed the service and let free the gods,
After Ea, the wise, had created mankind,
Had imposed upon it the service of the gods.

Finally, after building a lofty shrine in Babylon, the gods feast.

The great gods took their seats,
They set up festive drink, sat down to a banquet.[2]

HEBREW STORY OF CREATION (AFTER 1300 B.C.E.)

In the beginning when God created the heavens and the earth, the earth was a formless void and darkness covered the face of the deep, while a wind from God swept over the face of the waters.

[2] "The Creation Epic," from "Akkadian Myths and Epics," trans. E.A. Speiser, in *Ancient Near Eastern Texts Relating to the Old Testament*, 3rd ed., ed. James B. Pritchard, with Supplement. Copyright 1969 by Princeton University Press, renewed 1978, pp. 66–69. Reprinted by permission of Princeton University Press.

Then God said, "Let there be light"; and there was light. And God saw that the light was good; and God separated the light from the darkness. God called the light Day, and the darkness he called Night. And there was evening and there was morning, the first day.

And God said, "Let there be a dome in the midst of the waters, and let it separate the waters from the waters." . . . And it was so. And God called the dome Sky . . . the second day.

And God said, "Let the waters under the sky be gathered together into one place, and let the dry land appear." And it was so. God called the dry land Earth, and the waters that were gathered together he called Seas . . . And God saw that it was good . . . a third day.

And God said, "Let there be lights in the dome of the sky to separate the day from the night; and let them be for signs and for seasons and for days and for years, and let them be lights in the dome of the sky to give light upon the earth" . . . And God saw that it was good. . . . a fourth day.

And God said, " Let the waters bring forth swarms of living creatures, and let birds fly above the earth across the dome of the sky." And God saw that it was good . . . a fifth day.

And God said, "Let the earth bring forth living creatures of every kind: cattle and creeping things and wild animals of the earth of every kind."

Then God said, " Let us make humankind in our image, according to our likeness; and let them have dominion over the fish of the sea, and over the birds of the air, and over the cattle, and over all the wild animals of the earth, and over every creeping thing that creeps upon the earth." . . . male and female he created them. God blessed them . . . God saw everything that he had made, and indeed, it was very good. And there was evening and there was morning, a sixth day.

Thus the heavens and the earth were finished, and all their multitude. And on the seventh day God finished his work that he had done, and he rested on the seventh day . . . So God blessed the seventh day and hallowed it. . . .(Genesis 1:1-2:3, NRSV)

◆◆◆

What is the reason for creation in each of these stories?

The nature or character of the Gods(s) is reflected in these stories: How is it similar or different in each?

What is the character of the human being created in each account? What is the purpose for which the human was created?

What materials were used in creation? What is their origin?

◆◆◆

OTHER WESTERN UNDERSTANDINGS OF CREATION

These stories comment on the beginning of the universe; creation is an event in the past. Many interpreters regard these stories, whether Egyptian, Babylonian, or Hebrew, as attempts to express in symbolic language a basic religious understanding of the relation of the Divine to the natural universe and human life. There are other ways to understand creation, as the following passage shows. Martin Luther (1483–1546 C.E.) believed that the creative process continues; it is not something that happened only in the past.

Even as God in the beginning of creation made the world out of nothing, whence He is called the Creator and the Almighty, so His manner of working continues still the same.

Even now and unto the end of the world, all His works are such that out of that which is nothing, worthless, despised, wretched and dead, He makes that which is something, precious, honorable, blessed and living. Again, whatever is something, precious, honorable, blessed and living, He makes to be nothing, worthless, despised, wretched and dying. After this manner no creature can work; none can produce anything out of nothing.[3]

Luther also stressed the sustaining nature of God's activity.

I believe that God has made me and all creatures; that He has given me my body and soul, eyes, ears, and all my members, my reason and all my senses, and still preserves them, also clothing and shoes, meat and drink, house and home, wife and children, fields, cattle, and all my goods; that He richly and daily provides me with all that I need to support this body and life; that He defends me against all danger and guards and protects me from all evil; and all this purely out of fatherly, divine goodness and mercy, without any merit or worthiness in me; for all of which it is my duty to thank and praise, to serve and obey him.[4]

In many ways Luther's understanding of an ongoing creation and the continuing activity of the Divine in the natural order reflects a strand of ancient Christian insight into God's activity and, at the same time, resonates with modern scientific concepts of the nature of an expanding, still developing universe.

Because of emphasis on the uniqueness of the creation and its directedness toward a purpose under the creating and preserving, renewing activity of God, Western religious traditions have also emphasized that *time* is crucial. The ancient Greeks, though they held to cyclical views of time, pictured time in two figures: *Chronos*, an old gray-headed man, bent with the burden of the past of a world grown old, and *Kairos*, a young man running swiftly, the back of his head shaven smooth. Chronos, old Father Time, represents the moment-by-moment, day-by-day, year-by-year passage of time that robs us of youth and opportunity. With Chronos, we see the world grown old and tired. If we run with Kairos we know time as opportunity to be seized in the decisive moment. Judaism, Christianity, and Islam have seen time as Kairos, bringing hope and promise of a redeemed future for individuals and the world.

EASTERN ACCOUNTS OF CREATION

When we turn our attention from Western concepts of creation to those of the East, other distinctive aspects arise. Because Hindus stress the union of an individual's soul (Atman) with the world-soul (Brahman), they are less concerned with concepts of time and history (see Unit 10). Nevertheless, the importance of the creative process does not escape attention, as the following passage from the *Mundaka-Upanishad* shows. Notice the reincarnation and reunion motifs that underlie the statement.

This is the truth. As from a blazing fire sparks, being like unto fire, fly forth a thousandfold, thus are various beings brought forth from the Imperishable, my friend, and return thither also.

[3] Martin Luther, "The Magnifcat," *The Works of Martin Luther*, Vol. III (Philadelphia: Muhlenberg Press, 1930), p.127.
[4] Martin Luther, *Smaller Catechism* (St. Louis: Concordia Publishing House, 1943), p. 6.

That heavenly Person is without body, he is both without and within, not produced, without breath and without mind, pure, higher than the high Imperishable.

From him (when entering on creation) is born breath, mind, and all organs of sense, either, air, light, water, and the earth, the support of all.

Fire (the sky) is his head, his eyes the sun and the moon, the quarters his ears, his speech the Vedas disclosed, the wind his breath, his heart the universe; from his feet came the earth; he is indeed the inner Self of all things.

From him comes *Agni* (fire), the sun being the fuel; from the moon (Soma) comes rain (Parganya); from the earth herbs; and man gives seed unto the woman. Thus many things are begotten from the Person (purusha).

From him come the *Rig*, the Saman, the Yagush, the Diksha (initiatory rites), all sacrifices and offerings of animals, and the fees bestowed on priests, the year too, the sacrificer, and the worlds, in which the moon shines brightly and the sun.

From him the many Devas too are begotten, the Sadhyas (genii), men, cattle, birds, the up and down breathings, rice and corn (for sacrifice), penance, faith, truth, abstinence, and law.

The seven senses (prana) also spring from him, the seven lights (acts of sensation), the seven kinds of fuel (objects by which the senses are lighted), the seven sacrifices (results of sensation), these seven worlds (the places of the senses, the worlds determined by the senses) in which the senses move, which rest in the cave (of the heart), and are placed there seven and seven.

Hence come the seas and all the mountains, from him flow the rivers of every kind; hence come all herbs and juice through which the inner Self subsists with the elements.

The Person is all this, sacrifice, penance, Brahman, the highest immortal; he who knows this hidden in the cave (of the heart), he, O friend, scatters the knot of ignorance here on earth.[5]

Although Hinduism's picture of creation magnifies the mystery of the Brahman-Atman nature, Japan's ancient Shinto religion embodies a creation myth comparable to those in many Western traditions. Concerned only with the islands of Japan, it accounts for creation from a distinctively nationalistic viewpoint. The following summarization of this complicated Japanese tradition is by John Noss.

The Japanese islands are a special creation of the gods. After the primal chaos had in the course of events separated into heaven and ocean, various gods appeared in the heavenly drift-mist, only to disappear without event, until finally there came upon the scene the two deities who produced the Japanese islands and their inhabitants. These were the primal male and female, Izanagi, the Male-Who-Invites, and Izanami, the Female-Who-Invites. Their heavenly associates commanded them to "make, consolidate, and give birth to" the Japanese islands. These two beings descended the Floating Bridge of Heaven (a rainbow?), and when they reached its lower end, Izanagi pushed down his jeweled spear into the muddy brine and stirred it until the fluid below them became "thick and glutinous." Then he drew the spear up, whereupon "the brine that dripped down from the end of the spear was piled up and became an island." Stepping down on the island, they came together, and Izanami bore from her womb the eight great islands of Japan.

After the creation of a number of lesser deities Izanami dies and goes to the underworld. Izanagi unsuccessfully attempts to rescue her and a period of conflict and disorder ensues. During this period Izanagi produces the sun-goddess, the moon-god, and the storm-god.

[5] *The Upanishads*, E. Max Muller, trans. Vol. II (New York: Dover, n.d.), pp. 34–35.

Years later, we find the sun-goddess, Amaterasu, looking down from her seat in heaven and becoming concerned about the disorder in the islands below. The storm-god's son was ruling there, but she was not satisfied. She finally commissioned her grandson Ni-ni-gi to descend to the islands and rule them for her. . . .[In later times Ni-ni-gi's great grandson Jimmu Tenno became the first human emperor of the islands and established his capital on the central island, Honshu, in 660 B.C.E.]

Meanwhile, the leading families of Japan and the whole Japanese people were thought to have descended from the minor deities, or lesser kami, residing on the islands.

Thus, we are to understand that the emperor of Japan is a descendant in an unbroken line from the sun-goddess, Amaterasu, and that the islands of Japan have a divine origin, and so also the Japanese people.[6]

◆◆◆

Why have the world's religions been occupied with the attempt to explain the origin of the universe?

How many different accounts of the "nature and destiny of humanity and natural order" do you find in the accounts in this unit?

What is the relation of humans to God and to the natural universe in each account?

How will contemporary persons deal with the differences between the Hebraic affirmation of the natural order as basically good and the Hindu view of the world as illusory or unreal?

UNIT 81   RELIGIOUS VISION AND SCIENTIFIC METHOD

Recent scientific developments have added great interest to questions about the origin and nature of the universe. There is now perhaps a greater awareness of cosmology than has existed since the time of Copernicus, Kepler, Galileo, and Newton. In this unit we will examine the role of religious components in the creation of a new cosmology by examining the work of one of the great scientific investigators of an earlier period and explore the relation of scientific thought to religious vision in our time.

Religious concepts and images have been used in the past as a basis for scientific work and may well be continuing to function in the creative imagination that leads to scientific discovery. For example, Johannes Kepler was one of the founders of exact modern science, an astronomer who not only championed but also corrected and refined the Copernican model that placed the sun, rather than the earth, at the center of our planetary system. E.A. Burtt has described how a number of essentially religious conceptions about the nature of the universe (or cosmos) influenced Kepler to adopt the revolutionary new theory.

In his subsequently expressed reasons for accepting Copernicanism this central position of the sun is always included, usually first. This ascription of deity to the sun was covered over by Kepler with such mystical allegorization as was necessary to give it a hearing in

[6] Noss and Noss, A *History of the World's Religions*, pp. 359–361.

the prevailing theological environment, with especial reference to the doctrine of the Trinity. The sun, according to Kepler, is God the Father, the sphere of the fixed stars is God the Son, the intervening ethereal medium, through which the power of the sun is communicated to impel the planets around their orbits, is the Holy Ghost. To pronounce this allegorical trapping is not to suggest, of course, that Kepler's Christian theology is at all insincere; it is rather that he had discovered an illuminating natural proof and interpretation to it, and the whole attitude, with its animism and allegoriconaturalistic approach, is quite typical of much thinking of the day.... But the connexion between Kepler, the sunworshipper, and Kepler, the seeker of exact mathematical knowledge of astronomical nature, is very close. It was primarily by such considerations as the deification of the sun and its proper placing at the centre of the universe that Kepler in the years of his adolescent fervour and warm imagination was induced to accept the new system: But, his mind immediately proceeded, and here his mathematics and his Neo-Pythagoreanism come into play, if the system is true, there must be many other mathematical harmonies in the celestial order that can be discovered and proclaimed as confirmation of Copernicanism, by an intensive study of the available data. This was a task in exact mathematics, and it was very fortunate for Kepler that he was just plunging into such profound labours at the time when Tycho Brahe, the greatest giant of observational astronomy since Hipparchus, was completing his life-long work of compiling a vastly more extensive and incomparably precise set of data than had been in the possession of any of his predecessors. Kepler had joined Tycho Brahe the year before the latter's death and had full access to his magnificent accumulations.... Both Copernicus and Kepler were firmly convinced for religious reasons of the uniformity of motion, i.e., each planet in its revolution is impelled by a constant and never failing cause, hence Kepler's joy at being able to "save" this principle as regards the areas even though it had to be surrendered as regards the planet's path.[7]

Kepler's close identification of religion and science has often been lost in the modern world. Many people see a conflict between the knowledge gained through scientific investigation and that found in religious insights.

Particularly in the eighteenth and nineteenth centuries, many educated people felt that there was conflict and antagonism between the Newtonian concept of the natural order—often interpreted as leading to a view of the universe as a completely mechanical, "clockwork," deterministic machine—and religious views of the universe as alive and the scene of encounter between the human spirit and the Divine. The revival of modern day attacks on Darwinian concepts of evolution by "scientific creationists" reflects the belief of some Christians that there are conflicts between biblical accounts of creation and God's role in it and widely accepted results of modern scientific inquiry. Convinced that such conflicts exist, proponents of the scientific creationist position often seek to have creationism taught in American public schools as an "alternative theory" to that of biological evolution.

Yet this understanding of a conflict—alleged or real—is not shared by everyone. Interpreters of Hinduism and Buddhism have pointed to what they consider to be profound analogies between modern scientific cosmology and microphysics and concepts of Hinduism and Buddhism involving space, time, the evolving universe, and the self. After an initial impulse in late nineteenth- and early twentieth-century theology to separate

[7] E.A. Burtt, *Metaphysical Foundations of Modern Physical Science*, 2nd rev. ed. (London: Routledge and Kegan Paul, 1932), p. 48.

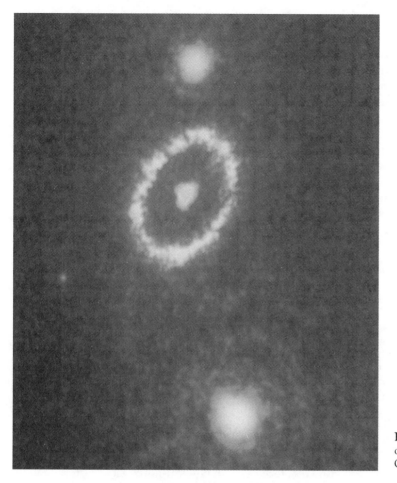

Figure 19.1 Celestial Photo of Stars (Nova Development Corp.)

science from religion (by saying that science deals with facts whereas religion deals with values, or value-laden interpretations of the significance of facts), an increasing number of Jewish and Christian thinkers have been interested in exploring the relationship between religious belief and the new science.

The Catholic priest and paleontologist Pierre Teilhard de Chardin interpreted the evolutionary process, as disclosed in geological, biological, and cosmological sciences, as under the guidance of the divine Spirit. He believed that contemporary scientific insight can sensitize us to the Divine's presence and purposes.[8] Though Teilhard's theories are controversial and opposed by some biologists, philosophers, and theologians, some interpreters are convinced that they are worthy of continued investigation.[9] His works provide an impressive synthesis of religious vision and scientific passion.

[8] See especially Pierre Teilhard de Chardin, *The Future of Man* (New York: Harper and Row, 1964).
[9] See Edward Dodson, *The Phenomenon of Man Revisited: A Biological Viewpoint on Teilhard de Chardin* (New York: Columbia University Press, 1984).

The writings of another contemporary thinker, Michael Polanyi, contain interesting speculations concerning the relation in contemporary scientific work of an intuitive vision of reality to exact scientific procedures. In *The Tacit Dimension*, Polanyi explored a dimension, or process, of mind that he called "tacit knowing." According to Polanyi, tacit—intuitive, nonreflective—knowing plays an essential role in scientific discovery, in guiding scientists to the problems that lead to new discoveries. Flashes of insight, lucky guesses, and intuitions are examples of tacit knowledge emerging into consciousness—in much the same way that new forms of life emerge from simpler forms.[10]

Alfred North Whitehead was another twentieth-century thinker who shared Polanyi's belief that exact scientific theorizing begins in an intuitive, feeling-level relationship to nature that may be called *religious* since it involves a sense of a relationship (that can never be given complete and exact conceptual expression) to the whole and potential wholeness of things. Mathematician, logician, philosopher of science, and metaphysician, Whitehead wrote,

> Nature is a process. As in the case of everything directly exhibited in sense-awareness, there can be no explanation of this characteristic of nature. All that can be done is to use language which may speculatively demonstrate it, and also express the relation of this factor in nature to other factors.
>
> It is an exhibition of the process of nature that each duration happens and passes. The process of nature can also be termed the passage of nature. Also the passage of nature is exhibited equally in spatial transition as well as in temporal transition. It is in virtue of its passage that nature is always moving on. It is involved in the meaning of this property of "moving on" that not only is any act of sense-awareness just that act and no other, but the terminus of each act is also unique and is the terminus of no other act. Sense-awareness seizes its only chance and presents for knowledge something which is for it alone.[11]

For discussion of the relevance to religion of contemporary theories of cosmology and the nature of the universe, especially of the Big-Bang theory, see Unit 58.

Many have found that not only the new cosmology, with its vision of a dynamic universe that embraces evolutionary processes on a physical-universal as well as biological-terrestrial scale, but also the newer theories of the microcosm, begun with Max Planck's and Albert Einstein's quantum physics (1900–1905) and continuing to the latest experimental and speculative theories concerning the physics of elementary particles, partly derive from and possibly support a dynamic religious vision of reality.[12]

---

[10] See Michael Polanyi, *The Tacit Dimension* (New York: Doubleday, 1966) and *Personal Knowledge* (Chicago: University of Chicago Press, 1958).

[11] Alfred North Whitehead, *The Concept of Nature* (Cambridge: Cambridge University Press, 1920), pp. 53–54.

[12] See especially, from the scientific side, such works as Nigel Calder, *The Key to the Universe* (New York: Viking Press, 1977); Gary Zukav, *The Dancing Wu LiMasters: An Overview of the New Physics* (New York: Bantam Books, 1980); Ilya Prigogine, *Order Out of Chaos: Man's New Dialogue with Nature* (New York: Bantam Books, 1984); Kitty Ferguson, *Stephen Hawking: Quest for a Theory of Everything* (New York: Bantam Books, 1992); Stephen W. Hawking, *A Brief History of Time* (New York: Bantam Books, 1988); and Paul Davies, *God and the New Physics* (New York: Simon and Schuster, 1983); William A. Dembski, *Intelligent Design: The Bridge Between Science and Theology* (Downers Grove IL: Intervarsity Press,1999); Francis J. Tipler, *The Principles of Immortality* (New York: Doubleday, 1994). For a discussion including scientists and theologians, see James E. Loder and W. Jim Neidhardt, *The Knights Move: The Relational Logic of the Spirit in Theology and Science* (Colorado Springs: Helmers and Howard, 1992).

During the past two decades, interest has been shown by many scientists, especially cosmologists and astrophysicists, as well as philosophers and theologians, in what has come to be called the Anthropic Principle.[13] The principle is an updated non-deistic version of the argument from design. The argument from design has been appealed to in philosophical theology from the time of Plato and was developed by Thomas Aquinas in the thirteenth century. It became very popular during the eighteenth century. It was then in "the Age of Reason" based on theistic inferences from the mechanistic picture of the universe drawn by many on the basis of Newtonian mechanics. According to this view, the universe is a machine planned, designed, and made by a Perfectly Wise Creator who imposed the laws of physics on his creation and left it to run in accordance with these laws. God's existence can be inferred from the order and design of the universe. This is the deistic form of the "Argument from Design" (see Unit 40).

During the eighteenth century, many orthodox Christians accepted the premises and conclusion of this deistic argument but amended it, holding that God occasionally intervened in the world He had made with a miracle that required suspension of natural law, thereby proving His existence in a way that went beyond deism. This or these forms of the argument from design fell into disrepute in the nineteenth century when evolutionary theorists explained many of the apparently well-designed features of the universe (such as parts and characteristics of animals that help them survive) as a result of blind and purposeless natural selection by the environment.

In more recent times, many theologians have objected to the eighteenth-century concept of God in both its deistic and orthodox forms. They have seen the concept of God as cosmic planner, designer, engineer, and builder as misleadingly literalistic and anthropomorphic, making God merely a finitelike being confined most of the time to the second, supernatural level of a two-storied universe.

The Anthropic Principle can reject both deistic and orthodox forms of the design argument but brings into discussions of cosmology and the sciences interesting suggestions related to purpose and directedness that may well serve as reasons for belief in a nonanthropomorphic deity. The principle has two forms. The weak form of the Anthropic Principle emphasizes the fact that in order for the universe to be comprehended or understood, it had to produce beings capable of understanding it. The strong, more interesting, form of the principle suggests that given the remarkable convergence of factors that had to come together to produce beings capable of understanding the universe, the universe must contain or be based on intelligent purpose.

For many people, contemporary physics discloses a sense of grandeur and mystery in its emerging vision of reality. Such elements constantly challenge traditional interpretations of the relationship of science and religion and perhaps leave room for a much closer identification of religion with science than has often been assumed.

Contemporary scientific research confirms that there are billions of galaxies in the presently known universe. Our sun and its assembly of planets is a tiny part of the huge galaxy called the Milky Way. When we look at this cloudy line across the sky, we are looking toward the nucleus of the galaxy. The cloud is the mass of millions of objects,

---

[13] See John D. Barrow and Frank J. Tipler, *The Anthropic Cosmological Principle* (Oxford: Oxford University Press), 1986; see also Errol E. Harris, *Cosmos and Theos* (Atlantic Highlands, NJ: Humanities Press International, Inc.), 1992.

stars, and star systems. It takes light, at the speed of 186,000 miles per second, approximately 70,000 years to travel across *this* galaxy alone, which is one of millions of galaxies. Many contemporary scientists combining this information with the "Big Bang" theory of the origin of the universe find it easier to entertain traditional religious affirmations concerning the nature and origin of the universe—affirmations that teach that creation is caused and sustained by a Divine principle.

Within the last decade of the twentieth century, questions arose about the possibility that there would soon be reached within the most basic of the sciences (physics, cosmology) an "end of science." Sometimes this meant only that government would become more and more reluctant to fund "big science" (such as the supercollider that was begun but later scrapped near Waxahachie, Texas) and therefore there would be no further progress in discoveries or in testing theories. Sometimes the prediction of "end of science" sounded pessimistic, meaning that everything that can be understood of the natural world by humans will soon have been discovered, leaving the rest of nature's secrets an impenetrable mystery. At other times the prediction of the "end of science" sounded wildly optimistic. Stephen Hawking suggested that humans might soon have discovered "all there is" of the basic laws of nature. Hawking saw such a possibility as real and imminent. It could happen within a few years, and it would be a great blessing to humans, because, Hawking thought, then scientific understanding would not be the exclusive privilege of trained scientists, but available to everyone. Hawking's writings about this took on an almost utopian flavor, as if the new ability of all humans to understand science and nature, once the basic laws are known, might take the place of traditional religion. Even though Hawking has been generally regarded as a skeptic or nonbeliever, though some of his scientific coworkers were known to be devout Christians, he spoke in reverent terms about what humans would be doing in understanding the basic laws of nature. They would be thinking God's thoughts after Him.

In terms of Unit 76's discussion of modernism and postmodernism as human orientations or attitudes, Hawking might be called a present-day scientific modernist, while a scientist such as David Bohm, who believed that every scientific achievement would still leave infinite levels of mystery beneath it, would be called a scientific postmodernist—or premodernist.

In Steven Weinberg's *Dreams of a Final Theory*, there is an interesting account of what it might mean for humans to grasp the ultimate basic laws of nature as Hawking thought possible (and an interesting account of the scuttling of the Texas supercollider that Weinberg had hoped would push this knowledge farther).[14]

David Dawkins, an eminent exponent of evolutionary theory, argues that the evidence of evolution reveals a universe without design. For a very different point of view from a scientist believing that important aspects of the sciences support religious belief, see John Polkinghorne, *Belief in God in an Age of Science*.[15]

---

[14] Steven Weinberg, *Dreams of a Final Theory* (New York: Vintage Books, 1992).

[15] David Dawkins, *The Blind Watchmaker* (New York and London: W.W. Norton & Co., 1987): John Pokinghorne, *Belief in God in an Age of Science* (New Haven and London: Yale University Press, 1998).

✦✦✦

Is Polanyi's theory about "tacit knowing" at least in part a theory about the role of religious vision in scientific knowledge?

Do Polanyi's and Whitehead's theories about tacit, or intuitive, knowing rest on a religious vision—or at least an intuitive vision about reality, the nature of human life, and its relationship to the rest of nature?

UNIT 82   THE TEMPORAL AND THE ETERNAL

Religions may be divided into at least two distinct types: those that understand the Divine as wholly or primarily eternal and those that believe the Divine has significant temporal as well as eternal aspects.

THE DIVINE AS PERSONAL

Judaism, Zoroastrianism, Christianity, and Islam illustrate the second type. These religions speak of the Divine in terms derived from personal experience, interpersonal relations, and the interaction of nations. Generally understood as a personal deity, the Divine may be characterized with words descriptive of human personality and can enter into personal relationships with individuals and groups. Being thus related to human concerns, God acts within the setting of earthly existence; therefore, within time. This fact infuses time itself with Divine significance.

There are numerous examples of this interplay and personal contact between the Hebrew leaders and Yahweh, the God of the Israelites. In Genesis 18, Yahweh has decided to destroy the cities of Sodom and Gomorrah because their inhabitants have participated in gross evil. God shares this intent with Abraham, and the following conversation ensues:

> Then Abraham came near, and said "Will you indeed sweep away the righteous with the wicked? Suppose there are fifty righteous within the city; will you then sweep away the place and not forgive it for the fifty righteous who are in it? Far be it from you to do such a thing, to slay the righteous with the wicked, so that the righteous fare as the wicked! Far be that from you! Shall not the Judge of all the earth do what is just?" And the Lord said, "If I find at Sodom fifty righteous in the city, I will forgive the whole place for their sake." . . . Then [Abraham] said, "Oh do not let the Lord be angry if I speak just once more. Suppose ten are found there." [Yahweh] answered, "For the sake of ten I will not destroy it." And the Lord went his way, when he had finished speaking to Abraham; and Abraham returned to his place. (Genesis 18:23-33,NRSV)

This example of an interpersonal relationship, wherein Abraham is in God's presence, talking to and even challenging God to be fully righteous, suggests how clearly the Israelites understood their relationship to God to be one of direct, personal contact, much like that with other humans. Note that Yahweh—the transcendent, all-powerful God of all creation—acts directly in history, creating, destroying, ruling, and chastening. Yet it is clear that Abraham does not understand himself to be equal to Yahweh: Abraham is anxious not to anger God. God is transcendent, not bound by human affairs or human history. Abraham may speak his mind and be heard by God, but it is God who acts in and controls history.

In contrast, the Hebrew realization of the transcendent nature of Yahweh, wherein the Divine is beyond comprehension or description, is expressed in the following passage from the prophet Isaiah:

> Have you not known? Have you not heard?
>   Has it not been told you from the beginning?
> Have you not understood from the foundations of the earth?
> It is he who sits above the circle of the earth,
>   and its inhabitants are like grasshoppers;
> who stretches out the heavens like a curtain,
>   and spreads them like a tent to live in;
> who brings princes to nought,
>   and makes the rulers of the earth as nothing.
> Scarcely are they planted, scarcely sown,
>   scarcely has their stem taken root in the earth,
> when he blows upon them, and they wither,
>   and the tempest carries them off like stubble.
> To whom then will you compare me,
>   or who is my equal? says the Holy One,
> Lift up your eyes on high and see:
>   Who created these?. . .   •
> The Lord is the everlasting God,
>   the Creator of the ends of the earth.
>   (Isaiah 40:21–26, NRSV)

As Isaiah indicates, the transcendent aspect of God is as important to the Hebrew understanding of God as is the concept of his relating to individuals and the nation on a personal basis.

Thus God is understood by the Israelites as transcending creation—including time—and at the same time as being involved in time and history. Such a concept is not without its tensions, for it requires a timeless transcendent Deity, unbound by creation and its time sequence, to be involved in the very history of that creation. In this tension, timeless transcendence threatens to overwhelm the concept of a personal historical involvement by God and the significance of human beings, creatures confined with the limits of time. Yet the Hebrews, along with Christians, Muslims, and Zoroastrians, maintain that the Divine manifests both elements so that people experience a personal God who is nevertheless transcendent; therefore, human beings can enjoy the reality of a personal relationship to the Divine.

THE DIVINE AS IMPERSONAL

Hinduism, Buddhism, philosophical Taoism, and Shinto speak of the Divine in terms derived from natural process. Generally understood as an impersonal power, the essence of the Divine is characterized with words not associated with human personality. Being impersonal, it does not enter into personal relationships with individuals and groups.

Thus the essence of the Divine transcends this existence and is therefore timeless, without beginning and without end. Time itself becomes only a passing episode in an unending, eternal process.

Heinrich Zimmer calls attention to an intriguing story in one of the Puranas, a story that speaks forcefully to our concern; "The Parade of Ants" opens with the figure of *Indra*, king of the Gods, after he has slain the Dragon who pent up the life-giving waters. Indra, to express and celebrate his kingly glory and splendor, has ordered *Vishvakarman*, the god of arts and crafts, to build splendid gardens, palaces, lakes, and towers. As he works, Indra's vision of what he desires gets bigger and bigger, so that finally Vishvakarman, in desperation, appeals to the "demiurgic creator, Brahma, the pristine embodiment of the Universal Spirit, who abides far above the Olympian sphere of ambition, strife, and glory," for help. Brahma himself appeals to Vishnu, the Supreme Being, who by a mere nod of his head indicates that the wish of Vishvakarman will be fulfilled. The next day a brahmin boy, "slender, some ten years old, radiant with the luster of wisdom," appears at Indra's gate. After inviting the boy into his palace, Indra asks, "O Venerable Boy, tell me the purpose of your coming."

> This beautiful child replied with a voice that was as deep and soft as the slow thundering of auspicious rain clouds. "O King of Gods, I have heard of the mighty palace you are building, and have come to refer to you the questions in my mind. How many years will it require to complete this rich and extensive residence? What further feats of engineering will Vishvakarman be expected to accomplish? O Highest of the Gods,"—the boy's luminous features moved with a gentle, scarcely perceptible smile—"no Indra before you has ever succeeded in completing such a palace as yours is to be."
>
> Full of the wine of triumph, the king of the gods was entertained by this mere boy's pretension to a knowledge of Indras earlier than himself. With a fatherly smile he put the question: "Tell me, Child! Are they then so very many, the Indras and Vishvakarmans whom you have seen—or at least, whom you have heard of?"
>
> The wonderful guest calmly nodded. "Yes, indeed, many have I seen." The voice was as warm and sweet as milk fresh from the cow, but the words sent a slow chill through Indra's veins. "My dear child," the boy continued, "I knew your father, Kashyapa, the Old Tortoise Man, lord and progenitor of all the creatures of the earth. And I knew your grandfather, Marchi, Beam of Celestial Light, who was the son of Brahma . . . "O King of Gods, I have known the dreadful dissolution of the universe. I have seen all perish, again and again, at the end of every cycle. At that terrible time, every single atom dissolves into the primal, pure waters of eternity, whence originally all arose. Everything then goes back into the fathomless, wild infinity of the ocean, which is covered with utter darkness and is empty of every sign of animate being. Ah, who will count the universes that have passed away, or the creations that have risen afresh, again and again, from the formless abyss of the vast waters? . . .
>
> "The life and kingship of an Indra endure seventy-one eons, and when twenty-eight Indras have expired, one Day and Night of Brahma has elapsed. But the existence of one Brahma, measured in such Brahma Days and Nights, is only one hundred and eight years. Brahma follows Brahma; one sinks, the next arises, the endless series cannot be told.
>
> "But the universes side by side at any given moment, each harboring a Brahma and an Indra: who will estimate the number of these? Beyond the farthest vision, crowding outer space, the universes come and go, an innumerable host. . . .
>
> A procession of ants made its appearance in the hall during the discourse of the boy. In military array, in a column four yards wide, the tribe paraded across the floor. The boy noted them, paused, and stared, then suddenly laughed with an astonishing peal, but immediately subsided into a profoundly indrawn and thoughtful silence.

"O Son of a Brahmin," the king pleaded presently, with a new and visible humility, "I do not know who you are. You would seem to be Wisdom Incarnate. Reveal to me this secret of the ages, this light that dispels the dark."

Thus requested to teach, the boy opened to the god the hidden wisdom. "I saw the ants, O Indra, filing in long parade. Each was once an Indra. Like you, each by virtue of pious deeds once ascended to the rank of a king of gods. But now, through many rebirths, each has become again an ant. This army is an army of former Indras.

"Piety and high deeds elevate the inhabitants of the world to the glorious realm of the celestial mansions, or to the higher domains of Brahmā and Shiva and to the highest sphere of Vishnu; but wicked acts sink them into the worlds beneath, into pits of pain and sorrow, involving reincarnation among birds and vermin, or out of the wombs of pigs and animals of the wild, or among trees, or among insects. It is by deeds that one merits happiness or anguish, and becomes a master or a serf. It is by deeds that one attains to the rank of a king or brahmin, or of some god, or of an Indra or a Brahma . . . In unending cycles the good and evil alternate. Hence, the wise are attached to neither, neither the evil nor the good. The wise are not attached to anything at all."

The boy concluded the appalling lesson and quietly regarded his host. The king of gods, for all his celestial splendor, had been reduced in his own regard to insignificance.[16]

In this story the Divine Reality is timeless, impersonal, solitary, and removed from the passing into and out of existence of the multitudinous universes. The Divine is oblivious to and detached from the concerns of "ambition, strife, and glory," exemplified by the god Indra.

Yet it is significant that the concern of the story is the meaning of individual identity, as expressed in Indra's desire for palaces, gardens, lakes, and towers celebrating his glorious achievements. Thus within the worldview that espouses timeless, eternal reality, a pressing problem still remains: What is the significance of time and human achievement?

Meanwhile, another amazing apparition had entered the hall.

The newcomer had the appearance of a kind of hermit. His head was piled with matted hair; he wore a black deerskin around his loins; on his forehead was painted a white mark; his head was shaded by a paltry parasol of grass; and a quaint, circular cluster of hair grew on his chest: it was intact at the circumference, but from the center many of the hairs, it seemed, had disappeared. This saintly figure strode directly to Indra and the boy, squatted between them on the floor, and there remained, motionless as a rock. The kingly Indra, somewhat recovering his hostly role, bowed and paid obeisance, offering sour milk with honey and other refreshments; then he inquired falteringly but reverently, after the welfare of the stern guest, and bade him welcome. Whereupon the boy addressed the holy man, asking the very questions Indra himself would have proposed.

"Whence do you come, O Holy Man? What is your name and what brings you to this place? What is the portent of that circular hair-tuft on your chest: why is it dense at the circumference but at the center almost bare? Be kind enough, to answer, these questions."

Patiently the old saint smiled, and slowly began his reply. "I am a brahmin. Hairy is my name. And I have come here to behold Indra. Since I know that I am short-lived, I have decided to possess no home; to build no house, and neither to marry nor to seek a livelihood. I exist by begging alms.

"As to the circle of hair on my chest, it is a source of grief to the children of the world. Nevertheless, it teaches wisdom. With the fall of an Indra, one hair drops. That is why, in

[16] Heinrich Zimmer, *Myths and Symbols in Indian Art and Civilization*, ed. Joseph Campbell, Bollingen Series VI (Copyright © 1946 by Billingen Foundation), reprinted with permission of Princeton University Press. pp. 4–8.

the center all the hairs have gone. When the other half of the period allotted to the present Brahma will have expired, I myself shall die. O Brahmin Boy, it follows that I am somewhat short of days; what therefore, is the use of a wife and a son, or of a house?

"Each flicker of the eyelids of the great Vishnu registers the passing of a Brahma. Everything below that sphere of Brahma is as insubstantial as a cloud taking shape and again dissolving. That is why I devote myself exclusively to meditating on the incomparable lotus-feet of highest Vishnu.

"Shiva, the peace-bestowing, the highest spiritual guide, taught me this wonderful wisdom. I do not crave to experience the various blissful forms of redemption: to share the highest god's supernatural mansions and enjoy his eternal presence . . . or even to be absorbed . . . in his ineffable essence."

Abruptly, the holy man ceased and immediately vanished. It had been the god Shiva himself; he had now returned to his supramundane abode. Simultaneously, the brahmin boy, who had been Vishnu, disappeared as well. The king was alone, baffled and amazed.[17]

This portion of the story not only reinforces the previous emphasis but also declares that the humanlike Indra and the Creator-God Himself—Brahma—are both ruled by the timeless, inexorable wheeling of eons.

Yet the story does not end here. And the ending itself underscores the demand within timelessness for temporal significance.

The king, Indra, pondered; and the events seemed to him to have been a dream. But he no longer felt any desire to magnify his heavenly splendor or to go on with the construction of his palace. He summoned Vishvakarman. Graciously greeting the craftsman . . . , he heaped on him precious gifts, then with a sumptuous celebration sent him home.

The king, Indra, now desired redemption. He had acquired wisdom, and wished only to be free. He entrusted the pomp and burden of his office to his son, and prepared to retire to the hermit life of the wilderness. Whereupon his beautiful and passionate queen, Shachi, was overcome with grief.

Weeping, in sorrow and utter despair, Shachi resorted to Indra's ingenious house-priest and spiritual advisor, the Lord of Magic Wisdom, Brihaspati. Bowing at his feet, she implored him to divert her husband's mind from its stern resolve. The resourceful counselor of the gods, who by his spells and devices had helped the heavenly powers wrest the government of the universe from the hands of their titan rivals, listened thoughtfully to the complaint of the voluptuous, disconsolate goddess, and knowingly nodded assent. With a wizard's smile, he took her hand and conducted her to the presence of her spouse. In the role, then, of spiritual teacher, he discoursed sagely on the virtues of the spiritual life, but on the virtues also, of the secular. He gave to each its due. Very skillfully he developed his theme. The royal pupil was persuaded to relent in his extreme resolve. The queen was restored to radiant joy.[18]

About this story, Zimmer says,

The wisdom taught in this myth would have been incomplete had the last word been that of the infinity of space and time. The vision of the countless universes bubbling into existence side by side, and the lesson of the unending series of Indras and Brahmas, would have annihilated every value of individual existence. Between this boundless, breath-taking vision and the opposite problem of the limited role of the short-lived individual, this

[17] Ibid., pp. 8–10.
[18] Ibid., p. 10–11.

myth effected the reestablishment of a balance. We are taught to recognize the divine, the impersonal sphere of eternity, revolving ever and agelessly through time. But we are also taught to esteem the transient sphere of the duties and pleasures of individual existence, which is as real and as vital to the living man, as a dream to the sleeping soul.[19]

The Hindu "Parade of the Ants " well illustrates Unit 25's discussion of the structuring of myths and how they function to bring balance to certain elements of life.

In this unit we have discussed, on the one hand, the way the Divine is conceived as personal, temporal, and in interaction with persons and nations, noting especially how Christianity, Judaism, Islam, and Zoroastrianism reflect this perspective. On the other hand, we have shown the Divine to be timeless and impersonal, as understood by Hinduism, Buddhism, and Taoism. Thus we have set the contrast between the temporal and the eternal in the world's major religions; we would emphasize, though, that all religions apparently maintain to one degree or another a dialectic between the temporal and the eternal.

✦✦✦

> In an earlier unit it was suggested that modern Hindu and Buddhist thinkers often see recent scientific evidence of an expanding seemingly unlimited universe as supporting their traditional explanations of the universe. How might the "Parade of Ants" story support this affirmation? What questions might it also raise for modern scientific theories?
>
> Compare the interrelationship between humans and the Divine in these Hebrew and Hindu examples.

[19] Ibid., p. 22.

INDEX OF
RELIGIOUS TRADITIONS

INDEX OF
NAMES AND SUBJECTS